"Finally, a handy, accessible history book written for students encountering the academic study of the Bible for the first time! Beth LaNeel Tanner's textbook is more than a primer; it is a rich and thought-provoking review of the historical and cultural issues that any seminary student must face in an introductory course. Developed and refined from her many years of teaching, Tanner proves to be an eminently reliable guide, both sensitive and challenging. Her textbook serves as the ideal invitation to delve deeply into the world behind the biblical text with an eye toward what lies beyond."
—William P. Brown, William Marcellus McPheeters Professor of Old Testament, Columbia Theological Seminary

"Studying the history behind the Bible can be perplexing, unsettling, and theologically challenging, especially for new students. With more than two decades of experience teaching, Tanner knows the most pressing questions, concerns, misconceptions, and biases that readers are sure to bring. More importantly, she knows how to address them. In this book, Tanner brings together established scholarship, new discoveries, her awareness of the limits of historical inquiry, and the contentions in charged debates about the history behind the Old Testament. Thankfully, she packages it in a way that is sensitive to students and to the real people who lived in the ancient world. One could not hope for a better balance of critical investigation and compassion."
—Justin Michael Reed, Associate Professor of Old Testament, Louisville Seminary

"Providing a succinct outline of the major historical events and cultural issues that undergird the Hebrew Bible, Tanner's compact and readable book brings to life the stories in the Hebrew text. As such, Tanner's work offers an accessible and engaging introduction to the study of the Hebrew Scriptures."
—Song-Mi Suzie Park, Associate Professor of Old Testament, Austin Presbyterian Theological Seminary

"Tanner's work fills a need for an introduction to the critical study of the Hebrew Bible for undergraduates and seminary students by focusing on the political, social, and material cultures that helped to shape these texts. Her prose reflects an engaging style, deals with foundational issues honestly, and reflects an erudite synthesis of the cultural milieus of the ancient world."
—James Nogalski, W. Marshall and Lulie Craig Professor of Hebrew Bible, Department of Religion, Baylor University

"In *Ancient Israel and Judah,* Tanner expertly guides the reader through complex issues in biblical scholarship while thoughtfully and conscientiously bridging the gap between faith-based, application-oriented approaches that tend to center the contemporary reader and contextualizing methods that biblical scholars use. The result is an accessible introduction to the history and culture of the Hebrew Bible that is both rich and engaging! Maps, charts, and images significantly enhance the presentation and clarity of the book."
—Rebecca Harris, Associate Professor of Bible, Messiah University

"It's often said that 'a text without a context is a pretext.' Finally, we have a book that presents the historical and cultural contexts of the Old Testament/Hebrew Bible with sensitivity, clarity, and expertise. Students and teachers alike will welcome this volume, and I predict that pretexts will become less common as a result."
—Carol M. Bechtel, retired Professor of Old Testament, Western Theological Seminary

Ancient Israel and Judah

Ancient Israel and Judah

Why History and Cultural Context Matter for Reading the Hebrew Bible

Beth LaNeel Tanner

© 2025 Beth LaNeel Tanner

First Edition
Published by Westminster John Knox Press
Louisville, Kentucky

25 26 27 28 29 30 31 32 33 34—10 9 8 7 6 5 4 3 2 1

All rights reserved. No part of this book may be reproduced or transmitted in any form or by any means, electronic or mechanical, including photocopying, recording, or by any information storage or retrieval system, without permission in writing from the publisher. For information, address Westminster John Knox Press, 100 Witherspoon Street, Louisville, Kentucky 40202-1396. Or contact us online at www.wjkbooks.com.

Unless otherwise indicated, Scripture quotations are taken from the New Revised Standard Version Updated Edition. Copyright © 2021 National Council of the Churches of Christ in the United States of America. Used by permission. All rights reserved worldwide.

Book design by Sharon Adams
Cover design by designpointinc.com

Library of Congress Cataloging-in-Publication Data is on file
at the Library of Congress, Washington, DC.

ISBN: 978-0-664-23498-0 (paperback)
ISBN: 978-1-646-98440-4 (ebook)

Most Westminster John Knox Press books are available at special quantity discounts when purchased in bulk by corporations, organizations, and special-interest groups. For more information, please e-mail SpecialSales@wjkbooks.com.

*To all the New Brunswick Theological Seminary students
I have had the privilege of teaching,
and to Jeanette Carrillo:
your quiet support and love have made the lives of all students and faculty better.*

Contents

List of Maps, Figures, and Charts	ix
Preface	xi
Acknowledgments	xiii
Abbreviations	xv
1. Introduction to the Academic Study of the Bible	1
2. Why Study the Historical Context of the Hebrew Bible?	11
3. Israel and Judah in Context	31
4. Life in the Afro-Asiatic Region	49
5. "In the Beginning": Genesis and Exodus	75
6. The Founding of a People in Canaan (1200–1000 BCE)	95
7. The Era of Early Monarchy (1000–927 BCE)	111
8. Two-Kingdom Rule: A Time of Expansion (927–840 BCE)	127
9. Israel Tumbles toward Destruction (840–722 BCE)	143
10. Judah under Assyrian Domination (722–639 BCE)	161
11. Battle for Control of the Afro-Asiatic Region (639–539 BCE)	173
12. The Persian Empire (539–330 BCE)	195
13. The Early Hellenistic Period (330–168 BCE)	225
14. The Maccabean Revolt and the Hasmonean Dynasty (168–63 BCE)	249
15. How the Hebrew Bible Became a Book	273

Glossary of Terms	293
Index of Scripture and Other Ancient Sources	301
Index of Subjects	308

List of Maps, Figures, and Charts

MAPS

1.	The Afro-Asiatic region	35
2.	Canaan	36
3.	Ancient Cisjordan and its immediately surrounding regions	41
4.	Fertile Crescent	44
5.	Topographical map of Canaan	45
6.	Main roads and cities of ancient Canaan	46
7.	Geographical spread of early Iron Age hill-country settlements	97
8.	Solomon's Jerusalem	117
9.	The Assyrian Empire at its greatest approximate extent	158
10.	Jerusalem at the time of Hezekiah	165
11.	The Persian Empire at its greatest approximate extent	199
12.	Persian Province of Judah among other provinces "Beyond the River"	201
13.	The Seleucid Empire	229

FIGURES

1.	Example of a tel. Reconstruction of Lachish, Level III	51
2.	Example of a four-room house in ancient Canaan	57
3.	The water system at Megiddo	63

4.	Interpretation of Jerusalem, the city of David in the time of Hezekiah	63
5.	Niche in replica of an Iron Age II house	65
6.	Standing stones at Gezer	71
7.	Arad temple	72
8.	Tel Dan Stela	114
9.	Black Obelisk of Shalmaneser III	150

CHARTS

1.	Multiple Hebrew Bibles in their designated order	4
2.	Chronology of the Afro-Asiatic region	32
3.	Early kings of the divided kingdoms (ca. 927–840 BCE)	132
4.	Kings after Jehu's coup (839–735 BCE)	146
5.	Kings of Israel and Judah (788–722 BCE)	152
6.	Kings of Judah (727–642 BCE)	161
7.	Last Kings of Judah (641–586 BCE)	173
8.	Differences in the Hebrew and the Greek texts of the book of Jeremiah	284

Preface

This book was designed for the classrooms of seminaries and colleges and for interested church readers. It outlines the history and context of the texts of the Hebrew Bible. The book notes the importance of the history of the periods described in the Hebrew Bible, yet it also explains the limits of recovering that history. It is intentionally brief, keeping the scholarly debates in archaeology and history to a minimum. However, it does discuss the most significant debates so students can understand the scope, rigor, and ongoing nature of this important scholarly work. The book also offers an introduction to academic biblical studies—to the field of history, the setting of the biblical texts in the worlds from which they emerged, and the cultural contexts of those texts. It discusses the importance of understanding a period's cultural context as background for better understanding the biblical texts.

As an author, I have stated my perspective in presenting the material and my philosophy of ancient history. I believe there is history in the Hebrew Bible, but that recording history was not the primary reason the biblical texts were written. This book also attempts to remove the colonizing names of the regions that provide the setting for the Hebrew Bible and instead adopts more neutral language. It also avoids using the divine name, known as the Tetragrammaton, a bad habit of Eurocentric Christian scholars.

I have taught the Introduction to the Old Testament class at New Brunswick Theological Seminary for twenty-six years. This book is the result of that teaching. Over the years, I saw students often overwhelmed and confused by multiple debates and long weekly reading assignments. This book is designed for a fourteen- or fifteen-week semester class where history is one of several objectives the professor must cover. It can also serve as a quick reference for studying a specific book or historical period, and the notes can lead students to other resources for more in-depth analysis. The book can also serve as a resource for a church-based class on history.

The Introduction to Old Testament class is usually one of the first classes students take in seminary. So, in the back, this book has an added glossary for students, to help them understand new terms and concepts. Hopefully, this book will serve as a doorway for students to enter the world of these concepts and resources and encourage them to engage in further research.

One unusual aspect of this book is that it covers the period of history overlapping with the Hebrew Bible until the fall of the Greeks and the rise of the Roman Empire. Many Hebrew Bible history books stop in the middle of the Persian period. However, what happens after King Darius II of Persia is crucial for understanding the events in the New Testament. This book covers that period during which Jewish practices were reshaped and the office of the high priest grew in importance and status. It also tells the story of the Samaritans and their relationship with Judah and the Greek Empire. These chapters will better prepare students for their New Testament studies.

Seminary studies can sometimes seem threatening to students' belief systems. In this book, I am conscious of this concern. If students feel their faith is being threatened, their learning can cease. I kept this in mind as I wrote this book. I hope this approach will help professors to keep students engaged for the entire semester.

Finally, when I began this book, we were unaware of AI; even now, we stand at the beginning of this revolution. While producing this book, I used Grammarly to make corrections and suggestions. In the last year, Grammarly added an AI portion to the program. I have not used this portion of the program, but for full disclosure, I need to state that I sometimes accepted the program's recommendations for better sentence structure. As I write this, universities are debating whether the use of Grammarly should be allowed, so in that spirit, I am informing readers of my use of it.

Acknowledgments

Many people have helped with a long project like this one. First and foremost, the current and former students of New Brunswick Theological Seminary. Your curiosity, questions, and struggles with the history and context in our Hebrew Bible classes shaped this book. For all of your questions and even your frustrations, I am eternally grateful. All of you have blessed my life and pushed me to be a better teacher

This book was an exercise in scholarly participation. I wanted to write a book that leaves the most colonizing language of Western European scholarship behind. In that effort, I engaged my colleagues at academic meetings, in our social-media groups, and over meals to discuss the ways forward. We debated which terms should replace the older European-centered names and acknowledged that even attempting to alter colonizing language was an uphill battle. Thank you to all who took the time to engage, weigh options, and discuss the best choices. Special thanks to John Bracke, Professor Emeritus of Eden Theological Seminary and my first Hebrew Bible professor; it was in your class that I found my calling for this work. You also took the time to read and comment on an early version of the book. Your input was so helpful.

The New Brunswick Theological Seminary Board of Trustees granted me the sabbatical time to complete this book; without that time and space, this book would never have been finished. Over the past twenty-six years, the NBTS faculty have served as colleagues and daily support for this work, and I am deeply appreciative of the work we share together. Likewise, the library staff and multiple librarians have found articles, purchased books, and aided with resources, always with good humor and a smile, especially Patrick Milas and Indira Douglas. My right-hand person for the last twenty years at NBTS is Jeanette Carrillo. She is quiet and works in the background, but her support of students, me, and my work has blessed my life.

My family and friends have aided me in so many ways. You have offered support, encouragement, and love. My life partner, Daniel Weaver, is a professor himself and has supported me while I was locked in my office writing. Daniel, I could not do life without you.

I also thank the Westminster John Knox staff, especially Bridgett Green and Julie Mullins, and copyeditor Dave Garber. I greatly appreciate your patience and understanding.

Abbreviations

ABC	A. K. Grayson, *Assyrian and Babylonian Chronicles*. Augustin, 1975; repr., Eisenbrauns, 2000.
ABD	David Freedman, ed. *Anchor Bible Dictionary*. 6 vols. Doubleday, 1992; Yale University Press, 2008.
ANES	*Ancient Near Eastern Studies*
ANET	J. B. Pritchard, ed. *Ancient Near Eastern Texts Relating to the Old Testament*. 3rd ed. Princeton University Press, 1969.
Ant.	*Jewish Antiquities*, by Josephus
BA	*Biblical Archaeologist*
BAR	*Biblical Archaeology Review*
BASOR	*Bulletin of the American Schools of Oriental Research*
BBR	*Bulletin for Biblical Research*
BR	*Bible Review*
COS	W. Hallo, ed. *The Context of Scripture*, vols. 1–3. Brill, 1997–2000.
CUSAS	Cornell University Studies in Assyriology and Sumerology
IEJ	*Israel Exploration Journal*
JBL	*Journal of Biblical Literature*
JBQ	*Jewish Bible Quarterly*
JSOT	*Journal for the Study of the Old Testament*
JSOTSup	Journal for the Study of the Old Testament Supplement Series
JTS	*Journal of Theological Studies*
NEA	*Near Eastern Archaeology*
PEQ	*Palestine Exploration Quarterly*
SBL	Society of Biblical Literature
VT	*Vetus Testamentum*
ZAW	*Zeitschrift für die alttestamentliche Wissenschaft*
ZDPV	*Zeitschrift des deutschen Palästina-Vereins*

1

Introduction to the Academic Study of the Bible

The purpose of this book is to orient learners to the history, culture, and worldview of the period when the individual books of the Hebrew Bible were composed. It is designed to set students on a path to becoming effective and responsible biblical interpreters by providing the necessary background to better understand the texts of the Hebrew Bible in their contexts. The book is brief and provides an overview of that history and context. Because of its brevity, it keeps scholarly debates to a minimum. Students wishing to write a paper about a single aspect of this history or context must consult history books that provide a more extensive background for the scholarly arguments and types of consensus in this field of study.

This book is also designed for today's seminary students. For many readers, your undergraduate degree is not in religious studies; for some, this is your first religious studies class. What you learned about the Bible, you primarily learned in church. So, seminary and the academic study of the Bible are a new world. When I began my academic studies, I wondered why I needed to know the history and context of the Hebrew Bible. I did not understand why the Bible itself was not enough. In addition, the professors and students with religious studies degrees spoke a language I did not understand, using terms such as *longue durée* (duration), *myth*, and *exegesis*. I felt overwhelmed. I had never thought about what the Bible meant in its own context or how I should read it. I just read it like other modern literature.

The traditional history books for studying the Hebrew Bible assume that students know the how and why of academic biblical study. They do not address the foundational questions. So this book begins with some of these foundational concerns. Chapter 1 engages students in the basics of the academic study of the Bible. Chapter 2 focuses on why the historical context is crucial to interpreting the Hebrew Bible. Chapter 3 outlines where the time of the Hebrew Bible fits into all of human history, the nations that developed in Canaan, and what geographic and topological considerations are essential for understanding the events of this period. Chapter 4 describes the lives of ancient people and how they lived, cooked, and worshiped. These are the people to whom and about whom the Hebrew Bible was written. The following ten chapters provide a brief history from 1500 BCE to 63 BCE. The final chapter discusses possibilities for how the individual narratives of the Hebrew Bible became books and then became the entire collection that Christians now call the Old Testament. This book will also help students by adding a glossary with brief definitions of terms that are part of academic discussions in biblical studies. But first, we will learn about the Hebrew Bible and why understanding it is not as simple as it seems.

A BRIEF HISTORY OF THE HEBREW BIBLE

The Bible is Holy Scripture. Holy Scripture is defined as a document or documents considered sacred and authoritative by a community. Many communities consider the Bible a single document from Genesis to Revelation. However, each book and story has its own life and history. Before the Old Testament existed, there were scrolls of Isaiah, Psalms, and Deuteronomy, and so on. Before the scroll of Genesis or any other book, there were oral stories about the flood, Abraham and Sarah, the Tower of Babel, and Joseph.

Where did the narratives and scrolls come from? How did God inspire them? This requires a long story to explore the possibilities, and some of the earliest traditions will be discussed in chapter 4. Let's focus on how the scrolls came together as individual documents and then as a collection of scrolls. It is known that from the establishment of the monarchy in Jerusalem in about 1000 BCE, sections of books and whole books began to be written down. Many books came from smaller stories originating as oral narratives told by community storytellers. This oral tradition was common because only a few people were literate, and those who could write worked for kings. These scribes were rare and honored. The rest of the communities and people in the ancient world shared stories by telling them over and over. A written record of the stories on scrolls was a costly endeavor that only kings and nations could afford. Exactly how the stories and poems came to be in larger books is a mystery. No records inside or outside the Bible describe the selection process or when each scroll/book was recorded in writing. More stories, poems, and prophetic books were in existence than we have today.[1] Some stood the test of time, while others did not.

All that can be generally said is that the stories were first gathered by the community storytellers in different groups of Israelites and Judeans beginning sometime after 1000 BCE, and the collecting continued for centuries after that. Even this time frame is debated among scholars. Some argue that the Hebrew Bible came together from 1000 to 600 BCE. Others say the Bible was not composed until much later, between 399 and 100 BCE, as a mythical work by Jewish nationalists.[2] Most scholars believe that many of the texts of the Hebrew Bible were written between 800 and 600 BCE. However, although these earlier scrolls were authoritative, they were also editable and were edited until around the time of the New Testament. Still, other books of the Hebrew Bible were not penned until the Hellenistic period, which began around 323 BCE and ended in 64 BCE. Many scholars believe that by the end of the second century CE, the Hebrew Scriptures were canonized and closed, meaning that no other books would be added and that the texts would no longer be edited or changed.[3] The Tanakh, the Jewish canon, consists of three sections: the Torah, the Prophets, and the Writings. It became the sacred Scriptures of the Jewish people. (See chap. 15 for more information about how the Hebrew Bible potentially took shape.)

Jesus and the disciples used the Torah, the Prophets, and the Psalms as faithful Jews and quoted them as recorded in the New Testament. At the time of the New Testament, these texts were authoritative but probably not yet considered Scripture as they are now. After Jesus' death, Christianity began as a sect of Judaism, and early Christians accepted the Hebrew books as sacred Scripture and cited them, often from a Greek version.[4] But the book's story did not end there. In 325 CE, the Christian church split into the Eastern and Western branches. The two Christian traditions developed separately and finally split in 1054 CE. As a result, two Old Testaments emerged, one used by the Catholic Church of Rome and the other by the Orthodox Church of Constantinople.

So, there were different collections of the Hebrew Scriptures depending on one's religion: the Tanakh written in Hebrew, the Catholic Bible in Latin, and the Orthodox Bible in Greek. Additional books were added to the Christian Old Testaments, not in the Tanakh (see chart 1 below). These three versions

---

1. For example, Num. 21:13–14 refers to a "Book of the Wars of the LORD"; 2 Sam. 1:18 speaks of "the Book of Jashar"; and 1 Kgs. 14:19 discusses "the Book of the Annals of the Kings of Israel" and 14:29, "the Book of the Annals of the Kings of Judah."
2. Philip R. Davies, *In Search of "Ancient Israel": A Study in Ancient Origins* (Bloomsbury, 1992).
3. Even the date of this codification of Scriptures is debated: see Lee McDonald and James Sanders, eds., *The Canon Debate* (Hendrickson, 2020).
4. Christopher Stanley, *The Hebrew Bible: A Comparative Approach* (Fortress, 2010), 17.

CHART 1: MULTIPLE HEBREW BIBLES IN THEIR DESIGNATED ORDER

Judaism	Christianity in three traditions (deuterocanonicals in italics)		
Hebrew Bible/ Tanakh	*Catholic Bible*	*Orthodox Bible*	*Protestant Bible*
Torah	**Pentateuch**	**Pentateuch**	**Pentateuch**
Genesis	Genesis	Genesis	Genesis
Exodus	Exodus	Exodus	Exodus
Leviticus	Leviticus	Leviticus	Leviticus
Numbers	Numbers	Numbers	Numbers
Deuteronomy	Deuteronomy	Deuteronomy	Deuteronomy
Prophets	**Historical Books**	**Historical Books**	**Historical Books**
Joshua	Joshua	Joshua	Joshua
Judges	Judges	Judges	Judges
	Ruth	Ruth	Ruth
Samuel (1 & 2)	1 Samuel	1 Kingdoms	1 Samuel
	2 Samuel	2 Kingdoms	2 Samuel
Kings (1 & 2)	1 Kings	3 Kingdoms	1 Kings
	2 Kings	4 Kingdoms	2 Kings
	1 Chronicles	1 Chronicles	1 Chronicles
	2 Chronicles	2 Chronicles	2 Chronicles
		1 Esdras	
	Ezra	Ezra + Nehemiah	Ezra
	Nehemiah		Nehemiah
			Esther
	Tobit	*Tobit*	
	Judith	*Judith*	
	Longer Esther	*Longer Esther*	
	1 Maccabees	*1 Maccabees*	
	2 Maccabees	*2 Maccabees*	
		3 Maccabees	

Judaism	Christianity in three traditions (deuterocanonicals in italics)		
Hebrew Bible/ Tanakh	*Catholic Bible*	*Orthodox Bible*	*Protestant Bible*
	Poetic & Wisdom	**Poetic & Wisdom**	**Poetic & Wisdom**
	Job		Job
	Psalms 1–150	Psalms 1–151	Psalms 1–150
		Job	
	Proverbs	Proverbs	Proverbs
	Ecclesiastes	Ecclesiastes	Ecclesiastes
	Song of Songs	Song of Songs	Song of Songs
	Wisdom of Solomon	*Wisdom of Solomon*	
	Sirach	*Sirach*	
Prophets (cont.)	**Prophets**	**Prophets**	**Prophets**
Isaiah	Isaiah		Isaiah
Jeremiah	Jeremiah		Jeremiah
	Lamentations		Lamentations
	Baruch, Letter of Jeremiah		
Ezekiel	Ezekiel		Ezekiel
	Daniel *(longer)*		Daniel
Hosea	Hosea	Hosea	Hosea
		Amos	
		Micah	
Joel	Joel	Joel	Joel
Amos	Amos		Amos
Obadiah	Obadiah	Obadiah	Obadiah
Jonah	Jonah	Jonah	Jonah
Micah	Micah		Micah
Nahum	Nahum	Nahum	Nahum
Habakkuk	Habakkuk	Habakkuk	Habakkuk
Zephaniah	Zephaniah	Zephaniah	Zephaniah
Haggai	Haggai	Haggai	Haggai

(continued on page 6)

Judaism (*cont.*)	Christianity in three traditions (**deuterocanonicals in italics**) (*cont.*)		
Hebrew Bible/ Tanakh	*Catholic Bible*	*Orthodox Bible*	*Protestant Bible*
Prophets (cont.)	**Prophets (cont.)**	**Prophets (cont.)**	**Prophets (cont.)**
Zechariah	Zechariah	Zechariah	Zechariah
Malachi	Malachi	Malachi	Malachi
		Isaiah	
		Jeremiah	
		Baruch	
		Lamentations	
		Letter of Jeremiah	
		Ezekiel	
		Daniel *(longer)*	
Writings			
Psalms			
Proverbs			
Job			
Song of Songs			
Ruth			
Lamentations			
Ecclesiastes			
Esther			
Daniel			
Ezra-Nehemiah			
Chronicles (1 & 2)			

of the Hebrew Bible remained the Scriptures of Jews and Christians until the 1500s. Martin Luther and the other Protestant reformers adopted only the books in the Tanakh for their Old Testament, omitting the additional books of the Catholic and Orthodox churches. Today, these four collections use different combinations of these ancient books: the Tanakh (Hebrew Bible), the Catholic Old Testament, the Orthodox Old Testament, and the Protestant Old Testament. Some Protestant Bibles have additional books used by the Roman Catholic and Greek Orthodox churches in a section between the Old and New Testaments called the apocryphal/deuterocanonical books.

Are you confused yet? I suspect you are, so please consult the chart above, which lists each tradition's books in the order they appear in their sacred Scriptures. The Old Testament differs depending on its context in the major Judeo-Christian religions.

So, to be completely accurate, Christians should specify whether they are referring to the Catholic, Orthodox, or Protestant Old Testament when they speak about these texts. This is one of the many reasons the term Hebrew Bible is often used in academic settings. The Hebrew Bible contains the books of the Tanakh only. This term also reminds us that Christianity came from Judaism. Protestants share the same individual books with Judaism, but the order differs. Others argue that Christians should use the term Old Testament, noting that the interpretation of the Scriptures in the Jewish and Christian traditions is fundamentally different, and thus the two titles are justified. Still others use the terms First Testament and Second Testament. This gives the two testaments equal treatment and reminds us that one came first and was the authoritative document in the second. In this book, I use the term Hebrew Bible to remind us of its shared status in Judaism and Christianity. But this is not a perfect solution, so I invite you to contemplate the multiple names for the Scriptures shared by different religious faith communities.[5]

THE ACADEMIC STUDY OF THE HEBREW BIBLE

How do you read the Bible? This sounds like a simple question. Before seminary, I never thought about how I read or interpreted the Bible. I read it like a novel, an instruction manual, or a life guide. I took it all at face value and never thought about the different authors, cultures, and traditions represented

---

5. This chapter does not touch upon the issue of English translations of the Bible, involving a complex and emotionally charged doctrinal debate. See, e.g., Harry Freedman, *The Murderous History of Bible Translations: Power, Conflict and the Quest for Meaning* (Bloomsbury, 2016).

in its pages. I also did not think much about a time frame; I just knew it was old. I read the Bible the way I saw others read it.

However, I sometimes did not understand what I was reading and had questions. For example, when I was young, I wanted to know how the sun stood still and whom Cain married if only Adam and Eve's family existed. Slowly, in my church context, I learned I should not ask those kinds of questions. Questions often made people upset and flustered. I knew I believed in the Bible but was unsure how to understand and believe each story. So I learned to overlook a lot as I read, but the Bible was important to me and my spiritual life. One of the reasons I went to seminary was to explore all the questions I had about the Bible, and I learned how to do that through academic study.

An academic study of the Bible will probably be different from how you have read and studied the Bible in the past. But please do not think that this way replaces the ways you have always read the Bible. Methods of academic reading are meant to add to, not replace, the ways you read now. You will read for new information and ways of interpreting, but this does not mean it is separate from your spiritual life. Learning new things and ways of thinking about the Bible should become part of your spiritual life and practice.

Academic study can be divided into three ways of thinking about the text: the world *behind* the text, the world *in* the text, and the world *in front of* the text. These three ways of looking at any text will ensure you have covered all aspects of responsible biblical interpretation. A text is defined as a section of the Bible. It could be a chapter, part of a chapter, or a psalm. Your focus could be as big as a whole book or as small as a few verses. The word *text* is shorthand for a section of the Bible you are exploring.

The world behind the text is concerned with the origin of the text. Here, you will ask questions such as where the text came from, who wrote it, when it was written, and why it was written. It is "behind" the text because the answers to your questions are not found in the text itself and usually must be researched. Reflections on these questions are found in books and articles written by scholars.

Another essential part of reading the world behind the text is the subject of this book. It concerns the history and context of the period when these texts were first composed and circulated. The next chapter discusses this background extensively. We will discuss why this background is essential for good biblical interpretation. This book will primarily present the world behind the text.

The world in the text relates to the words on the page. The world in the text involves literary criticism and study. It is the world the verses and chapters of the biblical text create on the page. This type of study will ask questions about the genre of the text and how that contributes to the text's meaning. The world in the text involves reading it in its original language to gain more insight into its meaning. Through this process, an interpreter will notice how the text tells its truth. Who are the characters? Who speaks and to whom? How do they say what they say? Who is without a voice? Does the text build to a crescendo? Are there twists and turns in the narrative, or is it consistent from beginning to end? Does the text move from one place to another, or do the characters remain in the same place? These are some of the questions that help one to explore the world in the text. This book will not primarily focus on this world except when it intersects with historical issues, but this skill is important and a key part of your class and biblical studies.

The world in front of the text is where the text meets the reader—in our case, the modern reader. It asks how a reader makes sense of a text and uses it. Countless readers and communities throughout history have read the biblical texts in different ways with different interpretations. This is also the so-called so what? of the text, meaning how this text applies to my life today. The world in front of the text is the world of sermon writing. Without incorporating the world behind the text and the world of the text, a pastor will read the text with only modern eyes. This way of reading singularly risks distorting the text and making it serve our purposes.

Chapters 2 and 3 demonstrate why all three worlds are essential to excellent biblical interpretation. For preachers, the world in front of the text may seem like the most important, but it requires the other two methods to inform the "so what?" to ensure that the interpretation honors the text.

As noted at the beginning of this chapter, this book will focus on the history and culture behind the Hebrew Bible. It is meant to aid students in understanding why studying the world behind the text is essential to sound biblical interpretation. The following three chapters, 2, 3, and 4, are designed to build the scaffolding of good academic study: the how and why of what we do as Bible scholars and why it is crucial to understanding the Bible.

This book's big "why" can be summed up in one word: *context*. Context is required to understand what you are reading. Let me give you one example. A few years ago, on a business trip, I was at breakfast and reading *The Indianapolis Star*, and the headline was, "Hey, we are going to Disney World!" Now, without the proper context, the headline would be nonsense. But this was probably not the case for the residents of Indiana that day. What the headline meant was that the Pacers had won the previous night's basketball game and advanced to the NBA playoffs in Orlando, Florida. Also, the phrase "I'm going to Disney World" is commonly used after an athlete wins a championship. Imagine that it is a thousand years in the future, and you are reading this old headline. How could you understand its whole meaning? The text could be misunderstood, misinterpreted, or seen as nonsensical without proper context. In that future, I might be able to discern what basketball is, who the

Pacers were, and what Disney World was, but I would still miss the fanatical place basketball holds in the hearts of the people of Indiana. Ancient texts are often like this. We need all the help we can get to understand what the biblical text was saying then, and what it is saying now. Context, or as much context as possible, will aid us in getting closer to the text's whole meaning. We need to solve the puzzle of the contexts of the past to understand the meaning of the Bible for us in our time. Learning about these contexts and how they help us interpret the biblical texts is a journey that begins here.

2

Why Study the Historical Context of the Hebrew Bible?

As we established in chapter 1, context matters. Every novel you read sets the context for what will follow. Context can be described as the book's who, what, when, and how. Most of us read the Bible in our own context, which makes sense. The Bible is the word of God for us. However, part of academic study is also to look at the world behind the text and its historical and cultural contexts. This chapter will begin this task by reviewing a scholarly understanding of history. Then we will turn to the related study of culture and why it is also part of good interpretation. Finally, we will discuss how the Bible uses multiple genres of literature to teach us its lessons. Each genre has its way of truth-telling, and understanding them helps us better interpret the texts.

WHAT IS HISTORY?

Historian John Fea begins his discussion of history by reminding his readers of a difference between the "past" and "history." The past is a record of events that occurred before this moment. The Bible was written in the past. King David lived in the past. History is something different. History is a literary genre and an academic discipline that takes those events in the past and provides a narrative or story to explain them. As Fea says, "It is the art of reconstructing the past."[1] History makes those events take flesh and color and content. It tries to explain the "why" surrounding past events.

History begins with the research of primary sources. Fea describes primary sources as "the stuff left behind—documents, oral testimony, objects—to make

1. John Fea, *Why Study History?* (Baker Academic, 2013), 3.

the past come alive."[2] Some events have multiple primary sources, while others have very few or none. Historians are collectors of the work done by other experts. These experts, such as archaeologists, archivists, librarians, epigraphers, and other specialists, use their expertise to identify and analyze primary sources. Especially in studying ancient history, these sources include physical artifacts such as buildings, walls, and cooking pots. Others are epigraphic artifacts, sources with writing on them, such as monuments with inscribed writing, clay tablets, narratives, and law codes. The last category is art in the form of paintings, wall carvings, and statues. All these primary sources require analysis by specialized scholars, who provide a peer-reviewed assessment of these primary sources. These assessments offer the artifact's age and a comparison of similar artifacts in the region. The epigraphic (written) artifacts are translated from their ancient languages.

There is often rigorous debate about ancient physical and epigraphic artifacts. Why is there debate? First, it is the nature of scholarship to debate findings. Scholars present physical artifacts and provide evidence of the time they came from. Other scholars will investigate their discoveries, evaluate their evidence, and either concur with the dating or disagree and offer another explanation. In the case of epigraphic materials, scholars will offer dating and translation. Others will study the artifact and the evidence and concur or disagree with the dating and the translation. Eventually, however, a scholarly consensus will usually emerge. This means that a large group of scholars agree on the dating of an artifact or its date and translation in the case of writing. However, even if the consensus of most scholars is reached, the debate is not always finished. Many of the primary sources presented in this book are still debated by scholars decades or centuries after their discovery. This level of debate is not uncommon, and a historian must always admit to providing only the best information available at any point in time. Another discovery can alter what we know about a specific event or even a series of events. Debating about the artifacts is part of the energetic discussion that continues to refine and improve what can be known about ancient times and people.

Historian John Arnold also asserts that all primary sources the researcher discovers must be interrogated. He explains, "The historian does not simply 'report from the archives.' . . . [Such a report] would probably repeat half-truths and confusions, if not downright lies. Sources are not innocent; their voices talk to certain ends, intend certain consequences."[3] For example, an ancient king's accomplishments written on his palace wall must not be taken at face value. Its claims need to be vetted against everything known about the

---

2. Fea, *Why Study History?*, 3.
3. John Arnold, *History: A Very Short Introduction* (Oxford University Press, 2000), 78.

Why Study the Historical Context of the Hebrew Bible? 13

period. To present themselves in a better light, kings were known to exaggerate their accomplishments or omit mention of battles lost.

This type of interrogation, or historical vetting, also applies to the biblical text, not to discount it as an essential theological document but to understand what it tells the historian about the past. This practice often surprises and may feel threatening to some readers because the Bible has been read as a source of inspiration and moral truth. Some see this way of reading as a threat to the Christian faith. Analyzing a text's historical claims is not a routine method of reading for most people who are not professionals in religious studies. So, it is not surprising that this method may feel unusual and even disconcerting to new students who read the Bible as a holy text. Many have been taught not to question the text. However, a text can be read in multiple ways, and historical inquiry is one. Carolyn Sharp equates different ways of reading the Bible with swimming in the ocean.

> You can also float peacefully and tranquilly on the sea; just so, the spiritually oriented reader who seeks comfort in familiar stories or meaningful verse of the Psalms is engaging Scripture in a valuable way that has sustained believers and communities for many centuries. On the other hand, scholars and others preparing to wrestle in a sustained way with Scripture are like those who go into the ocean for long training swims—to strengthen their muscles, improve endurance, and perfect their form. . . . There is not only one faithful way to read.[4]

Critical biblical study means reading the Bible in multiple ways to strengthen one's theological and historical understanding. This book focuses on the historical context in which the books of the Hebrew Bible were written, but this does not exclude or devalue other ways of reading. Exploring the Bible's historical settings is one of the many ways of reading that is important for trained religious leaders.

WHAT IS HISTORIOGRAPHY?

Placing the primary sources in a context is called historiography, or history writing. Using all available sources, the historian first gathers, orders, and assesses those primary sources. Then, the historian provides a context so the reader can understand the story of these sources. The product of this work is a history book or article that is researched and compiled while using clear

---

4. Carolyn Sharp, *Wrestling the Word: The Hebrew Scripture and the Christian Believer* (Westminster John Knox, 2010), xv.

criteria. Each historian will use different criteria, but there are general aspects concerning historiography that students need to keep in mind.

Historiography is not a science. By this, I mean that an experiment combining sodium and chloride will result in salt every time. It is fixed, and it does not matter which scientist performs the experiment; there is still a pile of salt in the end. Historiography tells a well-researched story while using the rules established by the discipline. It is an interpretive enterprise with different results depending on the historian. Historians from different cultures or ideologies will interpret events and artifacts differently. For example, many European historians credited Christopher Columbus with discovering the New World.[5] The perspective of other historians resulted in recognizing the experiences of people who lived in North and South America before the arrival of the southern Europeans. Columbus found a place where people had lived for centuries. The second perspective involves historiography that uses primary sources from those indigenous people, which the earlier European historians did not use. Scholars from other places and cultures increased the number of primary sources and included them in their history writing, changing how history was told. Archaeology, the discovery of artifacts, is a science,[6] but interpreting those artifacts and setting them in a historical and cultural context are acts of contextualization done with academic rigor and critical thought in the field of historiography.

All historiography is partial. In other words, a history does not contain all the information about people or places. This is the case for several reasons. First, a historian can only write what the primary sources allow. For the most part, the more ancient the period examined, the fewer primary sources exist. For example, historians trying to comment on the period of Abraham are faced with a lack of primary sources. Why? First, no clear time frame is specified in the Bible. This hampers the historian from knowing exactly where and when to search for those sources. Second, the Bible indicates that Abraham lived a nomadic lifestyle, so there is no specific place to look for what remains from his dwellings. So, without a particular time frame or a place to look, there are no artifacts to interpret. The historian's work is stymied before the writing even begins.

Second, historiography is partial because existing primary sources do not tell the whole story. For example, women were not considered important in most ancient cultures. Thus, little was said of their lives in ancient documents. Their stories cannot be easily recovered because they were rarely recorded in

---

5. D. Armitage, "Christopher Columbus and the Uses of History," *History Today* 42, no. 5 (May 1992): 50–55.

6. Ken Dark, "The Science of Archaeology," *Philosophy Now* (1991): 3, https://philosophynow.org/issues/3/TheScienceofArchaeology.

the first place. A historian is prevented from telling the story of ancient women because the primary sources excluded them. Ancient patriarchy impacts how history can be written.

Third, written sources do not narrate every event or even everything about a society. When studying the Hebrew Bible, one of the greatest frustrations is that, for the most part, a description of the actual worship practices of the Hebrew people is not part of the biblical text. The Bible does not contain a worship manual, so scholars must piece together what little is known and try to fill in the blanks. They use worship practices from later periods where more documentation is available. They also investigate how other ancient cultures worshiped to piece together the most likely ways the people worshiped privately and corporately. Unfortunately, what is known is often much less than what remains hidden in the historical inquiry of ancient people.

Fourth, any history book is partial because each historian focuses on a self-selected slice of the past. For example, this book centers on a specific time, region, and people. It places this time and people in its greater context, but its focus is still myopic. The book discusses other contemporary cultures in the region but does not provide a full exploration of those people or their literature. It will not tell the whole story of the ancient world during these periods.

One particular history book is also not the final word on the subject. John Fea notes, "While the past never changes, history changes all the time."[7] Historiography is a human endeavor. It is subjective, and as such, any history book joins the other books and articles written about a specific period of the past. Historians know that they enter a conversation with all the other texts written on the topic when they write a text. F. W. Dobbs-Allsopp explains the perspective of the biblical historian:

> Like the texts they study, [scholars] . . . are hopelessly embedded in their own cultures with all of that culture's attendant prejudices and biases. The positivist assumption that the critic can effectively efface [their] own cultural presuppositions is simply naïve. . . . In other words, critical historicists openly and enthusiastically embrace the utter subjectivity of all knowledge.[8]

The past is full of events, but the historian's task is to place those events in a context that involves a fair amount of educated guessing. The historian is also grounded in a specific place and time that shapes how one thinks and understands the world. Objective accounting is not possible. A good historian will

---

7. Fea, *Why Study History?*, 16.
8. F. W. Dobbs-Allsopp, "Rethinking Historical Criticism," *Biblical Interpretation* 8, no. 3 (July 1999): 242.

state their context so the readers know theirs is one perspective among many. A good historian writes *a* history, not *the* history. Any history book written is a contribution to the greater conversation.

All historiography sets individual primary sources in a historical and social context. As noted above, the first task of a historian is to identify and order the available artifacts with the aid of other experts in their fields, such as archaeologists and epigraphers. For example, when considering King Hezekiah, the historian would search in books by archaeologists for information about the period of Hezekiah's reign to learn about any building projects. This involves looking for written material from the period in Judah and other Mediterranean nations. These are all primary sources. But without a context, all we would know about King Hezekiah's reign would be a list of those primary sources.

Indeed, providing context is the bulk of a historian's work. Historians describe the culture that birthed the primary sources as best they can. John Arnold sees this as crucial: "We need to *interpret* the past, not simply present it. Finding a larger context for the story is an attempt to say not just 'what happened' but [also] what it meant."[9] One cannot say "what the past meant" without working to understand the culture—the system by which people make meaning—in which those events happened.

All history writing is the product of the historian's interests. Each scholar has a reason for spending years writing a book, impacting how the story is told. Some history books are written to be as comprehensive as possible. These books tend to be lengthy and not only cover, for instance, the history of Judah and Israel but also provide extensive coverage of the debates by historians concerning primary artifacts and their dates. Some books are written from a specific theological perspective and focus on whether the Bible is considered a perfect historical source or not. The variety of different history books demonstrates that history is far from settled. Like all academic fields, different perspectives help strengthen the field and historians' work.

This book is written for students studying the Bible for a limited time, such as a semester. It offers an overview of Israel and Judah's history and cultural context during the period covered in the Hebrew Bible. While making use of all the available information, both archaeological and epigraphic, it does not assume the biblical text to be a more reliable source of history than other sources, nor does it assume that the extrabiblical literary sources are more historically correct than the biblical text. It gives a slightly higher credibility to archaeological data, compared to the biblical and extrabiblical literary sources, for the purpose of historical study. The book will use the narratives in the Bible to fill in the story between available sources with the account of the

---

9. Arnold, *History*, 8.

biblical text. Still, when it does so, it will state that this section is "according to the biblical text," which cues the reader to understand that the information comes only from the Bible. Such a perspective is a middle-of-the-road one among the history books about this period, based on the extent to which a scholar views the Bible as historically accurate. This book does not spend much time discussing the debates about the history of this period. Still, the matter of the historical accuracy of the Bible is one significant debate that even a brief book must mention.

DEBATES IN HISTORICAL RESEARCH OF ISRAEL AND JUDAH

There are two major camps in the historical research of ancient Israel and Judah. However, even within these two categories, not all scholars agree with each other on every detail. One side, nicknamed the minimalists, claims to find no or minimal history in the books of the Hebrew Bible. The nickname comes from their argument for minimal history in the Bible. They believe the Hebrew Bible is literature written or at least heavily edited in the Persian or Hellenistic period (539 to 64 BCE) and that to treat it as history is more misleading than helpful.[10] These scholars produce articles and books that challenge historical claims about the Bible. Scholars who lean in this direction believe the meaning of the Bible is found in its theological message alone. There is something to be said for their approach because these scholars focus on the theological message of the text or what the text teaches about God and humans and their relationship.

On the other side, the so-called maximalists or traditionalists believe most of the books of the Hebrew Bible are historically accurate. The nickname again reflects their central belief that the Bible contains a maximal amount of historically accurate information. These scholars seek ways to explain instances where the biblical text contradicts itself or when the archaeological record and the biblical text conflict. James Maxwell Miller and John H. Hayes define this position in this way: "The presumption here is that the biblical accounts should be taken as historically factual unless there are overwhelming reasons not to do so."[11] This position also has positives because it provides reasons for scholars to study the primary sources further to verify the events in the Bible

---

10. See, e.g., Philip R. Davies, *In Search of "Ancient Israel": A Study in Ancient Origins* (Bloomsbury, 1992).
11. J. Maxwell Miller and John H. Hayes, *A History of Ancient Israel and Judah*, 2nd ed. (Westminster John Knox, 2006), 79–80.

and incorporate new archaeological discoveries into books on the history of ancient Israel and Judah.

Most scholars, including me, end up somewhere in the middle of the minimalist-maximalist debates. There is historical information about Israel and Judah surrounding the narratives, poems, sayings, and oracles of the books of the Hebrew Bible. Still, our knowledge of that history will always be partial. In addition, the biblical text itself has its own complex past. Today, a book is conceived and written by some person(s) who place their name on it. It is usually not altered once it has been published. This was not the case for the biblical texts. In the ancient period, texts were both authoritative and changeable. Many narratives were told through generations of people before anything was written on scrolls. This pre-textual activity is called oral tradition. Finally, biblical texts were edited for long periods even after they were committed to writing. Even after being placed in written form, any narrative or biblical book was not considered unchangeable or even what we would think of as Scripture for a long while. Later generations would add to and subtract from these texts. This long editing process impacts the historical value of the Hebrew Bible since original details could be altered over time. Such editing makes the work of historians more difficult. Yet I still recognize historical elements in the Hebrew Bible, even if some details do not match other primary sources. However, I also believe the central message and meaning of the Hebrew Bible is theological, not historical.

In addition to the amount of history a scholar believes is in the Bible, historians also adopt a philosophy of the context surrounding an ancient literary source like the Bible. Some historians assume that if a narrative's facts cannot be verified, then it has no basis in fact. For example, Victor Matthews looks at all the available evidence and writes, "Given these uncertainties, it is not possible to say with confidence that Abraham, Isaac, Jacob, and Joseph, as well as their wives and children, were real persons."[12] Matthews adopts an accepted and often published method of interpreting the available evidence. If minimalist and maximalist were on a continuum, Matthews would be toward the minimalist side. People of faith, however, may find such a stark statement disturbing. Matthews judges the available sources by using his clear criteria. However, in writing this book, I adopt a different approach. When the primary sources cannot verify the existence of persons such as Abraham or Moses, I state that I cannot confirm that a specific person existed or that an event transpired. I am in the middle of the continuum and thus remain open to the possibility that the narratives contain heavily edited stories of real people. Note that Matthews and I are using the same evidence. We simply choose to state the result of our analysis differently.

---

12. Victor Matthews, *A Brief History of Ancient Israel* (Westminster John Knox, 2002), 4.

This perspective on the existence of biblical persons points to my preconceptions. I seek to outline the facts I believe contribute to understanding the history and culture of ancient Israel and Judah, but I do not do this as an objective observer. I am an ordained Presbyterian minister and scholar who teaches at a Reformed seminary. I believe there is historical information in the Bible. However, the Bible is not a history book. What you are reading now *is* a history book that is a companion to the Hebrew Bible. This book is meant to help us better understand the words of the Bible in their context. I also believe the Bible is the word of God. By understanding its contexts, we can better interpret the Bible for proclamation to the faithful today.

WHY ARE HISTORICAL AND CULTURAL CONTEXTS IMPORTANT TO THE STUDY OF THE BIBLE?

For many families, all the important events are recorded in the family Bible: births, marriages, and deaths. It is fitting these records are found in the Bible because, for Christians, the Bible is also part of their family story. The stories of biblical heroes and biblical values help shape the family's story. Although this makes a beautiful theological statement, such a perspective can impede how we understand the Bible in its own context. If we are not attentive, we often collapse our cultural norms with those embedded in Scripture. Randall Bailey explains,

> Too often we have failed to look at the biblical text as a cultural production within its own time and geographical location, and we have not recognized that our interpretations of the biblical text have been prodded and shaped by our own cultural understandings and time. This has robbed us, as readers, of the rich textures of the text and, ironically, has inflated the importance of our own readings to equal the high status we have attributed to the Bible itself.[13]

The culture of the biblical world is foreign, which is often masked because the stories sound so familiar and sacred to us.[14]

Culture functions much like a computer's operating system. It analyzes, records, and stores all our information, but unless the computer crashes, we seldom think about how it shapes every part of our activity. Clyde Kluckhohn defines culture as how people live, including thinking, feeling, and believing, as "the communal storehouse of pooled knowledge and the standardized lens

---

13. Randall Bailey, "The Bible as a Text of Cultures," *The Peoples' Bible*, ed. C. DeYoung, W. Gafney, L. Guardiola-Sáenz, G. Tinker, and F. Yamada (Augsburg Fortress, 2009), 10.

14. David Lowenthal, *The Past Is a Foreign Country* (Cambridge University Press, 1985), 1–12.

through which they see the world."[15] Culture constructs the default position for everything we think and do: the way we see the world, the way we discern right from wrong, the way we interpret what we read, and the way we process incoming information. And yes, the way we read the Bible.

THE BIBLE COMES FROM A DIFFERENT CULTURE

In studying history, one enters another culture. Reading a history book should require a passport, a physical object to remind us that the cultures of the past we are studying are different from our own. Their values are not our values, and their ideas about truth are not our ideas about truth. For example, in Genesis 16, Sarai gives Hagar, a woman enslaved to her, to Abram so that Sarai and Abram can finally become parents through Hagar's womb (16:1–2). Today, this act is seen as morally abhorrent. However, the cultural norms of the biblical period were not the same as those of ours. Gordon Wenham notes, "Given the social mores of the ancient Near East, Sarai's suggestion was a perfectly proper and respectable course of action."[16] By knowing the cultural norms at the time, an interpreter can better comment on her act. Sarai acted properly for the time. The problem, the interpreter can now see, is that within her context, the text is indicating that she should have trusted God and acted against the cultural norm for childless couples. Knowing the ancient cultural norms leads to a better understanding of the biblical text. This does not mean we overlook the fact that Sarai gave another woman, treated as an object due to her enslavement, to her husband to be impregnated. Unfortunately, until feminist or womanist interpretations (readings that reflect the experiences and concerns of Black women) became part of the conversation about biblical texts, this point was often overlooked, and Hagar's personhood was ignored. Here is an excellent example of how the understanding of a text is transformed by careful study. First, ancient cultural norms aid the interpreter in understanding the situation. Second, new voices of women and womanists added Hagar's plight to an age-old interpretation.

For the student of the Bible, this task of historical and cultural interpretation is multiplied because it is not enough to understand only the cultures of the Bible on the one hand and the culture of the modern interpreter on the other. Another layer of understanding must be considered: how the text has

---

15. Clyde Kluckhohn, *Mirror for Man: The Relation of Anthropology to Modern Life* (Whittlesey House, 1949; repr., Routledge, 2018), 24–26.

16. Gordon J. Wenham, *Genesis 16–50*, Word Biblical Commentary (Word Books, 1987), 7.

been interpreted over time. The study of these traditions is called reception history. One simple example comes from the opening chapters of Genesis. We have all heard that an apple was the fruit that tempted the first people. But, if you read the Bible closely, it is simply called "fruit" (Gen. 3:6). Western culture's interpretation of the fruit as an "apple" is explained by Rebeca Rupp:

> The apple as Forbidden Fruit seems to have appeared in western Europe at least by the 12th century. Some researchers suggest that the apple got a bad rap from an unfortunate pun: the Latin *malus* means both "apple" and "evil," which may have given early Christians [such] ideas. A 1504 engraving by Albrecht Durer shows Adam and Eve with apples; and 16th-century paintings by Lucas Cranach and Titian show Adam and Eve under particularly tempting apple trees. Though Michelangelo's *Temptation and Fall* on the Sistine Ceiling features forbidden figs, apples, increasingly, were held responsible for the Fall. By the 17th century, when Milton wrote *Paradise Lost*, the forbidden fruit was an Apple with a capital A.[17]

The history of interpretation helps the student understand how interpretations have been added to what was written in the biblical text. Today, many Christians of European descent "know" that the apple caused the downfall of Adam and Eve. The interpretation has become more powerful than what was written in the biblical text itself. With each word we read, it is crucial to remember to read the biblical text on the page instead of the preconceived interpretation of the text we have been taught. Our cultural lens and centuries of tradition often impact how we read and interpret the Bible. Students of the Bible must learn to interrogate those interpretations and engage the text on the page.

The other reason to keep our physical passport in mind is our ingrained sense of cultural normativity. Without critical thought, our own cultural operating system will persuade us to think that our culture is the norm by which all others are to be measured. Leticia Guardiola-Sáenz and Frank Yamada note this as also something we have been enculturated to do: "Sadly, more often than not, we are socially trained to assimilate that which is similar to us and reject that which is different from us."[18] This often manifests itself in an interpreter's desire to "fix" the biblical text according to our cultural values. One example is the story of God and Cain in Genesis 4. The text is clear:

---

17. Rebeca Rupp, "The History of the Forbidden Fruit," *National Geographic*, July 22, 2014, https://www.nationalgeographic.com/culture/article/history-of-apples.

18. Leticia Guardiola-Sáenz and Frank Yamada, "Culture and Identity," in DeYoung et al., *Peoples' Bible*, 4.

> In the course of time Cain brought to the LORD an offering of the fruit of the ground, and Abel for his part brought of the firstlings of his flock, their fat portions. And the LORD had regard for Abel and his offering, but for Cain and his offering he had no regard. So Cain was very angry, and his countenance fell. (4:3–5)

No reason for God's actions is provided in the text. Gordon Wenham notes, however, that commentators have provided at least five reasons for God's actions:

> (1) God prefers shepherds to gardeners (Gunkel). This seems improbable in the light of 2:15, where Adam was appointed to till the soil. (2) Animal sacrifice is more acceptable than vegetable offerings (Skinner, Jacob). While blood sacrifices were obviously regarded as more valuable, every stratum of the law recognizes the propriety and necessity of grain offerings as well. (3) God's motives are inscrutable: his preference for Abel's sacrifice reflects the mystery of divine election (von Rad, Vawter, Golka, and apparently Westermann). Clearly the preference for Abel does anticipate a frequent pattern in Genesis of the choice of the younger brother (cf. Jacob/Esau, Isaac/Ishmael, etc.), but this type of explanation should only be resorted to if the text gives no other motives for divine action. (4) Inspired by Heb. 11:4, "By faith Abel offered to God a more acceptable sacrifice than Cain," some commentators (e.g., Calvin, Dillmann, Driver, König) suggest that it was the differing motives of the two brothers, known only to God, that accounts for their different treatment. (5) The commonest view among commentators, ancient and modern, is that it was the different approaches to worship that counted and that this was reflected in the quality of their gifts. Whereas Cain offered simply "some produce of the land," Abel offered the choicest animals from his flock, "firstlings" and "their fat portions." The sacrificial law underlines frequently that only perfect, unblemished animals may be offered in sacrifice (Lev. 1:3; 22:20–22, etc.). "I will not offer burnt offerings to the LORD . . . that cost me nothing" (2 Sam. 24:24). Since this is the first account of sacrifice in the OT[,] we might well expect an allusion to this fundamental principle in this story.[19]

Scholars, it seems, go to great lengths to provide a reason for God's choice so God does not appear capricious.[20] Their modern understanding of God drives scholars to offer reasons for God's action, and these reasons become as powerful as the biblical text itself. The ancient culture from which this text

---

19. Gordon Wenham, *Genesis 1–15*, Word Biblical Commentary (Word Books, 1987), 104.
20. Angela Kim, "Cain and Abel in Light of Envy: A Study in the History of Interpretation of Envy in Genesis 4:1–16," *Journal for the Study of the Pseudepigrapha* 12, no. 1 (2001): 76.

Why Study the Historical Context of the Hebrew Bible? 23

sprang felt no such compulsion. The text offers no reason for the choice; it is this point we should grapple with instead of providing answers for a gap in the biblical text. Some traditions, such as Jewish midrash, engage in this type of gap-filling interpretation, but the purpose is more a philosophical and spiritual exercise than a definitive interpretation. For preaching and teaching, students should learn to deal with the text before them as it is. If there is a gap or puzzlement in the text, biblical interpreters should try to lean into the concern instead of fixing it to adhere to our cultural beliefs.

As these first two examples point out, the Bible is an ancient document from an ancient Eastern culture that is very different from our own. Understanding the Bible as a product of another culture or cultures will take study and practice. Another way the Bible can be puzzling to modern readers is its focus on agricultural life.[21] For example, Psalm 72 is a coronation hymn for the king of Judah. Right from the beginning, it connects righteous rule with the fruitfulness of the land.

> Give the king your justice, O God,
> and your righteousness to a king's son.
> May he judge your people with righteousness
> and your poor with justice.
> May the mountains yield prosperity for the people,
> and the hills, in righteousness. (72:1–3)

In this hymn human actions in ruling a kingdom are related to the fruitfulness of the land. In a world ever impacted by climate change, perhaps we can see how these ancient metaphors can help us reconnect with the land and its essential role in our world. Maybe we need to reconnect with the Bible's understanding of how human actions can and do impact the fruitfulness of the land. Other examples may not be so apparent. Isaiah 24 is a prophetic oracle that states, "For thus it shall be on the earth and among the nations, as when an olive tree is beaten, as at the gleaning when the grape harvest is ended" (24:13). According to J. J. M. Roberts, this is a metaphor representing the remnant of Israel or the ones who remain faithful even after the Babylonians' destruction of the temple in Jerusalem.[22] Olive trees are shaken or beaten during harvest to retrieve the last olives, but some will stay on the branches even then. Likewise, grapes are picked from the vines, but some are overlooked. To understand the message of the text, the reader needs to know how olives and grapes are harvested. Specific books called commentaries can help readers

---

21. Ellen Davis, *Scripture, Culture, and Agriculture: An Agrarian Reading of the Bible* (Cambridge University Press, 2009).
22. J. J. M. Roberts, *First Isaiah*, Hermeneia (Fortress, 2015), 315.

understand the agricultural metaphors of the Hebrew Bible and their meaning, as well as many other contextual meanings.

Another example of differences between our culture and those of the biblical period is how we measure time. Our time is defined by hours, minutes, seconds, and sometimes even hundredths of seconds or milliseconds. We always know what time it is, and the clock rules much of our lives. The ancients did not own wristwatches. Time was measured by the sun, moon, planets, stars, seasons, and harvest, not by a clock and calendar. Their way of understanding and valuing time is different from ours. One example is in Genesis 1. This refrain repeats with only the number of the day as variation: "And there was evening and there was morning, the first day." Why did the ancients state days in this way? Our day starts at sunrise. The ancients used a moon calendar, so their day began when it became dark—backward from the way we think.

Another example is how the Bible refers to the reigns of the kings. Our historical documents would have a birth, coronation, and death date, sometimes even to the minute. The writers of the Bible remembered the reigns of the kings this way, "In the twentieth year of King Jeroboam of Israel, Asa began to reign over Judah" (1 Kgs. 15:9). The coronation of one king is based not on a date, but on the regnal year of the king in the opposite kingdom. This was the writers' custom. Our way and the ancient way of accounting time are both valid; it simply is a matter of different cultural norms. These are two small examples, but they demonstrate that the cultures in the Bible and ours are quite different. If I visit another culture, I need to know as much as I can about that culture, or I will make mistakes, be misunderstood, and appear arrogant by assuming that my way of living is superior to all others. The same applies to the Bible.

One of my mentors, Jimmy J. M. Roberts, always reminded his students that those who wrote, edited, and preserved the Bible were not stupid or unsophisticated. They wrote the narratives the way they did with intention. They knew nothing of apples but understood the word "fruit." They presented a dilemma in Genesis 4 by not telling the reader why God acted the way God did. They knew a good king with a fair rule would impact everything, even the harvest in the fields. And they used the measurements of time that made sense to them. Their culture and its norms had their own integrity. We should realize that if we desire to fix the text, offer a rationale beyond the text, or apply our sense of time or governing to the text, that is our desire to make the text understandable and comfortable for *us*. The issue lies with us, not with the text and its ancient culture. The Bible, read in its cultural context, should challenge our own cultural preconceptions and how we think the world is organized. Reading outside our culture takes practice. It will force us to name our cultural operating systems and challenge our desire to make whatever we read conform to it.

THE BIBLE IN MULTIPLE CULTURAL CONTEXTS

The context of a biblical text, in its own time and place, matters. However, all the narratives in the Bible are not interchangeable, nor are they written in a vacuum. What happened at a specific time and place impacts the texts written during that time. For example, the prophets Jeremiah and Ezekiel prophesied in roughly the same period. However, they provide two different views of their situation. Jeremiah speaks of God's sorrow and tears over the sin of the people: "O that my head were a spring of water and my eyes a fountain of tears, so that I might weep day and night for the slain of the daughter of my people!" (Jer. 9:1). The picture is of an intimate God in pain as the people break God's heart. On the other hand, Ezekiel cannot even bring himself to describe the holy God, only describing "the appearance of the likeness of the glory of the LORD" in the temple as "like the bow in a cloud on a rainy day" (Ezek. 1:28). God, as described by Ezekiel, is lofty and majestic. It is a very different image from the one in Jeremiah. What can account for these two prophets' different descriptions of God?

We can begin to see how to understand these two prophets' words by studying their different contexts. Jeremiah was in Jerusalem, where the Babylonian army had surrounded the town, waiting for the inhabitants to starve. The context for these writings was one of the grimmest events in all biblical literature. The sorrow of that event is reflected in Jeremiah's message. God was present in the brokenness and sin of the people. As God saw their suffering, God cried. On the other hand, Ezekiel was exiled to Babylon. He was speaking from a majestic empire. The world of the Babylonians was one of massive architecture that proclaimed its tremendous power and privilege as the reigning empire. The statues of its gods were huge and impressive. Ezekiel provided an image of God as majestic and powerful as the gods the people saw in exile in Babylon. Babylon and its gods may be large and impressive, Ezekiel is saying, but *our* God is so large and holy that God does not even fit into these massive human-made places. The two contexts of Jerusalem and Babylon impacted how the prophet spoke of God to the people. If one does not know the context of each message, the two messages appear to offer wildly divergent characterizations of God. As good preachers, the prophets shaped their messages to fit their contexts. Both books then appear in the Bible, testifying to how the writers formed the message to suit the needs of the people in a specific place and time: context matters.

HISTORY, GENRE, AND TRUTH

For thousands of years, humans have used art to reflect their lives.[23] The date for the invention of writing has been debated, but most scholars place it in Mesopotamia, approximately 3200 BCE. It was used initially for accounting purposes.[24] The next development was narrative poetry.[25] The Sumerians, a people from Mesopotamia, told epic stories and then wrote them in cuneiform, a type of ancient writing. In later centuries, the purpose of writing was to record the narratives of a people, preserving a sense of who they were, where they came from, and their relationship with their god or gods. These stories did not take the form of history but of legend. A legend is a story shared by a culture, often in oral form, which cannot be verified and usually contains supernatural elements.

Modern history writing, or historiography, requires reflection on past events from many sources. History is a singular genre that uses clear and authenticated evidence to explain what happened and why. The invention of history writing is debated, but most scholars believe it originated in the Greek Empire in 452–450 BCE.[26] Herodotus (ca. 484–ca. 425 BCE) was one of the first historians; in his book, he states the purpose of his works:

> Herodotus of Halicarnassus herein puts on display the result of his inquiries so that man's past may not fade into oblivion over time nor the great and amazing deeds displayed by both Greeks and barbarians be without renown, with particular attention to the reason why they went to war with each other.[27]

The difference in Herodotus's works was not in simply telling the story of the war but also in recording events from eyewitnesses and analyzing why it happened. This kind of work marks the beginning of history writing, which seeks to explain and interpret past events by using and examining witnesses. T. James Luce reports that Herodotus traveled and listened to the reflections

---

23. The oldest cave paintings found to date are about 40,000 years old; M. Albert et al., "Pleistocene Cave Art from Sulawesi, Indonesia," *Nature* 514, no. 7521 (2014): 223–27. However, others question the definition of art: if "art" is seen as human traces of lines or squares, then this evidence of human activity is much older. Amy McDermott, "What Was the First 'Art'? How Would We Know?," in *Proceedings of the National Academy of Sciences of the United States of America* 18, no. 44 (2021), https://doi.org/10.1073/pnas.2117561118.

24. Piotr Michalowski, "The Presence of the Past in Early Mesopotamian Writings," in *Thinking, Recording, and Writing History in the Ancient World*, ed. Kurt Raaflaub (Wiley Blackwell, 2014), 145.

25. Michalowski, "Mesopotamian Writings," 145.

26. T. James Luce, *The Greek Historians* (Routledge, 1997), 1.

27. Herodotus, *Herodotus with English Translation*, ed. A. D. Godley (Harvard University Press, repr., 1960), 1:2.

of the people involved in the events.[28] He also clearly states the reason for his inquiry. We do not know when or even if the writers and editors of the Hebrew Bible knew of Herodotus and his writings, which represent some of the earliest history writing. Not till 331 BCE did Alexander the Great conquer the Persian Empire, of which Judah was a part. Whether or not the biblical authors knew of Herodotus, the Bible does not contain the same sense of researched history. It is more focused on the relationships between God and humans than on the historical reporting of human events. This is not to say there is no historical information in the Bible; there is. The difference is clear: Herodotus declares that he is writing a history book. The Hebrew Bible makes no such claims; its primary purpose is to tell about God and God's people.

The Hebrew Bible uses multiple genres and literary devices to explore who God is and God's relationship with the world. Each genre requires a different understanding of how it is conveying truth. Below, I introduce several genre examples within the Hebrew Bible to demonstrate this point and discuss how these can and cannot be understood as history. The genre of a given biblical text matters for its correct interpretation. Not all biblical texts can be read in the same way, nor do all texts have a historical perspective. A student of the Bible must take the genre into account when interpreting texts. There are at least six genres in the Hebrew Bible.

The first genre category is *saga*. Multiple sagas begin the Hebrew Bible in Genesis 1–11. The great theologian Karl Barth defined this section of Genesis as "an intuitive and poetic picture of a pre-historical reality."[29] Likewise, William Placher explains how this genre functions: "In its intuitive poetic way, saga communicates truths about the ultimate origins of things."[30] Another name for this genre is *myth*. In our modern culture, myths and sagas are often seen as untrue or fiction. But just because sagas and myths cannot be verified historically does not mean they are not true. They are true because they describe human nature and our relationship with our Creator and nature. These are statements of belief and faith, not history. They are true in the same way that God being represented as a rock in the Psalms is true. These genres give witness to a reality beyond what the eyes can see. Their meaning comes from other ways of knowing. Barth states, "We are no less truly summoned to listen to what the Bible has to say here in the form of saga than to what it has to say in other places in the form of history, and elsewhere in the form of address, doctrine, law, epigram, epic and lyric."[31]

---

28. Luce, *Greek Historians*.
29. Karl Barth, *Church Dogmatics*, III/1, trans. J. Edwards, O. Bussey, and H. Knight (T&T Clark, 1960), 81.
30. William Placher, "Is the Bible True?," *Christian Century* 112, no. 28 (2001): 925.
31. Barth, *Church Dogmatics*, III/1:83.

Legend is another genre of biblical texts that many modern readers often confuse with history. Legends are like sagas, but legends mix the ordinary with the extraordinary. The legends in the Hebrew Bible were probably once based on actual historical events, but over time, the telling of an event expanded, so the original historical event is hard to determine. One large section of legends begins in Genesis 12, with Abraham and Sarah, and runs through all the narrative sections of the remainder of Genesis, Exodus, and Numbers. Concentrating primarily on the narratives in Genesis 12–50, legends have several features. The first is that the stories originated as and are preserved by oral tradition. They are stories told over and over to generations of ancient people before they were placed in written form.[32] The second characteristic is that they tell stories of smaller events. Modern history writing is usually concerned with significant events in a nation, such as presidential elections, significant policies, social events, and wars, but not the story of two sisters married to the same man (Gen. 29). Gunkel notes, "History would be expected to tell how and for what reasons David succeeded in delivering the Israelites from the Philistines; legend prefers to tell how the boy David once slew a Philistine agent."[33] Also, Gunkel asserts that legends "report things which are quite incredible,"[34] such as serpents and donkeys who talk (Gen. 3:1–6; Num. 22:1–40), people who live hundreds of years (Gen. 5:27), and a sun that stands still (Josh. 10:12-14). Legends also have a lesson to teach us only when we consider their genre as different from a historical accounting of events. For example, the whole of Israel and Judah's story in the Bible demonstrates how their disobedience to God led to their loss of rule in their own land. The lesson is not so much historical as theological.

The Bible also contains *legal codes* in Exodus, Deuteronomy, and Leviticus. The legal codes are another genre and are not in historical order. Jewish tradition holds that there are 613 commandments in the Hebrew Bible.[35] However, the codes are not date-stamped, so knowing when a specific law was added is impossible. We do not know which laws were the first or added last. However, the laws are of historical value because they define the ancient culture's community rules. For example, Exodus 22:14 tells us, "When someone borrows an animal from another and it is injured or dies, the owner not being present, full restitution shall be made." This law code explains how the community lived out their commitment to God and their neighbor.

Like law codes, *proverbs* teach us how the community practiced its faith and beliefs. Again, this genre is not strictly historical but opens a way to access the

---

32. Hermann Gunkel, *The Legends of Genesis*, trans. W. H. Carruth (Open Court, 1901), 4.
33. Gunkel, *Legends of Genesis*, 5.
34. Gunkel, *Legends of Genesis*, 7.
35. Israel Drazi, *Maimonides and the Biblical Prophets* (Gefen Publishing, 2009), 209.

community's wisdom: "A gentle tongue is a tree of life, but perverseness in it breaks the spirit. A fool despises a parent's instruction, but the one who heeds admonishment is prudent" (Prov. 15:4–5).

A third of the Hebrew Bible is *poetic*, including the psalms, most prophets, and wisdom books such as Ecclesiastes, Job, and Song of Solomon. Poetic texts are known for the literary device of metaphor. A metaphor is when one thing is substituted for another as a poetic comparison. A metaphor makes a point about the essence of something. For example, a saying from Proverbs, "The mouth of the righteous is a fountain of life" (10:11), is not meant to be an anatomical description. A poem from Psalms does not mean God is a literal "rock" (28:1). Likewise, a prophetic oracle comparing Israel to a grapevine is used to make a greater point (Jer. 6:9), not as a statement of fact. These are metaphors that make a point about human nature being a source of abundance or the strength of God. Metaphorical speech is not historical speech: it has another purpose. Like other genres, poetic texts contain kernels of historical events, which are often generalized by poetic devices, making them mostly useless for modern historical purposes.

The final genre category is the group of so-called *historical books*. The name seems to indicate that the purpose of these books is historical narrative. These are the books of Joshua, Judges, 1 and 2 Samuel, 1 and 2 Kings, and 1 and 2 Chronicles. The category "historical books" is modern. In Jewish tradition, the first six books in this list are in the Prophets section, and 1 and 2 Chronicles are in the Writings. These books narrate how Israel and Judah became nations, grew, and then were overtaken by other empires. Many historical elements are in these books, but history is not their central purpose. For example, the battles in Joshua probably had a historical event or events associated with them. As the story was told and retold over time, the narrative grew and became an epic legend. So the scholar uses these books as a source for writing history while realizing that these books are not strictly historical in their purpose.

Historiography, or history writing, has also evolved and changed since the first works of Herodotus, who admits the influence of the gods but puts the stress on human character and actions. Today, history books deal with human acts and the reasons behind them. Contemporary history writing never involves the realm of God. But in the Bible, God is the book's central character and its very purpose. There are many genres in the Hebrew Bible, but none are solely about humans and their political and personal reasons for their actions. Stated as clearly as I can, if God is a character in the narrative, then the text is not modern historiography. This does not mean that the stories in the Bible are not true. It also does not mean that the narrative did not happen. This means that the perspectives presented in these books are not strictly historical. There may be historical elements, but the purpose of the biblical texts is not a historical accounting of events and their context.

Historiography uses multiple sources for its information. Written accounts, archaeological discoveries, and all available art and artifacts are used as witnesses to the past. The most reliable historical points have more than one verification method, such as an event mentioned in a biblical text confirmed by archaeological discovery. The purpose of modern history books that seek to understand the ancient world of the Bible is not to challenge or discredit the Bible. The historians enhance our understanding of the world of the Bible, its context and events. History books do this when students use them to aid their study of biblical texts. This book aims to help students do just that. It is designed as a companion for critical study: it does not replace or challenge the truth of the Bible.

SUMMARY

Historiography is a discipline that places the available primary sources from a time period in context. It involves gathering available artifacts and resources, interpreting them while using specific criteria, and placing them in a context to tell a story about how and why past events took place. As a result, it is an interpretive enterprise. It is always partial, because of both the available resources and the specific perspective of the scholar. It is never the only word because historians are embedded in their own contexts, and those contexts shape the way they see and understand the world. A history book of the ancient period of the Hebrew Bible does not replace the Bible. Its purpose is to contextualize the past by using all available resources and artifacts. All this is done in the service of good biblical interpretation.

We need to be reminded that the world of the Bible is not our world. We cannot assume that the culture of the Bible is the same as our own. Texts need to be interpreted within their ancient contexts and not be expected to conform to our culture's norms. This means remembering that the Bible is a theological book containing multiple genres, and these genres tell their truth in various ways. It also means understanding that the purpose of the Bible is not to provide a history of Israel and Judah but to tell the theological story of the relationship between God and God's people, even as there are historical elements within the narratives and poetry of the Bible.

3

Israel and Judah in Context

In twenty years of teaching, I have noticed that students often struggle to remember the knowledge gained from their secular education and connect it with their religious education. A student in my class noted, "The world of the Bible was taught as a world unto itself. I knew about Hammurabi,[1] but I never realized his laws related to the Bible." Students will affirm that the oldest humans were found in Africa, and a moment later, they will affirm that Adam and Eve of Genesis were the first people on earth. You may also feel this disconnect. This is not a failure by students but by the teachers, pastors, and culture that have not encouraged a connection between religious and general education.

This chapter will engage this divide and aid students in understanding a fuller history of the Afro-Asiatic region and where the Hebrew Bible fits into the overall time frame of the prehistoric and ancient history of this region. Second, it will present the geographical context of the area and how its topography and location are essential for understanding the Bible. Finally, the chapter will present some of the region's rich literary traditions, which sheds additional light on the context of the biblical texts.

First, it is important to define the areas of the world discussed in this book. The chronology below applies to the whole earth. Still, this book focuses on the continents of Africa and Asia, specifically focusing on northeastern Africa and (south)western Asia. For this book, this region is named the Afro-Asiatic region because it is where the two continents come together, and people in this region receive influence from both cultural contexts.

---

1. Joshua J. Mark, "Hammurabi," *World History Encyclopedia*, April 16, 2018, https://www.worldhistory.org/hammurabi/.

CHART 2: CHRONOLOGY OF THE AFRO-ASIATIC REGION

Prehistoric Periods	
Paleolithic	before 10,000 BCE
Mesolithic	10,000– 8000 BCE
Neolithic	8000–4000 BCE
Chalcolithic	4000–3200 BCE
Ancient Times	
Early Bronze Age	3200–2000 BCE
Middle Bronze Age	2000–1550 BCE
Late Bronze Age	1550–1200 BCE
Iron Age I–III	1200–500 BCE
Persian Period	539–330 BCE
Classical Times	
Hellenistic Period	330–63 BCE
Roman Period	63 BCE–324 CE

THE WORLD BEFORE THE PEOPLE OF THE BIBLE

Archaeologists have identified the oldest human fossilized skeleton in South Africa, thought to be about 3.67 million years old.[2] During the Paleolithic Era (before 10,000 BCE), humans were hunter-gatherers. During this prehistoric time, human achievements included toolmaking and the discovery of fire. Humans evolved slowly at first in the Paleolithic and Mesolithic Eras, with few changes over thousands of years. During these periods, humans developed stone tools (Paleolithic) and improved those stone tools (Mesolithic). Human progress was moving forward, but at a slow rate of change and improvement.

---

2. Elaina Zachos, "3.6 Million-Year-Old Human Ancestor Unveiled to the Public," *National Geographic*, December 6, 2017, https://www.nationalgeographic.com/science/article/million-year-old-human-ancestor-unveiled-to-public-spd.

The invention of farming marked the beginning of the Neolithic Period (8000 to 4000 BCE), significantly changing humans' lives.[3] Some nomadic groups of the past transitioned slowly to a more sedentary farming community-based existence in fertile regions. Others continued the nomadic lifestyle for centuries. For the first time, new farming techniques provided excess food that could be sold to others. The additional development of pottery for food and water storage provided the means for the first cities to appear. Scholars are divided on which city developed first, but Shedet in Egypt, Uruk in Mesopotamia, and Jericho in the West Bank were all developed around 7000–6000 BCE.[4]

The Bronze Age, which began in 3200 BCE, is so named because of the discovery of metallurgy by mixing copper and tin. This process produced a more rigid metal that could be fashioned into metal tools and weapons. These inventions, along with rapid increases in the availability and quality of pottery, increased food production and distribution. Because of these improvements, cities became more extensive and more plentiful. Commerce resulted in the need for a record-keeping system: as a result, writing was invented, marking a change in the epoch from Prehistoric times to the Ancient Age. The Ancient Age began with the invention of writing.

Mesopotamia and Egypt grew into some of the first empires during this period. Empires built monumental structures and controlled large regions of land. Both features required a government with laws, skilled workers, and a military. Egypt constructed the pyramids and the Sphinx between 3000 and 1500 BCE, during the Early and Middle Bronze periods. At this time, humankind in the Afro-Asiatic region was a mix of nomads, farmers, and urbanites. Empires emerged from this growing ability to farm, build, and create armies.

From the first cave drawings dating back to Paleolithic times, humans wanted to tell their stories. Writing continued to develop during the Bronze Age, moving from being used in business to recording human stories. One of the first major works was the Epic of Gilgamesh, a legend first told by Babylonian storytellers in about 2000 BCE.[5] It was finally recorded on twelve clay tablets about 1200 BCE, during the Late Bronze period. Empires also needed laws. King Hammurabi of Babylon developed one of the first known written law codes around 1750 BCE.[6]

The importance of these early written pieces is hard to overestimate in human history. Written laws now govern humans. These ancient cultures also

---

3. K. L. Noll, *Canaan and Israel in Antiquity: A Textbook on History and Religion*, 2nd ed. (Bloomsbury T&T Clark, 2013), 108.

4. The debate centers on differing definitions of what distinguishes a city from a village.

5. Benjamin R. Foster, trans. and ed., *The Epic of Gilgamesh: A New Translation, Analogues, Criticism, and Response*, 2nd ed. (Norton, 2019). Original author unknown.

6. Mark, "Hammurabi."

began writing epic poetry to preserve, remember, and celebrate their culture and past. All these achievements happened before the nations of Israel and Judah were established. This world and its cultures are the prehistory for our oldest stories of faith. This was the larger world into which the narratives and poetry of the Hebrew Bible would be birthed.

EARLY CANAANITE INHABITANTS
(14,000–3200 BCE)

Canaan is a smaller area within the Afro-Asiatic region, which encompasses the area that will become ancient Aram, Phoenicia (NRSVue: Sidon/ians), Israel, Judah, Ammon, Moab, Edom, and Philistia by the biblical period.[7] The region's name first appears in a fifteenth-century BCE text from Mari (in present-day eastern Syria [Aram], on the Euphrates), a northern Afro-Asiatic city that names Canaan as a region or land.[8] Canaan is also a term used in the earliest stories of the Bible, from Genesis through Joshua, but rarely afterward. In this book, the Afro-Asiatic region refers to the lands that stretch from Egypt to Mesopotamia (map 1).

Canaan is used for the smaller region (map 2). It is a name that predates the Bible and was used by the people who lived in that region. Other familiar modern names, such as Palestine and the Levant, are names assigned to the region at later times by colonizing empires.[9]

The oldest evidence of humans in Canaan is a 55,000-year-old skull discovered in the Manot Cave in western Galilee. It is the oldest skull identified outside of Africa.[10] This skull places humans in Canaan during the Paleolithic period (before 10,000 BCE). Many scholars also believe the invention of farming began in the Afro-Asiatic region in communities such as the Natufian

---

7. Philip Schmitz, "Canaan (Place)," *ABD* 1:828–31.

8. *ANET*, 577. Henry Baker Tristram argues that "Canaan" is a native name meaning lowlands. *Biblical Places: Topography of the Holy Land* (SPCK, 1897), 336.

9. Other common names were assigned to the region by colonizing empires; Palestine is of Greek origin, and the Levant is a French word meaning "rising," as in the East. Europeans used it in the 15th century to name this region, and so did a French mandate in 1920–46; David Graf, "Levant," *The Oxford Encyclopedia of Greece and Rome*, vol. 1, ed. Michael Gagarin and Elaine Fantham (Oxford University Press, 2010), 247–48.

10. John Pickrell, "Oldest Human Fossil outside of Africa Discovered," National Geographic Society, January 25, 2018, https://news.nationalgeographic.com/2018/01/oldest-human-outside-africa-discovered-fossil-jaw-israel-science/. This was the oldest skull until 2019, when a skull discovered in Greece was deemed 210,000 years old. This is a new development and still requires additional vetting. Maya Wei-Haas, "Enigmatic Skull May Be the Oldest Modern Human outside Africa. But Questions Abound," July 10, 2019, https://www.nationalgeographic.com/science/2019/07/enigmatic-skull-may-be-oldest-modern-human-out-of-africa/.

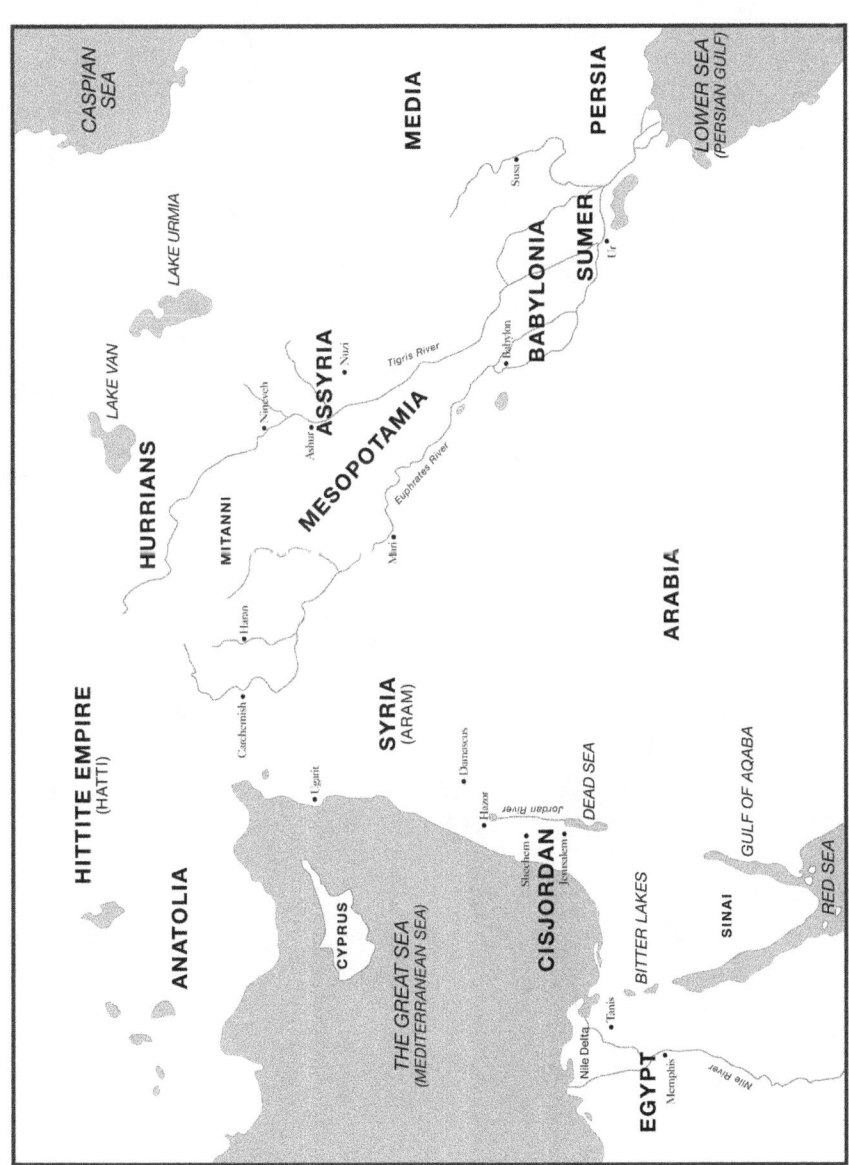

Map 1. The Afro-Asiatic region. (Courtesy of Karla Bohmbach)

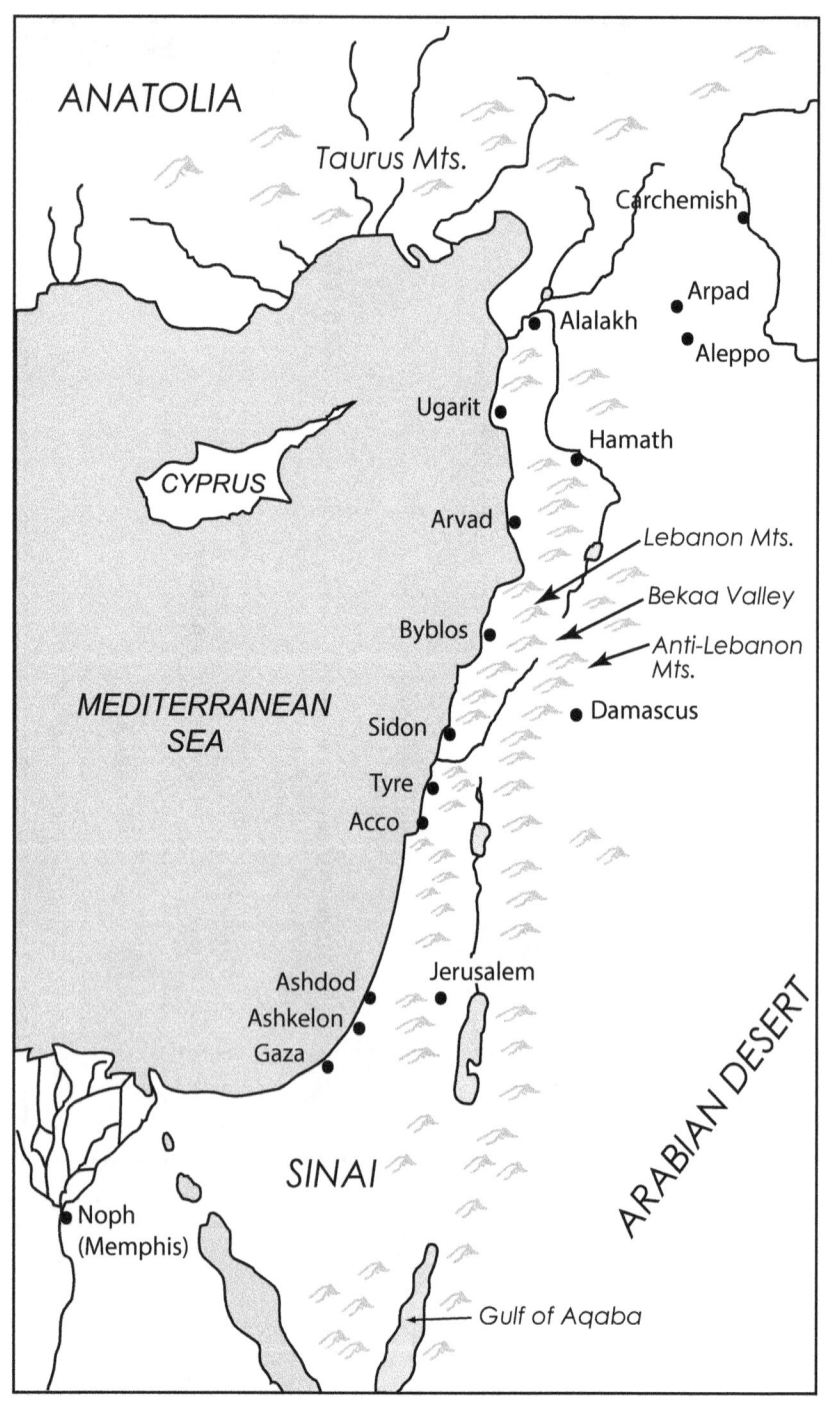

Map 2. Canaan. (Courtesy of Westminster John Knox Press)

village of Ain Ghazal, located in ancient Canaan.[11] These communities of Canaan developed social organization and used a combination of food gathering, farming, and hunting, using stone and flint tools.[12] This occurred during the Mesolithic Age (10,000–8000 BCE).[13]

During the early Neolithic Age (8000–6000 BCE), these communities grew along the Jordan River Valley, and Jericho was established as one of the first cities in the world. The inhabitants of Jericho raised city walls to protect the settlement. Building walls demonstrates a growing governmental and social structure: such a project requires cooperation and pooled resources and labor.[14]

The Ghassulian tribe is another group that emerged later in Canaan (4000–3200 BCE). In addition to occupying the Jordan Valley, they established small settlements in the peripheral southern desert regions, the coastal plain, the northern Negev, and the southern Sinai Peninsula.[15] The Ghassulians were also the first group to move to multiple places widely scattered across Canaan, adapting to various environments. These multiple sites helped the region take a big step toward becoming an interrelated nation-state. These groups are all precursors to those who wrote and preserved the Bible.

AFRO-ASIATIC EMPIRES DIVIDE CANAAN (3200–1500 BCE)

The Early Bronze Period (3200–2000 BCE) marks the beginning of what historians call ancient times, which saw the rise of the empires of Egypt and Sumer (the southern region of Mesopotamia), which divided the Afro-Asiatic region. The Sumerian Empire of Mesopotamia had more influence in the northern sections of Canaan, especially Syria (Aram), sharing culture, material items, and trade connections. The southern region of Canaan shared more resources and cultural influences with Egypt.[16] However, the whole region reflected a mix of resources, literature, and cultural influences of both empires. Like the earlier Ghassulian villages, small and unfortified villages continued to develop

---

11. O. Bar-Yosef and F. Valla, "The Natufian Culture and the Origin of the Neolithic in the Levant," *Current Anthropology* 31 (1990): 433. Melinda Zeder argues that farming was established in several areas of the Fertile Crescent simultaneously and independently: "The Origins of Agriculture in the Near East," *Current Anthropology* 54 (2011): 223–26.

12. Amihai Mazar, *Archaeology of the Land of the Bible: 10,000–586 B.C.E.* (Doubleday, 1990), 36.

13. Mazar, *Archaeology*, 36. They call this the Epi-Paleolithic Age.

14. Mazar, *Archaeology*, 42.

15. David Ussishkin, "The 'Ghassulian' Temple in Ein Gedi and the Origin of the Hoard from Nahal Mishmar," *BA* 34, no. 1 (1971): 23.

16. Mazar, *Archaeology*, 92.

in Canaan.[17] In fertile regions, settled agricultural villages replaced nomadic herding. Larger fortified cities grew, and the inhabitants built shared water and grain storage facilities and monumental public buildings.[18] Cities such as Dan, Hazor, Beth-Shean, Megiddo, Jericho, and Lachish developed during this period. These cities continued to grow and appear in later biblical narratives. The development of organized city planning and massive structures for food and water storage required an increasing development of a centralized government in Canaan.

The first known information about the people who would become Israel and Judah is believed to appear in the region near the close of the Late Bronze Age (1550–1200 BCE), but most of their story occurs in the subsequent Iron Age. By the Late Bronze Age, "the peaks of ancient Egyptian civilization—the Old Kingdom, Middle Kingdom, and New Kingdom—had already come and gone. The Sumerian city-states, Hammurabi's Babylonian kingdom, the Hittite Empire, and the Minoan and Mycenaean civilization—all of this was past history."[19] The people portrayed in the Hebrew Bible were latecomers to an active and growing Afro-Asiatic region.

This history is often surprising for students. Many Christians have been taught that the Bible contains the first and only stories of humanity, a claim the Bible never makes for itself. Indeed, the Bible speaks of other civilizations surrounding the first people presented in the Bible (Gen. 4:14–16). The people who told and shared the stories of Genesis knew other groups of people surrounding them, and they probably heard the stories of those who came before them.

CANAAN AND THE GROWTH OF SMALL NATION-STATES (1500–1000 BCE)

Ever since there were people on the earth, they organized themselves into larger family units, often called clans or tribes. The people of Canaan were no exception. Several tribes would join to form clans for worship, trade, and mutual protection. Several clans were then incorporated into nation-states under kings. These kingdoms were not the same as modern-day nations, which have strict borders and passports. The edges of ancient kingdoms were much more porous, with the borders changing based on the territory held by various tribes and families. However, genetically, the people of these tribes were not

---

17. Mazar, *Archaeology*, 94.

18. Aharon Keminski, *The Rise of an Urban Culture: The Urbanization of Palestine in the Early Bronze Age, 3000–2150 BC* (Israel Ethnographic Society, 1978), 235–41.

19. J. Maxwell Miller and John H. Hayes, *A History of Ancient Israel and Judah*, 2nd ed. (Westminster John Knox, 2006), 3.

different. Most people in the Canaanite region shared a common ancestry. They formed different kingdoms but were ethnically descendants of the same group of Afro-Asiatic peoples.

Where did the people of Israel and Judah come from, and when did they arrive in Canaan? This is a difficult question to answer. Genesis 11:31 notes that Abram's father, Terah, journeyed with his family from their hometown, Ur-Kasdim, which is translated in English as "Ur of the Chaldeans." This traditional translation places Ur in southern Mesopotamia. However, a trip from this city would not place the family in Haran, a city in southeastern Turkey. A better fit for the narratives of Abraham is Ur-Kasdim in Turkey, as Muslim traditions suggest (modern-day Urfa). This city, located further north, aligns with Abram's family's work as herders, and it is a suitable origin point for a journey that includes a stop in Haran,[20] about 500 miles north-northeast of Megiddo. This city was part of the Aramaean portion of Mesopotamia, as stated in Deuteronomy 26:5, and in the northern edge of ancient Sumer's influence. Information of the dating of this journey is likewise difficult to know with certainty. All available evidence shows that the Abram and Sarai story occurred in the Late Bronze Age (1550–1200 BCE).

This period has little historical information because all the major kingdoms of the area were in decline, and major cities, along with their written records, were destroyed. Historical records tell us that a mixed group of people moved in and took over the area earlier controlled by these city-states. Abram and Sarai were possibly part of this migration to Canaan. We do know that the people who would become Israel and Judah come from the same genetic pool as those who populated Canaan in the Late Bronze and Early Iron Ages. These tribes were known collectively as Canaanites. Slowly, the tribes grew into small nation-states.

A group of small Canaanite nation-states made up the near neighbors to the emerging Israel and Judah. These small nation-states were either allies or at war with Israel and Judah at various times. At other times, they were all controlled by larger and more powerful empires. All the people in Canaan may have been members of different nation-states, but they all looked the same and shared the same overall culture. They cooked using the same utensils. They farmed in the same ways. Their houses were made the same way. What was different was whom they affiliated with and some of the gods they worshiped. Canaan is a region, not a people. The region was made up of different tribes of people. These tribes would soon become nation-states.

---

20. Gary A. Rendsburg, "Ur Kasdim: Where Is Abraham's Birthplace?," *TheTorah.com*, 2019, https://thetorah.com/article/ur-kasdim-where-is-abrahams-birthplace.

THE NATION-STATES OF CANAAN
(1000–586 BCE)

The nation-states of Canaan were neighbors (map 3). Natural disasters such as earthquakes or famine impacted all of them. Part of telling the history of Israel and Judah involves these neighboring nations. This helps to remind us that Israel and Judah were not alone. Often the Bible will set Israel and Judah against "the Canaanites," but in this small region, the fate of one nation-state was tied to what happened in the others. Israel and Judah alongside these other six nations—Aram, Phoenicia, Ammon, Moab, Edom, and Philistia—were all part of Canaan. Each nation-state had its own customs, government, and tribal alliances, but they all were Canaanites.

You may have noticed that this book refers to Israel and Judah as separate states. This is because, for most of their history, they were. Judah was in the southern region, south of the Valley of Aijalon. Israel was a larger nation to the north. As will be seen in chapter 4, the hill country of Israel was developed first, with the territory of Judah being occupied later in the settlement period of 1200–1000 BCE. This settlement from north to south was probably related to weather. Northern areas received more rain and thus produced more crops. The regions of Judah are more arid. The official split into two nations occurred after the death of King Solomon (about 930 BCE). However, tensions between Israel and Judah are seen as early as the books of Joshua and Judges. For most of their existence, Israel and Judah were two nation-states whose people worshiped the same God. At times, the two nations were in a beneficial and peaceful relationship; at other times, they were antagonistic or even in a state of war.

To the north of Israel was the Kingdom of Damascus, also called Aram (now modern-day Syria and Southern Turkey). The Aramaeans were a group of tribes from Mesopotamia. Deuteronomy 26:5 states that Abraham was a wandering Aramaean, and Genesis 12:4 says he was from Haran, a city on the northern border of ancient Aram. The kingdoms of Damascus and Israel shared close ties because of their proximity and the shared international road that ran through their nations (map 6—see further discussion of road routes on p. 44). Aram was more involved in the story of Israel and Judah than any other Canaan nation-state.

To the east of the Jordan River were the kingdoms of Ammon, Moab, and Edom. The map shows these countries stacked on top of each other. Ammon was located to the north. Its northern border was the Jabbok River. The river appears in the narratives of Jacob and Esau (Gen. 32:22, 23) and Joshua (Josh. 12:2). Judah or Israel often controlled Ammon. David used conscripted labor from it (2 Sam. 12:31). Ammon did not reach its zenith until the Assyrian and Babylonian Empires, when the power of Israel and

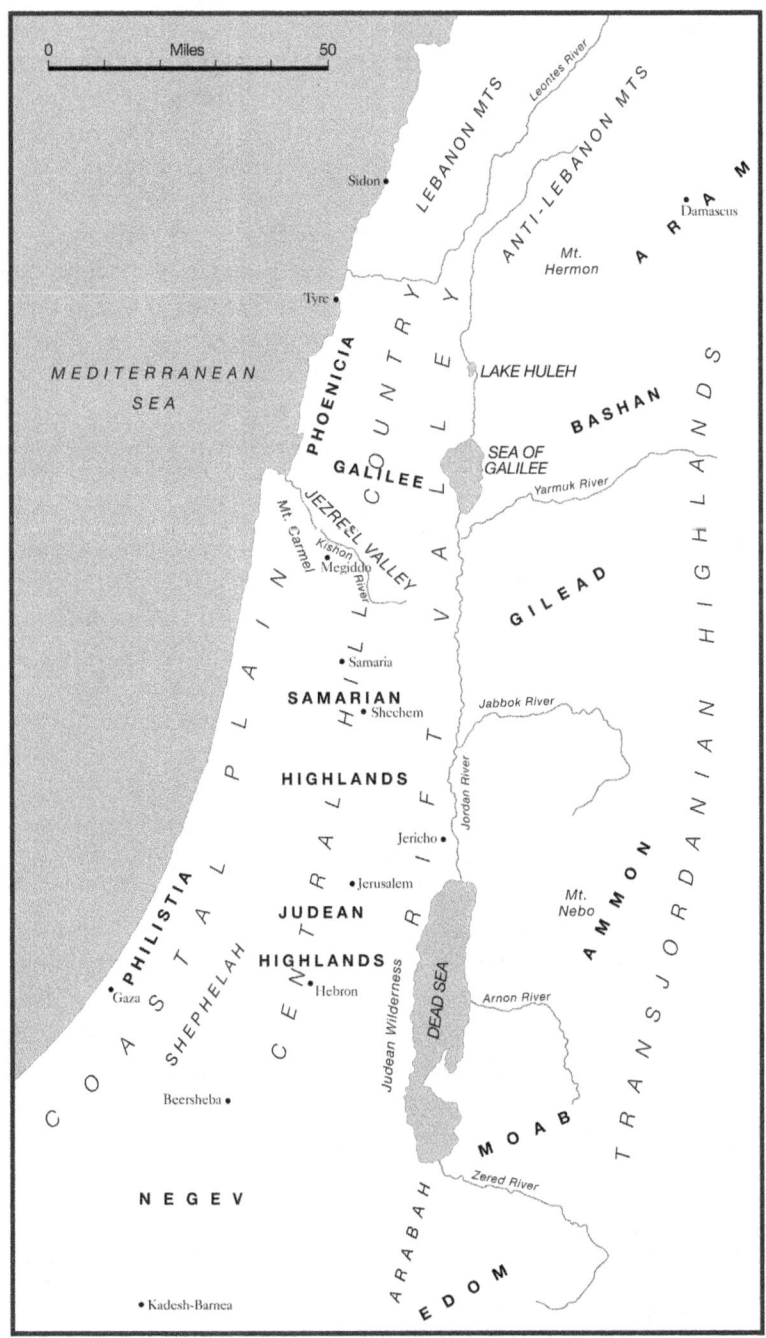

Map 3: Ancient Cisjordan and its immediately surrounding regions. (Courtesy of Karla Bohmbach)

Judah waned.[21] Moab was directly south of Ammon and east of the Dead Sea, across from Judah. It was a small country, and Israel often controlled the northern plain of Moab, along the Jordan. Moab appeared to emerge at about the same time as Israel/Judah. According to Deuteronomy 34:1–5, Moses died in Moab, on Mount Pizgah. The beginning of the book of Ruth is also set in Moab (1:1).

The country to the southeast of Judah was Edom, just south of the Dead Sea. It was a desolate area; until recently, little was known about its inhabitants during biblical times. It was claimed to be taken by David in the early monarchy (2 Sam. 8:14). Psalm 137 remembers Edom as an ally of Babylon. Because of the arid landscape, it was a nomadic area, without many permanent cities. Nomadic cultures were considered relatively poor and lacked the governmental organization of more settled areas. Recent archaeological excavations in Faynan and Timna have challenged these beliefs. These very arid regions were rich in copper deposits. Copper was required to make bronze, so these mines were active from the second half of the twelfth century until the second half of the ninth century BCE, using hundreds of nomadic workers.[22] Excavations at these mines have shown that even though the Edomites were nomadic, "operating the mines was centralized and hierarchical, and its social complexity was at a level that can be attributed to an early state."[23] In short, there appears to have been a more organized governmental structure and income from copper mining in Edom than previously thought. Do these findings have ramifications for other nations in the region? That remains to be seen as research on this nomadic culture and its copper mines continues. This is an example of how a new discovery prompts more research and a reevaluation of nomadic cultures in Canaan.

To the southwest of Judah was the country of Philistia. The Philistines were the only people in the region who were not native to Canaan. The Bible says they originated in Crete (Amos 9:7), but archaeologists cannot verify their exact origins. Most agree they originated from the Mediterranean Islands.[24] Recent DNA testing from Philistine graves confirms that their genes came from regions other than Canaan, probably the Greek Islands.[25] There is a debate among archaeologists as to the period of their arrival in Canaan, but it

---

21. R. W. Younker, "Rabbah (Place)," *ABD* 5:599.
22. Erez Ben-Yosef, "The Architectural Bias in Current Biblical Archaeology," *VT* 69 (2019): 365.
23. Ben-Yosef, "Architectural Bias," 367.
24. Eric Cline, *1177 BC: The Year Civilization Collapsed* (Princeton University Press, 2014), 4.
25. Kristen Romey, "Ancient DNA May Reveal Origin of the Philistines," National Geographic Society, July 3, 2019, https://www.nationalgeographic.com/culture/2019/07/ancient-dna-reveal-philistine-origins/.

was either Late Bronze or Early Iron Age I.[26] The Philistines developed on the coast, controlling and further developing the cities of Gaza, Ashkelon, Ekron, Gath, and Ashdod. They battled with Israel and Judah during the early formation of the Canaanite nations.

All this demonstrates that the region had a long history and was inhabited by many peoples other than the Judeans and Israelites. Other nations were also developing at the same time. Except for the Philistines, the people of the Canaanite nations originated in the Afro-Asiatic region. Israel and Judah were among the nations in the Canaanite region.

The larger Afro-Asiatic region (often called the Middle East) sits at the borders between three continents: Africa to the southwest, Asia to the east, and Europe to the northwest. Canaan comprised the countries listed above, at the eastern end of the Mediterranean Sea, and was situated on some of the most critical lands in the ancient world. This location, where the continents meet, would significantly impact Judah and Israel's history.

GEOGRAPHIC AND TOPOLOGICAL REALITIES

During the period described in the Hebrew Bible, Canaan's importance was its function as the land bridge between Asia and Africa. Canaan was bound by the Mediterranean Sea to the west, with deserts to the east and south. Between Babylon and Canaan is the Arabian Desert: 900,000 square miles of a sandy, arid environment with a summertime temperature of 100–110 degrees. Its vast size and scarce water and food made it impassable in this ancient period. Thus the shortest land path between Babylon and Egypt, the Arabian Desert, was impossible to traverse. For most land-based nations, the only way to travel from Asia to Africa was counterclockwise around the so-called Fertile Crescent (map 4).[27] This swath of cultivatable land is often called a land bridge. In the east, this land bridge begins at the mouth of the Persian Gulf. It is bound on either side in the southeast by the Tigris and Euphrates Rivers. At the top (northern arch) of the crescent is the southeastern edge of the Anatolian

---

26. David Ussishkin reports the lack of Philistine pottery at Lachish, a major trading city in the region, indicating that the Philistines settled in the area later than the destruction of that Canaanite city in 1130 BCE; "Archaeology of the Biblical Period: On Some Questions of Methodology and Chronology of the Iron Age," in *Understanding the History of Ancient Israel*, ed. H. Williamson (Oxford University Press, 2007), 136. Others argue that the Philistines arrived earlier, before 1150 BCE; L. Stager, "The Impact of the Sea Peoples in Canaan," in *The Archaeology of Society in the Holy Land*, ed. T. Levy (Leicester University Press, 1995), 332–48.

27. Editors of *Encyclopedia Britannica*, "Fertile Crescent," March 13, 2019, www.britannica.com/place/Fertile-Crescent.

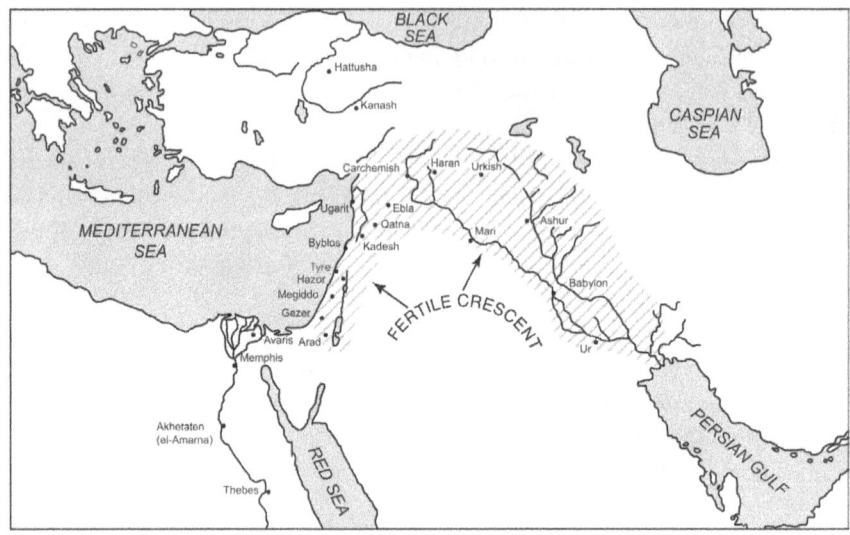

Map 4. Fertile Crescent. (Courtesy of Westminster John Knox Press)

plateau and the northern edge of the Arabian plate. The crescent turns southwest and follows the Mediterranean coast into Canaan and then into the fertile lands of Egypt, fed by the Nile, thus into Africa. This central arch of the Afro-Asiatic region was the area with the most livable land. As a result, it was the most populated and the most desired.

Geographically, Canaan made up the southwestern portion of the Fertile Crescent. Its topography includes mountains and plains (map 5). Two mountain ranges run north to south, with the Jordan River and its valley between them. This severely limited how one could travel from east to west in Canaan. But these two mountain ranges were not the only problem. A mountain range also runs to the southeast from the Mediterranean Sea, the Carmel Range. This also blocked traffic from moving quickly from north to south, so all the traffic in this region had to use a few roads.

Two of the most important roads were the north-south routes. The first road ran from Damascus through Ammon, Moab, and Edom in the Transjordan and down the Arabian Peninsula (map 6). It was named the Transjordanian Route and called the King's Highway (Num. 20:17; 21:22).[28] This route ran on the fringe of the desert and was blocked to the west by the Jordanian mountains and to the east by the Arabian desert. It connected the kingdoms and peoples east of the Jordan River. This vital route was probably why Judah

---

28. Miller and Hayes, *Ancient Israel and Judah*, 22.

Map 5. Topographical map of Canaan. (Courtesy of Frank Ramspott)

tried to capture the countries of Ammon and Moab in the biblical period. The road was essential to controlling the eastern part of the region.

The second road was named "The Way of the Sea." It ran southward along the Mediterranean coast, going eastward into the Plain of Esdraelon (also called Valley of Megiddo or Jezreel Valley) to avoid the Carmel Mountain, and exiting the plain near Megiddo. The trek upward past Megiddo and into the Wadi ʿĀrah, leading southwest to the coastal plain, was one of the most dangerous places on the Way of the Sea because of mountains on each side of the valley. The people traveling on the road could be easily attacked from the hills above. Whoever controlled the land above this valley also controlled this critical travel route. They could charge those passing by to use it and sell them supplies. It would also be impossible to gain control of the region without controlling this section of the route. The road then returns to the plain by the sea, a much

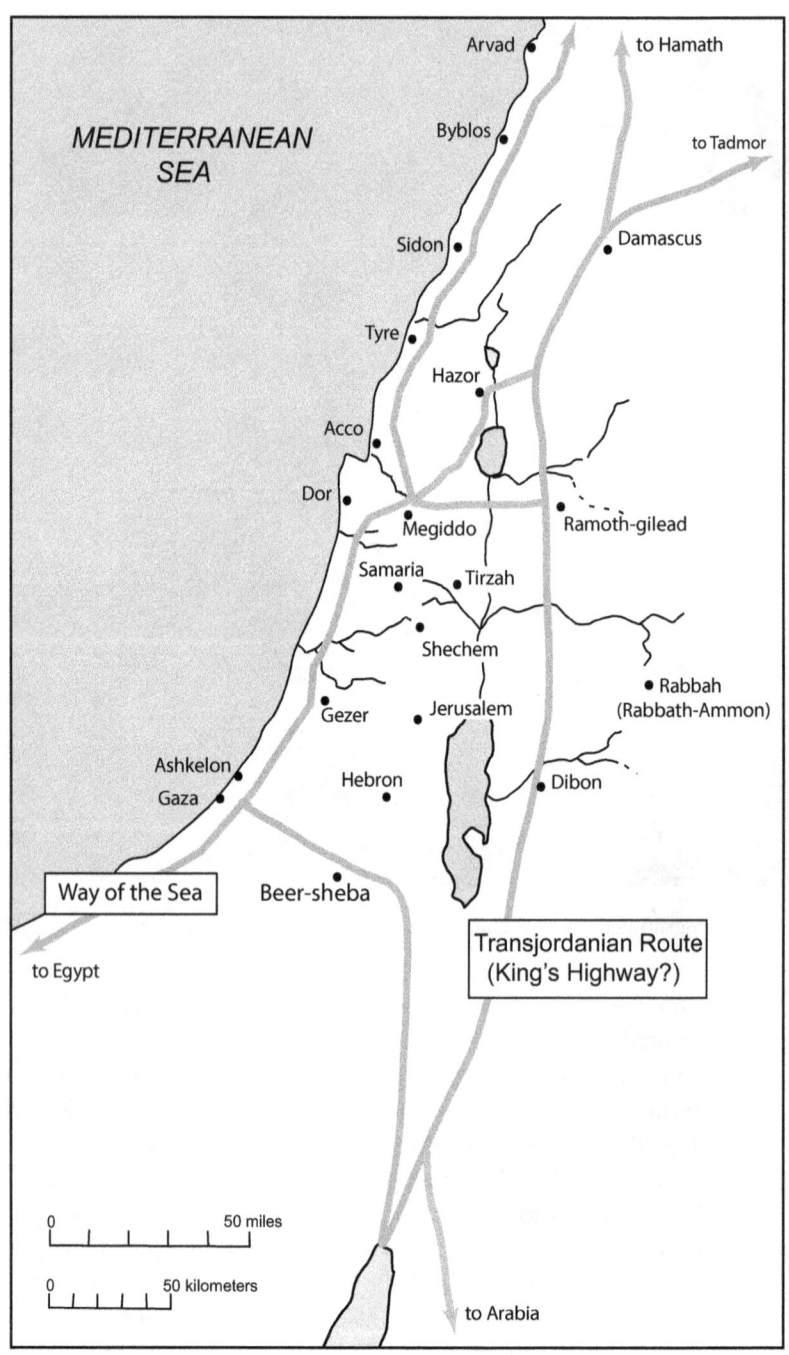

Map 6. Main roads and cities of ancient Canaan. (Courtesy of Westminster John Knox Press)

broader and flat area, before exiting southwest Israel near Gezer into Philistia and on into Africa via Egypt. This was the most accessible and the easiest of the two roads to travel. With its easier terrain and available resources, the Way of the Sea was the quickest way to transport goods and move troops.

Two major east-west roads connected the Way of the Sea and the Transjordanian Route. The northern route ran southwest from Damascus through the Hulu (Huleh) Valley of the Jordan River to Hazor, then traversed hilly terrain before meeting the Way of the Sea at Megiddo. The southern route was in the Sinai, far south of the Dead Sea, crossing the Sinai near Kadesh-Barnea before intersecting the Way of the Sea near Egypt. The southern route was out of the way: some significant hills and barren regions of the Sinai had to be negotiated.

There were also less desirable routes that cut between the Way of the Sea and the Transjordanian Route, but they had significant elevation changes to deal with. One of the most used cuts was between Ramoth-Gilead on the King's Highway in the east, westward through Beth-Shean near the Jordan River, and on up through the Jezreel Valley and through the Plain of Esdraelon to Megiddo, where it intersects the Way of the Sea. This path was an essential route for Israel. A second path began further south at Rabbath-Ammon to Jericho, where it turned southwest to Jerusalem and past Gezer to the Way of the Sea, making it an important route for Judah.[29]

The land's topography forced most travel into these pathways (map 5). This explains the placement of the major cities in Canaan. Hazor was the northernmost major fortified city, guarding the Hulu Valley. Gezer (map 4) in the southwest was at the intersection of another connection point and the Way of the Sea, protecting the road from armies and robbers from the south. However, by far, the most crucial city for protection was Megiddo. Whoever controlled the Jezreel Valley and the Way of the Sea controlled the region's access. Megiddo loomed over the valley as a military fortification and a city for replenishing supplies. This strategic road was the reason for needing to control Israel and Philistia and, to a lesser degree, Judah. It was essential for any empire that wanted to move between the two continents.

Also, because of these mountain ranges, Canaan had a variety of climates even though it was small, roughly the size of New Jersey. The geography ranged from dense forests in the north to the deserts of the east and south. There were primarily two seasons: the wet winter and the dry summer. The rainfall was higher in the north, making those lands more suitable for crops. In the southern areas, there was less rainfall and vegetation. On the coastal plain,

---

29. Not shown on map 6; other paths headed south from Jerusalem and went through Hebron or Arad, two other fortified cities on these roads.

the breezes off the Mediterranean made the temperatures pleasant all year and allowed cultivation even in the south. These climate conditions impacted the location of agricultural communities and smaller cities.

In summary, the area of Canaan was small, and the topography further limited the options for travel, farming, and development. Over the years, this topography resulted in local battles to control the best land. Like the roads, the farmable land areas impacted what happened in this region. The topography of Canaan takes some patience to understand, but it is crucial to what happened to this region during the period of the Hebrew Bible.[30] The land sits at a critical crossroads of the two continents, which has shaped its fate repeatedly. The roads were essential for moving between Egypt and Mesopotamia, so any empire wishing to conquer the region needed to capture the roads and surrounding lands. Since the Way of the Sea ran through Israel but only skirted Judah, Israel was always a target of growing empires. The farmable lands in Israel and Judah were often the targets of other Canaanite nation-states, and there were constant battles over control of that farmland. Terraces, cisterns, wells, and irrigation enabled farming marginal land. The only easily farmable land in the south was called the Shephelah (lowland), located between Judah and Philistia. This land was one of the reasons for the early wars between Israel and Philistia. In short, the empires would attack Canaan to capture the trade routes, and the Canaanite nation-states would fight over farmable land and water.

SUMMARY

The Bible is neither separate from its culture and the surrounding cultures in Canaan nor from the history of the world. The words on the pages of the Hebrew Bible have a physical, geographical, and topographical context, and that context impacted how the biblical narratives were shaped. The people of the Hebrew Bible are more than just those in Israel and Judah. Israel and Judah share a history with all Canaanite nation-states and the empires that overtook the region. The area has a long history, with the oldest skull outside of Africa found in Canaan, dating to about 52,000 years before the first stories that became the Hebrew Bible began to circulate. So, as you read the Hebrew Bible, remember the context behind the words and the stories, for they, too, are part of the biblical text's meaning.

---

30. Aryeh A. Leifert, "Virtual Israel Touring," 2015, a topographical resource, https://www.youtube.com/watch?v=8KW2OyFUZz0.

4

Life in the Afro-Asiatic Region

The previous chapter focused on the greater world surrounding the people of the Hebrew Bible. This chapter will focus on their lives. What was their everyday existence like? What was the typical family structure? How was rural living different from life in a city? How did they worship? What did they eat? What were the social and political structures? This chapter will draw from the collective knowledge of archaeologists, anthropologists, and historians. Much of this information comes from archaeological discoveries instead of written sources, including the Bible.

The Bible uses a lot of imagery from daily and rural life. However, it is also "a national document."[1] This means that while we have narratives about people, families, and events, there is not enough detail to understand daily life; it is assumed that those reading or hearing the text would know those details already. However, this daily life provides essential context for the Hebrew Bible's narratives and poems. This chapter will provide background context for life during the time of the writing and editing of the Hebrew Bible.

ARCHAEOLOGY AND ITS DISCOVERIES IN THE AFRO-ASIATIC REGION

Archaeology is a discipline that focuses on discovering physical artifacts of ancient cultures. Through exploration, excavation, and evaluation, it unearths the places people lived, the items they used, and how their cities and villages

---

1. Carol L. Meyers, "The Family in Early Israel," in *Families in Ancient Israel*, ed. L. Perdue, J. Blenkinsopp, J. Collins, and C. Meyers (Westminster John Knox, 1997), 1–47, here 4.

were constructed. But while these artifacts can tell us the "what," "when," and "where" of a group of people, they are not able to reveal nearly as much about the "who," "why," and "how." We may be able to learn about the type of houses people lived in and the type of pottery they used; we can even see where a town was burned or damaged. What we cannot know is *why* they lived in that way, *why* they preferred this type of pottery, or *how* exactly they worshiped. Archaeological studies can reveal a fire during a town's history, but the cause of the fire often remains elusive. Although archaeology can tell us a great deal about a people's lives and culture and what happened to a place over time, it has its limits.

Archaeology is a social science. It uses scientific techniques but must also depend on academic paradigms that can be altered based on new discoveries. The most significant point of contention in the archaeology of the Afro-Asiatic region is determining the "when." Assigning dates to ancient events is a challenging and complex task. Archaeologists excavate multiple sites in an area. A site often contains many occupation levels stacked on top of one another in a mound called a *tel* (see fig. 1). Each level represents different periods in the history of the people who occupied that site. For example, one site may have eight layers of a long-term city that constitute an almost continuous occupation for one thousand years. Another site may contain the ruins of two cities built upon the other, with a 500-year occupation gap between them.[2] A large part of the evaluative process is to assign dates for the pottery and other physical remains found in each layer. Pottery and other artifacts can be dated because the method of making material goods changed over time. Archaeologists worked for decades to develop a progression of these pottery changes, allowing them to provide a range of dates for a specific city layer. Dating each of the hundreds of sites in this region creates an overall view of a specific time. If a new artifact changes the dating of one site, it would most likely impact the relative dating of all the related sites. This is a complex and incomplete methodology because only so much information is recoverable after all these centuries. Knowledge about a particular period is always partial and subject to change with each new excavation.[3]

---

2. For more information, see William Dever, *Who Were the Israelites?* (Eerdmans, 2003); or Lester Grabbe, *Ancient Israel: What Do We Know and How Do We Know It?* (T&T Clark, 2007). This applies only to larger cities. Smaller settlements that leave no trace on the topography of the land are often found by chance during modern excavation for roads or buildings.

3. Radiocarbon dating is not usually helpful at these sites for three reasons. First, the samples need to be unique, and this is difficult since one group of people builds on the ruins of the last. Second, only organic items can be tested, such as wood or seeds, and must be identified as part of a wall or gate; there is still concern that the organic material is not contemporary with the building structure. Finally, radiocarbon dating has a significant margin of error ranging from 20 years for a good sample and up to 100–150 years for some other samples. This significant margin of error often exceeds the time frame between settlements for

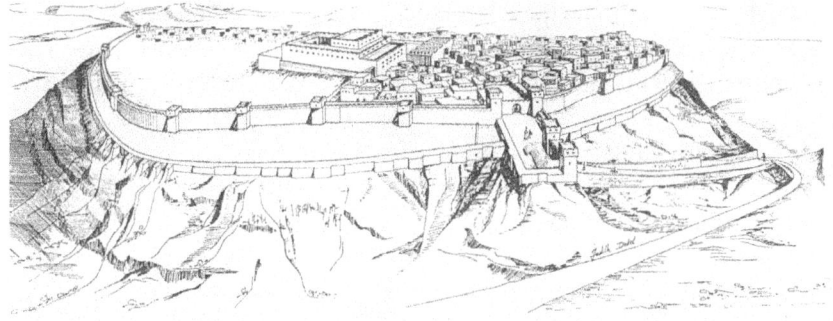

Figure 1. Example of a tel. Reconstruction of Lachish, Level III. (Courtesy of the Expedition to Lachish, David Ussishkin, Director; Drawing: Judith Dekel)

Archaeology provides significant insights into a culture and can help determine a timeline of certain events. Archaeological research tells us when cities were occupied or destroyed. It also provides a picture of life in small villages and towns. Thus it offers valuable information on the context of the Hebrew Bible. However, archaeology is not designed to vindicate or vilify the narratives in the biblical text. It is an independent discipline that provides valuable information to biblical scholars, historians, and students. Its purpose is to create a picture of a certain people at a specific time.

LITERARY CONTRIBUTIONS

Another piece helps us understand the ancient Israelite and Judean contexts: the available written sources. These written sources can aid us in understanding the questions archaeology cannot answer, such as Who? Why? and How? We read stories about the people and their gods. These texts tell us about their lives and their values. The last chapter focused on the history of the immediate world, Canaan, and the countries that surrounded Israel and Judah. The literature of those nations is also crucial to understanding the history and context of the time. Israel and Judah originated in a world already populated by multiple tribes and nations, each with its own literary traditions. These writings range from monumental inscriptions to epic poetry to law codes.

The literary corpus of a people is often subjective, usually drawing from collected memories and favoring the group telling the narrative. These writings

---

the Iron Age period. See Lily Singer-Avitz, "Archaeological Views: Carbon 14—The Solution to Dating David and Solomon?," *BAR* 35, no. 3 (May/June 2009): 28.

left behind must be critically evaluated and questioned to discover their purpose and meaning in their original context. For example, as mentioned earlier, a king's memorial stela often speaks of his benefits and successes but rarely mentions his defeats or setbacks. As an incomplete accounting of a king's reign, it must be interrogated by using other sources to understand how it fits into a historical framework. For example, the Black Obelisk (erected in 825 BCE) of Shalmaneser III, an Assyrian king, records a battle with Ben-Hadad of Aram and Ahab of Israel in this way: "He brought along to help him 12,000 chariots, 1,200 cavalrymen, and 20,000 foot soldiers of Adad-'idri [Ben-Hadad] of Damascus, . . . 2,000 chariots, and 10,000 foot soldiers of Ahab the Israelite."[4] A historian cannot take the number of troops listed at face value because the Assyrian king has a vested interest in increasing the number of defeated troops to make the battle look more significant. A historian would vet this finding before stating the army size under Ahab of Israel.

Even with critical evaluation, the literature from other nations enhances the work of the biblical scholar in two ways. The first purpose is historical, providing contextual information and verifying dates and events. For example, the stela quotation above tells the historian about a military campaign in Canaan. This event can be compared to the records in Israel and Aram to verify the attack, even if the numbers listed are less reliable. As noted in chapter 1 (above), these sources are vetted by scholars to determine their authenticity, integrity, and usefulness for the historical enterprise. The most essential ancient literary sources for our study of the Hebrew Bible are discussed in this book. Still, hundreds of these literary sources from the surrounding cultures are available to scholars and students for more in-depth exploration. Other written materials, such as receipts or land deeds, are more objective documentation and can be considered more reliable in developing a people's history. Like archaeological discoveries, written sources tell part of a people's story.

The second purpose of these written sources is to enable comparison. Comparative studies, applied to biblical scholarship, read the texts of other Afro-Asiatic peoples alongside the biblical ones. Christopher Hays explains the importance of this endeavor:

> One simple answer to the question *Why compare?* is that comparison brings things into focus. Humans form their self-identities by comparison every day: Am I tall? Am I well spoken? Am I talented at math? Categories such as "tall," "well spoken," and "talented" turn out to be relative. . . . Literature and theological features come into focus through comparison as well.[5]

---

4. *ANET*, 278–88.
5. Christopher Hays, *Hidden Riches: A Sourcebook for the Comparative Study of the Hebrew Bible and Ancient Near East* (Westminster John Knox, 2014), 4–5.

For example, J. J. M. Roberts discusses the place of biblical laws in comparative studies. His work compares biblical laws and the laws from several Mesopotamian kingdoms, which all predate the biblical texts. This comparison demonstrates a common-law tradition that "was basically shared throughout the region of Mesopotamia, Syria [Aram], and Palestine."[6] Therefore we know that the laws found in the Torah are not the first laws of the region. As the Code of Hammurabi (1750 BCE) demonstrates, there was a basic understanding of right and wrong long before the law codes appeared in Exodus.[7]

Many modern readers assume that the laws in the Bible are unique and that all other laws originate from them, a claim the Bible itself never makes. This is an example of our modern blinders. Through comparative study, Roberts explains that it is not the biblical laws' uniqueness but their theological context that sets them apart.[8] In the Bible, the laws were not handed down by a king but, as recorded in Exodus 19–23, were given to the people in a covenant ceremony by God. The law was God's gift to the people. Also, outside of the Hebrew Bible, the laws are exclusively concerned with civil law concerning humans and their property. In the Hebrew Bible, the laws are mixed, reflecting both civil law and religious regulations and requirements. This mixture, seen in the Hebrew Bible in the Ten Commandments and the Covenant Code (Exod. 20:22–23:19), is another distinction of the laws in the Torah.

Without comparative studies, this essential theological understanding would not be fully understood. Instead of undermining the uniqueness of the Bible's law codes, comparative studies aid the interpreter in understanding the full context and gift of the law. What can we learn about the lives of the people from these common-law traditions? These laws demonstrate what the community valued. Scholars often discuss two types of laws.[9] The first type is apodictic laws, which define a society's boundaries. These are clearly stated in Exodus 20:1–17, known as the Ten Words, or Ten Commandments. The apodictic laws are distinguished by the phrase "You shall not," meaning this line is not to be crossed:

- 20:4: You shall not make for yourself an idol.
- 20:7: You shall not make wrongful use of the name of the LORD your God.
- 20:13: You shall not murder.
- 20:14: You shall not commit adultery.

---

6. J. J. M. Roberts, "The Ancient Near East," in *The HarperCollins Bible Commentary*, ed. J. Mays (Harper Collins, 2000), 50.

7. Hays, *Hidden Riches*, 137–38, lists seventeen similarities between Hammurabi's code and Exodus 21–23.

8. Roberts, "Ancient Near East," 51.

9. Hays, *Hidden Riches*, 139.

- 20:15: You shall not steal.
- 20:16: You shall not bear false witness against your neighbor.

These boundary laws are both simple and complex.[10] They are short, simple statements but complex in meaning, requiring interpretation. For example, what are the parameters of the prohibitions? Does murder cover war or the death penalty? Almost as soon as the words appear in the Exodus text, the next chapter discusses situations when the death penalty should be applied (Exod. 21:12–26). These interpretations of the boundary law codes resulted in the second type of law, casuistic, or case laws. These are the if-this-happens, then this-is-the-result laws. For example, Exodus 21:12 states, "Whoever strikes a person mortally shall be put to death." These are an exception to the "You shall not murder." As with our laws today, ancient people saw that the general prohibition could be violated in some circumstances. Other instances of laws in the Torah are case laws that again arise from the court in adjudicating disagreements between citizens. An example of case law is found in Exodus 21:35–36:

> If someone's ox hurts the ox of another, so that it dies, then they shall sell the live ox and divide the price of it, and the dead one they shall also divide. But if it was known that the ox was accustomed to gore in the past and its owner did not restrain it, the owner shall restore ox for ox but keep the dead animal.

In summary, comparison studies help to point out what is unique about Israelite and Judean laws and what is shared with other societies around them. Concerning the law, comparative studies demonstrate that there is a shared ethical perspective concerning murder, stealing, adultery, and lying in all nations. What is unique about Israelite and Judean laws here in Exodus is that God gives the law, and laws concerning religion and civil law are intermingled. This intermingling provides us with a theological insight that the people's religious and ordinary lives are also intermingled. How one lived before God mattered to the community, and how one treated others mattered to God. This is one of many examples of how comparing the literature of Israel and Judah's neighbors can aid the interpreter in understanding what the laws mean for the people who used and preserved them.

The Hebrew Bible is the literature of Judah and Israel. However, it was also penned in a world of other nations and people with long traditions of writing,

---

10. Boundary laws are not as simple as they appear. Many of the laws in the Covenant Code (Exod. 20:22–23:19) and in the books of Deuteronomy and Leviticus serve to interpret these boundary laws. Patrick Miller declares, "There is a continuing tension between the universality and the particularity of the Commandments," in *The Ten Commandments* (Westminster John Knox, 2009), 4. A discussion of these tensions is beyond the scope of this book.

farming, and religious life. These ancient people may not have known how long the history of humans stretched behind them, but they knew they were not the first or the only people in the region or on earth. Their history is part of the history of the world. Outside sources contribute to developing a picture of the ancient peoples and their lives. This was demonstrated above in the laws of the Covenant Code. Such laws arose in each nation from real-life situations, such as the ox laws above. Because the laws come from real life, they also show how a society structures itself and how people are expected to treat each other. This adds to our knowledge of how the people lived together.

LIFE IN ISRAELITE AND JUDEAN RURAL COMMUNITIES DURING THE IRON AGE

The family was the center of life in rural areas in Israel and Judah. The nuclear family was patriarchal, and the center of all family life was their compound, or *bāyît*.[11] The family unit began with the parents' marriage, which *their* parents arranged for economic reasons, not romantic ones.[12] As Philip King and Lawrence Stager report, "Marriage was not considered a religious rite but a civil contract."[13] The contract included a bride-price or dowry, which the woman's parents paid. The typical age of marriage in ancient Israel and Judah is unknown. However, Wilma Bailey makes a compelling thesis that ancient women could not bear children until around eighteen, so the age of marriage would have been similar.[14] King and Stager also observe, "It is estimated that as a result of nursing babies for as long as three years, Israelite women gave birth to an average of four children."[15] Infant mortality rates and maternal death rates in ancient Canaan are thought to have been around 50 percent.[16] Thus, the typical couple averaged 4 to 6 births, and about half

---

11. Lawrence Stager, "The Archaeology of the Family in Ancient Israel," *BASOR* 260 (Autumn 1985): 20.

12. Philip King and Lawrence Stager, *Life in Biblical Israel*, ed. D. Knight (Westminster John Knox, 2001), 55.

13. King and Stager, *Life*, 56.

14. Wilma Bailey, "Baby Becky, Menarche and Prepubescent Marriage in Ancient Israel," *Journal of the Interdenominational Theological Center* 37 (2011): 119. She argues this based on a comparison with other ancient literature and a few biblical texts. Carol Meyers (in "Family," 27) gathers that childbearing would begin soon after puberty. King and Stager (in *Life*, 27) argue that women married "while still in their teens, sometimes their early teens," thus disagreeing with Bailey. Bailey argues that the barrenness theme in Genesis may have been because Leah, Rachel, and Rebecca were each prepubescent at the time of her marriage.

15. King and Stager, *Life*, 41.

16. Israel Finkelstein, "A Few Notes on Demographic Data from Recent Generations and Ethnoarchaeology," *PEQ* 122 (1990): 49.

of those babies survived to adulthood. However, it would also not be uncommon for larger families as well. Factors in these statistics were proper nutrition, drinkable water, and sanitation, which varied from place to place. In other words, with proper nutrition and a healthy water supply, women could bear children sooner and have more children, and more children could have survived. These are averages, and each family was dependent on specific circumstances.

Life expectancy in the time frame of the Hebrew Bible is likewise unknown. Skeletons analyzed from the later Hellenistic and Roman periods indicate about 17 percent of the population was over 50 at the time of death.[17] However, these were upper-class tombs, and scholars estimate that the life expectancy for the rural and poor populations was probably lower.[18] Joseph Blenkinsopp came to a similar conclusion by calculating the age of kings from biblical accounts, determining the average age of the 11 kings who lived out their reigns to be 53.2 years.[19] In summary, ancient people had a probable life expectancy of 35–60 years, assuming they survived early childhood.[20] A couple would marry when the woman was in her teens and the man was somewhat older.[21] Marriage was the social norm. Men who lost their wives would remarry, but women would usually remain widowed until their deaths.[22]

As noted above, families lived in small compounds, providing a home and a courtyard. They lived in houses called four-room pillared mud-brick homes (fig. 2). These homes were typical throughout the Afro-Asiatic region.[23] This style of home was the norm in both rural and urban environments, but the plan of the home varied.[24] These structures provided space for a nuclear family, including two parents and unmarried children, usually five to eight occupants. Larger pillared dwellings housed extended families consisting of the nuclear family and married sons with their families, older unmarried

---

17. Patricia Smith and Joseph Zias, "Skeletal Remains from the Late Hellenistic French Hill Tomb," *IEJ* 30, nos. 1/2 (1980): 111.

18. Smith and Zias, "Skeletal Remains," 115.

19. Joseph Blenkinsopp, "Life Expectancy in Ancient Palestine," *Scandinavian Journal of the Old Testament* 11, no. 1 (1997): 49–50.

20. Other studies of the Iron Age in the area have a lower life expectancy, but these consider the high infant mortality rate. A. Alesan, A. Malgosa, and C. Simó, "Looking into the Demography of an Iron Age Population in the Western Mediterranean: I. Mortality," *American Journal of Physical Anthropology* 110 (1999): 285–301.

21. In *Life*, 37, King and Stager state, "Men waited until well into their twenties or even early thirties before marrying."

22. King and Stager, *Life*, 53.

23. Avraham Faust and Shlomo Bunimovitz, "The Four Room House: Embodying Iron Age Israelite Society," *NEA* 66, nos. 1/2 (March-June 2003): 22.

24. William Dever, *The Lives of Ordinary People in Ancient Israel: Where Archaeology and the Bible Intersect* (Eerdmans, 2012), 149, 158.

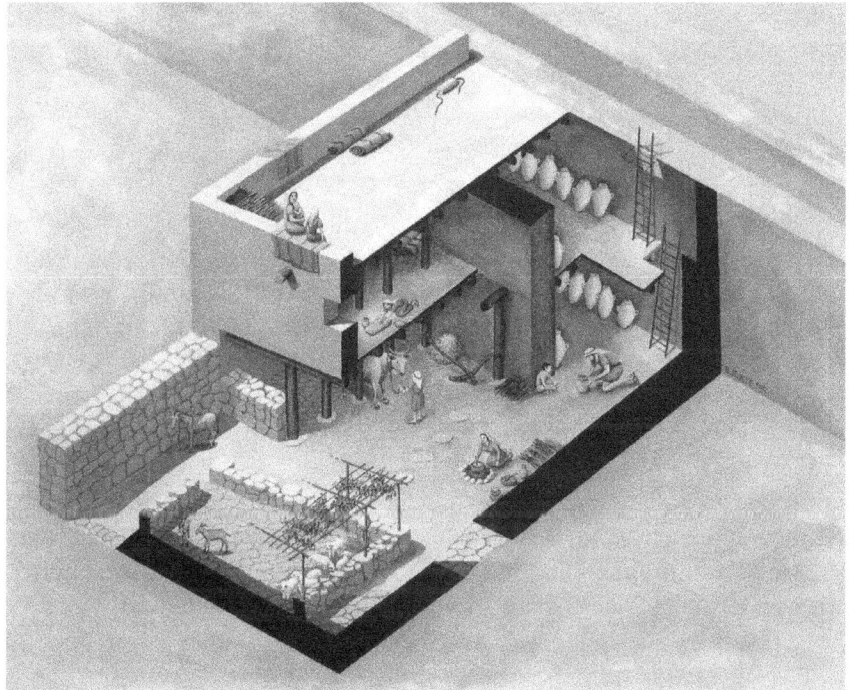

Figure 2. Example of a four-room house in ancient Canaan. (Courtesy of the Madaba Plains Project excavations at Tall al-'Umayri, Jordan. Artist: Rhonda Root © 1999 Professor Rhonda Root [Andrews University])

adults, and servants.[25] The houses were two stories tall, with an interior ladder between floors. There was a second ladder to the roof from the ground, which was also usable family space. Wealthier families could have an exterior staircase in addition to the ladders. The lower floor had multiple uses. It often served as a stable for animals and a place to process, preserve, and store food. It had a firepit and a baking oven for cooking.[26] The doors and windows of the lower floor provided ventilation and drew the smoke from the fire out of the house.[27]

The second floor, accessed by a ladder or an exterior stone staircase, was the family living space. It also served as another work area for activities such as weaving and needlework.[28] There may have been distinct rooms

25. Dever, *Ordinary People*, 158; Yigal Shiloh, "The Casemate Wall, the Four Room House," *BASOR* 268 (November 1987): 5–6.
26. King and Stager, *Life*, 33.
27. King and Stager, *Life*, 30.
28. King and Stager, *Life*, 34.

upstairs, depending on the size and wealth of the family.[29] The furnishings were simple. People sat and slept on mats. Tables were low to the ground and ordinarily used for serving meals and other tasks.[30] Rooftops were also living and working spaces. The inhabitants probably slept outside in the warm, dry months. The roof (Josh. 2:6) also served as a place to dry grain and fruits in the sun and store materials.

Most daily activities centered on food production for the family and commercial use. Goods were usually not sold for money but were often used to barter or to pay taxes. The climate was subtropical, with two seasons—the dry, hot summer and the wet, cooler winter. The winter could be cold: it snowed in the northern mountains and hill country and, occasionally, as far south as Jerusalem. Crops were planted at the beginning of the cool, wet season and harvested in the late spring/early summer. Grapes and olives were harvested in the late fall, usually around the New Year festival.[31] The ancients were primarily vegetarians, with a diet of grains, legumes, vegetables, and fruits. Having only a few tools, clearing land, yearly planting, and harvesting were labor-intensive propositions. Once harvested, grains and legumes were dried and stored. Small family compounds would store dried grain in large pottery jars. Olives and grapes were further processed by using presses to produce oil and hewn vats for treading grapes to make wine. The oil and the wine were used for consumption and to pay taxes or barter for other goods unavailable on the farm. For example, a farmer might have traded olive oil or grain for the pottery needed to cook or store materials. Water was another vital resource. Some farms were fortunate to have a natural spring or human-made well on the property, but most farms and villages had cisterns that collected rainwater during the rainy season.[32] These resources were precious and susceptible to drought, insects, and other natural calamities. Any problem with food production or a lack of rain would jeopardize the family or village. Starvation was a genuine and ongoing concern.

The final agricultural resource was animals. The subtropical environment was suitable for small animals. Sheep were raised for their wool, meat, milk, and hides. Some farms also had small cattle for milk, food, and sacrifice to God. Because of the climate, these herds required movement over a large area to prevent overgrazing, with the father and/or sons serving as shepherds (1 Sam. 16:11). Goats provided twice the milk of sheep[33] and would be kept close to the family compound for daily milking. Many farms also had a donkey

---

29. Stager, "Archaeology of the Family," 16.
30. King and Stager, *Life*, 63.
31. King and Stager, *Life*, 88.
32. King and Stager, *Life*, 126.
33. King and Stager, *Life*, 114.

for transporting goods and people and an ox for farming purposes.[34] In this ancient time, a family's wealth was measured by the number of animals they kept, demonstrating their value to the family.

The family's work was divided by gender, but each family member played an important role in the survival of the whole. The lives of men centered on animals, crops, and farm maintenance. This hard, back-breaking work was done without the aid of machines. Men cleared the land, built structures out of the available fieldstones, and made mud bricks for the construction of houses, silos, and cisterns. They traveled with the flocks to graze them. Periodically, men would be called to defend the land, possibly leaving for extended periods. This event could be a local disagreement with another tribe or clan. In the case of the Philistines, some men may be called on to fight in a national army.

Women had a prominent role in the family. While the men worked outside the home, women were responsible for processing, preserving, and cooking all the food. They also made clothing and other household goods by processing animal skins and weaving the wool into cloth. Women also tended the animals close to the family compound and shepherded some of the flocks (Gen. 29:9). The women were responsible for the early education and socialization of the children, both male and female. Each family member was put to work as soon as they were old enough: agriculture production required the work of each member of the household. Patriarchy was how society functioned, but on a day-to-day basis, parents and children worked on daily tasks to feed and house the family.

Rural inhabitants lived regionally. Residents would only travel more than a few miles from their homes for occasional religious festivals or military service. The rugged terrain and mountainous routes encouraged regional living since the closest town, "as the crow flies," may not have been readily accessible by foot. The only way to travel was by walking or riding an animal, which made long-distance travel difficult. Victor Matthews notes that the average distance for a day of travel on foot was twenty miles.[35] For example, this meant that the Mediterranean Sea was a two-day walk from Jerusalem. Farming also required some family or servants to remain at the compound to feed and tend the animals. Planting and harvesting required all family members to get the work done.

All these factors kept rural families close to home. Goods would be bartered at the nearest market. Marriages were arranged with neighbors or at

---

34. King and Stager, *Life*, 116.
35. Victor Matthews, *Studying the Ancient Israelites: A Guide to Sources and Methods* (Baker Academic, 2007), 48.

least within one's clan. The community would gather for worship regionally, rarely traveling to the larger temples and shrines. Small family compounds would slowly grow as children matured, established their own family units, and built new compounds. These smaller compounds would then develop into small farming villages. A single-family house could become a small farming community within a few generations. A village would develop when these family compounds grew and possibly abutted the compounds of other families. This village might have had a low wall, but the wall would have been more for containing of animals and children than for protection from invading armies.

The number of persons living in rural Israel and Judah during the Iron Age is impossible to know, but an educated guess can be made from several studies. Israel Finkelstein notes that by 1000 BCE, the estimated population of Canaan was 150,000, with the population primarily in rural areas.[36] By the eighth century BCE, the population had grown to approximately 460,000.[37] Of that 460,000 estimate, Yigal Shiloh suggests the population of the 60 cities and towns in Iron Age Judah and Israel to be about 150,000 persons, leaving 310,000 living in rural areas.[38] This means that in the eighth century, 2 people lived in rural areas for every person in a town or city. Thus, we can safely say that most of the population lived on small farms and in rural villages throughout the Iron Age (1200–500 BCE).

Rural life did not change much throughout the Iron Age. Late in the period, better infrastructure made the transportation of goods easier. But later, beginning with Assyrian domination (722–609 BCE), empires imposed heavy taxes on the citizens, making the burden of farming more difficult. Empires also conscripted their sons for warfare; in addition, quartered troops took over the supplies stockpiled for the family. Agriculture remained the primary engine of commerce throughout the Iron Age in Israel and Judah, especially in the valuable and portable resources of olive oil and wine.

LIFE IN URBAN CENTERS IN THE IRON AGE

As the population grew (described above), urban areas also began to grow. William Dever divides the population of cities and towns based on the overall Iron Age II population (1000–700 BCE):

---

36. Magen Broshi and Israel Finkelstein, "The Population of Palestine in Iron Age II," *BASOR* 287 (August 1992): 54.

37. Broshi and Finkelstein, "Population of Palestine," 54.

38. Yigal Shiloh, "The Population of Iron Age Palestine in Light of a Sample Analysis of Urban Plans, Areas, and Population Density," *BASOR* 239 (1980): 32.

- Tier 1: Capital Cities: Jerusalem, Samaria, Damascus (population: 20,000 +), District Administrative Centers: Dan, Hazor, Megiddo, Beth-Shemesh, Gezer, Lachish, Beersheba, Arad (population: 5,000–20,000)[39]
- Tier 2: Urban Centers or True Cities (population over 1,000)
- Tier 3: Towns (population 300–1,000)
- Tier 4: Villages (population 50–300)[40]

Tiers 1–3, urban areas, demonstrated a degree of urban planning.[41] Some began as villages and were expanded and rebuilt as the population and importance of the city grew. Others, such as Megiddo and Jerusalem, were already significant cities during the Bronze Age (3200–1200 BCE). These cities were either abandoned or taken by Israel and Judah and became part of their territory. Each city has its own characteristics, but the layouts are similar overall.

Cities that were capitals and district administrative centers were built in elevated locations, either on human-made tels[42] or a natural hill or mountain. The purpose of elevated cities was both for defense and to demonstrate the nation's power and prestige. Barrier walls and fortified gates surrounded these cities. The exterior walls lining the outside of the city were usually of solid construction and thick enough to prevent them from being damaged by a battering ram.[43] The city gates provided entrance to the city and were an important defense system. The gates were also a place of commerce, where farmers and skilled artisans sold their goods.[44] The barter system of the rural communities was also used in cities. However, in the largest cities, there was a rough monetary system based on the weight of precious metals, usually silver. Silver was so standard that the ancient Hebrew word for "money" also means "silver."[45] The weight of the silver varied in different regions, but it allowed commerce among the local farmers, artisans, and the people traveling through the areas. The Bible also reports that the city gates served as the place for public and social functions (Ruth 4:1) and as a court to settle disputes (Amos 5:15). These

---

39. The populations of capital cities and administrative centers were not provided by Dever; his estimates were based on Broshi and Finkelstein, "Population of Palestine," 47–60.

40. Dever, *Ordinary People*, 50.

41. Yigal Shiloh, "Elements in the Development of Town Planning in the Israelite City," *IEJ* 28, nos. 1/2 (1978): 36.

42. A tel (or tell) is an elevation of human creation. "Tell (archaeology)," 2025, https://en.m.wikipedia.org/wiki/Tell_(archaeology).

43. The broad wall attributed to the reign of Hezekiah in Jerusalem is 7 meters (22 feet) thick. Mazar notes that these outer walls were from 2 meters (6 feet) to 7 meters, depending on the site. Amihai Mazar, *Archaeology of the Land of the Bible: 10,000–586 B.C.E.* (Doubleday, 1990), 465.

44. Mazar, *Archaeology*, 469.

45. King and Stager, *Life*, 195.

large cities provided protection in times of war, when the local rural farmers would move into the cities with the regular inhabitants, and the gates would be closed to outsiders.

Larger cities arranged public and governmental buildings near the city center or acropolis, indicating the importance of these structures.[46] Scholars speculate on the use of these buildings. One probable function was that these cities protected the major trade routes of the territories they governed, and the buildings served a military function. Another function was probably as a governmental administrative center.

In addition to these administrative buildings, other public-use structures stored food and provided access to water. Some cities had in-ground silos for grain storage. The largest one was at Megiddo, where the silo had a capacity of 4,000 cubic feet.[47] Massive food storage in these cities served two functions. The first was commerce. Megiddo stood on the Way of the Sea and probably provided supplies for travelers. However, in times of attack, these food stores supplied the residents and the surrounding farming families who moved to the city during the war. The second vital resource for cities was a secure water supply. Cities required a constant supply of water, usually from a natural spring. In times of threat, the community also needed to be able to access this water supply from inside the locked city. Most of the natural springs were located outside the city. The city's government needed to create secure access to the water inside the city. However, access from inside the city was a complicated and labor-intensive endeavor. The method used in most major cities was a series of shafts dug and chiseled into the tel (the elevated area where the city is located). At Megiddo, the first shaft began in the city and was dug 100 feet (30.5 meters) straight down to bedrock (ca. seven building floors). Then, the horizontal shaft was chiseled 229 feet (70 meters) through the bedrock to reach the spring. The exterior spring entrance was then blocked: there was no external access.[48] Sites without a spring built deep cisterns that captured the rain runoff during the winter.[49] These water features were a major multiyear building project (fig. 3).

Cities also contained residential areas with evidence of social stratification. Most of the residential areas inside the city were populated with the four-room houses of the working class. These houses followed the same pattern as the rural ones but often shared common walls with the house next door. The people living in these homes worked within the city, probably as merchants, soldiers, tradespeople, artisans, or builders/maintenance workers.

---

46. Dever, *Ordinary People*, 121.
47. Dever, *Ordinary People*, 123.
48. Mazar, *Archaeology*, 478–79; and https://www.bibleplaces.com/megiddo/.
49. Dever, *Ordinary People*, 128.

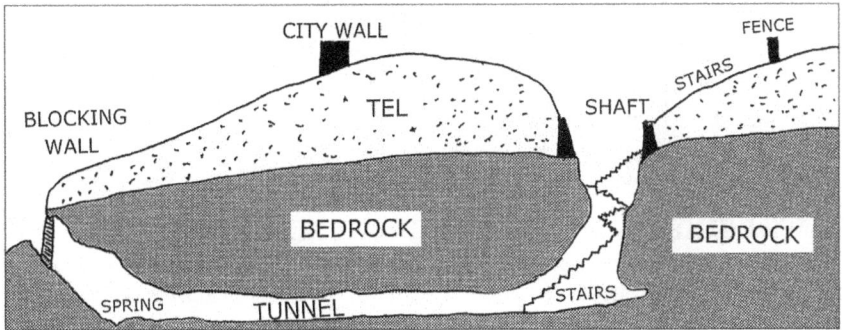

Figure 3. The water system at Megiddo. (Courtesy of Ferrell Jenkins)

Urban residents were often trained in crafts such as pottery, weaving, or metallurgy. Urban families performed many of the duties of rural ones, such as food preservation and preparation, the maintenance of some small animals, and child-rearing. The women were primarily responsible for those duties, and the men worked on their crafts instead of farming.

In the capital cities of Jerusalem and Samaria, the elite lived in somewhat isolated compounds behind a second set of walls (fig. 4). In Jerusalem, the king had palaces adjacent to the temple. However, palaces have also been found in Lachish and Megiddo, which are administrative center cities. Whether these belonged to the king or other high officials is unknown. Larger homes were also in the cities, district centers, and capitals. They were placed in the center or in expansion areas if the town had moved the defensive walls to allow for a

Figure 4. Interpretation of Jerusalem, the city of David, in the time of Hezekiah. (© L. E. Stager; illustration by C. S. Alexander, as in Philip J. King and Lawrence E. Stager, *Life in Biblical Israel* Ill. 98; courtesy of Harvard Museum of the Ancient Near East)

larger population.[50] These residences and their accompanying luxury goods indicate a small elite or ruling class who lived in the larger cities throughout Israel and Judah. Dever notes that this elite class was probably no more than 1 percent of the population.[51]

WORSHIP IN ISRAEL AND JUDAH BEFORE THE EXILE

Some of the first biblical references to worship practices are found in Genesis. Noah built an altar and offered sacrifices in Genesis 8:20–22. Abram built altars and offered sacrifices in Genesis 12:7–8, 13:18 (in Hebron), and 22:1–19 (Moriah). Jacob built an altar at Bethel (Gen. 35). All these were acts of a patriarch. This type of individual or family worship was central to worship life.

By the time of the narratives of 1 Samuel–2 Kings, it appears that the religious life of the people was an orthodox system of strict monotheism in the ways stipulated in the book of Leviticus. However, a closer reading of these books and the prophets tells a much more complex narrative of how worship differed through time, in different regions, and even with families and individuals. Like the developing nations of Israel and Judah themselves, the worship rituals and piety of the people varied and continued to change, depending on location and local traditions. In addition, worship practices and their development cannot be placed on a timeline. While one can certainly talk about worship before and after the temple in Jerusalem was built, the building of the temple did not mean that family, tribal, clan, and regional worship ceased in regions outside Jerusalem. Also, while archaeological discoveries will tell us about the religious items found in homes, villages, and cities, they do not tell us how these items were used or about people's actual worship practices. This means that while we can identify *places* of worship in Israel and Judah, the actual worship *practices* and when they began and transitioned to a different phase cannot be pinpointed.

Regular worship was practiced in the family home or compound in rural areas, towns, and cities. Household shrines have been found in both Judah and Israel and throughout Canaan and typically included "some combination of platforms or benches, alcoves or niches, stone altars or incense stands, and *masseboth* [*maṣṣēbôt*, standing stones]."[52] The first ritual place was in the

---

50. Avraham Faust, "Residential Patterns in Ancient Israel," *Levant* 35 (2003): 138.
51. Dever, *Ordinary People*, 233.
52. Beth Alpert Nakhai, "Varieties of Religious Expressions in the Domestic Setting," in *Household Archaeology in Israel and Beyond*, ed. A. Yasur-Landau, J. Ebeling, and L. Mazow (Brill, 2011), 353.

Figure 5. Niche in replica of an Iron Age II house; *Houses of Ancient Israel*, exhibit installation, circa 2004. (Photograph by Beth LaNeel Tanner. Courtesy of Harvard Museum of the Ancient Near East)

common household area inside the house (fig. 5).[53] Here, prayers and small offerings such as wine and incense were offered. The second area was the roof, where offerings were given.[54] It is not known if these rituals were daily or weekly. Also unclear is when each was used and if each site in the compound was for a specific purpose. The prominence of multiple household shrines indicates this as an important family practice. We do not know the liturgy and prayer that accompanied these ritual acts. What we gather is that regular worship was part of daily life.

Scholars are divided on who led family worship. Dever writes, "It has been suggested that wives and mothers were often the real 'ritual experts,' not priests. They would have officiated in various religious rites, perhaps daily, surrounded by their families."[55] Leo Perdue disagrees: "Male heads of households, at least early on, were the priests who led the family worship, offered sacrifice, and performed other family rituals. . . . Women were excluded from the official priesthood and perhaps performing the role of priests in

---

53. Patrick Miller, *The Religion of Ancient Israel* (Westminster John Knox, 2000), 63.
54. Miller, *Religion*, 63.
55. Dever, *Ordinary People*, 267.

the household."[56] There are some accounts of family worship in the book of Judges. In Judges 17, the family provides an idol, a shrine, and a priestly coat and appoints the son as a priest at the family shrine (17:1–6). This seems to support Perdue's argument that men led family worship. However, the event is from the book of Judges, where part of the book's point is "In those days there was no king in Israel; all the people did what was right in their own eyes" (17:6): this potentially undermines the idea that this family was following a widespread tradition. Since the worship practices were passed on from generation to generation, it would also be expected that they would vary in different areas of Israel and Judah and that they could change over time. Both Dever and Perdue may be correct, depending on the location. Even today, some denominations ordain women, and others do not. This is a good lesson to remember: not all biblical narratives reflect the same cultural values. The actual practices of most of the populations in Israel and Judah varied depending on the time frame, area, and inherited traditions.

The Names for God

The Hebrew Bible uses several names for their God. Some biblical books or narratives prefer one name over the other. For example, Genesis 1 uses the name *Elohim* (*ĕlōhîm*) for God, while Genesis 2 uses the compound name, combining the Divine Name and *Elohim*, translated as the LORD God. What are these names, and how are they used?

Elohim is a Hebrew word that English Bibles translate as "God." This generic name is also used for other gods, with the distinction that the word is not capitalized (Ps. 82:6). In a similar way, the generic name for "God" in English is also translated into many different languages: *Dios* in Spanish, *Gott* in German, *Dieu* in French, *Allah* in Arabic, and so on. Most Christians do not understand that *Allah* is the name for God in Arabic-speaking countries, and Arabic-speaking Jews and Christians pray to Allah just as we pray to God.

Adoni (*ădōnāy*) is a Hebrew word that means "Lord" or "Master." In English, it is usually represented by "the Lord." This name reminds readers that we humans are the servants of God.

Another common name for God in the Hebrew Bible is the Divine Name, which in Jewish tradition is never pronounced aloud or fully written (to guard against misuse; Exod. 20:7). This name appears over six thousand times in the Bible. The name is four Hebrew consonants: *yod-he-waw-he* (YHWH). In the

---

56. Leo Perdue, "The Israelite and the Early Jewish Family: Summary and Conclusions," *Families in Ancient Israel*, 205.

Hebrew language of the Bible, vowels are a series of dots and dashes printed under the consonants. The scrolls of the Hebrew Bible were written without the vowels. The vowels were added by a group of scribes called the Masoretes in the Middle Ages (ca. 400–1000 CE) to preserve the pronunciation of the original Hebrew text. The Masoretes knew the divine name was never pronounced or written, so they added the vowels for a different word, *Adoni* (Master, Lord), another name for God. It was a signal to substitute Adoni for the divine name. Jews will not write or pronounce the divine name, reading "Adoni," "Hashem" (the name), or "the Tetragrammaton" (the four-letter word [YHWH]) instead. However, many Christian scholars use the name YHWH in academic publications. It is a common practice. However, we are not even sure how to pronounce this divine name. Its most common translation was adopted in the nineteenth century by German scholars such as Wellhausen.[57] To use this name for God is, to me, unnecessary; that practice could be understood as anti-Semitic. *In this book*, the name *Adoni* represents the Hebrew name *Yahweh*, a name used only here so students can know what the word is.

Another problem with all these names is that they take the male pronoun "he" in Hebrew. This has led to the problem of assuming that God is male. Hebrew has only two genders for pronouns. Just like God's mysterious divine name, God is also mysterious and lives in and around and above genders, races, or a specific religion. The divine name's origin and meaning are equally obscure, adding to the mystery. The divine name is revealed to Moses when he asks for it in Exodus 3:13–15. God's answer to Moses is "I am who I am," which also means "I am what I am" or "I will be what I will be." God's name is not a proper noun like Baal or Zeus, but a state of being or existence. Even in naming God's self, the name is a mystery. Hence, the language used in this book reflects a decision to honor the text and the Jewish faith by not writing out the divine name or assigning a gender to God.

In addition, archaeological evidence demonstrates that monotheism, worship of only one God, *Adoni*, was not the norm during the Iron Age in Israel and Judah. Archaeologists have discovered about 3,000 terra-cotta figurines in the region of Israel and Judah, with dates of origin ranging from the 12th century BCE to the early 6th century BCE, with most of them coming from the 8th to 7th centuries (799–600 BCE).[58] Many such figurines were judged to be originating from the time of the exodus until the early Persian occupation

---

57. Johanna W. H. Bos, "Writing on the Water: The Ineffable Name of God," in *Jews, Christians, and the Theology of the Hebrew Scriptures*, ed. A. Bellis and J. Kaminsky (Society of Biblical Literature, 2000), 48.

58. Dever, *Ordinary People*, 280.

(after 539 BCE), thus contemporaneous with the independent nations of Israel and Judah.

These figurines are all female, with overemphasized breasts. Dever explains that they probably represent the Goddess Asherah and were used for fertility rituals.[59] Who is Asherah? That is a complicated question. In ancient Canaanite traditions, she was the consort or wife of the supreme god 'El (*'ēl*).[60] In the Hebrew culture, 'El was another name for *Adoni*, so some have suggested that this goddess was considered *Adoni's* consort or wife."[61] Other scholars explain the figurine as Astarte, the consort of the god Baal (*ba'al*). Baal is seen in the Hebrew Bible as a competing god in the hearts of the people, as recorded in the narratives of 1 and 2 Kings (e.g., 1 Kgs. 16:31–34). Also, all the Canaanite nations used the same ritual elements, such as platforms or benches, alcoves or niches, stone altars or incense stands, and standing stones (*maṣṣēbôt*), so it can be challenging to understand which god or gods a family worshiped.

What are we to make of these other god figurines found in homes throughout Israel and Judah? The fertility of the land and the family was essential for survival, and these female gods and Baal were known as gods of fertility. In the ancients' thinking, worship of these gods assured a successful harvest, baby animals, and even children. Ignoring the fertility gods would be a risk to their future. In addition, the worship of multiple gods and goddesses was common throughout the Afro-Asiatic region for centuries. Monotheism was a new idea. The archaeological discovery of the female gods in multiple households in Israel and Judah helps confirm the conflicting messages in the Hebrew Bible about monotheism and polytheism. The social norm in independent Israel and Judah would have been to worship *Adoni* and other gods. The archaeological evidence for these female deities is overwhelming. Add this to the complaints of the prophets concerning such idols (see Hos. 10:1–8; Isa. 42:17; 44:9–17; Jer. 44:15–25), and the picture emerges that monotheism was a new concept; it took time to change the ways of people, who followed the rituals handed down from their ancestors. So instead of strict monotheism, the people's practices were that of henotheism, which is a belief in *Adoni* as the supreme god while recognizing the existence of multiple gods (Ps. 82), and/or polytheism, which is the worship of multiple gods.

The final edited edition of the Bible is hard on the people for worshiping other gods. Still, the evidence suggests that worshiping *Adoni* alone was not

---

59. Dever, *Ordinary People*, 280.
60. Dever, *Ordinary People*, 280.
61. André Lemaire, "Les inscriptions de Khirbet el-Qôm et l'Ashérah de YHWH," *Revue biblique* 84, no. 4 (1977): 595–608.

a common practice until the postexilic period (539–330 BCE). This is when the other figurines finally disappear from the archaeological evidence. It is also clear that monotheism alone was the norm in the temple in Jerusalem. However, even in that temple, there is biblical evidence of the worship of other gods, especially when Jerusalem was controlled by another empire (for example, 2 Chr. 29:3–31:21 tells of Hezekiah cleansing the temple of other gods).[62] Hence, this is a situation where the Bible presents a norm that may have been practiced by the priests in Jerusalem, but it would take centuries for it to become the practice of all the people.

We might be tempted to paint the people as unfaithful for their worship practices, but we should also remember that until at least 600–400 BCE, there were no set laws; even then, the biblical laws were not understood in the same ways throughout the region. The continual editing of the scrolls of the Hebrew Bible means the last edits to Israel and Judah's laws and religious rules happened over time. By the time Exodus, Numbers, and Deuteronomy were in their final form, it would appear in the text as if all the laws were declared simultaneously during the time with Moses at Sinai. But the final form of the text was shaped over many years, and most people of Israel and Judah only gradually gained knowledge of the laws and practices described in the text. The reality was, as Devers notes, that most ancient Israelites and Judeans never went to Jerusalem, saw the temple, or participated in its rituals "and remained largely polytheistic (and naturalistic) until the end of the monarchy [approximately 586 BCE]."[63]

This final shaping of the biblical story came from a group of people living primarily in Jerusalem who are not representative of the whole of the people. The leaders in Jerusalem were focused on worship in the temple, not on daily family worship as practiced by most people in Israel and Judah. This point reminds us that the ancient people cannot be considered the same as us or even the same as the later generations described in the Bible. Throughout the Hebrew Bible, these ancient cultures created what we now take for granted as a fixed whole. In reality, worship practices were family traditions, which took a long time to change, especially in people who believed that their worship of multiple gods assured the success of their crops, animals, and families.

---

62. Excavations in Jerusalem have uncovered figurines and seals dedicated to other gods: Christopher Eames, "Excavations Reveal Idol Worship in Ancient Israel," December 23, 2019, https://www.nationalgeographic.com/science/article/million-year-old-human-ancestor-unveiled-to-public-spd. Students should note that the term *idol worship* is a derogatory term. Historians normally use more neutral language when describing worship practices.

63. Dever, *Ordinary People*, 251.

Before moving on, we need to discuss an important term. We use the terms "religion," "worship," and "church" in our world. When speaking about the ancient world, scholars use the words "cult," "cultic activity," and "cultic sites." The problem, of course, is that the term "cult" is not favorable in our modern world. Merriam-Webster's online dictionary first defines a cult as "a religion regarded as unorthodox or spurious."[64] It is not until the third definition that this modern dictionary defines the term as the scholars of ancient peoples intend: as "a system of religious beliefs and ritual . . . *also*: its body of adherents."[65] "Cult" in academic writings refers to worship and worship spaces in ancient contexts. With this understanding of terminology, we can describe ancient cultic worship practiced within the tribal and clan structures of ancient Israel and Judah. This is important because we cannot equate "cult" in its modern sense to the Jewish faith. Scholars using these terms are not disparaging the ancient faith nor betraying anti-Semitic sentiments. A discussion of ancient worship practices cannot be extrapolated onto modern Judaism.

Alongside their household worship, the family, or at least the men of the family, would also worship at the clan's cultic center (1 Sam. 1:1–19). Such centers were regional and used to celebrate the festivals tied to the celebration of the harvests. These regional religious festivals were not uniform throughout Israel and Judah and developed before organized religious practices celebrated *Adoni* in Jerusalem (e.g., Gen. 35:1–15; Exod. 19:1–25; Num. 7:1–89; Josh. 24:1–28). Some of these sites are mentioned in the biblical text (1 Sam. 9:12; 10:8; 2 Sam. 1:19; 1 Kgs. 3:2) but have rarely been discovered by archaeologists because of their remote locations.[66] They are located on hilltops near towns and villages; thus are called high places, *bāmôt*; and are marked by cultic objects such as large standing stones, altars, and basins. However, these high places were essential to the cohesiveness of the larger clan. Shared religious rituals and praise festivals were part of a yearly cycle of piety and faith development in Israel and Judah (fig. 6).

Cultic activities have also been identified in larger cities. Some residential rooms contain space for worship and cultic items such as altars (Megiddo, Lachish, Taanach, and Tel Amal).[67] Larger installations have also been identified. Tel Dan was noted in the Bible as a cultic site for the northern kingdom of Israel (1 Kgs. 12:26–33). A large cultic foundation (62 feet or 19 meters in length) for a temple and an altar was discovered in the Tel Dan excavations.[68]

---

64. Merriam-Webster, "Cult" (2025), https://www.merriam-webster.com/dictionary/cult.
65. Merriam-Webster, "Cult."
66. Mazar, *Archaeology*, 500.
67. Mazar, *Archaeology*, 500.
68. Mazar, *Archaeology*, 492–93.

Figure 6. Standing stones at Gezer. (Photograph by Beth LaNeel Tanner)

A temple was also identified in a royal area of Tel Arad in Judah (fig. 7). This temple was active during the monarchy.[69] These temples appear to be for the worship of *Adoni* but could have also been used for other gods. The site at Arad contradicts the rule that Jerusalem was the only place of sacrifice and ritual worship in Judah (2 Kgs. 18:3–4). In 2024, an excavation report from a site on the eastern slope of the city of David in Jerusalem described a series of rock-cut rooms. From the contents of the rooms, the archaeologists determined this was an ancient worship site that included an altar. The site was used from the Middle Bronze Age (2000–1550 BCE) until the mid-eighth century BCE when it was intentionally boarded up. This site near the temple in Jerusalem was used for worship, but whether it was for other gods is not clear. More research in the coming years will seek solutions to the question of why there was another worship site close to the Jerusalem temple.[70] These urban cultic

---

69. Y. Aharoni, "Arad: Its Inscriptions and Temple," *BA* 31, no. 1 (1968): 18–23. This temple had the same westward orientation as the one in Jerusalem and the same width (20 m, or 65 feet) but not the same length.

70. Eli Shukron et al., "Evidence of Worship in the Rock-Cut Rooms on the Eastern Slope of the City of David, Jerusalem," *'Atiqot* 116 (2024): 77–124.

Figure 7. Arad temple. (Photograph by Beth LaNeel Tanner)

sites were probably staffed by professional priests who offered regular worship and sacrifices. They were also places for festivals for the urban dwellers and the surrounding rural communities.

Worship continued throughout the Iron Age in a variety of ways. The center of the rituals remained in the home and constituted the day-to-day rhythm of personal and family piety. Regional cultic sites in high places provided occasions for public worship with and without professional priests. These sites existed in Israel and Judah, where *Adoni* and possibly other gods were celebrated during the settlement in Canaan (Abraham to Saul) and within the monarchies of Israel and Judah (1000–586 BCE). Likewise, the temples in larger cities such as Dan and Arad, and certainly Jerusalem, provided pilgrimage destinations to even larger groups for public worship. Like most of the history and culture of this period, we know less than we would like about their exact rituals and elements of worship. Yet it is clear that these various worship centers worked together to provide the people with a complete worship life. Worship served to bring the larger community together and provided cohesion (Josh. 24). Much of the biblical text centers on the temple in Jerusalem and its practices. But even then, we know less than we wished. Worship during the monarchy should be understood as developing. Rituals were different, depending on the area of the country, family traditions, and shared beliefs. The practices were not the same in all places or at all times. Monotheism took a long time to develop fully.

Life in the Afro-Asiatic Region

What we read in the Hebrew Bible needs to be studied and understood as one perspective of worship from the viewpoint of those involved in temple worship. Family and regional worship continued in Israel and Judah for centuries.

SUMMARY

One way to enter the world of the biblical text is by seeking to understand the people these texts first engaged. This is done by using the insights of archaeologists and other experts who uncover and translate the artifacts of ancient people. As this chapter has pointed out, the ancient Israelite world differed from ours. Except for a small class who were part of or close to the royal family or other elites, people lived regionally on farms or in urban centers. Their economy revolved around agriculture, and families were constantly threatened by drought, flood, pests, war, or anything else that could disrupt their food or water supply. Worship was usually a family event except on festival days, and even then, the gathering place was not in Jerusalem for most, but at their local cultic site.

In contrast to this reality, most of the Bible was written in urban centers and reflects an exclusive urban life that revolved around the temple cult in Jerusalem and the lives of those closest to the king. In its final form, the Hebrew Bible is a national document that reflects the highest circles of power. This is not a criticism but a statement of fact. Like all documents, it has a purpose and intended audience. These scrolls carry the official view of those in the Jerusalem circles. This does not mean the religious regulations prescribed in the Hebrew Bible were universally practiced or reflected all the theological diversity of the people. Just as the Bible today is interpreted in many cultures and traditions, it was composed in a world with multiple beliefs, cultural practices, and ways of life.

How does this context help students to read and interpret the Hebrew Bible better? There is an old saying among Bible scholars, "The Bible was not written *to* you, but it was written *for* you." This means we are not the original audience. Everything in the Hebrew Bible happens in a context vastly different from ours. For example, the Bible says nothing directly about modern moral issues. It is not a book of history, nor is it here to provide us with crystal clear answers. It is more of a guide for our inner lives and our relationships with God and others. The Bible offers us principles to follow from its own time, like this: "You shall also love the stranger, for you were strangers in the land of Egypt" (Deut. 10:19; cf. Lev. 19:34). It does not explain how this impacts a modern country's immigration policy.

The people, culture, and society reflected in the Hebrew Bible should not be dismissed either. I have heard a lot of sermons where the people in the Bible are quickly condemned for being faithless. This is an easy shot to take. It has the air of "Well, we know better." How would that sermon sound if the pastor and the people were in the same situation and culture as the rural people of Israel and Judah? Who would you pray to if your family faced starvation? Would you pray only to your God, or would you consider the gods of your neighbors who have food? What would it take for you to abandon the worship of gods that your ancestors have worshiped for generations? As preachers and teachers, instead of judging the people of the Bible, we should place ourselves in their context. These essential questions provide faith formation and aid us in developing empathy for others. Writing them off as faithless does not grow faith formation; it confers an air of superiority over others in different contexts.

5

"In the Beginning": Genesis and Exodus

The Bible begins with a book that transports readers back to a "beginning." The stories are colorful, engaging, and enlightening. But what does the word "beginning" mean in the Hebrew Bible? Is it to be understood chronologically or metaphorically? Is it meant as science or philosophy? Does it belong in a history book? Most history books that focus on the Hebrew Bible begin with the exodus or, more commonly, the settlement of the land of Israel. Why? This chapter explores this issue as we learn how texts function in Genesis and Exodus. We also discuss these texts' genres, editing, and traditions. Finally, we ask: If the Bible is not history, then what is it?

Jews and Christians believe the Bible is a sacred text inspired by God. This recognition, however, does not tell us *how* we are to read the text. Do we read it as a newspaper, expecting an objective report on the events of the day? Or as law and instruction used as a moral guide for living? Or is it a book of poetry and narratives teaching us about God and ancient people? Without realizing it, we often bring a whole philosophy of reading to this or any text. We also bring the traditions of our church, family, and culture to a reading of the Bible.

As noted in chapter 2, having our passports in hand when we pick up the Bible might be helpful to remind us that we must enter the Bible as we would a foreign culture. The Bible was written thousands of years ago in a place that bridges Africa and Asia, where people spoke ancient Hebrew and Aramaic, among other languages. The Hebrew Bible was not written in the language of our culture nor with the norms of our culture. Pastors and teachers are meant to be guides who help bridge the gap between the ancient world and contemporary issues. To start to bridge this gap, we will begin at "the beginning."

IN THE BEGINNING (GENESIS 1–11)

The Hebrew Bible begins with two distinct accounts of creation (Gen. 1:1–2:4a and 2:4b–3:24); these two accounts say something about ancient ways of thinking and how they are different from our ways. Why are there two different accounts? What does this teach us about reading the Bible? The rest of the opening chapters (4–11) tell of human disobedience, murder, a genealogy from *adam* (the human) to Noah, and more disobedience, including a strange story about "the sons of God" and human females, the flood narratives, and the story of the Tower of Babel. These stories are supernatural and bizarre, so what are the best ways to read and understand them?

First, the people who wrote, preserved, and canonized the Hebrew Bible knew there were two creation accounts in Genesis, along with additional creation accounts in Psalm 104 and Proverbs 8:22–31. Right at the beginning, the book's very form, presented in two distinct narratives, tells the reader something. But what is that message?

The two accounts are different. Genesis 1 describes an ordered creation. God, *Elohim*, spoke everything into existence. Humans were created last and made in God's image, male and female. It was all pronounced "very good" (Gen. 1:27, 31). In the second account, the Lord God (note the different name) created *ādam* first to till and keep the garden. Then, the *Adoni* God made that garden, formed the animals from the dirt, and took them to *ādam* to name. Later, God puts *ādam* to sleep, takes one of his sides,[1] and creates a helper and partner. A way to understand these texts is to use the interpretive skills discussed in the previous chapters. What will comparative studies of other ancient cultures teach us? What can be learned from archaeologists and other experts? How will the genre of the text aid in its interpretation? Are these texts history?

Some Notes on Hebrew in the Genesis Creation Accounts

Genesis 1:27 in the NRSVue states, "So God created humans." The rest of creation was spoken into creation. God created humans. The word *bārā'* in 1:27 is a verb reserved chiefly for God's creating work. In Hebrew, humans can "make," "form," and "fashion," but only God can create from nothing. This essential theological message is often overlooked without knowledge of Hebrew.

---

1. Most English Bibles translate this word as "rib." Interestingly, the Hebrew word *ṣēlā'* means "rib" only here. The meaning the other thirty times it appears is the side of the tabernacle, temple, or house.

We know the word "Adam" as a proper name. That is true in English but not in Hebrew. The word *ādam* simply means human and is paired with another word in the text. This feminine counterpart, *ădāmāh*, means earth or dirt and is not related to the name Eve at all. At this point, *ādam* is the earth human prior to its split. The text does not actually give the human we call Adam a proper name, but it teaches another theological lesson. God is God. Humans are intimately connected to the earth and created by God. Their parallel is to the earth, not to God. I try to provide the same connection in my classes by identifying Adam and Eve[2] as dirt boy and dirt girl. We sever this connection to the earth by assigning them proper names.

We are all told that the woman was formed from one of the man's ribs (Gen. 2:21). This time, it is the English Bibles that add a layer of misogyny, for the Hebrew word most often means the entire side, usually of a temple or other building! God splits the *ādam* to create the corresponding partner. The NIV translation carries a footnote with this meaning but still sticks with the traditional "rib" in the text.

Comparative studies shed light on why there are multiple accounts of creation in the Hebrew Bible. Christopher Hays advises, "It is best to set aside certain preconceived notions at the onset. For example, many readers may expect that each civilization has one creation story—a *single* account of origins. . . . Instead, wherever we have large bodies of preserved literature from the ancient Near East [Afro-Asiatic region], we also find multiple accounts of origins."[3] So, from comparative studies, we discover that various origin accounts were accepted in the ancient world. So, within its own context, Genesis follows the ancient parameters for origin stories.

When these nonbiblical origin stories from other nations were first shared in the early 1900s, this discovery resulted in turmoil in many Christian communities. Claus Westermann reports: "When the parallels to Genesis 1 were first made known, Christian theologians, almost without exception, regarded them as a threat to the revelation of the biblical story of creation. The interpreters of the Bible . . . took up an attitude which prejudged the question, and which sought to demonstrate the unique character of the religious superiority of the biblical account."[4] This preconception of the uniqueness of the Genesis

---

2. The name "Eve" is not assigned until after they leave the garden in 4:1. It is not a name given in the creation narratives.

3. Christopher Hays, *Hidden Riches: A Sourcebook for the Comparative Study of the Hebrew Bible and Ancient Near East* (Westminster John Knox, 2014), 61.

4. Claus Westermann, *Genesis 1–11: A Continental Commentary*, trans. J. Scullion (Fortress, 1994), 19.

creation story is still a commonly held belief. Instead of seeing other stories as threats, in our study here we will see what we can learn from them.

While a comprehensive discussion of this topic is not possible, a few quick insights will introduce readers to the possibilities of a comparative literature review. For example, as noted above, this comparative literary study reveals that multiple accounts of origins were common and that the Bible is no exception. The other examples will come from comparing and contrasting the Genesis narratives with a well-known Mesopotamian creation account called the Enuma Elish. The exact date of origin for the Enuma Elish is unknown, but most scholars have assigned it to the First Babylonian Dynasty (1894–1594 BCE).[5] The precise dates of the circulation of the Genesis texts are also unknown but are certainly after the First Babylonian Dynasty.

Did the author or authors of the Genesis creation accounts know the origin myths of others? It is impossible to state with certainty, but in a world where stories were told and retold because they served the function of education, entertainment, and community cohesion, it is reasonable to believe they knew some of these myths. The Enuma Elish begins with an account of the origin of the gods.[6] In contrast, the Hebrew Bible never speculates on God's origin. When Genesis opens, God simply is, without explanation. God's origin remains a mystery. Interestingly, this fits with the divine name of the Hebrew God, introduced in Exodus 3:13–22 and discussed in chapter 4.

Another point of comparison can be made regarding the creation of humans. In the Enuma Elish, the god Marduk creates humans to do the work of the gods so the gods can rest.[7] Contrast this to the two reasons in the Genesis account. In Genesis 2, the *Adoni* God created *ādam* to till and keep the garden, not for the sake of God but for the human and the creation. Humans being created to work resembles the Babylonian account, but the reason is not. In Genesis 1, humans were created in God's image to multiply and fill the earth. The humans were created to *be*, not to work for the gods. This contrast tells us that God did not create humans to work for God but to work and exist in God's image in the world. These examples demonstrate how comparative studies can enhance our understanding of texts in the Hebrew Bible.

Next, we move to the archaeologists and other experts. Do they shed light on these early Genesis texts? Unfortunately, they do not. These first eleven chapters are not datable. The statements like "In the beginning" (Gen. 1:1) and "These are the generations of the heavens and the earth when they were

---

5. Alexander Heidel, *The Babylonian Genesis: The Story of Creation*, 2nd ed. (Chicago: University of Chicago Press, 1951), 14.

6. W. G. Lambert, *Babylonian Creation Myths*, Mesopotamian Civilizations 16 (Eisenbrauns, 2013), 51.

7. Lambert, *Creation Myths*, 111.

"In the Beginning": Genesis and Exodus 79

created" (2:4) do not provide a time frame for the archaeologist to discover anything. Archaeological discoveries provided parallel creation stories from other nations, thus adding to our knowledge of their ancient contexts. However, no direct evidence of these early Genesis narratives has been found elsewhere.

So far, we have looked at the history behind the texts with comparative studies and the history in the text with archaeological inquiries. Next, we tackle the question of how the Bible is true. This exploration will provide some historical background into how different Christians today read the Bible. This discussion is not specifically about the first eleven chapters of Genesis; instead, these questions often arise for students embarking on an academic study of the Bible. Therefore, it is essential to deal with these questions here. This entails some abbreviated discussions of the history of biblical interpretation.

Until the 1500s, the Catholic and Orthodox Churches were the two major Christian denominations worldwide. During this period, the Bible was not commonly read or studied by people other than priests and scholars. The Jewish traditions were quite different, with robust debates among rabbis and other Jews about biblical understanding and interpretation from the Talmud and Midrash traditions. In the 1500s, the Protestant reformers believed in *sola Scriptura*, Scripture alone. This coincided with the development of Gutenberg's printing press (ca. 1450). The Bible was translated from Greek, Hebrew, and Latin into the peoples' languages. But this did not mean that all the reformers had a universal understanding of Scripture.

Martin Luther (1483–1546) understood Genesis as what was literally written, instead of conveying an allegorical meaning. He writes, "Moses spoke in a literal sense, not allegorically or figuratively, i.e., that the world, with all its creatures, was created within six days, as the words read." He says further, "We know from Moses that the world was not in existence before 6,000 years ago."[8] We see with Luther a process of biblical interpretation based on the author's intention, an author he understood to be Moses, a traditional assumption. In this way, he sought to understand the text in its ancient context.

John Calvin (1509–65) read the texts of Genesis differently, saying: "Since the infinite wisdom of God is displayed in the admirable structure of heaven and earth, it is impossible to unfold the History of the Creation of the World in terms equal to its dignity. For while the measure of our capacity is too contracted to comprehend things of such magnitude, our tongue is equally incapable of giving a full and substantial account of them."[9] Calvin argues

8. Martin Luther, *Lectures on Genesis, Chapters 1–5*, in vol. 1 of *Luther's Works*, ed. Jaroslav Pelikan et al. (Concordia, 1958), 4–5.
9. John Calvin, *Commentaries on the First Book of Moses Called Genesis*, trans. J. King (Baker, 1979), 1.

that creation is a great act of God that we cannot comprehend or adequately write about. He is not reading Genesis as historical but as a theological text that points to the great mysteries of God.

Luther and Calvin represent the tensions among biblical interpreters as a result of the Enlightenment. The age of reason meant that the questions about historicity and authorship applied to other literature began to be applied to the Bible. It was a question of faith and reason coming together in a quest for meaning. This debate between faith and reason continued and is still part of the debate about how to interpret the Bible today. There are as many ways to interpret the Bible as there are readers of the Bible; even the terms *biblical literalism*, *inerrancy*, and *infallibility* do not mean the same thing to all denominations and persons. I present what I and most other mainline Protestant scholars use as our guide when it comes to this debate. First, for me, the Bible is true in matters of faith and testimony about God and God's relationship with humans. This does not mean the Bible is historically accurate in all things. It is also not a science textbook. Its focus is theological, yet it does not have one single theological perspective. Indeed, the Bible often talks to itself about issues of the day, and it debates back and forth about them. I also believe that the Bible testifies to a mystery that human words cannot adequately capture. It is, therefore, not God's only revelation in the world.

From these observations, one can see that understanding the "beginning" as described in Genesis must encompass both of these creation narratives and their context. Objectively, we cannot state that one or the other of these Genesis texts is "history" because history as a category of writing did not exist, and the texts do not read as a history. So, if they are not history, how are these narratives true? These foundational myths were designed not as history per se but as confessions of faith. In essence, these myths instructed an ancient audience about God while seeking to communicate some truths about humans and how we act against God and our best interests. The texts in context confess that God is and always has been. The story of God and humans begins with God speaking the world into existence (Gen. 1) and creating the world with the human (Gen. 2). The text confesses that they were created in God's image (Gen. 1) and given the earth to till and keep it (Gen. 2). It is a statement about God's relationship with the world and humans. Genesis 3–11 continues to teach about God's relationship with humans. It tells a story that will be repeated again and again in the Hebrew Bible. Humans do something to fracture their relationship with God, and God finds another way to continue the relationship with humans. Victor Matthews sums up Genesis 1–11 this way: "It is more likely that these narratives function to explain the origins of the world and society (etiology) rather than provide scientific or objective historical accounts."[10] Just as in the creation accounts, the meaning of the texts in Genesis 3–11 should be sought in theological terms instead of historical ones.

Just as with Genesis 1–4 and its stories about Adam and Eve and their children, the flood narrative in Genesis 6–9, for instance, cannot be verified by archaeological or geological evidence despite repeated efforts to do so.[11] However, it is a type of narrative found in cultures worldwide.[12] Scholars have understood floods in ancient narratives as representations of disaster and chaos. Floods suddenly come into this region with terrifying results. The stories try to make sense of these tragic events and to understand God's role in them.[13]

Before we leave Genesis 1–11, there is one more point to discuss. In these chapters so far, the Bible reads more like a collection of short stories than a cohesive whole. For example, the vocabulary and even the name of God are different in the two creation narratives. As Luther assumed, Moses was seen as the traditional author of the Bible's first five books, as also accepted during ancient times. However, authorship was not considered a copyrightable function in the ancient world. The community shared the stories and passed them on from generation to generation. Often, to provide the narratives with authority, a legendary figure at the time was said to be the author. But does the Bible need an authority figure to be authoritative?

THE MATRIARCHS AND PATRIARCHS (GENESIS 12–50)

Beginning with the Abraham and Sarah cycle in Genesis 12, there is a change in how the stories in Genesis are presented. The texts are full of places and people, and these details appear to provide evidence for historical inquiry. As modern readers, we recognize these elements as what we expect in historical narratives. However, a closer inspection demonstrates that the Genesis 12–50 narratives do not provide concrete dates or enough specific information to set them in a definite historical time frame. Think of it this way: many family stories contain faraway places and details that make the story exciting

---

10. Victor Matthews, *A Brief History of Ancient Israel* (Westminster John Knox, 2002), 2.
11. The Wikipedia article on searches for the ark is an interesting read: "Searches for Noah's Ark," 2025, https://en.wikipedia.org/wiki/Searches_for_Noah%27s_Ark.
12. J. Frazer reported the existence of 250 flood sagas across the world, in *Folklore in the Old Testament* (Macmillan, 1919), 63–82. Many of these flood sagas, collected by Mark Isaak (2002), are at https://www.talkorigins.org/faqs/flood-myths.html.
13. Westermann, *Genesis 1–11*, 399.

and grounded in real life. Yet these stories are the product of memories, and often those memories are passed on from generation to generation. Details get garbled or lost, and one would be hard-pressed to return to the area and discover the places described. Also, even though many places are listed in the biblical texts, there is currently no archaeological evidence to prove that these matriarchs and patriarchs were there. This lack of written and archaeological evidence is not unusual when studying ancient cultures. The matriarchs and patriarchs lived as seminomads. Nomads do not build large structures or leave behind a cache of physical remains that archaeologists can excavate later. From a strictly historical perspective, nothing is known about this period.[14]

Indeed, we are not even sure of the time frame within which to look for archaeological remains. The only way to provide some guidance on the time frame is to give an educated, reasoned guess from what we know about the ancient world. So, we begin with the first historically verifiable date that suggests the existence of the people of Israel and Judah, which is via the Merenptah Stela, discovered in Thebes, Egypt, and dated around 1203 BCE: it describes a people known as "Israel" located in Canaan. Counting backward, using the biblical texts as the only reference, a possible time frame for the matriarchs and patriarchs is the Middle Bronze (MB) era, between 2200 and 1550 BCE. The biblical text comes from multiple sources transmitted via oral tradition long before it was written down. Some traditions in the text fit with the Middle Bronze era, while others are clearly from a later time. For example, there are several anachronistic details, such as the groups of people mentioned in the text that were not in the area until later, in the Iron Age. The Philistines (Gen. 21:32; 26) did not arrive in Canaan until the Late Bronze Age or Early Iron Age, 1500–1100 BCE. Also, Abraham and Jacob are said to have camels (Gen. 12:16, 30:43); but camels were not domesticated in the eastern Mediterranean area until the tenth century BCE.[15] Does this mean the matriarchs and patriarchs were not real people, that Abraham did not exist, or that Joseph was never a valued official of Pharaoh? There is simply no evidence to say one

---

14. This is the reason many history books do not discuss the book of Genesis, and strictly speaking, they are correct. Since nothing can be stated with historical certainty, the narratives of Genesis are not discussed. See J. Maxwell Miller and John H. Hayes, *A History of Ancient Israel and Judah*, 2nd ed. (Westminster John Knox, 2006), 69–81.

15. Multiple examples of this appear in scholarly literature: many of the people whom Abraham encounters come from a later period (Sea Peoples, Aramaeans, Arabs, and Chaldeans, for example); the nomadic lifestyle was not exclusive to this early period; and so on). Lester Grabbe, *Ancient Israel: What Do We Know and How Do We Know It?* (T&T Clark, 2007), 53. Studies show the camel was not domesticated in this region until 930 BCE: Mairav Zonszein, "Domesticated Camels Came to Israel in 903 B.C., Centuries Later Than the Bible Says," *National Geographic*, February 10, 2014, https://www.nationalgeographic.com/culture/article/140210-domesticated-camels-israel-bible-archaeology-science.

way or the other.[16] The narratives of this period can teach readers about the relationship between humanity and God, but they do not add anything to an understanding of the history of the Middle Bronze Age or Early Iron Age.

The story of Israel and Judah began as a family story based on a promise given by God (Gen. 12:1–3). It is not a pretty story. It is filled with family dysfunction and deceit. The promise given by God that "in you all the families of the earth shall be blessed" (12:3) is quickly forgotten as brother is set against brother. Since the humans act like humans, the hero of this story is God, who remains faithful to God's promise to this family, even in the face of their dysfunction. The book of Genesis opens with God's great act of creation and the pronouncement "It is very good"; it ends with the children of God's promise surviving in a foreign land. The text's message, from "very good" to existing in exile, lies in its theological character, not in its historical reporting of traceable events.

THE EXODUS FROM EGYPT (EXODUS 1–15)

The book of Exodus opens with the story of God's deliverance of the people of Israel from suffering under a new regime. It is a story of God's care and salvation for enslaved people, and its message has stimulated hope for generations of believers. However, as with Genesis, historical uncertainties continue. It is easy to see how some scholars have questioned whether the exodus from Egypt was an actual event.

First, the biblical text does not provide the specifics of the event, such as the date or the name of Pharaoh. Why are these specifics absent? A look at the whole of the Hebrew Bible shows that many of the specifics we seek were not important to the original audience. The Bible does not contain precise dates. Instead, it uses relative dating: "Now a new king arose over Egypt who did not know Joseph" (Exod. 1:8). The ancients told their stories according to relationships and generations. This makes the task of creating a chronology of Judah and Israel difficult and tentative. In addition, there may be other reasons for the omission of information. For example, in Exodus 1, the two midwives, Shiphrah and Puah, are remembered by name, while Pharaoh is not given the same honor. The purpose may have been to dishonor the king

---

16. The Nuzi texts may provide some information on social customs during this period. Discovered in the 1920s, the texts present the practices of adoption in Northern Mesopotamia and have much in common with those described in Gen. 16 (*COS*, 1:251–52). Information like this from a neighboring culture can clarify biblical texts but does not greatly aid in the dating of a specific practice.

of Egypt by purposely *not* remembering him. In other words, the slight could serve a theological purpose rather than a historical one.[17]

Historians must use the specifics that do exist in this ancient text to discover a possible time frame. In the case of the exodus event, the evidence is all indirect. Exodus 1:11 mentions the store cities of Pithom and Rameses as the places the enslaved people built. Can these city names be connected to actual ancient cities? Archaeologists have identified Pithom as Tell el-Maskhuta, but studies show it was abandoned for five centuries beginning in 1550 BCE.[18] The city of Rameses was identified as Tell el-Dabʻa. It was also destroyed in 1550 BCE but was rebuilt during Rameses II's reign (1279–1213 BCE), presumably by those enslaved by the Egyptians.[19] Thus, Tell el-Dabʻa is a possible match to the biblical account during the most probable time of the exodus, but Tell el-Maskhuta is not because it was abandoned until about 1000 BCE; by that time, Israel was forming its monarchy in the region of Canaan.

A Lesson in How Historical Evaluations Can Change

Above is the standard scholarship concerning the two Egyptian cities in Exodus 1:11. The assumption was that the names of these two cities were another anachronistic substitution since Pithom and Rameses existed from the sixth century onward and thus were added to the biblical text later. Recently, James Hoffmeier and Gary Rendsburg looked at more recent archaeological discoveries in the area and at Egyptian documents from the reign of Rameses II. They argue that Pithom should be associated with Tell el-Retaba, not Tell el-Dabʻa, and Rameses should be associated with Qantir. Both were significant cities during Egypt's Nineteenth and Twentieth Dynasties (1292–1077 BCE).[20] If their investigation is proven sound, the association of these cities would be changed. Others will look at the evidence presented in the article and either agree or disagree. It can take decades for a majority of scholars to agree with a new discovery.

---

17. Other scholars provide other reasons for the omission; see James K. Hoffmeier, who argues that it was an Egyptian practice not to name an enemy: *Israel in Egypt: Evidence for the Authenticity of the Exodus Tradition* (Oxford University Press, 1997), 110–11. On the other side, Ronald Hendel argues that the lack of a name is "providing a movable boundary of inclusion for those [over time] who share this memory"; "The Exodus in Biblical Memory," *JBL* 120, no. 4 (2001): 604.

18. William Dever, *Who Were the Early Israelites and Where Did They Come From?* (Eerdmans, 2006), 14.

19. Dever, *Early Israelites?*, 14.

20. James K. Hoffmeier and Gary Rendsburg, "Pithom and Ramses (Exodus 1:11): Historical, Archaeological, and Linguistic Issues," *Journal of Ancient Egyptian Interconnections* 33 (March 2022): 1–19.

"In the Beginning": Genesis and Exodus   85

While there is no direct evidence connecting the building of the city of Rameses to the enslaved of the biblical text, Amihai Mazar argues that there was a sizeable Afro-Asiatic population living in this region of Egypt during this period.[21] The people of Exodus 1 could have been some of those people who were also enslaved. At the same time, there is also no direct evidence that the Pharoah in Exodus was Rameses II; more evidence is needed. Other discoveries add to the knowledge of this period. Ronald Hendel notes that Egypt's taking some Canaanites into bondage was common. They captured Canaanites as prisoners of war, for vassal tribute, or even for the financial gain of ancient traffickers.[22] The matriarchs and patriarchs lived in Canaan as nomadic or seminomadic people, and the biblical text records them as going to Egypt during a famine only to become enslaved later; their enslavement is historically plausible. The Canaanite region was an important source of enslaved people for the growing Egyptian Empire during the late New Kingdom (1550–1050 BCE). James Hoffmeier reports a relief on the wall of the tomb for an Egyptian official, Rekhmire, who served Thutmose II (1479–1425 BCE): it depicts laborers making bricks with an inscription that describes them as prisoners of war from the southlands and the northlands, presumably the Canaanite region.[23] This demonstrates that prisoners or enslaved people made bricks for buildings during at least part of the New Kingdom period (1550–1050 BCE). Again, this is an indirect piece of information from an earlier period before Rameses II's reign and the rebuilding of Tell el-Dab'a. Still, it shows that enslaved people participated in building Egyptian cities, which fits the description in the biblical text of the Hebrew enslaved people making bricks (Exod. 1:13–14).

The following two pieces of evidence help narrow the time frame for the enslavement and exodus from Egypt. The Amarna letters, discovered in Egypt, are 350 pieces of correspondence between the Egyptian rulers and the kings of Canaanite city-states. Most of these letters were written during the reign of Amenhotep IV from 1353 to 1336 BCE.[24] In all of these letters, there is no mention of the people "Israel,"[25] even though many of the letters deal

21. Amihai Mazar, "The Patriarchs, Exodus, and Conquest Narratives in Light of Archaeology," in *The Quest for the Historical Israel*, ed. Israel Finkelstein et al. (SBL, 2007), 59.
22. Hendel, "Exodus in Biblical Memory," 607.
23. Hoffmeier, *Israel in Egypt*, 112–14. This time frame is several centuries before the most probable time of the exodus. However, Egypt remained in control of the region for the entire period; there is no reason to assume that slave functions changed significantly during Egypt's control of the Afro-Asiatic region.
24. Priscilla Scoville, "Amarna Letters," *World History Encyclopedia*, November 6, 2015, http://www.ancient.eu/Amarna_Letters/.
25. Some have asserted that the *Habiru* and *Shasu* in these letters are actual references to the earliest Israelites; see Norman Gottwald, *The Tribes of Yahweh: A Sociology of the Religion of Liberated*

with local disputes and military actions between city-states in Canaan. This indicates Israel was either not an entity or was too small to be noticed by the city-state rulers during this earlier period.

The other commonly used marker for the exodus event comes from the Merenptah Stela.[26] This stela, discovered in his mortuary temple at Thebes, praises Pharaoh Merenptah for turning back a Libyan invasion. However, the bottom of the monument commemorates a military campaign through the Canaanite region in approximately 1203 BCE. The important line for our purposes reads, "Israel is laid waste, his seed is no more."[27] Additionally, the stela does not use the hieroglyphic sign for a foreign nation, but the one used for a nomadic people.[28] It is the first definitive extrabiblical evidence of the existence of the people called Israel. This mention of Israel helps to narrow the timeline of the exodus to sometime between the last of the Amarna letters (1336 BCE) and the campaign of Merenptah (1203 BCE). Unfortunately, with the decline of Egypt and other empires, epigraphic evidence disappeared during the twelfth century and the Afro-Asiatic region entered "the early dark-age centuries of the Iron Age."[29] There is evidence from archaeological surveys of widespread disturbance in the area in approximately 1200–1150 BCE as Egyptian power declined.[30] However, as Eric Cline notes, this was not just a decline in Egyptian power; it was also a decline in almost all the powerful countries of the Bronze Age, from Egypt to the Aegean.[31] Also, in the thirteenth century, small settlements began to appear in the highland regions of Canaan.[32] These findings clearly indicate significant changes consistent with the resettlement and the movements of people as all the powerful empires waned. The smaller highland settlements did not introduce new styles of pottery or building materials, indicating the people resettling in the area were

---

Israel, 1250–1050 B.C.E. (Orbis Books, 1979), 401–9. This connection, however, is not certain and has been abandoned by many historians, such as Miller and Hayes, *Ancient Israel and Judah*, 37.

26. "Merneptah Stele [Merenptah Stela]," Wikimedia Foundation, 2025, https://en.wikipedia.org/wiki/Merneptah_Stele.

27. Anson Rainey, "Israel in Merenptah's Inscription and Reliefs," *IEJ* 51 (2001): 57–74. Rainey demonstrates that "His seed is no more" is a term that refers to a military victory. Thus the claim does not necessarily indicate complete destruction.

28. Carol A. Redmount, "Bitter Lives: Israel in and out of Egypt," in *The Oxford History of the Biblical World*, ed. Michael D. Coogan (Oxford University Press, 1999), 97.

29. Miller and Hayes, *Ancient Israel and Judah*, 45.

30. Eric H. Cline declares, "The magnitude of the catastrophe was enormous; it was a loss such as the world would not see again until the Roman Empire collapsed more than fifteen hundred years later." Cline, *1177 B.C.: The Year Civilization Collapsed* (Princeton University Press, 2021), xix.

31. Cline, *1177 B.C.*, 9.

32. Israel Finkelstein, *The Archaeology of the Israelite Settlement* (Israel Exploration Society, 1988).

Canaanites. Enslaved people escaping a weakened Egypt could be some of the people who established themselves in Canaan during this time.

Given all this, what can be said about the historical evidence of the exodus? Scholars previously assigned a date of 1250 BCE for the exodus. But it is probably best not to speak of a specific year but of a probable time frame. Thus, using the date for the Amarna letters as the earliest point possible date (1336 BCE) for the exodus, and the campaign by Merenptah as the point where "Israel" as a collective entity is recorded in Canaan (1203 BCE)—this provides a range for the exodus event between 1336 and 1203 BCE. Any further attempt to narrow the time frame would be speculation.[33] There is insufficient historical information to do so.

Then, there is the question of the size of the exodus. The biblical text in Genesis tells us that Abraham and Sarah were seminomads in Canaan. Two generations later, Jacob's sons went to Egypt to escape a famine in Canaan. Then, we learn, "a new king arose over Egypt who did not know Joseph" (Exod. 1:8). The Pharoah enslaves their descendants because "the Israelite people are more numerous and more powerful than we" (1:9). Was this the case? Or is it a literary hyperbole? This issue appears again near the end of the exodus story. Exodus 12:37 reports that 600,000 men left Egypt in the exodus. With the addition of women and children, the number would swell to approximately 3.5 million,[34] or roughly 300,000 less than the population of Los Angeles, California! Were there 3.5 million enslaved Israelites in Egypt? Israel Finkelstein estimates the entire population of Israel and Judah to be 55,000 about two hundred years *after* settling in the land.[35] Certainly, more people would have been in Israel and Judah after two hundred years of settlement than the former slaves who left Egypt. Does this mean the claim that the enslaved Hebrews were more numerous than the Egyptians and that 600,000 men leaving Egypt is false or an exaggeration? Again, this question arises from a modern perspective on reading the Bible. Ancient peoples did not think in the same ways we do. The word we translate as "thousand" can have a range of meanings in Hebrew, including a "clan," "tribe,"[36] or even a section of a tribe. Thus, the meaning of the text would be 600 "something"

---

33. Even stating this period is not without controversy. Some traditionalists use the 480-year time frame from 1 Kgs. 6:1 and thus place the exodus in 1446 BCE, but that date conflicts with the archaeological data discussed. Others argue that the exodus was not a single event but a layering of several escape events weaved into one narrative (Dever, *Early Israelites?*, 18–21; Hendel, "Exodus in Biblical Memory," 602).

34. Lester Grabbe, "*Adde Praeputium Praeputio Magnus Acervus Ecrit:* If the Exodus and Conquest Had Really Happened," *Biblical Interpretation* 8 (2000): 24.

35. Finkelstein, *Israelite Settlements*, 334; most archaeologists concur.

36. Ludwig Koehler and Walter Baumgartner, *The Hebrew and Aramaic Lexicon of the Old Testament*, rev. J. Stamm, trans. M. E. J. Richardson (Brill, 2001), 60.

of men.[37] The number is not to be read as a definitive head count but as a theological expression of God's abundance in the flourishing of the people despite their slavery. We see a number and treat it as a fact; the ancients used a term with various meanings to demonstrate God's fulfillment of promises.

Were the Israelite people all descendants of the matriarchs and patriarchs? This issue will be discussed further in the next chapter, which will explore the founding of the people in Canaan. The Bible remembers that they were all members of the same family, but this seems unlikely from a historical perspective. Enslaved people were often displaced from their extended families, and, according to the Bible, the people's slavery in Egypt lasted several hundred years. At that time, there were probably other Canaanites in slavery as well. Indeed, Exodus 12:38 states that Israel went out of Egypt, and "a mixed crowd also went up with them." Again, this question lies beyond what we know, but it seems unlikely that the people who left Egypt were all from a single family.

Additionally, while there is some ancillary information that provides a possible time frame for the exodus—between the writing of the Amarna letters and the campaign of Pharaoh Merenptah—the question of the events in the book of Exodus, such as the plagues or the Red Sea escape, are simply beyond the scope of historical inquiry. There is no record of these events except the biblical one, and the purpose of the biblical account is not to provide a historical account that conforms to our modern standards. This does not mean that these events are absolute fiction; it simply means that we know little about the history of this period.

Acknowledging this dilemma, many scholars have questioned whether the exodus can be called a historical event. Some historians state that it cannot. Niels Lemche notes, "It is generally acknowledged by scholars that the traditions about Israel's sojourn in Egypt and the *exodus* of the Israelites are legendary in nature. . . . There is accordingly no real reason even to attempt to find a historical background for the events of the Exodus."[38] In contradiction to Lemche's assessment, other scholars think his point is overstated. The physical evidence is slight, but as Graham Davies argues, "The [exodus] tradition is *a priori* unlikely to have been invented; the biblical evidence is widespread and can be followed back to a respectable antiquity, within at most two hundred years of the supposed event; some elements of it have a particular claim to authenticity; and in various ways what is said corresponds more closely to the realities of New Kingdom Egypt than one would expect from a later wholly

---

37. G. Mendenhall, "The Census Lists of Numbers 1 and 26," *JBL* 77 (1958): 52–66.

38. Niels Peter Lemche, *Ancient Israel: A New History of Israelite Society*, The Biblical Seminar 5 (JSOT Press, 1988), 109.

fictitious account."³⁹ In other words, physical evidence is not all that historians weigh. In this case, the weight of the tradition in the biblical texts, in addition to the indirect evidence stated above, are all used by historians to test the veracity of the exodus account. It is common to have little evidence for an ancient event. Thus, the debate about the history of such an event is usually vigorous, as it is here with the pivotal exodus event. It is good to remember that none of these scholars is saying the exodus is not important theologically for the story of the Bible. Theirs is a historical argument based on only the lack of clear evidence.

THE WILDERNESS AND MOUNT SINAI (EXODUS 15–20)

Many Bibles contain a map of the path taken by the Israelites when they left Egypt. These biblical maps represent a literary account of the wilderness path based on the biblical text and a biblical scholar's interpretation. Depending on the scholar's opinion of the biblical text, these maps outline multiple paths. These maps can be misleading for modern readers, implying that the path and the marked places are as accurate as satellite technology-powered Google maps.

Unfortunately, little is clearly known about the trip from Egypt to the hill country of Canaan. Archaeological exploration in the northern Sinai east of the Nile Delta has been complicated by the destruction of many places and landmarks in the region by centuries of building and a higher water table, which has buried the earlier cities.⁴⁰ In the southern section of the Sinai, the land is arid, rocky, and mountainous, making sites challenging to identify and excavate. In addition, many of the people who traversed and lived in this area were nomads and semi-nomads, leaving little archeological evidence behind.⁴¹

The exact site of Mount Sinai remains a mystery. Its location is not precise in the biblical text, stated simply as "the wilderness of Sinai" (Exod. 19:1). In 530 CE, St. Catherine's Monastery was built by Byzantine Emperor Justinian I (ruled 527–565 CE). This traditional site of the burning bush and the giving of the law was not discovered through archaeological discovery but through religious fervor and a desire to establish a church on Sinai. For the ancient people who wrote the Exodus text, it appears that the encounter with

---

39. Graham Davies, "Was There an Exodus?," chap. 2 of *In Search of Pre-exilic Israel: Proceedings of the Oxford Old Testament Seminar*, ed. John Day (T&T Clark, 2004), 36.

40. Donald Redford, *Egypt, Canaan, and Israel in Ancient Times* (Princeton University Press, 1992), 102–3.

41. Israel Finkelstein, *Living on the Fringe: The Archaeology and History of the Negev, Sinai, and Neighbouring Regions in the Bronze and Iron Ages* (Sheffield Academic, 1995), 101.

God was the focus of the narrative, not mapping the location of the mountain nor the physical path the people wandered.

Can something be said about the history of this foundational event of lawgiving at the mountain (Exod. 19–24)? As with both the exodus and the journey to Mount Sinai, there is no direct evidence of God's covenant with the people and the laws written on stone tablets. Historically, we are in the same position as we are with all of Genesis and Exodus. We do not have physical proof of the events recorded in the biblical text. The laws or instructions are included as part of the Torah, or Pentateuch (the first five books of the Bible). These laws begin in Exodus 20 with the Ten Words, or Commandments, and continue, with a couple of narrative interludes, until the end of Leviticus. Yet these laws are recognized as coming from various sources throughout the history of Israel and Judah, not just the time at Sinai, as the biblical text describes.[42]

According to the biblical chronology, the worship of *Adoni* and the giving of the law code at Sinai occurred early in the wilderness period, ending in the second year. The following law codes demonstrate some of the complexity historians face in using the Bible to determine the history of the Hebrew people. Exodus 19 reports the people arriving in Sinai. Then following the giving of the Ten Words in Exodus 20 is the Book of the Covenant (Exod. 20:22–23:19). These laws are broad and share much in common with the law codes of neighboring lands. Laws much like the ones recorded here in the Bible were established in Mesopotamia in the late third and the second millennia BCE, during the reigns of Ur-Nammu of Ur (2112–2095 BCE),[43] Lipit–Istar of Ur (1934–1924 BCE),[44] and Hammurabi (1792–1749 BCE).[45] These codes were instituted hundreds of years *before* Israel's exodus and wilderness events. Like the creation narratives, the people who wrote and preserved the words concerning law in the Pentateuch were aware of the laws of other cultures. As argued by Jimmy J. M. Roberts, the importance of these laws was not found in their uniqueness.[46] Their importance was that the laws were understood to be given to the people *by God* in a worship setting. Human kings dictated the other law codes in surrounding nations.[47]

---

42. The traditions in the law code come from the E, J, and P sources. John Collins, *A Short Introduction to the Hebrew Bible*, 3rd ed. (Fortress, 2018), 82–83.

43. Martha Roth, *Law Collections from Mesopotamia and Asia Minor*, Writings from the Ancient World 6 (SBL Press, 1995), 13–22.

44. Roth, *Law Colllections*, 23–35.

45. Roth, *Law Collections*, 71–142.

46. J. J. M. Roberts, "The Ancient Near East," in *The HarperCollins Bible Commentary*, ed. J. Mays, rev. ed. (Harper Collins, 2000), 51.

47. John Durham, *Exodus*, Word Biblical Commentary, vol. 3 (Word Books, 1987), 317–18.

The Book of the Covenant, or Covenant Code, is followed by narratives of the peoples' impatience: the idolatrous actions of the people waiting for Moses to come back down the mountain, and the ramifications of that act and God's renewal of the covenant with them, including additional laws (Exod. 32:1–34:35). Exodus then ends with the construction of the tabernacle (chaps. 35–40).

A second set of law codes is found in the book of Leviticus. It is a complex set of laws that grew over time. Leviticus first presents laws about worship, sacrifices, offerings, priests, clean and unclean regulations, and the Day of Atonement in chapters 1–16. The laws of chapters 17–26 contain the holiness codes regulating how the people of God are to live. John Hartley surmises, "[The law] seems to have undergone growth after the settlement in Canaan, for it provides laws on issues faced by a growing urban population, e.g., the laws on buying and selling of houses in walled cities (25:29–34)."[48] These law codes from a much later time are placed here because all of the laws of God's people were seen as originating from the Sinai event, when God gave the law to the people. The placement of the laws here makes it difficult for the historian to state just when the laws originated. They probably grew over the centuries that cover the time of the Hebrew Bible.

THE POST-SINAI WILDERNESS YEARS (BOOK OF NUMBERS)

The book of Numbers begins with a census of the people at Sinai. The people finally move on from Sinai in chapter 10, which, according to 10:11, was "in the second year, in the second month, on the twentieth day of the month." According to Exodus 19, the people arrived at Sinai about three months after leaving Egypt ("on the third new moon," 19:1) and then remained at the mountain for almost two years. The rest of the book of Numbers narrates the further time in the wilderness. Joshua 5:6 states that the time in the wilderness lasted forty years. However, this is not a firm historical number because forty is part of a symbolic pattern of measuring time in the Genesis–2 Kings narratives. In addition to the wilderness, the reigns of David (2 Sam. 5:4) and Solomon (1 Kgs. 11:42) are forty years. The time from the exodus to the building of the First Temple is 480 years (1 Kgs. 6:1). Thus, the numbers are not reliable for the historical reconstruction of this period. The point of the verse is not the exact time frame of forty years but that those who left Egypt "perished, not having listened to the voice of [*Adoni*]" (Josh. 5:6). The original generation

---

48. John Hartley, *Leviticus*, Word Biblical Commentary, vol. 4 (Word Books, 1992), xlii.

of the exodus gave way to the next, who will move from the wilderness into the promised land.

There is no extrabiblical information from this post-Sinai period. Israel Finkelstein sums it up this way: "There is not even a single shred left by a tiny fleeing band of frightened refugees."[49] Part of the reason for this is the same as for the rest of these early narratives. The biblical text was edited for several centuries after the events took place. This caused place names and even peoples to be added or substituted to reflect the places and people groups that existed during the time of that further editing. For example, the census list of Israel in the first chapter of Numbers 1 is more extensive than this desert environment could actually support.[50] Also, the itinerary in Numbers 33 lists cities, such as Migdol, that were not occupied until the 7th–6th centuries BCE, much later than the possible time frame for the wilderness period.[51] This is but one example of the cities mentioned in Numbers that were occupied only after this time. These additions are part of the ancient biblical tradition that made sense to the writers but made it difficult for historians to piece together the actual events.

Does this mean these events did not happen? Again, it is impossible to say. The lack of any trace of external evidence for this time in the desert cannot be easily explained away. It is possible that the chronology of the period and the size of the group were part of the communal memory preserved via oral tradition and, as such, were conflated or inflated over time. Thus, we have no sure historical foundation. The wilderness narratives remain a story of God's provision for the people in a frightening and inhospitable place. This message would have resonated with the people of Israel and Judah, who often became refugees as empire after empire swept through the region. This message of divine deliverance and provision, despite the disobedience of the people of God, stands as the central meaning of this story instead of its historical certainty.

SUMMARY

To say that the historical proof for the two opening books of the Bible (as well as Leviticus and Numbers) is paltry is an understatement. This surprises many because of the preconceptions we place on historical accuracy from our modern perspective. However, becoming entangled in the historical proof and the arguments that swirl around the historicity debate leads to missing the point that these ancient texts are trying to tell readers. Historical accuracy was not

---

49. Israel Finkelstein, *The Bible Unearthed: Archaeology's New Vision of Ancient Israel and the Origin of Its Sacred Texts* (Simon & Schuster, Touchstone, 2002), 63.
50. Dever, *Early Israelites?*, 18.
51. Dever, *Early Israelites?*, 19.

the central point or probably not even an important consideration in compiling these stories. It is more accurate to think of these texts as explanations of who God is, who the people were, and how they lived together in this complex divine-human relationship.

Why, then, discuss the history or lack of proof in these books?[52] One could say there is value in simply being able to clearly state what we know, even if only to understand something about the probable period in which these texts were set. A more critical answer, perhaps, is to realize that historical probability is not the only measure of a text's worth to the church and the broader culture. This challenges Western cultural norms about history and history writing. To put it in the most straightforward form, these are texts of faith and not texts of history. For some readers, this threatens how they understand the Bible. But what is being threatened in this statement is our Western way of reading, not the Bible itself. Brandon O'Brien and Randolph Richards note, "We see the world dualistically. Things are true or false, right or wrong, good or bad. We have little patience for ambiguity or for the unsettling reality that values change over time."[53] Western culture has taught us that if one thing in a story is not historically accurate, then the whole is suspect. These historical debates stifle the intended messages of these stories. As colorful and engaging texts, they teach us about God and ourselves, and therein lies their value.

---

52. Many recent texts do just that and say nothing about this early period of the matriarchs and patriarchs and the exodus: see, e.g., Miller and Hayes, *Ancient Israel and Judah*.

53. Brandon O'Brien and E. Randolph Richards, *Misreading Scripture with Western Eyes* (IVP Books, 2012), 32.

6

The Founding of a People in Canaan (1200–1000 BCE)

The last chapter ended with the people of Israel wandering through the wilderness of the Transjordan. This chapter focuses on what is known about the rise of this people in Canaan and traces their development through the period of the first Israelite leader, Saul. More information is available for this period. These primary sources allow scholars to agree on a broad historical outline of the period. However, the details regarding specifics—for chronologies, events, and the groups involved—are more difficult or impossible to state with certainty.

MAJOR DISRUPTIONS IN THE AFRO-ASIATIC REGION (1200–1000 BCE)

The Iron Age begins in roughly 1200 BCE. Marking the Iron Age is the transition from tools and weapons formerly made of bronze to the harder and more durable iron. It is ironic, then, that as tools and weapons improved, the civilizations of the Mycenaeans (Greek isles), the Hittites (Turkey), and Canaan, including the important city-state of Ugarit, all first collapsed and then disappeared.[1] There was a perfect storm in which shifting weather patterns caused drought conditions along with the collapse of major empires.[2] Like all global events, Eric Cline summarizes, "The progression [of collapse] wasn't linear; the reality was much messier. There probably was not a single driving force or trigger, but rather some different stressors, each which forced the

---

1. Amihai Mazar, *Archaeology of the Land of the Bible: 10,000–586 BCE* (Doubleday, 1990), 235.
2. K. L. Noll, *Canaan and Israel in Antiquity: A Textbook on History and Religion*, 2nd ed. (Bloomsbury T&T Clark, 2013), 143–44.

people to react in different ways to accommodate the changing situation(s)."[3] These sweeping changes across the greater Afro-Asiatic and Aegean areas allowed people to move and settle in areas formerly occupied by the imperial powers.

In Canaan, several cities were destroyed or heavily damaged in this period, including Hazor, Megiddo, Gezer, and Lachish. The destruction is apparent, but what is less clear is who or what caused it. There are several possibilities, including Pharaoh Merenptah, the Israelites, the Philistines, or other groups participating in the chaos of the Late Bronze Age, as well as the possibility of destruction by natural forces such as earthquakes or fires. Yet clearly, this pattern of destruction is not consistent with the presentation of the battles in the book of Joshua, as the Israelites are described making a conquest of Canaan. The archaeological data does not match the narratives of the Bible. The people known as Israel probably did destroy some cities or small settlements, but all these destroyed sites cannot be attributed to them or any other group. The inability to attribute the destruction to specific people or causes is unsurprising. Archaeology can uncover a layer of destruction in a city, but the army or event causing the destruction is not easy to discern.

A second major event in the region was the arrival of the Sea Peoples, or Philistines, in the coastal area. The Philistines were not from Canaan or the Afro-Asiatic region. As noted in chapter 3, recent DNA testing of Philistine graves identifies them as originating in the Aegean area of the Mediterranean.[4] They brought with them distinctive material items and a culture that had previously not been seen in Canaan. Archaeologists debate the period of their arrival, but it was either the Late Bronze Age or the early Iron I Age (cf. 1 Sam. 13:19–22).[5] The Philistines established the cities of Gaza, Ashkelon, Ekron, Gath, and Ashdod on the Mediterranean coast.

The third significant change was the growth of small settlements in the highland region of Canaan. The highland region in Israel is in the middle of the country, with the Sea of Galilee and the Jordan River to the east and the seacoast to the west (map 7). At first glance, compared to the other two

---

3. Eric Cline, *1177 B.C.: The Year Civilization Collapsed* (Princeton University Press, 2014), 170.

4. Kristen Romey, "Ancient DNA May Reveal Origin of the Philistines," National Geographic.org, July 3, 2019, https://www.nationalgeographic.com/culture/2019/07/ancient-dna-reveal-philistine-origins/.

5. Ussishkin reports no Philistine pottery at Lachish, a major trading city in the region, indicating that the Philistines settled in the area later than the destruction of the Canaanite city in 1130 BCE: "Archaeology of the Biblical Period," in *Understanding the History of Ancient Israel*, ed. H. Williamson, Proceedings of the British Academy 143 (Oxford University Press, 2007), 136. Others argue that the Philistines arrived before 1150: L. Stager, "The Impact of the Sea Peoples in Canaan," in *The Archaeology of Society in the Holy Land*, ed. T. Levy (Leicester University Press, 1995), 332–48; cf. https://www.eisenbrauns.org/sample_chapter/Stager_introduction.pdf.

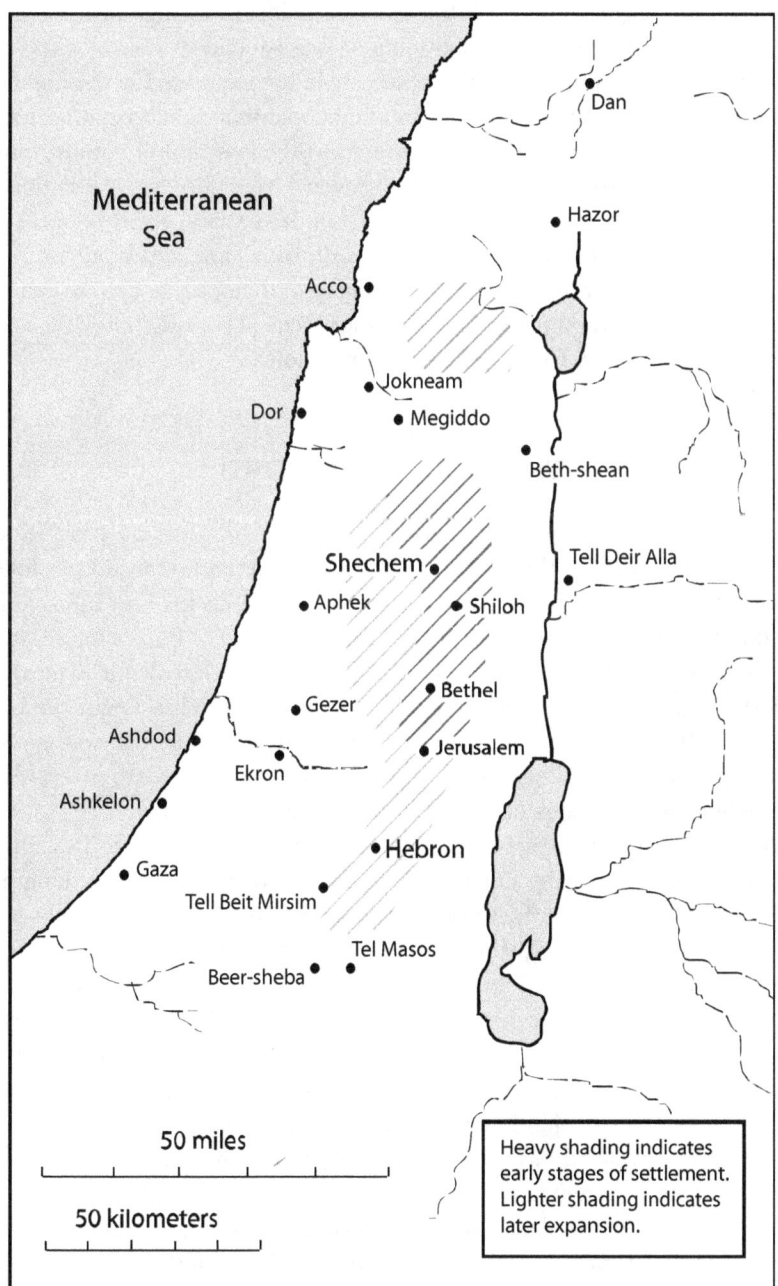

Map 7. Geographical spread of early Iron Age hill-country settlements. (Based on Israel Finkelstein, *Archaeology of the Israelite Settlement*, 325, 329.) (Courtesy of Westminster John Knox Press)

changes, this might seem to be the most insignificant change in the region, but this last change marks the beginning of Israel-Judah. Archaeologists have identified over 250 sites that developed early in the Iron Age I in the highland region.[6] These sites were occupied by the people that would become Israel. Most of the settlements were concentrated in the central hill country north of Jerusalem and running further north toward Megiddo (heavy shading on map 7). Throughout approximately two hundred years, steady population growth occurred in outlying areas to the west, with some development to the south in Judah and north of Megiddo. These outlying areas did not reach a significant population until well into the monarchical periods (900–700 BCE). Like all other nations, Israel-Judah took form slowly.

THE BIBLICAL RECORD

Information concerning this period is recorded in Joshua, Judges, and 1 Samuel. But reading these books is not easy. The narratives do not follow an expected chronological order, and some crucial events and information are omitted, while others are repeated more than once. For example, there are questions in the narratives about Joshua himself. His death is narrated in Joshua 24:29, followed by "after the death of Joshua" to begin the book of Judges. But, in Judges 2:6, Joshua appears and leads the tribes, then dies (again?) in 2:8. Clearly, there are two traditions of Joshua's death preserved in the Bible, one in the book of Joshua and the other in Judges.

Another example of these puzzling conflicts is the case of Jerusalem. In Joshua 10, Joshua's army defeated a coalition led by Jerusalem's king and "took all these kings and their land at one time" (10:42). It appears that Jerusalem was in the hands of Joshua and his forces. Joshua 12 confirms that Jerusalem and the land of the Jebusites were taken (12:7–24). The Jebusites were the people who controlled Jerusalem and the surrounding lands at the time. But that does not appear to be the whole story. Judges 1:8 declares that the people of Judah fought against Jerusalem and set it on fire. In contrast, Judges 1:21 reports, "The Benjaminites [one of the tribes of Israel] did not drive out the Jebusites who lived in Jerusalem; so the Jebusites have lived in Jerusalem . . . to this day." Finally, 2 Samuel 5 claims that David took Jerusalem as his own. These conflicting claims about Jerusalem are confusing and do not help the historian understand what happened during this period. It is possible that

---

6. Israel Finkelstein, *The Archaeology of the Israelite Settlement* (Israel Exploration Society, 1988), 19.

the city changed hands often during this time. But if it did, these changes did not leave a discoverable archaeological trace.[7]

What are we to make of these uneven and sometimes contradictory stories in Joshua, Judges, and 1 Samuel? First, except for a clause that begins Judges and is thought to be added in the editing process,[8] there is no indication of a linear timeline for these books. The narratives of battles, judges, and covenants are discrete and not necessarily in chronological order. This seemingly haphazard presentation of narratives is a good representation of memories preserved by oral tradition. Ancient editors who recorded such stories would preserve some and leave others out. These books are more like the conversations at a family reunion than a timeline leading to war, as would appear in *The New York Times*. The point of these texts is to be a theological narrative and not a historical account of battles. Some things are omitted. Some events have two important traditions around them, such as the death of Joshua, and both are recorded.

In short, to understand these books, we must read them as ancient literature, recognizing that our modern paradigms do not apply. As in family narratives, people or groups will remember conflicts and other events differently. Indeed, one of the marks of the Bible's authenticity as an ancient document is the uneven character of these stories. The discrepancies, time gaps, and contradictions were not removed, smoothed over, or fixed. The narratives do not conform to our modern Western ways of reading. These books are collected memories.

Also, little additional written material exists to corroborate the events of this period. Canaan during Iron Age I was, by and large, an illiterate society.[9] The stories in these books were told and retold just as the narratives of Genesis and Exodus were. Later, others wrote it down. Moreover, the stories were placed together long after the events occurred. A firm chronology was unknown, and later editors stitched together narratives from this two-hundred-year period. Just as later laws were added in the Sinai corpus, other battles may have been added here in Joshua and Judges by those later editors. Events that were remembered differently by the various groups of people were also included in the narrative simultaneously, creating contradictions and repetitions.

Unsurprisingly, archaeological records can confirm some events and battles in Joshua, Judges, and 1 Samuel, but not others. The most well-known

---

7. Jane Cahill, "Jerusalem at the Time of the United Monarchy: The Archaeological Evidence," in *Jerusalem in Bible and Archaeology*, ed. Andrew Vaughn and Ann Killebrew (SBL Press, 2003), 54–55.

8. "After the death of Joshua" (Judg. 1:1).

9. Noll, *Canaan and Israel*, 147.

example of this discrepancy is the battle of Jericho in Joshua 6. While not as well known now as it was to earlier generations, it is a story of Bible legend and the subject of a hymn, even sung by Elvis Presley, "Joshua Fit the Battle of Jericho." Despite the popularity of the story, multiple archaeological excavations resulted in most scholars accepting that Jericho was abandoned at the time of the early Iron Age, remaining empty during this two-hundred-year period, and so the armies of Joshua did not conquer Jericho during the Iron Age I.[10] As with the wilderness wanderings, the archaeological evidence cannot be ignored or swept away. Some biblical narratives align with the archaeological record, while others do not. In addition, the battles in the Bible were not the only ones happening in the area, and it is often impossible to know which group was responsible for any given destruction during this time. This was a period when the entire Afro-Asiatic region was unstable.

Some scholars and students are disturbed by the fact that the narratives in the Bible and the archaeological record do not align. Others are shocked by the content of the narratives themselves. The text states that the Israelites commit what seems like genocide in the towns of Jericho and Ai, among others: "So the people shouted, and the trumpets were blown. As soon as the people heard the sound of the trumpets, they raised a great shout, and the wall fell down flat, so the people charged straight ahead into the city and captured it. Then they devoted to destruction by the edge of the sword all in the city, both men and women, young and old, oxen, sheep, and donkeys" (Josh. 6:20–21).

Is this order from God historically accurate? First, I will remind the reader to return to the definition of history. It is the description of the acts and events of humans; history cannot evaluate the realm of God. Second, in ancient literature, it was common for a king or a people to declare the utter destruction of another city and its inhabitants. It was the typical language of the day, even if it was not historically accurate.[11] These texts are disturbing, but recalling that this is ancient literature can help the modern reader interpret them better.

Although these stories do not always reflect the historical account of the period, the biblical narratives reflect how people lived and worked together in groups, clans, and tribes. We know that in these approximately two hundred years, groups of people were organized into tribes who collectively called themselves "Israel" and came to control part of Canaan. To claim much more is to

10. John Bright, *A History of Israel*, 3rd ed. (Westminster, 1981), 130.
11. The Merenptah Stela brags, "Israel's seed is no more." Anson Rainey, "Israel in Merenptah's Inscription and Reliefs," *IEJ* 51 (2001): 57–74. Rainey demonstrates that "His seed is no more" is an expression that declares a military victory. Thus, the claim does not necessarily indicate complete destruction.

claim too much. They told their stories because they believed God brought them to this promised land and helped them become a nation in this area.

BECOMING A NATION

The biblical, archaeological, and epigraphic sources from this time period (1200–1000 BCE) all point to the central hills as the place where "Israel" begins.[12] The archaeological research verifies the growing population in the central hill country. Many places discussed in Joshua were either in that central hill country or on its fringe. Finally, as discussed earlier, the Merenptah Stela confirmed a people called "Israel" in this region around 1203 BCE. More accurately, later biblical authors and editors called them Israel. The twelve tribes are the subjects of the books of Joshua and Judges, but the two books also use the name Israel for the collective. It is unknown how the people of this time period referred to themselves.

Extensive excavations have provided a wealth of information about how people lived in these highland villages. These settlements were all rural and agricultural, with no urban centers. The largest villages had a population of fewer than a hundred people.[13] Small compounds contained four-pillared mud-brick houses for a nuclear family of five or six. Farming and food preparation occupied the spaces on the first floor, with family living space on the second, covered by a flat roof used for drying grain and skins in the sun.[14] Two or three of these houses would make up a walled compound with a central courtyard; a village would be several of these walled compounds close to each

---

12. Traditionally, this category is presented via the three models: (1) *conquest*, by William F. Albright, "The Israelite Conquest in the Light of Archaeology," *BASOR* 74 (1939):11–23; (2) *peaceful infiltration*, first presented by Albrecht Alt, "The Settlement of the Israelites in Palestine," in his *Essays in Old Testament History and Religion*, repr. (JSOT Press, 1989), 133–69, and expanded by Martin Noth, *The History of Israel*, trans. rev. P. R. Ackroyd, 2nd ed. (A&C Black, 1960); and (3) *peasant-revolt theory*, first presented by George Mendenhall, "The Hebrew Conquest of Palestine," *BA* 25, no. 3 (1962): 66–87, and then significantly altered by Norman Gottwald, *The Tribes of Yahweh: A Sociology of the Religion of Liberated Israel, 1250–1000 BCE* (Orbis Books, 1979). The models are presented, and the strengths and weaknesses are discussed, with the end result being that none do a complete job of describing this period. This method has been intentionally abandoned here. First, scholars have produced many more models than these three: see William Dever, *Who Were the Early Israelites and Where Did They Come From?* (Eerdmans, 2006), chap. 8. Second, since all the models are deficient in some way, a better way may be to simply state what is known and to leave it at that, with as little speculation as possible.

13. Noll, *Canaan and Israel*, 176.

14. P. King and L. Stager, *Life in Biblical Israel*, ed. D. Knight (Westminster John Knox, 2001), 28–35.

other.[15] These villages were generally not fortified, although some sites reused older Middle Bronze Age fortifications.[16]

The inhabitants of these villages lived regionally (close to home), including for worship. Worship practices changed as the highland villages were populated. Dever observes, "The temples and their elaborate paraphernalia that are so typical of the Late Bronze Canaanite society simply disappeared by the end of the 13th century BCE."[17] When Israelite families gathered for worship with their clan for festivals in the early Iron Age, it was in nonspecialized spaces instead of the old Bronze Age temples.

Throughout these two hundred years, life centered on agriculture.[18] Most of the family dedicated their time to creating hillside terraces to cultivate crops, care for grazing animals, and produce food. Life was hard, and the hours were long. Most of the family lived within the same compound. Families worked, worshiped, looked for mates, and made alliances, all within a short distance from home. As time progressed, farming methods became more efficient. Settlements became more extensive as the population grew and as farmers were able to provide more food for larger villages. Alliances with other families further from home began as they traded and worked with others. Conflict occurred between some groups over land, and other concerns flared up occasionally. Near the borders of nations, fighting with neighboring nations over holding the land happened regularly. The Philistines and the Israelite tribes began to fight over land ownership.

Although archaeologists have made many discoveries about how the early people of Israel lived, they have had difficulty pinpointing significant aspects of their history and culture. Questions can only be answered imperfectly, questions such as these: Who are these people? How did they form into a nation? How did they worship? We will rely upon archaeological findings, the biblical text, and all other available resources to address these questions.

Scholars have gathered information on how people in the region, and therefore in Israel, were organized, drawing from biblical, archaeological, and comparative sources. The basic organized unit was the family, or *bēyt 'āb*, meaning "house of the father." Several extended families living close together would form a group for trade, marriage, grazing animals, and defense from outside intruders. This extended group was called *mišpāḥâ*, meaning "clan." A

---

15. Dever, *Early Israelites?*, 105.
16. Finkelstein (*Israelite Settlement*, 263) notes that this was the case in Beth-Zur.
17. Dever, *Early Israelites?*, 126.
18. The information for this 200-year period comes from archaeologists performing surface surveys. They only excavate some of the sites fully but use topographical surveys of the land to identify where other small sites are, based on land disturbance. It is impossible to excavate hundreds of small sites. Dever, *Early Israelites?*, 92–96.

clan would probably contain at least one village governed by the elders, the patriarchs of the individual compounds. Finally, clans would join in larger regional alliances called *šəbāṭîm*, "tribes." Eventually, these tribes would join into one large group called *bənê-Yiśrāʾēl*, "the sons of Israel," probably for defense against the Philistines and others in the region. In fact, during this period in Iron Age I, it is better to think of "Israel" as a group of people who could gather a militia against an outside threat instead of a nation with borders, an organized central government, and an army. Both the physical borders and the members of these tribal groups would have been in flux, depending on formal and informal alliances. These alliances were not necessarily along family lines. Clan and tribe memberships were geographical first and also possibly familial.

The formation of Israel was a complex process. Were the people who were included only from the exodus and wilderness groups? Indeed, the book of Joshua is, in part, concerned with the purity of the people, even to the point of calling for the extermination of the people called the "Canaanites, Hittites, Hivites, Perizzites, Girgashites, Amorites, and Jebusites" (Josh. 3:10). On the other hand, the books of Joshua and Judges declare that others in the Canaanite region were not conquered (Josh. 13:2–6; Judg. 3:1–6). From an archaeological perspective, according to K. L. Noll, "Israelites are invisible" as a group or culture.[19] They are invisible because the material culture of these hill-country villages is identical to that of their neighbors; the houses, cooking utensils, tools, and all other items are the same as everyone else in the region. It is impossible to distinguish an Israelite compound from all the others in the area. Indeed, this lack of obvious distinction may have fueled the concern in the book of Joshua for isolation from other groups. For group cohesion, the Israelites would need something that set them apart from everyone else in the region.

Likewise, modern scholars often search for what made the Israelites distinctive. Recent interest has focused on not finding pig bones in these Israelite settlements. Some scholars argue that this absence could be directly linked with the prohibition against eating pork (Deut. 14:8; Lev. 11:7–8), which set kosher restrictions in this early period as an ethnic marker of being "Israel."[20] Later studies discount this earlier observation. Hesse and Wapnish investigated patterns in the entire region of pastoralist or nomadic people and the more settled or farming peoples. Their study demonstrates that, as people became less nomadic and more settled into farms, their patterns of animal husbandry

---

19. Noll, *Canaan and Israel*, 147.
20. Lawrence Stager, "When Canaanites and Philistines Ruled Ashkelon," *BAR* 17, no. 2 (March/April 1991): 24–29, 31, 35–37, 40–42.

changed, and they raised and ate fewer pigs, not just in the highland regions but also throughout the area. They conclude, "Since this environment generated widespread pig avoidance, the unremarkable nature of this foodway made [the lack of pig bones] an unlikely candidate for establishing a boundary with any specific group, save, perhaps, for the Philistines."[21] In other words, the effort to identify what makes "Israelites" different in genetics or lifestyle during this early period has eluded researchers. The Israelites are simply indistinguishable from the other population of Canaan.

If we claim to know how these people became an organized group called "Israel," that asserts too much. Biblical scholars have presented models over the years. However, when vetted by others, each model has proven inaccurate via biblical and archaeological evidence.[22] What can be said is that the emergence of Israel was probably like the emergence of any group that chooses to become a "nation." Building on the work of years of scholarship using many relevant sciences, Ann Killebrew has suggested that early Israel was a "mixed crowd" of all the people uprooted in this region at the time (cf. Exod. 12:38).[23] She uses the sociological term of ethnogenesis to describe the process whereby a group identity emerges from unrelated but indigenous smaller groups of persons over time.[24] Herwig Wolfram identifies three central aspects in this coming together, or ethnogenesis: (1) a shared story or stories of a miraculous event or miracle, (2) the group had a religious experience or transformation as a result of that event, and (3) there was an enemy that threatened the group and thus cemented their unity.[25] This theory has much to commend it, as we shall soon see.

The first point in Wolfram's theory of the development of a people is a shared story or, more importantly, *stories* of miraculous event(s). Indeed, the exodus was such a story and was central to the theology of the people in its later periods. The process of ethnogenesis also allows for more than one story

---

21. Brian Hesse and Paula Wapnish, "Can Pig Remains Be Used for Ethic Diagnosis in the Ancient Near East?," in *The Archaeology of Israel: Constructing the Past, Interpreting the Present*, ed. N. Silberman and D. Small, JSOTSup 239 (Sheffield Academic, 1997), 263; and Robert Redding, "The Pig and the Chicken in the Middle East: Modeling Human Subsistence Behavior in the Archaeological Record[,] Using Historical and Animal Husbandry Data," *Journal of Archaeological Research* 23 (2015): 325–68.

22. There are many models or theories, but the most commonly discussed are by Albright and Alt, followed by Noth and Mendenhall, followed by Gottwald. See note 12 above for details.

23. Ann Killebrew, *Biblical Peoples and Ethnicity: An Archaeological Study of Egyptians, Canaanites, Philistines, and Early Israel, 1300–1000 B.C.E.* (Society of Biblical Literature, 2005), 149.

24. Killebrew, *Biblical Peoples*, 149.

25. Herwig Wolfram, "Einleitung oder Überlegungen zur Origo Gentis," in *Typen der Ethnogenese unter besonderer Berücksichtigung der Bayern: Berichte des Symposions der Kommission für Frühmittelalterforschung*, ed. H. Wolfram and W. Pohl, vol. 1 (Verlag der Österreichischen Akademie der Wissenschaften, 1990), 19–34.

for a given group. Adopting the stories of others joining the group enables a fuller narrative and is the mark of oral tradition.

A simple example will help. When I married my husband, I had stories of my life, and he had stories of his. Our children will adopt some of each of our stories as part of their story. Eventually each will find a partner, and their individual stories will merge for their children into another story with elements of all those family stories. Some of our stories will be told by our children to their children, and some will be forgotten. The biblical text, as we have it, follows a similar process. Not every event was recorded, and a group may not tell their great-grandmother's story exactly as she would; but her story is part of their narrative, and they pass it on to their children.

Another method of group sharing and cohesion is the inclusion of lengthy genealogies in the Pentateuch (Gen. 10; 11:10–32; Num. 1:1–4:49; etc.). These genealogies, like family stories, are less about DNA-verified family trees and more about social, political, and cultural ties.[26] As another simple example, I was raised in a farming community, and I had many aunts and uncles who were not related by blood, but they were part of our extended family. The biblical genealogies serve the same purpose, to unite a group of unrelated people into a community or "family."

Stories bind diverse groups into a single "nation." Indeed, Judeo-Christian tradition still functions in this way. We are a people of God, and thus the stories in the Bible become part of our shared story, to which we add our own stories and the stories of others we know.

Wolfram's second point is that the group has a religious experience or change in their religious practices. The shared religious experience occurred in conjunction with identity formation through the stories. Again, the examples from the biblical narrative are multiple: the worship of *Adoni*, the Passover celebration, and the giving of the Law. The book of Joshua also has examples of shared experiences that unite the people. It begins with a five-chapter introduction that concludes with a circumcision ceremony followed by the celebration of the Passover (Josh. 5:2–15). After the first stories of the conquest of Jericho and Ai, Joshua builds an altar, makes sacrifices, copies the laws, and reads them in the hearing of the people, marking a second time the people come together (8:30–35). Then, the book of Joshua ends with an assembly at Shechem, where the people are called on to choose the God or gods they will serve (24).[27] These ceremonies

---

26. L. Stager, "Forging an Identity: The Emergence of Ancient Israel," in *The Oxford History of the Biblical World*, ed. M. Coogan (Oxford University Press, 2001), 150.

27. Lawson Stone states a similar proposal in "Early Israel and Its Appearance in Canaan," in *Ancient Israel's History*, ed. Bill Arnold and Richard Hess (Baker Academic, 2014), 156. With a different methodology, Gottwald also suggested a mass conversion of some of the Canaanite city-states; *Tribes of Yahweh*, 556–63.

call the people together to commit to this God and this people. The ceremonies themselves suggest a need for membership or citizenship ceremonies as more people joined "Israel." Stager says it clearly in observing that "Israel developed its self-consciousness or ethnic identity in large measure through its religious foundation—a breakthrough that led a subset of Canaanite culture, coming from a variety of places, backgrounds, prior affiliations, and livelihoods, to join a supertribe united under the authority of and devotion to a supreme deity, revealed to Moses as *Adoni*."[28] There is ample evidence that Israel continued to grow by sharing stories and religious traditions.

Wolfram's third point is that forming a new group identity is also stimulated and forged from an external threat. This threat developed as the Philistines organized and began to attack not just one region in Canaan but several, first taking the Shephelah region (hills between the Judean mountains and the coastal plain) and then moving to try to conquer the highland region of the Israelites around 1100 BCE.[29] The ongoing Philistine attacks were probably the final factor that pulled this "mixed multitude" in the central hill region together into a people known as Israel, whose connection to each other was a shared faith in *Adoni* instead of merely a shared bloodline. A people who could sing as children do in Sunday school, "Father Abraham had many sons, many sons had Father Abraham; I am one of them, and so are you."

The formation of Israel is reflected in the last ten chapters of Joshua, which details the territory of each of the twelve tribes. This naming of the tribes of Israel served to knit them into one people by providing shared memories and faith. How the people formed themselves into a nation had to be gleaned from many sources. Their path to nationhood is not unique among the Afro-Asiatic peoples. Indeed, it is the story of all the surrounding nations that grew from the turmoil of the early Iron Age. "Israel" is one of the several Canaanite "nations" that developed in this period.

SAMUEL, SAUL, AND THE FORMING OF A NATION (1150–1000 BCE)

The settlement and growth of Israel from farms in the central hill country, to forming regional alliances, and further to developing a territorial state with centralized and regional administrative processes in place—all this took about two hundred years, approximately overlapping Iron Age I (1200–1000

28. Stager, "Forging an Identity," 142.
29. Stager, "Forging an Identity," 168.

BCE).³⁰ A territorial state was an entity based on an agreement among peoples sharing infrastructure, culture, religion, and military forces. It was more porous and flexible than the nations with secure borders of today.

The book of 1 Samuel begins during what scholars estimate to be the late Iron Age I, in the heart of the central hill country at Shiloh of Ephraim. Shiloh (12 miles, or 19 km, south of Shechem; 20 miles, or 32 km, north of Jerusalem) was a settlement that reused earlier Bronze Age walls and built pillared houses within those walls. The biblical text and excavations at the site confirm that "Shiloh was the first inter-regional cult center in Israel," meaning it was a center of worship for different communities.³¹ The archaeological data also confirms that the people of Israel were in a transitional period. They formed alliances and moved from smaller governments and worship centers to larger ones. While no specific historical information about him exists, Samuel appears in the biblical text as a figure who bridged the gap of that transition. He is a judge (1 Sam. 7:15) and a prophet (3:19–21) who called Israel into account (7:6). He also served as a priest under Eli at Shiloh (3:1) and anointed Saul (10:1). Each of these offices—judge, prophet, and priest—would be separate in later periods, but here Samuel is said to serve in all these roles during this period of formation and transition.

As with Samuel, no clear historical evidence points to an early leader named Saul. However, the territory under Saul's control listed in 2 Samuel 2:9 (Gilead, Asher, Jezreel, Ephraim, and Benjamin)³² fits with the occupation of the area during this period, as determined by archaeological discoveries in the highland regions.³³ His headquarters, or home, was in Gibeah, which many scholars identify as Tell el-Fûl.³⁴ Despite several explorations, none of the excavation levels in Tell el-Fûl can be definitively linked to Saul or the probable period of his reign.³⁵ This is made more difficult since the exact time frame of Saul's reign is itself challenging to determine since the biblical text is unreadable and possibly intentionally corrupted (" Saul was . . . years old

---

30. Diane Edelman, "Saul," *ABD* 5:989.
31. Finkelstein, *Israelite Settlement*, 231.
32. Second Samuel 2:9 is the territory of Saul's son Ishbaal, but it has the areas controlled by his father.
33. The text claims that Saul held the territories of Asher, Jezreel, Ephraim, and Benjamin. The next phrase, "and over all of Israel," matches other statements in Judges and was probably formulaic. Lester Grabbe, *Ancient Israel: What Do We Know and How Do We Know It?* (T&T Clark, 2007), 113.
34. William Albright, *Excavations and Results at Tell el-Fûl (Gibeah of Saul)*, ed. B. W. Bacon (American Schools of Oriental Research, 1924). But recently, Israel Finkelstein has debated this identification in "Tell el-Ful Revisited: The Assyrian and Hellenistic Periods (with a New Identification)," *PEQ* 143, no. 2 (2011): 106–18.
35. Finkelstein, *Israelite Settlement*, 56–60.

when he began to reign, and he reigned . . . and two years over Israel,"1 Sam. 13:1).[36] Some scholars have estimated his reign to be about twenty years, based on the number of battles described during his reign and the fact that his children are grown fighting men when he dies.[37] However, this estimate is based on backdating from more secure later time frames. The best possible time frame for Saul is around 1000 BCE, at the end of Iron Age I.[38] However, this date remains a tentative estimate.

Saying that the biblical text presents a mixed picture of Saul would be a massive understatement. He was loved and hated, first by Samuel and then by David. Also, many of the narratives in 1 Samuel are discrete, appearing to come from different traditions. For example, in 1 Samuel 16, David is called to the court to play for and soothe Saul, yet in the very next chapter, when David slays Goliath, Saul does not know who David is (1 Sam. 17). In battle, Saul is portrayed as a great warrior-hero. Indeed, almost all the positive images of Saul in the biblical text depict him in battle, defeating enemies on all sides. He is also portrayed as sinning against God (13:8–15; 15:1–23) and as mentally unstable (16:14; 18:10–11). Unfortunately, from a historical perspective, nothing can help sort out this mixed picture. Samuel and Saul are part of the biblical record but not part of the historical or archaeological account. The biblical narratives about them fit with this late Iron Age I period, but any further discussion is nothing more than speculation.

During this transition period, as Israel grew and consolidated itself, the biblical text indicates that there were questions concerning how these new people would be governed and who would govern them. At this time, kingship was the only form of government known at a national level in the Afro-Asiatic region, so the next logical step to nationhood would be for this new group to install a king. The biblical text contains conflicting messages regarding the evolving significance of kingship in the developing nation of Israel.

The first issue of kingship is whether a king suited the people of God. From the viewpoint of Judges and 1 Samuel, kingship is a great evil and a rejection of God (Judg. 8:22–23; 1 Sam. 8:6–18; 12:12, 17–20). This theology argued that the people already had God as their king. However, the book of Judges indicates that the people could not stay faithful to God without a leader (Judg.

---

36. Hans Hertzberg noted that the formula in 13:1 has sections missing. Both Josephus and Acts 13:21 list his reign as 40 years, but that is not certain either: Hertzberg, *1 and II Samuel* (Westminster, 1965), 103.

37. Iain Provan, V. Philips Long, and Tremper Longman III, *A Biblical History of Israel* (Westminster John Knox, 2003), 200.

38. Miller and Hayes concur and refuse to give a length of reign or firm date for Saul and his battles: J. Maxwell Miller and John H. Hayes, *A History of Ancient Israel and Judah*, 2nd ed. (Westminster John Knox, 2006), 130.

17:6; 19:1–21). Later, kingship under God's authority is praised as a hallmark of the nation and, after the exile, seen as the hope for the future (Pss. 2; 20; 72; Isa. 9:2–7; 11:1–16). According to the text, kingship becomes the accepted and praised office in Israel, and then also in Judah once the monarchy is divided. Even Samuel finally conditionally accepts kingship, saying, "If you will fear [*Adoni*] and serve him and heed his voice and not rebel against the commandment of [*Adoni*], if both you and the king who reigns over you will follow [*Adoni*] your God, it will be well" (1 Sam. 12:14). From a historical perspective, despite some reservations, Israel and Judah's kingship can be seen as another critical step to becoming a nation. Since kingship was the only form of government known at the time,[39] the development of kingship for Israel and Judah seems inevitable from a historical vantage point.

The second issue of ambivalence is with Saul's kingship, specifically. Samuel stood in a time of transition, and Saul did too. Saul is the first to be anointed king (1 Sam. 10:1) and is acclaimed by the people as king (10:17–27). However, he is also called a *nagid*, or leader. This Hebrew term was used for kings (10:1; 25:30), military leaders (1 Chr. 13:1), and even some clan chiefs (9:11). According to the biblical text, Saul's home, Gibeah, did not have a palace. Also, Saul's story tells of his leadership on the battlefield. Saul does not build a kingdom nor encourage trade with other nations. In other words, though he is anointed as the first king, he acts more like a military commander than a king in the narratives of 1 Samuel. Many scholars argue that Saul was nothing more than a foil in the text to make David look good.[40] But if this were the only reason for Saul, why raise up Saul as the first king in the national story at all? Saul may have been part of a struggle for power between two clans (Saul's and David's), but this does not diminish his leadership as the first king and military commander of Israel.

SUMMARY

As with the previous discussions of the matriarchs and patriarchs and the exodus from Egypt, there is not enough archaeological and historical evidence to say a great deal about the formation of these Hebrew tribes into a nation. Early models were based on the idea that this group, known as Israel, was distinct from the rest of the Canaanite peoples. As shown, no compelling evidence distinguishes these people who settled in the hill country from the rest of

---

39. At a smaller level, there were tribal chiefs, but as tribes combined into a nation-state, the form of government became kingship.

40. W. L. Humphreys, *The Tragic Vision and the Hebrew Tradition* (Fortress, 1985), 63.

the Canaanite population. Some biblical texts described the Israelites as intentionally separate from the Canaanites. Other texts in Joshua and Judges speak of others joining their ranks and sharing the land. Both might have been true. One group may have begun with the strict divisions argued for in the book of Joshua. Others perhaps also worshiped the God *Adoni* from the ancestors' period and shared their stories of living in the land. Through interactions over two hundred years, these groups of people with ancient stories came together, sharing stories and cultic festivals. Studies by sociologists, anthropologists, and archaeologists make clear that the formation of the people group called Israel was not all that different from the formation of other peoples all around the globe. The point, then, that we can glean from the biblical text is not that the rise of this one group was unique or that it can be proven archaeologically, but that God was their God as they struggled to become a united entity.

This early period also saw the first two leaders of Israel emerge in the late part of Iron Age I, Samuel and Saul. However, historians have not found reliable information about this period and its leaders. According to the biblical text, Samuel and Saul were developing their roles as they led the people. It was a time of transition and change. Samuel, for the most part, was a religious leader. Saul was named and anointed the first king. Even without historical evidence, their roles as transitional leaders would have been an intermediary step in nation formation. The biblical narratives fit with how people groups typically develop into a more formalized nation.

7

The Era of Early Monarchy (1000–927 BCE)

David and his son Solomon are second only to Moses as the best-known persons in the Hebrew Bible. Their acts are legendary, and even non-Christians know about David and Goliath and "the wisdom of Solomon." They are models for leadership both in the church and in the world. Not only were they great leaders: they were also known as writers. David is traditionally known as the writer of the Psalms, and Solomon as the author of wisdom books (Proverbs, Ecclesiastes, and Song of Solomon). Their reigns are the ones by which all others are measured. As with all legendary figures, however, the historical picture is mixed. This chapter will divide the legend from what can be known historically. From the beginning, it is essential to realize that the archaeological record during the period of David and Solomon is heavily debated. In this period, the minimalist and maximalist scholars wage their academic wars.[1]

THE BIBLICAL SAUL AND DAVID: GROWING TENSIONS

Judah was considered one of the twelve tribes in the book of Joshua (15:1–12). Yet in 1 Samuel, the narrative changes. The Bible reports that "Israel" and "Judah" were different and possibly even warring clans (2 Sam. 2:1–11; 5:1–5). First Samuel 11:5–11 details the first of Saul's battles at Jabesh-Gilead, and Judah is listed as a separate fighting entity from Israel (11:8). Likewise, in the Goliath narrative, Judah is seen as a separate group (17:52). Thus, the "nation of Israel" appears to de-form even while forming. One possible reason for the

---

1. Minimalists claim to find nothing historical in these narratives. Maximalists accept the biblical texts as mostly historically accurate.

split was tribal rivalry between "the house of Benjamin," Saul's tribe, and "the house of Judah," David's tribe (2 Sam. 3:1).[2] However, the actual reason or reasons are unknown.

According to the biblical text, David's story was initially intertwined with Saul's. As groups came together to form a nation, they engaged in warfare with their neighbors to control the region. The Philistines were a growing threat, attacking deep into Judah and Israel's territory. They shared a long border with Judah; at first, it may have been a fight over the important farming region of the Shephelah (hills between the Judean mountains and the coastal plain). But it soon expanded to a battle for more territory in Canaan.

The biblical text is the only written information for this period. First Samuel 16 briefly discusses the biblical report of David as a young boy in service to Saul. David's rise begins in 1 Samuel 16 when Samuel comes to David and secretly anoints him king. The text reports this after the withdrawal of Samuel's, and presumably God's, support of Saul (15:10–33). The Bible then reports a series of events where Saul and David confront each other (1 Sam. 18:10–16; 19:1–17). However, intertwined in these texts, David maintains a friendship with Saul's son, Jonathan (18:1–5); and marries Saul's daughter, Michal (18:20–30). Since David was Saul's son-in-law, this was also a family fight. As the family drama continues, David is forced to flee to the less populated area of his homeland, Judah, or even to Philistine territory (21:10; 27:1–4).

In Judah, David begins his rise to power. He is able to raise a personal army (1 Sam. 22:1–5), make his own alliances (22:3–5; 27:1–4), and attack his enemies (23:1–6). David becomes the leader of Judah. Saul continues his leadership of Israel. These two early anointed kings were the leaders of two competing political entities. The text reports that as they fight each other, they also fight the Philistines.

THE HISTORICAL DAVID AND SOLOMON

The reign of King David and his son Solomon became the model for all other kings of Judah. The biblical text reports that during their consecutive reigns, the city of Jerusalem was taken by David and his men (2 Sam. 5:6–10), the ark of God was brought to Jerusalem (6:1–23), and the temple was constructed (1 Kgs. 6:1–38). The biblical text states that Solomon allied with the Afro-Asiatic region's kings and even welcomed the Queen of Sheba from Southern

---

2. Jacques Vermeylen, "La maison de Saül et la maison de David: Un écrit de propagande théologico-politique, de 1 S 11 à 2 S 7," in *Figures de David à travers la Bible: XVIIe congrès de l'ACFEB, Lille, 1er–5 septembre 1997*, ed. L. Desrousseaux and J. Vermeylen (Cerf, 1999), 34–74.

Arabia (1 Kgs. 10:1–13). With this amount of construction and international interactions, one would expect a significant increase in archaeological and epigraphic artifacts. However, the historical proof for these narratives of the Bible is scant.

Extrabiblical epigraphic evidence does not mention the kings David and Solomon. There is no equivalent to the Merenptah Stela confirming these kings or their countries. No trade records have been found with Hiram of Tyre or the Queen of Sheba. There are no monumental inscriptions of local kings that mention this pair. Unfortunately, the records of other countries have yielded nothing. Also, no Israelite or Judean records outside the Bible relate directly to David or Solomon.

This changed in 1993–94 when archaeologists discovered the Tel Dan Stela (fig. 8).[3] What is of interest here are the names on the stela. It reads in part, "[and I killed Jo]ram, son of A[hab,] king of Israel, and [I] killed [Ahazi]yahu, son of [Joram, kin]g of the house of David . . ."[4] This stela shows that there was a dynasty called "the house of David," confirming for most scholars the existence of David's dynasty by an independent source.[5] But does the text confirm the existence of an actual physical David? Scholars are divided. Some argue that the obscured, partial inscription "proved that King David from the Bible was a genuine historical figure and not simply the fantastic literary creation of later biblical writers and editors."[6] William Schniedewind notes that the term "house of David" is rare in biblical texts and is used most often in opposition to the "house of Saul."[7] This lends credibility to the phrase "house of David" as a title used contemporaneously with David's reign and his tensions with Saul's family (2 Sam. 3:1). One must also consider that the term may be contemporaneous with the early monarchy. The Tel Dan Stela's creation is attributed to Hazael, the king of Aram, with a date of 150–200 years after David. It confirms that the royal house of Judah was called "the House of David." For most scholars, that is enough to claim the existence of David definitively. While the find does not provide a direct physical link to King

---

3. "Tel Dan Stele," 2024, https://en.wikipedia.org/wiki/Tel_Dan_Stele.

4. William Schniedewind, "Tel Dan Stela: New Light on Aramaic and Jehu's Revolt," *BASOR* 302 (1996): 75–90, esp. 77–78. The letters in brackets are faint or missing and reconstructed by scholars tasked with interpreting the text.

5. A minority of scholars have argued that this is not the reading; among others, see P. R. Davies, "'House of David' Built on Sand: The Sins of the Biblical Maximizers," *BAR* 20, no. 4 (1994): 54–55.

6. Biblical Archaeology Society staff, "The Tel Dan Inscription: The First Historical Evidence of King David from the Bible," 2019, https://www.biblicalarchaeology.org/daily/biblical-artifacts/the-tel-dan-inscription-the-first-historical-evidence-of-the-king-david-bible-story/.

7. Schniedewind, "Tel Dan Stela," 80.

Figure 8. Tel Dan Stela. ("House of David" inscribed on a victory stele, Dan, Iron Age II, 9th century BCE, Basalt, H: 34; W: 32 cm, Israel Antiquities Authority IAA: 1996-125, 1993-3162. Collection of the Israel Antiquities Authority. Photo © The Israel Museum, by Meidad Suchowolski)

David, it leaves little doubt he was the founder of the royal line who reigned in Jerusalem. If the inscription does indicate a historical David, this is the single piece of outside evidence for David or Solomon that has been identified.

DATING THE REIGNS OF DAVID AND SOLOMON

In the modern world, a king's years of reign would not take a whole section to explain. But everything is different when dealing with ancient events. The exact dates of David and Solomon's reigns, like all the kings of Israel and Judah, are not exact. This will be an ongoing problem because the reigns of the kings listed in the Hebrew Bible do not use dating based on the cycles of the moon or stars, but relative dating using the reigns of other kings as the reference. The second problem with the dates of the early monarchy is the result of the missing dates in 1 Samuel 13:1 for the reign of Saul. This omission made it impossible to establish when the monarchy and the nation began. As stated in the preceding chapter, Saul's reign was calculated as based on later events and remains a guess. The third issue is the text's dating of David and Solomon's reigns. The biblical text states that David was king of Judah for seven years and six months before becoming king of Israel too, the northern tribes, making his full reign in Judah forty years and six months (2 Sam. 5:1–5). Likewise, Solomon's reign was recorded as forty years (1 Kgs. 11:42). While it is possible that both father and son reigned for forty years, the number was probably symbolic since there is a biblical precedent for the numbers forty and four hundred being used in this way.[8] This is another reminder that we are reading ancient literature, where exact dates were not a priority.[9]

Many scholars use an external event to estimate the reigns of David and Solomon. First Kings 14:25–27 describes an attack by Pharaoh Shishak against Jerusalem in the fifth year after Solomon's death:[10]

> In the fifth year of King Rehoboam, King Shishak of Egypt came up against Jerusalem; he took away the treasures of the house of [*Adoni*] and the treasures of the king's house; he took everything. He also took away all the shields of gold that Solomon had made, so King Rehoboam made shields of bronze instead and committed them to the hands of the officers of the guard who kept the door of the king's house.

A relief in the Temple of Amun in Karnak, Egypt, describes an invasion of Israel by Pharaoh Sheshonq (believed by many scholars to be Shishak in the biblical text). This attack was assigned a firm date of 925 BCE,[11] which would place the death of Solomon in 920 BCE. Using the biblical statement of a forty-year reign, Solomon began his reign in 960 BCE; therefore, David's

---

8. There are many examples: Isaac and Esau were both 40 when they married (Gen. 25–26); the people of God wandered for 40 years (Num. 14:33) and ate manna for 40 years (Exod. 16:35); Joshua was 40 years old when he began his work with Moses (Josh. 14:7).

9. K. L. Noll, *Canaan and Israel in Antiquity: A Textbook on History and Religion*, 2nd ed. (Bloomsbury T&T Clark, 2013), 218–19.

10. This invasion has served as a firm archaeological peg for the dating of the chronology of this period since its discovery and translation along with the Megiddo fragment; see, e.g., John Bright, *A History of Israel*, 3rd ed. (Westminster, 1981), 233–34; or the first edition of J. Maxwell Miller and John H. Hayes, *A History of Ancient Israel and Judah* (Westminster, 1986), 245–46.

11. K. Kitchen, *The Third Intermediate Period in Egypt (1100–650 BC)* (Aris & Phillips, 1973), 272–312.

reign would be from 1000 to 960 BCE. These dates are often used in older textbooks, but are they accurate?

First, is the Shishak of 1 Kings the same as the Shoshenq, Ruler of the Twenty-Second Egyptian Dynasty? Is this just a difference in spelling? Many scholars have assumed so. It seemed to make sense and provided a firm date. However, Egyptologists later identified a second Pharaoh named Shoshenq, who probably reigned in 885–773 BCE, beginning about forty years later than 925 BCE.[12] The biblical text could refer to either of the two pharaohs. Also, a closer investigation of the relief from the Karnak Temple lists about 150 places that were destroyed or conquered. All the locations are outside Jerusalem and Judah: "The readable names are of cities or regions in Israel, the Transjordan, and the region between Hebron and Gaza."[13] These places coincided roughly with an attack northward along the Way of the Sea route, which would have bypassed Jerusalem (in the low mountains). The relief does have broken places where the Judean cities could have been written, but that is far from certain. In short, further research is required, perhaps revising our reconstruction of an event we previously thought provided a definite date for David and Solomon's reign. What was once considered a firm date for an event is now questionable. Again, it is best to use a rough time frame of 1000–900 BCE for the reigns of David and Solomon instead of specific dates. This example again reminds us that what we know about that ancient time will always be less than we wish we knew.

THE ARCHAEOLOGICAL RECORD IN JERUSALEM

Next, we turn to the archaeological information from Jerusalem. The questions center on what was built in Jerusalem during the time of David and then Solomon. According to 2 Samuel 5:6–10, David took Jerusalem from the Jebusites and named it "the city of David" (2 Sam. 5:9). Like Saul, David was a warrior king early in his reign, not a builder of kingdoms. According to the biblical text, only two buildings were added in Jerusalem during David's reign: David's house (2 Sam. 5:11; 1 Chr. 15:1) and "a place for the ark of God" (1 Chr. 15:1). Later, the biblical text reports that Solomon built the temple and other monumental buildings in Jerusalem. Can the archaeological record confirm these biblical statements?

---

12. Peter James et al., *Centuries of Darkness: A Challenge to the Conventional Chronology of Old World Archaeology* (Rutgers University Press, 1993), 253.

13. Frank Clancy, "Shishak/Shosenq's Travels," *JSOT* 24, no. 86 (1999): 3–4.

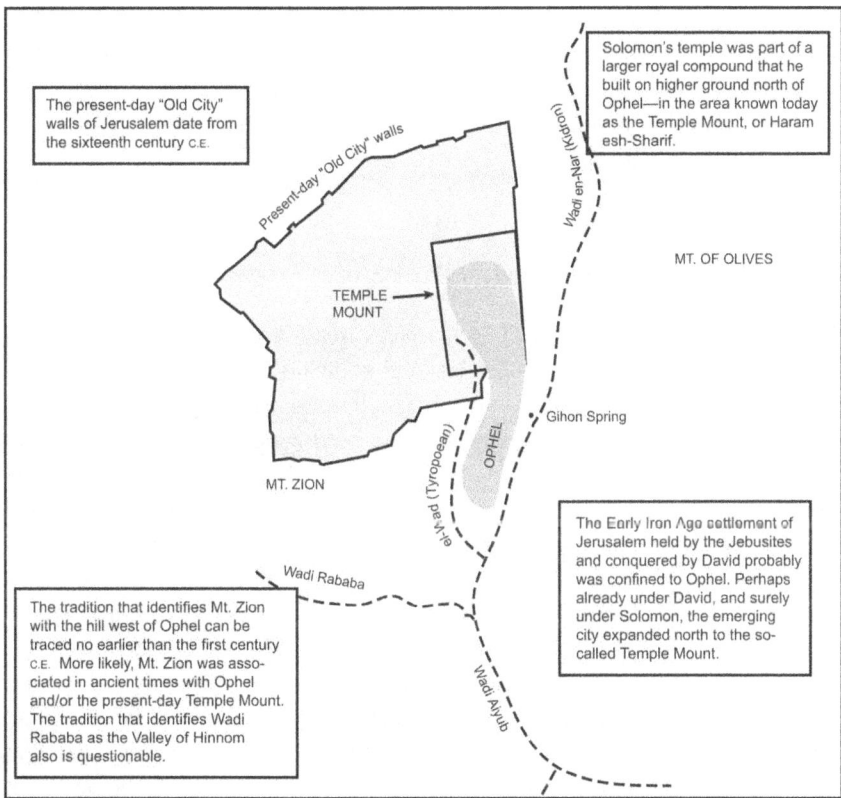

Map 8. Solomon's Jerusalem. (Courtesy of Westminster John Knox Press)

Early Jerusalem, initially built by the Jebusites, was much smaller than the modern-day city and even the Old City (map 8): notice that the Ophel region and part of the Temple Mount were the extent of Jerusalem during the early monarchy. It was located south of the current Temple Mount in a narrow area bounded by the Kidron Valley to the east and the Tyropoean (Cheesemakers') Valley to the west.[14] Unfortunately, the building projects of later empires destroyed much of early Jerusalem. Kathleen Kenyon (1906–78) excavated this area extensively and explains, "Evidence of early occupation on the summit area [of the city of David] does not exist. This is mainly because Roman quarrying and Byzantine buildings destroyed all earlier structures and occupation."[15] The same is true for the Temple Mount. Israel Finkelstein

---

14. Amihai Mazar, *Archaeology of the Lord of the Bible: 10,000–586 B.C.E.* (Doubleday, 1990), 374.
15. Kathleen Kenyon, *Digging Up Jerusalem* (Praeger, 1974), 94.

summarizes, "So here on the Temple Mount, at least, the archaeological search for David and Solomon reached a dead end."[16] However, the biblical descriptions of the temple (1 Kgs. 5:16–6:38) and Solomon's palace (7:1–12) were consistent with similar buildings in the region at the time, helping to affirm the biblical account.[17]

Archaeological Work Still in Process

Recent excavations in the city of David have discovered some exciting remains. An ancient bulla, seal impression, was the equivalent of an ancient envelope with a return address. In ancient times, a small stone inscribed with a name and image was often worn as a ring. The person would write a letter on papyrus-like paper, roll it up, and wrap a string around the middle. A small amount of clay would be used to fasten the string, and the mark in the ring would be pressed into the clay, entrapping the strings. This was a marker of either ownership or an indication of the author of a letter. In 2019, one of these clay bullae was discovered in the small area of "the city of David." It was dated to the First Temple period with the words "[belonging] to Nathan-Melech, Servant of the King." The name Nathan-Melech appears once in the Bible, in 2 Kings 23:11, where he is described as an official in the court of King Josiah.[18] Josiah will be discussed later in the book; this discovery helps confirm that archaeologists are looking in the right place for royal remains, even if they do not date back to the period of David and Solomon. This may seem like a small find. However, it is an exciting discovery with so little from the Judean kings available.

What, then, can be said about David and Solomon's Jerusalem? There is insufficient archaeological information to state anything other than the beginning of a dynasty named after David. There is no firm evidence of Solomon or his building projects. We can say that, at some point, David took over the city from the Jebusites and called it "the city of David" (2 Sam. 5:9). The city already had some impressive fortifications and buildings erected by the Jebusites, so it is difficult to know what was built previously and what was built

---

16. Israel Finkelstein and Neil Silberman, *David and Solomon: In Search of the Bible's Sacred Kings and the Roots of Western Tradition* (Free Press, 2006), 268.
17. Mazar, *Archaeology*, 376–79.
18. Adam Eliyahu Berkowitz, "Rare Seal Bearing Biblical Name Found in City of David," Biblical News, Israel 365 News, March 31, 2019, https://israel365news.com/329867/2600-year-old-seal-bearing-name-of-servant-of-the-king-found-in-city-of-david/. This find needs to be vetted further, but it appears to be a correct reading.

by David and Solomon. According to the biblical text, a palace and temple were added by the end of Solomon's reign. Any other building projects in Jerusalem are unknown.

THE ARCHAEOLOGICAL RECORD OUTSIDE OF JERUSALEM

The biblical text does not attribute any cities built outside Jerusalem to Saul or David. Solomon is credited with constructing cities outside of Jerusalem (1 Kgs. 9:15–25). Outside Jerusalem, there has been a wealth of archaeological discoveries. Major excavations uncovered archaeological remains in Hazor, Megiddo, and Gezer. The Bible lists these cities as Solomon's storage cities for military personnel and materials (9:19). At each site, archaeologists have discovered similar, massive city gates.[19] These gates and the attached casemate walls surrounded and protected the city. But were the cities built by Solomon? Yigael Yadin (1917–84), a prominent archaeologist, noted in 1958, "[This] not only confirms quite clearly the biblical narrative . . . that Megiddo and Hazor were both rebuilt by Solomon but even suggests that both gates were built by the same royal architect."[20] Further research eroded this confident statement. After more extensive excavations in the region, David Ussishkin (1935–) reports, "Summing up the indirect evidence, it seems clear that the six-chambered gate type was popular throughout the country during the 10th–9th centuries B.C., rather than being an exclusive type of gate constructed only in Solomon's royal cities. All the gates constructed were similar though they differ in size and style."[21] In other words, this type of gate was used both before and after the time of David and Solomon. Recently, Finkelstein and Ussishkin proposed that the monumental buildings at Megiddo belong not to the period of David and Solomon but to that of Omri and Ahab (ca. 880–850 BCE) based on this and several additional factors.[22] Their arguments for

---

19. Editors of the Madain Project, "Solomonic Gates," 2022, https://madainproject.com/solomonic_gates.

20. Y. Yadin, "Excavations at Hazor, 1957, Preliminary Communique," *IEJ* 8 (1958): 3.

21. David Ussishkin, "'Solomonic' City Gate at Megiddo Built by King Solomon?," *BASOR* 239 (1980): 17. The six-chambered gate is also found in Ashdod, a Philistine city.

22. The arguments for the later date are complex and involve many different factors: the claims of the Pharaoh's stela, the placement of the broken piece in Megiddo, the dating of the period of red-slipped, hand-burnished pottery, the estimated population of Judah during the period of the United Monarchy. See David Ussishkin, "The Chronology of the Iron Age Israel: The Current State of Research," *ANES* 45 (2008): 218–34; Israel Finkelstein, "State Formation in Israel and Judah: A Contrast in Context, A Contrast in Trajectory," *NEA* 62 (1999): 35–52. In this article, Finkelstein states that, based on the archaeological evidence, he is retracting his previous position for the lower chronology.

a later date for the construction of these cities are convincing. Still, the dating of these cities continues to be a point of debate among scholars.

Another site is now part of the discussion of the reigns of David and Solomon. Khirbet Qeiyafa, a site first excavated in 2008 (20 miles or 32 km SW of Jerusalem), has led to some scholars declaring David as the builder of several cities in Judah during his reign. Yosef Garfinkel (1956–) began excavating the Khirbet Qeiyafa site, a fort on the Philistine border overlooking the Elah Valley. His team discovered a casemate wall surrounding the city with a four-chambered city gate, similar to the six-chambered gates of Megiddo, Hazor, and Gezer.[23] The pottery, gates, and city wall are similar to those at other Iron Age II sites. Garfinkel, Hershel Shanks (1930–2021), and others claim that this site proves David had an administration with store cities.[24] Not surprisingly, other scholars doubt these findings. They believe Garfinkel's and Shanks's evaluations are clouded by their desire to prove King David existed and was a historical figure.[25] Finkelstein argues that the site dates from the Middle Bronze Age (2000–1550 BCE) to Early Iron Age I (1200–1000 BCE), the Early Iron Age I being slightly earlier than the time frame for the early monarchy. There is no definitive evidence that David or Solomon was responsible for the construction of the site.[26] The scholarly debate continues, with each side accusing the other of ulterior motives. At this point, there is not yet a scholarly consensus about Khirbet Qeiyafa.

Students of the Hebrew Bible must understand that archaeology is not an objective discipline. Indeed, archaeology was named "biblical archaeology" in its early days. The first ones to dig up what they then called "the Holy Land" were not trained archaeologists. They were biblical scholars. Towering scholars like William Albright (1891–1971) learned archaeology as they dug; their objective was often to prove the Bible to be historically accurate. Today, some scholars and archaeologists are more religiously conservative than others. Each side accuses the other of religious instead of scientific motives. Whether these accusations are true or not, they enter the debate. In modern-day Israel

---

23. Hershel Shanks, "Newly Discovered: A Fortified City from King David's Time," *BAR* 35, no 1 (January/February 2009): 38–43.

24. Yosef Garfinkel and Hoo-Goo Kang, "The Relative and Absolute Chronology of Khirbet Qeiyafa: Very Late Iron Age I or Very Early Iron Age IIA?," *IEJ* 61, no. 2 (2011): 171–83; and Hershel Shanks, "Newly Discovered: A Fortified City from King David's Time," *BAR* 35 (2009): 38–43. Interestingly, as noted above, these scholars place the building in the time of David, not Solomon.

25. Israel Finkelstein and Eli Piasetzky, "Khirbet Qeiyafa: Absolute Chronology," *Tel Aviv* 37 (2010): 84–88.

26. Finkelstein and Piasetzky, "Khirbet Qeiyafa," 57.

and Jordan, archaeology is always enmeshed in religion and politics.[27] This makes the debates more continuous and personal.

Many characterize these arguments over the dating of these sites in Hazor, Megiddo, Gezer, and Khirbet Qeiyafa as driven by religious motives. Those placing these dates in the David-Solomon era are seen as religious zealots. In contrast, those adopting a later time frame for these monumental building projects are seen as intentionally trying to undermine the Bible. Neither of these is the case. If one can strip away the religious overtones for a moment, what remains are two groups of archaeologists who disagree about the dating of sites from a specific 200-year period. This is a common occurrence in the field of archaeology and history. Let's review what is at stake in this debate and why.

Given the current body of archaeological knowledge, most scholars lean toward a later chronology for the gates in Hazor, Megiddo, and Gezer. One reason for the change was a large-scale Iron Age dating project that began in 2003.[28] This project recognized that the traditional date for the gates and its materials is 1000–930 BCE. This is equivalent to the dates assigned to David and Solomon. But a second possible time frame for these building projects was determined by archaeologists to be during the Omride period of 880–840 BCE. These dating differences were determined by analyzing all the sites in the region, looking at the architecture, the pottery types, and the items used by the inhabitants. This analysis was helpful but not definitive since the architecture and material items remained the same between 1000 and 850 BCE. Another way of determining age is by carbon 14 dating. However, this test can only be performed on *organic* material, so archaeologists must search for seeds or wood from the sites. Scientists using carbon 14 dating, where possible, have determined a time of 920–880 BCE.[29] This would place these monumental buildings at these store city sites *later* than David and Solomon's reigns, meaning the building of the three cities cannot be attributed to them. The other reasons why these building projects should be dated late is the success of the later Omride dynasty, which included massive building projects in cities such as Megiddo.

The discussion above highlights a few issues in determining the archaeological record of ancient civilizations. In archaeology, a change in the dating

---

27. Archaeological discoveries that do not align with the biblical text are seen by some Jews and Christians as designed to undermine modern Israel's right to the land, even when the archaeologist does not connect the new discovery to modern politics.

28. Israel Finkelstein and Eli Piasetzky, "The Iron Age Chronology Debate: Is the Gap Narrowing?," *NEA* 74 (2011): 50–54. This testing was done prior to the discoveries at Khirbet Qeiyafa.

29. Finkelstein and Piasetzky, "Iron Age Chronology," 51.

of ancient periods is not surprising. Each time a site is excavated or science advances, there is a possibility that past assumptions made by archaeologists will change. It is also not uncommon to have different groups of archaeologists debate each other over these issues. A lot of educated guesswork is in this process. This may feel like a problem to some biblical interpreters because these investigations can seem to "prove" or "disprove" the Bible. But we must remember that modern archaeology is a discipline in and of itself and should not be concerned with the truth claims of the Bible. Whether Jerusalem was as large as the text says at the time of David and Solomon is ultimately unknown. However, the evidence points to a smaller, more modest settlement than the one reported in the biblical text, written much later.

ARCHAEOLOGICAL DISAGREEMENT AND THE BIBLE

What should we make of a smaller Jerusalem during this period? Does this challenge our faith or the Bible? Not at all. First, as noted above, no monumental buildings were attributed to David. The record of Solomon is the issue. Evidence currently leans toward attributing the extensive fortifications outside Jerusalem to the Omride dynasty, but there is not enough evidence to say that definitively. Ronald Hendel sums it up in this way: "If these fortified cities were not Solomonic, Solomon's kingdom would not be as strong or as centralized as the Bible portrays, but this doesn't mean that Solomon wasn't king or that his kingdom didn't exist. It just means that it was a kingdom on a smaller scale, like many such kingdoms in the ancient world. It was a tribal kingdom, not a massive institutional state."[30]

So, were the biblical writers exaggerating? Not really. The descriptions of a larger Jerusalem and kingdom may simply reflect the size of Jerusalem at the time of a later editor who would assume that the Jerusalem he saw before him was indeed the Jerusalem of David and Solomon.[31] This phenomenon is known as "mnemohistory," remembered history. Another possibility is that it was common to attribute all the buildings of a kingdom to the first leaders, such as the house of David, even if the actual construction took place later.

---

30. Ronald S. Hendel, "What Difference Does a Century Make?," *BR* 19, no. 1 (February 2003): 10, 49.

31. This is a common occurrence. For example, the medieval paintings of biblical scenes picture Jesus and the disciples in medieval-period clothing and in clearly European landscapes. The artist read the text and made his painting based on the way his world looked. A later editor of the biblical text could do the same, assuming the buildings that he sees before him have always been part of Jerusalem. This phenomenon is known as "mnemohistory," remembered history, not actual verified historiography.

The Era of Early Monarchy 123

This is similar to all the laws of Israel and Judah being presented as coming from the meeting at Mount Sinai, even the ones written much later.

The same can be said for the extent of Solomon's kingdom in 1 Kings 4:24 (5:4). The text states: "For he [Solomon] had dominion over all the region west of the Euphrates, and he had peace on all sides."[32] However, there is no evidence that Judah and Israel ever held a territory that reached from the Euphrates River to the border of Egypt. "More likely," J. Maxwell Miller and John H. Hayes reflect, "Solomon's realm remained essentially what he inherited from David: the bulk of western Palestine (but excluding the Mediterranean coast) and some of northern Transjordan. . . . Solomon's cities are said to have fortified all [areas that] fall within these smaller territorial limits, as do the cities/areas from which his twelve officers collected produce."[33] Except for 1 Kings 4:24, the biblical text matches the archaeological record. David and Solomon ruled over a kingdom that grew in later generations—but never extended from the Euphrates to Egypt. Disagreements among scholars are common. The stakes only seem higher here because of the religious and political ramifications. Building projects or even territorial claims for kings of this region may not fit the archaeological record, but since we know the texts were written long after the actual events, we are not surprised.

To some, this argument among scholars and people of faith seems trivial. However, the image of an untarnished and wildly successful David and Solomon is not just an ancient concern. Why are the images of David and Solomon so well-known and enduring? Finkelstein proposes a critical evaluation of Western culture:

> The figures of David—shepherd, warrior, and divinely protected king—and of his son Solomon—great builder, wise judge, and serene ruler of a vast empire—have become timeless models of righteous leadership under God's sanction. They have shaped western images of kingship and served as models of royal piety, messianic expectations, and national destiny.[34]

In other words, we, in Western culture, have a great deal vested in the story of these two rulers and its paradigm for our Judeo-Christian pride. European kings often thought of themselves as heirs of David and Solomon. These first kings were also part of the story of Jesus and take precedence over all the ancestors in Jesus' line. Such traditions cement David and Solomon's place

---

32. Here in 1 Kgs. 4:24 (5:4), the NRSVue (2021) is reading the Greek text, but the NRSV (1989) is translated from the Hebrew text, which adds, "from Tiphsah to Gaza, over all the kings west of the Euphrates."
33. Miller and Hayes, *Ancient Israel and Judah*, 206.
34. Finkelstein and Silberman, *David and Solomon*, 5.

in Western culture, fortifying the image of their great power and expansive kingdoms. Our responsibility is to ask who benefits from the claims made.

THE UNITED MONARCHY

The "United Monarchy" is one of the names for the period when David and Solomon reigned over one kingdom, and the widespread understanding is that this kingdom was named "Israel." However, a close reading of 1 and 2 Samuel tells of not one but two kingdoms. As early as 1 Samuel 11:8, Judah was considered a separate entity. David was crowned king of Judah (2 Sam. 2:1–5), while Abner, the commander of Saul's army, brought Saul's son Ishbaal to Gilead to become king of Israel (2 Sam. 2:8–11). Approximately seven years later, Ishbaal was murdered, and "then all the tribes of Israel came to David at Hebron" (2 Sam. 5:1) and made him king over Israel in a separate ceremony.[35] Further evidence of the two kingdoms continued with the selection of Jerusalem as David's city. The early capital of Judah, Hebron, was likely too far south to satisfy both kingdoms. Jerusalem was still in Judah, but close (ca. 9 miles or 14 km south of Israel). Also, this new choice of a center was called "the city of David." The king provided a city that earlier did not belong to either group as his headquarters. The evidence suggests that David was the ruler of both nations, but a united single nation of Israel was never achieved.[36] Judah and Israel had the same king but still understood themselves as separate people.

Likewise, when David ordered the anointing of Solomon as his successor, the text names the two entities of Israel and Judah: "Let him enter and sit on my throne; he shall be king in my place, for I have appointed him to be ruler over Israel and over Judah" (1 Kgs. 1:35). At Gibeon, a northern Israelite cultic site (ca. 9 miles NW of Jerusalem), Solomon offered "a thousand burnt offerings on that altar" (1 Kgs. 3:4), likely indicating that worship within the territory of Israel was an important act of the king. Other texts reflect attempts at unification during the reign of Solomon. For example, when Solomon conscripts labor for building projects as part of the taxation of the people, he appears to force them to come from the entire kingdom (1 Kgs. 5:13–18).[37] Also, the building of the temple is in "the fourth year of Solomon's reign over

---

35. King Menes (aka Narmer) was the king of both Upper and Lower Egypt around 3000 BCE. Thomas Heagy, "Who Was Menes?," *Archéo-Nil* 24 (2014): 65–74, https://www.persee.fr/doc/arnil_1161-0492_2014_num_24_1_1071.

36. Arthur E. Cundall, "The United Monarchy: Fact or Fiction?," *Vox Evangelica* 8 (1973): 33–39.

37. Cundall, "United Monarchy," 37.

Israel" (1 Kgs. 6:1), an apparent reference to a united kingdom. When Solomon dies, he is remembered as one who "reigned in Jerusalem over all Israel" (1 Kgs. 11:42).[38] Thus, it is possible that there was a move during Solomon's reign toward a unified nation called "Israel."[39] But if so, that development did not last long.

The definitive evidence of the two nations' separate entrenchment comes after Solomon's death. The northern tribes of Israel negotiated with the new king, Rehoboam (1 Kgs. 12:1–11). When negotiations failed, the Israelites anointed Jeroboam as their king, separating from the southern kingdom of Judah entirely.

SUMMARY

The biblical texts in 2 Samuel and 1 Kings portray the two leaders of the (somewhat) unified kingdom as faithful and flawed. David is portrayed as a complex character, part mercenary, part rival leader, part sinner, part military leader, part king, and part faithful worshiper. Solomon was said to be endowed with great wisdom, but he also conscripted the labor of the people of Israel to build the temple and other projects, amassed wealth, and married many foreign wives for political purposes. While the historicity of this period is impossible to know, the stories here speak of both the good and the bad of these two leaders. Their legend would grow with time, but the text remembers two very human kings who were faithful and imperfect.

Did David and Solomon take these two regions of Israel and Judah from an organized group of tribes under Saul to a nation? The archaeological record is debated. In addition, as Raz Kletter points out, the definitions of ancient areas are fluid because the terms "chiefdoms," "states," and "empires" are ill-defined.[40] The same could be said today about our words "town," "city," and "metropolis." They also lack exact definition and remain in the eyes of the beholder. Just as in ancient days, the definition of cities or towns depended

---

38. This term does not have a single meaning and can mean the entirety of Israel and Judah, as in Josh. 23:2; 2 Sam. 5:5; or it can mean the Northern Kingdom, as in 1 Kgs. 12:20. The meaning of "all Israel" needs to be interpreted based on the context each time it appears.

39. Others argue that this narrative was shaped long after Solomon's death. Indeed, it was after the fall of Israel in 722 BCE, when many refugees had escaped the northern lands to reside in Judah; this was an attempt at that time to create one nation by weaving the stories of both together, say Finkelstein and Silberman, *David and Solomon*, 141–44. This is a strong argument, and its ramifications will be discussed later. Note that the only source here is the biblical text itself. A united monarchy is not verified by other sources.

40. Raz Kletter, "Chronology and the United Monarchy: A Methodological Review," *ZDPV* 120 (2004): 13–54.

on the perspective of the one assigning it a category. While some scholars see Jerusalem as a small chiefdom, others argue that it was an imperial city. Conversely, almost every scholar agrees that portraying Israel as a large, connected, fortified kingdom stretching across from the border of Egypt to the Euphrates River was an exaggeration. But the size of the territory or the success of David and Solomon is not the key point of the biblical text; to focus only on what was or was not the size of the kingdom misses the text's theological purpose. It is a narrative about some very human leaders and about God, who remained in relationship with these less-than-perfect people.

8

Two-Kingdom Rule: A Time of Expansion (927–840 BCE)

King Solomon died in about 927 BCE and was succeeded by his son, Rehoboam. This chapter focuses on the period from Solomon's death up to the assassination of the kings of Judah and Israel in 840 BCE. It was a time of some hostilities between Israel and Judah. It was also a time of growth and expansion in both kingdoms.

ISRAEL BECOMES INDEPENDENT

There is no extrabiblical evidence for the permanent split between Israel and Judah; the only record is the biblical one. However, ancillary evidence, such as the Tel Dan Stela, written about one hundred years later, confirms the existence of the two kingdoms. The stela states that the king of Aram killed "Jehoram, son of Ahab, king of Israel" and "Ahaziahu of the House of David," indicating two distinct kings of two different kingdoms.[1] Tensions between northern Israel and southern Judah eventually led to the formation of two nations with different governance and theological understandings of God. As in the previous chapter, the historical and archaeological record is scant for much of this period.

The reality of building a nation required a growing administration and the building of an infrastructure. David (2 Sam. 20:24) and Solomon (1 Kgs. 5:11–18) conscripted labor from all the tribes to build Jerusalem. This labor force was used for construction projects and served as a form of taxation on

---

1. Avraham Biran and Joseph Naveh, "The Tel Dan Inscription: A New Fragment," *IEJ* 45, no. 1 (1995): 1–18.

the people. According to the biblical text, Solomon died after a forty-year reign. Rehoboam, his son, succeeded him (1 Kgs. 11:43). This dynastic succession created a stable government in Judah, with the son succeeding the father, usually without conflict or competition for the throne.

There was not the same pattern of succession in Israel. Rehoboam went to Shechem, an important city in the northern kingdom, about 50 miles (80 km) north of Jerusalem (1 Kgs. 12:1). The text reports, "All Israel had come to Shechem to make him king," but it is unclear if Rehoboam went for a negotiation or for a coronation, so "all Israel" could make him king.[2] Neither David nor Solomon were associated with Shechem.[3] The most probable reading of the text is that "all Israel" intended to negotiate with Rehoboam concerning their status and the issue of conscripted labor before they allowed him to be king of Israel. Once Rehoboam arrived, the people announced, "Your father made our yoke heavy. Now, therefore, lighten the hard service of your father and his heavy yoke that he placed on us, and we will serve you" (12:4). The Bible reports that when Rehoboam refused to negotiate, the Israelite group rejected the house of David (12:16), and Rehoboam fled back to Jerusalem. "All Israel" then made Jeroboam the king of the northern kingdom of Israel (12:20). Jeroboam had previously fled to Egypt from King Solomon (12:2).

THE TWO KINGDOMS, ISRAEL AND JUDAH

First Kings 12:16 to 2 Kings 17:41 tells of the time of the two kingdoms. As with all ancient documents, it narrates some of the events but not all. In addition, these narratives are centered on the royal houses and do not explain how most of the population of these two countries lived and worshiped. The Bible also speaks of other national sources, such as the Book of the Annals of the Kings of Israel (1 Kgs. 14:19) and the Book of the Annals of the Kings of Judah (14:29). Unfortunately, no trace of these books has been found. Much of what we know of this period is from 1 and 2 Kings and the prophetic books. Several extrabiblical sources also supplement this period.

The nation of Israel in the north stretched from the Mediterranean Sea in the west to the Trans-Jordan in the east and from near Mount Hermon in the

---

2. This has led some scholars to state that "all of Israel" as mentioned in 1 Kgs. 12 means Judah as well; Iain Provan, V. Philips Long, and Tremper Longman III, *A Biblical History of Israel* (Westminster John Knox, 2003), 259. Yet that does not seem reasonable since the biblical text states in 11:43 that Rehoboam was now king in Jerusalem.

3. According to 2 Sam. 5:1–5, "all the tribes of Israel" came to David in Hebron to make him king. Solomon's acceptance by Israel is unclear, saying only that he sacrificed at Gibeon, about 5 miles NW of Jerusalem (1 Kgs. 3:4).

north to Bethel in the south, making it approximately twice the size of Judah. Also, a significant section of the Asia-Africa trade routes traversed or were close to the nation. The trade routes, the Way of the Sea and the Transjordanian Highway, allowed Israel access to the entire Afro-Asiatic region and facilitated trading goods and selling services to travelers (see map 6). The route was also crucial to maintaining a military advantage in the region. Therefore, this prime location put Israel at risk of invasion. Any nation that desired to dominate the Afro-Asiatic region had to control the trade routes. This was especially important because the Way of the Sea route passes through the narrow valley, Wadi ʿĀrah, that connects the coastal plain with the Plain of Esdraelon. This narrow passage made any traveling military unit vulnerable to the large, raised city of Megiddo.[4]

On the other hand, Judah was landlocked, blocked from the sea by Philistia to the west and on the east by the Dead Sea and Edom. It was not on or even near either of the trade routes.[5] Judah was out of the way, smaller, and had no intrinsic value to outsiders. These geographical differences would be a significant factor in the fate of these two nations.

Another factor in Israel's growth was its topography and climate. The northern regions provided fertile valleys for growing crops and hills that supported olive and grape farming.[6] The regions of the north also received more rain over a more extended season.[7] Judah's terrain was more arid and received less rainfall per year. It also contained large areas of desertlike wilderness. In short, the northern region of Israel contained more farmable land with good rainfall. This allowed Israel to feed its citizens and trade agricultural products, mainly olives and grapes. Judah's land was not as fertile and thus did not grow the population or commercial potential at the same rate.

These geographic differences are borne out in archaeological surveys of the land from 1200 to 900 BCE. While different camps of archaeologists debate the exact numbers, all agree that the population density of Israel was greater than that of Judah. Israel's population also expanded quickly throughout this period. Growth in the Judean region was slower and began

---

4. J. Maxwell Miller and John H. Hayes, *A History of Ancient Israel and Judah*, 2nd ed. (Westminster John Knox, 2006), 22; Eric Cline, *The Battles of Armageddon: Megiddo and the Jezreel Valley from the Bronze Age to the Nuclear Age* (University of Michigan Press, 2000).

5. One north-south trade route runs near the sea, and portions run through Israel's Plain of Megiddo and the Jezreel Valley; the other is east of the Jordan River, on the edge of the desert, crossing into the Sinai Peninsula at the head of the Gulf of Aqaba. Neither intersects with Judah.

6. Israel Finkelstein and Neil Silberman, *The Bible Unearthed: Archaeology's New Vision of Ancient Israel and the Origins of Its Sacred Texts* (Free Press, Touchstone, 2001), 157.

7. Miller and Hayes, *Ancient Israel and Judah*, 24.

much later, impacting the development of the state and the infrastructure required to support commerce.[8]

As two nations, Israel and Judah used different governmental structures. In Judah, from the reign of David forward, a dynastic monarchy was the normal course of governance, meaning that a son followed the father. As a result, the succession was smooth and usually without bloodshed. This dynastic succession was also directly tied to the worship of *Adoni* in the Jerusalem temple. The king was important in governance and worship (Pss. 2; 72). Seen as the quintessential human, the king was serving Judah's true king, God (Pss. 93–99). Psalms 2 and 72 show how God and governance are connected. As a royal psalm, Psalm 2 declares, "He [God] said to me, . . . 'Today I have begotten you'" (v. 7). Yet this does not make the king different from the rest of humanity; there is no elevation of the person to the status of a god, as in Egypt. Likewise, Psalm 72 does not place a mantle of privilege on the king but one of responsibility:

> Give the king your justice, O God, and your righteousness to a king's son.
> May he judge your people with righteousness and your poor with
>   justice. . . . [So that the king will be one who]
> delivers the needy when they call, the poor and those who have no helper.
> He has pity on the weak and the needy and saves the lives of the needy.
> From oppression and violence he redeems their life, and precious is their
>   blood in his sight.
>
> Ps. 72:1–2, 12–14

Here is a concept of kingship as a theocracy, where the king was to carry forth the edicts of God's kingdom, not his own whims. This was known as royal, or Zion, theology and accounted for more political stability in Judah.[9]

The northern kingdom of Israel did not have the same understanding of kingship. Coups after the king's death were common, and there seemed to be no understanding of a hereditary monarchy. James Maxwell Miller and John H. Hayes calculate that from 924 to 722 BCE, seven of Israel's kings were assassinated or executed, each resulting in a dynastic change.[10] The result of multiple dynastic changes was political instability. Why was there a difference, especially when Israel's economy had advantages over Judah's? The Bible does not answer the question directly, so we are left to offer possible reasons. Israel did not draw its monarchical history back to one person or

---

8. Lester Grabbe, *Ancient Israel: What Do We Know and How Do We Know It?* (T&T Clark, 2007), 71.

9. J. J. M. Roberts, "The Davidic Origin of Zion Tradition," in *The Bible and the Ancient Near East* (Eisenbrauns, 2002), 313–30.

10. Miller and Hayes, *Ancient Israel and Judah*, 267.

family as Judah did. The throne was something to be taken when the opportunity presented itself. Multiple families ruled Israel. Also, the Israelite king did not have the same religious role as in Judah. The temple in Judah was associated with the king and was located directly beside the palace in Jerusalem. Israel had several places of religious importance, such as Bethel and Dan (1 Kgs. 12:29), plus other "high places" (12:31). Judah had centralized worship in Jerusalem. Israel did not.

As noted above, Israel was larger and more prosperous than Judah. Yet readers notice how the focus of 2 Samuel–2 Kings is on Jerusalem, the temple, and the Davidic succession. This perspective means that the archaeological record will diverge significantly from the biblical narrative. The biblical texts were not favorable or even balanced when describing Israel, its kings, and its people. Scholars attribute this section of the Bible (Joshua to Kings) to a so-called Deuteronomistic source (Dtr). A source should not be confused with a single writer. It is better defined as a perspective or position in telling the story. This perspective would impact how the reigns of Judah's and Israel's kings were reported. Kings were not measured by economic success, support of the poor, or the growth of the population. The measure of a good king, according to the Deuteronomistic source, was strict adherence to worship in the temple in Jerusalem and the destruction of any public worship site outside the Jerusalem temple. This perspective is helpful for those investigating the religious devotion of the kings but provides little assistance for historians.

A second set of texts from this period appears in 1 and 2 Chronicles. For most historians, 1 and 2 Chronicles serve as a secondary document, using much of the material from 1 and 2 Kings and focusing almost exclusively on Judah. The books are considered the work of one author or authorial group and are dated quite late in the history of these nations, during either the Persian or Hellenistic Empires (539–64 BCE). These books are some of the latest in the Hebrew Bible to be composed. Because of their distance from actual events, the books are considered by most to be less reliable from a historical standpoint than 1 and 2 Kings and the prophetic books.

The biblical text reports in 1 Kings 15 that the two countries remained at war with each other for several decades (15:6, 16, 32). There is not much biblical or extrabiblical information for the rest of the reigns of Rehoboam (in the south) and Jeroboam (in the north) or their sons or grandsons. Chart 3 below lists the kings of Judah and Israel and the approximate times of their reigns from approximately 927 to 840 BCE. In 1 Kings, the biblical assessment of the kings becomes formulaic. Kings either did what was right in the sight of the *Adoni* or did what was wrong (e.g., 1 Kgs. 14:22; 15:11), and then slept with their ancestors. Without clearly established dates, the years

CHART 3: EARLY KINGS OF THE DIVIDED KINGDOMS (CA. 927 TO 840 BCE)

Kings of Israel	Kings of Judah
Jeroboam 927–906	Rehoboam 927–910
Nadad (son of Jeroboam) 905–904	Abijam 909–907
Baasha 903–882	Asa 906–878
Elah (son of Baasha) 882–880	
killed by	
Zimri 880 (?)	
Omri 880–869	Jehoshaphat 877–853
Ahab 868–854	
Ahaziah 853–852	
Jehoram/Joram 851–840	Jehoram/Joram 852–840
	Ahaziah 840
Jehoram of Israel and Ahaziah of Judah killed by Jehu	

of reigns should be considered estimates.[11] The length of kings' reigns mentioned in the biblical text also do not always correspond with these approximate historical dates. The problem continues through all the kings' reigns in both Judah and Israel.

Judah remained stable during the first three decades after the united monarchy, with the son succeeding his father. Each king's reign reported the continuing war with Israel. King Asa of Judah went as far as allying with the king of Aram, who then supposedly attacked Israel (1 Kgs. 15:16–24), probably in response to Baasha's fortifying of Ramah, which was close enough to (ca. 5 miles or 8 km north of) Jerusalem to cause a continuous threat.

In Israel, the political scene was not as steady. Israel had neither a stable dynasty nor a fixed capital city. Jeroboam's son, Nadad, was killed after two years, and another family gained control. Baasha moved his capital from

---

11. Dates vary from scholar to scholar, and all are estimates based on the biblical text and extrabiblical sources. The dates in chart 3 adopt Miller and Hayes's schema, although theirs is not superior to another textbook, such as K. L. Noll, *Canaan and Israel in Antiquity: A Textbook on History and Religion*, 2nd ed. (Bloomsbury T&T Clark, 2013); or Victor Matthews, *A Brief History of Ancient Israel* (Westminster John Knox, 2002).

Jeroboam's Shechem to Tirzah, possibly his home city. His son, Elah, reigned for two years, then he and his entire family were murdered by his army commander, Zimri (1 Kgs. 16:8–14). Some in leadership named another commander, Omri, their king (16:16–20). When Zimri heard of all of this, he killed himself and burned down the king's house in Tirzah. But that did not settle the matter; the people were divided on who should be king. Some supported Omri, and others turned to Tibni (16:21). The would-be kings fought over the throne for several years. Israel's palace intrigue is worthy of *Game of Thrones*![12] Instead of an idyllic picture of the two nations ordained by God, Judah and especially Israel's stories were ordinary, violent, and very human. From a historical perspective, there are no extrabiblical records for this period, so the biblical account remains the only source. From either a sociological or theological perspective, humans were acting just like humans: grabbing power, waging war, and killing each other in a contest for control.

ISRAEL'S RISE

The biblical narrative omits the most significant historical facts about the northern kingdom of Israel. This is because the Bible is not a history book but a story of God and God's people told from a particular perspective. Remember, the Bible does not cover everything. Its judgments are not historical, so its narration of events is incomplete. In Western culture, many are taught that the Bible contains everything, yet this is not a claim the Bible ever makes of itself.[13] According to the archaeological records, Israel, under the Kings of Omri and his son Ahab, built a capital, controlled surrounding nations, amassed wealth, and engaged in massive building projects. Yet none of these are covered in the biblical text.

During the ninth century, Israel became a powerful regional nation. It built a significant infrastructure and captured some territory from its neighbors. However, Israel was not alone in its expansion of territory. Another player during this period was Aram under King Ben-Hadad. "Ben-Hadad" is a throne name, like Pharaoh, meaning "son of Hadad," a god of Aram. Hadad is also another name for Baal, which accounts for its multiple appearances

---

12. George R. R. Martin, *Game of Thrones*, Season 1–5 (Running Press, 2015).
13. The closest verse is 2 Tim. 3:16–17, "All scripture is inspired by God and is useful for teaching, for reproof, for correction, and for training in righteousness, so that [everyone who belongs to] God may be proficient, equipped for every good work." This is quoted by many as proof of perfection. Yet the Scripture states that it is useful for teaching, and it is. Often the teaching is missed because a modern reader focuses on historical truth instead of theological insight.

throughout the Hebrew Bible. Aram and its king would be an ally and an enemy of Judah and Israel at different times in this period.

Further to the northeast, Assyria, with its king Ashurnasirpal II (883–859 BCE), was gaining strength even as Israel created the most successful period of its history. This period marked the rise of the first superpowers in the Afro-Asiatic region, and these powers would change the fortunes of the people residing in every nation.

ISRAEL'S RISE UNDER THE OMRI DYNASTY (880–840 BCE)

As reported in the section above, this period began with a civil war between those who supported Omri and those who supported Tibni. Israel often broke into civil unrest when a king died. In this instance, the reported war can be matched by the archaeological record. In Tirzah, the capital of Israel at the time, archaeologists discovered a layer of burned debris, which matched the statement in 1 Kings 16:18 that the city burned. Further, archaeologists found that the city was partially rebuilt but was not completed. This also matches the biblical narrative that Omri abandoned Tirzah for the new capital, Samaria (1 Kgs. 16:24).[14] The area known as Samaria was in a better location (ca. 7 miles, or 11 km, NW of Shechem), on the west side of the central hill country, with easier access to the Way of the Sea. The city Omri established was named Samaria, after the region. It was an elevated city, allowing for better defense.[15] Also, in establishing his own city, Omri may have been patterning his dynasty after the house of David, who moved his dynasty to his own city of Jerusalem. The entire biblical report of Omri is brief: his only noted accomplishment was moving the capital from Tirzah to Samaria six years into his reign (1 Kgs. 16:21–28).

The archaeological and historical record tells a different story. Samaria was impressive, built atop the hill and with a large, reinforced wall. The builders filled the space between the wall and the hill with earth to create a five-acre royal acropolis.[16] On top of this base construction, a large palace made of high-quality ashlar stone was built. The interior walls of the palace were made with carved ivory decorations, a rare commodity reserved for the wealthiest monarchs. It is not known when the building was started or completed, but

---

14. Roland de Vaux, "Tirzah," in *Archaeology and Old Testament Study*, ed. D. W. Thomas (Oxford University Press, 1967), 371–83.

15. Miller and Hayes, *Ancient Israel and Judah*, 303.

16. Finkelstein and Silberman, *Bible Unearthed*, 181. The construction of Samaria is strikingly similar to the other debated cities of Megiddo, Hazor, and Gezer.

the project was probably begun by Omri and completed by his son Ahab. The town of Jezreel was also built during this time and was a second residence for Ahab.[17] Jezreel was on a spur of Mount Gilboa and at the head of the Valley of Jezreel, sloping to the Jordan and part of an ancient trade route between the Jordan Valley and the Way of the Sea. Omri established alliances with other regional powers. The alliance with the Phoenicians resulted in his son Ahab's marriage to Jezebel, a daughter of King Eth-Baal of Sidon, Phoenicia, and worshiper of Baal (1 Kgs. 16:31).

The Israelite monarchs were also named in the written records of surrounding nations. A stela erected by Mesha, the neighboring king of Moab, mentions Omri and his son in lines 4–9:[18]

> Omri was king of Israel, he humbled Moab for many days, for Kemosh was angry with his land. And his son succeeded him and he said—he too—"I will oppress Moab!" In my days, he spoke [so], but I looked down on him and on his house, and Israel has gone to ruin forever![19]

This stela is known as the Moabite Stone, or Mesha Stela. It reports that Omri had conquered Moab, which Ahab then controlled. Mesha regained control from one of Ahab's sons.[20] This stela is the first extrabiblical evidence of an Israelite or Judean king and, thus, a significant historical artifact.[21] From this stela, historians can confidently state that Omri existed and was regionally powerful, controlling other nations.

Another extrabiblical stela confirms that Ahab, Omri's son, built on his father's success as a military leader. But this time, the stela was not by a regional king but by a rising empire builder. The Kurkh Monolith lists kings that King Shalmaneser III of Assyria defeated at Qarqar (NW Syria/Aram); among them is the line "2,000 chariots and 10,000 soldiers of Ahab the Israelite."[22] Most scholars agree that the number of chariots and troops stated was probably

---

17. Miller and Hayes, *Ancient Israel and Judah*, 295.
18. André Lemaire, "'House of David' Restored in the Moabite Inscription," *BAR* 20, no. 3 (1994): 30–37. Lemaire argues that the Moabite stone also contains the words "House of David," but to date other scholars have not concurred.
19. *COS*, 2:137. The inscription continues for several stanzas, describing the areas the king took back from Israel.
20. Recently some scholars have questioned whether one *or* two kings are named Omri: their complaint is basically concerning the 40 years, which do not match the reigns of Omri and Ahab (see Grabbe, *Ancient Israel*, 144–46, for more information), but there is no significant doubt as to the Omri connection here, especially since it is on a victory stela of a king who was forced to be a vassal for years.
21. The Tel Dan Stela tells of "the house of David." As noted in the last chapter, scholars are divided on whether this is a direct reference to King David. The Moabite Stone clearly refers to the persons of Omri. It remains the first definitive evidence for the king of Israel.
22. *COS*, 2:263.

more propaganda than fact.[23] However, even if the numbers in Ahab's army were exaggerated, he *was listed* among the leaders of the region, confirming that Israel had a significant military presence. Both the archaeological evidence within the territory of Israel and the epigraphic evidence from other kingdoms confirm the existence of and power within the Omride dynasty.

The one debated question is the extent of Omri's building projects in other major cities. The central issue is which king was responsible for the massive city defensive structures at Megiddo, Hazor, and Gezer. Many scholars believe the archaeological evidence indicates that their construction took place during the Omri dynasty (Kings Omri, Ahab, Azariah, and Jehoram). Others, as noted in the last chapter, attribute the fortification of these cities to Solomon. There is no clear resolution to this impasse.[24] However, given the evidence of the extensive building and fortifications in Samaria, the addition of defensive fortifications in these three cities near major trade routes best fits the period of the Omride dynasty. Everything indicates that the nation was a significant regional power.

As observed, the biblical record of Omri and Ahab does not mention these great building projects or their regional military power. The 2 Kings account barely mentions Omri, and the Ahab narratives are focused on Elijah and his conflicts with the king and his wife, Jezebel. Ahab and Jezebel are portrayed as evil apostates. Indeed, the narratives of this period speak much more about the acts of Elijah and his successor, Elisha, than those of Omri and Ahab. The books of Chronicles ignore King Omri except as a relative to the wife of a Judean king (2 Chr. 22:2). Second Chronicles (18) also tells of a marriage alliance between Ahab and Jehoshaphat, king of Judah, and the circumstances of Ahab's death.

According to the biblical account, after Ahab's death (about 854 BCE), the reign of his son Ahaziah was brief, lasting hardly two years till he died without an heir. Moab broke free of Israelite domination during his reign or shortly thereafter, as recorded on the Mesha Stela (described above).[25] As Israel struggled, Shalmaneser III of Assyria continued to attempt control of the region

---

23. K. Lawson Younger, "Neo-Assyrian and Israelite History in the Ninth Century: The Role of Shalmaneser III," in *Understanding the History of Ancient Israel*, ed. H. Williamson, Proceedings of the British Academy 143 (Oxford University Press, 2007), 253.

24. Steve Ortiz, "United Monarchy: Archaeological and Literary Sources," in *Ancient Israel's History: An Introduction to Issues and Sources*, ed. B. Arnold and R. Hess (Baker Academic, 2014), 238.

25. The exact date of Moab's freedom is uncertain. First, "Omri's son" can mean his son or his descendants. Second Kings 3 details a battle between Jehoram and Moab, but this records an Israelite victory. André Lemaire argues that the stela not only indicates victory but subsequent rebuilding, and he dates it to 810 BCE; "West Semitic Inscriptions and Ninth Century BCE Ancient Israel," in *Understanding the History of Ancient Israel*, ed. H. Williamson, Proceedings of the British Academy 143 (Oxford University Press, 2007), 288.

and gave several defeats to a coalition of countries in 849, 848, and 845.[26] It is unclear if Israel was part of the coalition after the death of King Ahab.

JUDAH DURING THE OMRIDE DYNASTY (880–840 BCE)

Judah, during the first half of the ninth century (900–840 BCE), was in somewhat of a dark age, both biblically and historically. We find little information on how the nation fared. First Kings is brief and formulaic; 2 Chronicles offers an expanded narrative of a peaceful Judah during Asa's early reign. The books of Kings and Chronicles report hostilities between Asa of Judah and Baasha of Israel (1 Kgs. 15:16; see chart 3). Asa's son, Jehoshaphat, made peace with "the king of Israel" (1 Kgs. 22:44), and 2 Chronicles 18:1 notes a marriage alliance between the two houses of Judah and Israel.[27] First Kings 22 says the two armies of Israel and Judah fought together against Aram and later against Moab (2 Kgs. 3:4–27). Historically, these alliances are challenging to validate because there are no records of Judah during this time outside the Bible. The archaeological record of Judah reflects a growing nation, as the cities of Jerusalem, Arad, Lachish, and others were expanded and fortified,[28] but their growth was slower than in Israel.[29] According to biblical evidence, the two nations experienced some early battles against each other but then settled into a peaceful coexistence for the rest of the period. This information fits with evidence of the fortification of Judean cities as Israel and Judah grew into more developed nations.

LAST YEARS OF THE OMRIDE DYNASTY (854–840 BCE)

The next period of kingship is mysterious. The nation of Israel appears in the biblical text to be losing its grip on the surrounding countries at this time, as the Mesha Inscription supports. The Assyrian Empire was growing, and its power was felt by the nations of Canaan, as attacks on them were increasing. The archaeological record does not demonstrate significant changes.

---

26. The Black Obelisk and other Assyrian documents describe these campaigns and omit the king of Israel and the other kings, listing only Ben-Hadad of Damascus and the twelve kings from the seacoast: *ANET*, 279–80.
27. The text of 1 Kgs. 22 only refers to "the king of Israel"; however, 2 Chr. 18 names Ahab as the king of Israel at the time.
28. Amihai Mazar, *Archaeology of the Land of the Bible: 10,000–586 B.C.E.* (Doubleday, 1990), 417–44.
29. Miller and Hayes, *Ancient Israel and Judah*, 267.

Jehoram of Israel and Jehoram of Judah became kings within a year of each other. Ahaziah, the king of Israel, was Ahab's son, died without an heir, and was succeeded by someone named Jehoram in 851 BCE (2 Kgs. 1:17–18). The Greek text states Jehoram was Ahaziah's brother, and most English translations follow that text. The Hebrew text does not state Jehoram's relationship to Ahaziah. Is it possible that Jehoram was one person who ruled both Judah and Israel after the untimely death of Ahaziah, instead of two people with the same name? Scholars are divided, and the arguments are based on several assumptions.[30] There is not enough evidence to declare that there was only one king for both countries. In addition, if someone from the Davidic line again became king of Israel, thus reuniting the "nation" of David and Solomon, it would be surprising for the Bible to be silent about this monumental event.[31]

The other player in this period is Athaliah, either Ahab's sister or daughter. She was married to the king of Judah, Jehoram, and she gave birth to Ahaziah, the same name as the deceased king of Israel. Marriages between royal houses were a common ancient practice to seal political alliances (for example, Solomon and his foreign wives, Ahab and Jezebel). She was also the aunt of Jehoram of Israel (2 Kgs. 8:26).[32] The intermarriages between the two royal houses and the similar names make it difficult to sort out the genealogy. Usually a king's wife who is related to the monarch of a neighboring country was not historically significant, but Athaliah was a key figure in what unfolded later.[33] Little else is known of the reign of Jehoram of Judah; he died, and his son, Ahaziah, succeeded him in 840 BCE.

In summary, Israel became a regionally recognized power under Omri and Ahab and may have gained control of all the surrounding nations, as evidenced by the Mesha Inscription.[34] Their time in ruling the region was one of growth, trade, prosperity, and military power. For most of the ninth century BCE, the Omride dynasty in Israel had an alliance with Aram and either voluntarily or involuntarily controlled the region's other countries.

---

30. See Miller and Hayes, *Ancient Israel and Judah*, 321–22; and John Strange, "Joram, King of Israel and Judah," *VT* 25 (1975): 191–201.

31. Strange (in "Joram," 201) argues just the opposite, that the editors' dislike of Israel was so strong that they would not have allowed any Davidic king to be associated with that nation.

32. Reuven Klein, "Queen Athaliah: The Daughter of Ahab or Omri?," *JBQ* 42 (2014): 11–20. The biblical text is unclear: she is either Ahab's sister or daughter (2 Kgs. 8:18); W. Boyd Barrick, "Another Shaking of Jehosophat's Family Tree: Jehoram and Ahaziah Once Again," *VT* 51 (2001): 9–25. It would be possible for her to have been born late in Omri's reign or early in Ahab's reign and be the age required to marry Jehoram. Either way, Ahaziah of Judah is Athaliah's son.

33. Strange, "Joram," 201.

34. Miller and Hayes (*Ancient Israel and Judah*, 304) argue that Israel also held Judah as a vassal during this period; perhaps so, but no clear confirmation of this has been found either in or out of the biblical text.

Why is the biblical account so different from the archaeological evidence and the written records of the other nations? Israel Finkelstein proposes a reason:

> The true character of Israel under the Omrides involves an extraordinary story of military might, architectural achievement, and (as far as can be determined) administrative sophistication. Omri and his successors earned the hatred of the Bible precisely *because* they were so strong, precisely because they succeeded in transforming the northern kingdom into an important regional power that completely overshadowed the poor, marginal, rural-pastoral kingdom of Judah to the south.[35]

Finkelstein sees this as a way for the Judeans composing these books to discredit this powerful family. Probably Finkelstein is correct, but remember that these narratives were also edited long after the end of the Omride dynasty. Within a hundred years, the nation of Israel would be destroyed (722 BCE). By the time this story was included as part of the whole story of Israel and Judah, the Omride dynasty was gone, and their acts were a memory. The authors of the Bible had a different perspective on this northern dynasty, possibly because they were taking a longer view of these events. Perhaps in light of Israel's destruction, Omri was remembered as unimportant, and Ahab's reign and his marriage to Jezebel exemplified why they failed. The narratives of the nation of Israel in the Hebrew Bible portrayed the reasons for that failure as religious. In the end, there are multiple reasons for the biblical writers to shape the stories as they did.

THE RELIGION OF THE OMRIDE DYNASTY

Monotheism, defined as the belief in one god,[36] appeared as a foundational principle from the beginning to the end of the Hebrew Bible, when the text was finally complete and stabilized, as discussed in chapter 4. The reality of monotheism in ancient Israel and Judah was much different. The account of Ahab and Jezebel is an example of religious life during the Omride dynasty.

Before discussing monotheism and the ancient world, it is essential to note the differences between modern and ancient worldviews. In modern culture, we choose to believe in higher powers or not. This choice would be an alien

---

35. Finkelstein and Silberman, *Bible Unearthed*, 194–95.
36. Donald McKim, "Monotheism," in *Westminster Dictionary of Theological Terms* (Westminster John Knox, 1996), 177.

concept in the ancient world. There was little or no atheism as we know it. They did not deny the existence of other gods. Ancient people knew and took their gods and the gods of others very seriously. The ancient people believed in many gods during most of the period of the Hebrew Bible, which makes monotheism somewhat of a misnomer. A more accurate understanding of the worldview of the ancients would be to ask *which* god or gods they served.[37]

An example of the ancient religious worldview comes from the narratives of Ahab and Jezebel, which end 1 Kings and begin 2 Kings. The biblical text states that Ahab and his foreign wife, Jezebel, not only allowed but also encouraged the worship of Baal over the worship of *Adoni*. As a document of ancient culture, these narratives depict a battle for the hearts of the Israelites. Loyalty to *Adoni* alone was a constant struggle among ancient Israelites and Judeans, as these texts make clear.[38]

A close reading of the biblical text demonstrates a common political and religious practice. The marriage of Ahab and Jezebel was part of a political alliance between Israel and Phoenicia. Jezebel was a Baal worshiper, and it was expected that Ahab would provide her with a place to continue to worship her god, as reported in 1 Kings 16:31–32. This was a typical practice in the ancient world (cf. Solomon in 1 Kings 11).

Did Ahab forsake his God and follow Baal? It isn't very likely. For example, Ahab's sons have names that incorporate the name of the Israelite God into their given names. Their names indicate the primary God they served.[39] Ahab would not have given his sons the names Ahaziah (held by Yah) and Jehoram (Yah is exalted) if he were a Baal worshiper. So, at best, Ahab is a mixed character, serving *Adoni* and possibly other gods. At this time, the people of Israel and Judah were polytheistic, believing in a council or family of gods (see Ps. 82). The question for these ancient people was not, Which God do you exclusively serve? Psalm 82 is an example of how the gods were often portrayed in a council of gods. The chief god of the pantheon was Israel's God, but that did not eliminate the lesser gods of Baal and Asherah and others. The archaeological record includes the discovery of terra-cotta figurines of other

---

37. As an example, Joshua's charge to the people is not just to believe in only one god but "Now, therefore, revere [*Adoni*] and serve him in sincerity and in faithfulness; put away the gods that your ancestors served beyond the River and in Egypt and serve [*Adoni*]" (24:14). Joshua does not argue that the god of the ancestors was not real. The stress is on choosing *Adoni* now.

38. The religion of ancient Israel and Judah is a topic unto itself that a small volume such as this cannot address in any detail; see Patrick Miller, *The Religion of Ancient Israel*, Library of Ancient Israel, ed. Douglas Knight (Westminster John Knox, 2000).

39. Obadiah (chief minister) and Ahaziah and Jehoram (Joram) are Yahwistic names (Grabbe, *Ancient Israel*, 156). In addition, before the battle, Ahab consulted the prophets of *Adoni*, not Baal.

gods during the entire time of the two kingdoms, confirming the people's worship of many gods.[40] These texts display the tension between how the people of this era worshiped and how the Hebrew Bible was finally shaped. Monotheism was portrayed as the norm of the people, but it was not fully adopted until the postexilic period.

SUMMARY

The division of the two kingdoms resulted in Israel controlling more resources, but with internal instability. Judah had internal stability and fewer resources. For the first few years after the division upon the death of Solomon, the two countries fought over control.

Later, the Omride kings of Israel built a powerful dynasty, a nation, and a strong military. During their reign, Israel had a stable and inherited dynasty. They moved the capital to Samaria and fortified the nation. In the records of other nations, they appear as a regional power. Under the Omride kings, Israel thrived. Judah also grew but at a slower pace than Israel. During Israel's dynasty, the kings made peace with Judah and ratified their relationship with intermarriage within the royal houses. The people of both nations continued to worship in the ancient ways of belief in a pantheon of gods. Both nations grew during this period and were prosperous and stable. By the end of the Omride period, this stability began to erode. First, with the death of Azariah of Israel, there was no direct heir to succeed him. Second, the shadow of Assyria lengthened and threatened both countries.

---

40. William Dever, *The Lives of Ordinary People in Ancient Israel: Where Archaeology and the Bible Intersect* (Eerdmans, 2012), 280.

9

Israel Tumbles toward Destruction (840–722 BCE)

The successful Omride dynasty established in the northern kingdom of Israel would soon end. The Assyrians under Shalmaneser III (859–823 BCE) attacked multiple times, trying to gain control of the region. Israel was also engaged in conflicts with the surrounding nations. This chapter traces internal and external challenges for control of Israel. The Assyrian threat continues to grow, but there are also extended times of peace, when conflicts decrease.

THE MURDER OF THE TWO KINGS

The period began with the kings of Israel and Judah leading their armies and fighting to control Ramoth-Gilead in the Trans-Jordan in 840 BCE. They were fighting Aram, the nation directly north of Israel, which formerly was a friendly nation. Jehoram of Israel was wounded in a battle and withdrew to Jezreel along with King Ahaziah of Judah, the son of Jehoram of Judah; Ahaziah succeeded Jehoram of Judah in 840 BCE (2 Kgs. 8:28–29). Ahaziah, the new king of Judah, was the cousin of Jehoram of Israel.[1]

Jehu, son of Jehoshaphat, son of Nimshi, was one of the commanders of the troops at Ramoth-Gilead. He was first introduced when the prophet Elisha sent another prophet to him. The prophet sought him out as commanded, anointed him, and then presented a violent word of God.

---

1. As discussed in the preceding chapter, the relationships are unclear, but Athaliah, his mother, was probably Ahab's sister.

"Thus says the LORD the God of Israel: I anoint you king over the people of the LORD, over Israel. You shall strike down the house of your master Ahab, so that I may avenge on Jezebel the blood of my servants the prophets and the blood of all the servants of the LORD. For the whole house of Ahab shall perish; I will cut off from Ahab every male, bond or free, in Israel. I will make the house of Ahab like the house of Jeroboam son of Nebat and like the house of Baasha son of Ahijah. The dogs shall eat Jezebel in the territory of Jezreel, and no one shall bury her." Then he opened the door and fled. (2 Kgs. 9:6–10)

There is no introduction of Jehu in the text other than his name (2 Kgs. 9:2). Another wrinkle is that the message above is expanded from the one Elisha instructed the prophet to give (9:3). Elisha's instructions encompassed only the first sentence. Did Elisha and God condone the violent acts Jehu is instructed to carry out? This question is beyond the scope of historical inquiry but adds to the mystery of what occurred.

Of course, coups happened occasionally in Israel, and military commanders like Jehu were usually the culprits. The text reports that Jehu first murdered both kings—Jehoram of Israel and Ahaziah of Judah—and all who were with them, then killed Jezebel and all of Ahab's descendants, including the children. Finally, he turned to all the Baal worshipers, tricking them into coming to Baal's temple for a worship and sacrifice service. Jehu then slaughtered them (10:18–27). After these events, Jehu took the throne of Israel for himself. Even to the most dedicated and zealous follower of God, Jehu's actions, based on God's orders, are theologically troubling, especially in a world where this kind of religious hatred continues. Notably, Jehu was not remembered as a good king when the biblical text assessed his kingship. He was also condemned by the prophet Hosea for his murderous actions (2 Kgs. 10:28–36; Hos. 1:3–4).[2]

Precisely, who was Jehu? No evidence was given other than his father's and grandfather's names; and his grandfather Nimshi is unknown except for that single mention. Tammi Schneider argues that Jehu was from the house of Omri and was determined to overthrow the two kings. She offers several reasons, including an Assyrian relief that refers to him as "son of Omri" and the peculiar prophecy given to him that was directed strictly to "the house of Ahab," not the ancestral house of Omri.[3] Her argument is intriguing. We do not know who Jehu was or where he came from. It is even unclear if he was from Israel or Judah since the attack on Aram was a joint Israel and Judah

---

2. No king of the Northern Kingdom is counted as worthy by the scribes; this may be why they condemned Jehu.

3. Tammi Schneider, "Did King Jehu Kill His Own Family?," *BAR* 21, no. 1 (January/February 1995): 26–33, 80.

operation. He could have been a commander from either country, either royal house, or unrelated to the two dynasties in any way.[4] His pedigree was not of interest to those who compiled the narratives.

Historically, the account of this massacre of the kings and their relatives is only in the biblical account. There are, however, two extrabiblical sources that, while not directly related to the massacre, help in understanding what occurred. Several sources refer to "Jehu, son of Omri," including the Black Obelisk of Shalmaneser III.[5] According to the Black Obelisk, in 841 BCE, Jehu paid tribute to Assyria shortly after becoming king of Israel.[6] This Assyrian record confirms the Bible's report that Jehu was the king of Israel. Also, the Tel Dan Stela adds to the understanding of the assassination. Most scholars agree that the stela was written in the first person by Hazael, king of Aram. The stela claims, in Hazael's voice, "[and I killed Jo]ram, son of A[hab,] King of Israel, and [I] killed [Ahazi]yahu, son of [Joram, kin]g of the house of David. . . ."[7] In other words, the Tel Dan Stela describes Hazael, not Jehu, as the murderer of Joram/Jehoram of Israel and Ahaziyahu/Ahaziah of Judah. Was the king of Aram the one who killed Jehoram and Ahaziah? Why does the Tel Dan Stela not mention Jehu or his part in the murders? Is the biblical account correct, or is this stela historically accurate?

So, which account is more trustworthy for historical reconstruction? Scholars weigh in on the different possibilities. André Lemaire proposes that the biblical account should be accepted, arguing that it was more contemporaneous with the event than the stela, which was part of Hazael's propaganda.[8] James Maxwell Miller and John H. Hayes argue that the inscription should be used for historical reconstruction since it was more contemporaneous with the

---

4. Bible scholars, almost exclusively, assume that Jehu was an Israelite, probably because he takes the throne in Samaria, but since he was in Samaria, the taking of that throne makes sense. He may have intended to also take the throne in Jerusalem. In short, we cannot assume he was definitely an Israelite without further evidence.

5. Three other Assyrian inscriptions refer to Jehu, 841 BCE, and "Jehu son of Omri": The Aleppo Fragment, in "Die Assur-Texte Salmanassars III (858–824)," *Die Welt des Orients* 1, no. 4 (1949): 255–71; the Kurba'il Statue, "The Kurba'il Statue of Shalmaneser III," *Iraq* 24 (1962): 90–115; and Fuad Safar, "A Further Text of Shalmaneser III," *Sumer* 7 (1951): 3–21.

6. "I received tribute of Jehu, of Bīt Ḫumrî [son of Omri]: silver, gold, a golden bowl, a golden goblet, golden cups, golden buckets, tin, a staff of the king's hand, and javelins": *COS*, 2:270; http://www.britishmuseum.org/research/collection_online/collection_object_details.aspx?objectId=367012&partId=1.

7. William Schniedewind, "Tel Dan Stela: New Light on Aramaic and Jehu's Revolt," *BASOR* 302 (1996): 77–78. Brackets indicate reconstruction by scholars. Many scholars have argued that the last part of line 11 can be reconstructed to read "[Jehu ru]led over Is[rael]," but the full reconstruction of Jehu's name here seems tentative and remains uncertain.

8. André Lemaire, "The Tel Dan Stela as a Piece of Royal Historiography," *JSOT* 23, no. 81 (1998): 11.

CHART 4: KINGS AFTER JEHU'S COUP (839–735 BCE)

Kings of Israel after 840	Kings of Judah after 840
Jehu 839–822	Athaliah (queen) 839–833
	House of Omri
	Joash/Jehoash 832–803
	House of David and Omri
Jehoahaz 821–805	
Joash 804–789	Amaziah 803–786
Jeroboam II 788–750	Uzziah/Azariah 785–742
	Jotham 742–735

actual events, and the biblical text was not recorded until years later.[9] William Schniedewind and Matthew Stith suggest a compromise between these two views. They propose that Jehu and Hazael formed an alliance, which resulted in the murders of the two kings and their families.[10] In short, Jehu had the help of the very king Israel and Judah were fighting against. Why would Hazael support Jehu? The first reason was to settle the current fighting and gain control of the entire region. The second was that Hazael needed Israel and possibly Judah's forces to prevent the further incursion of the Assyrians. What we do know is that in a few short years, Hazael would be the power in the region, and Jehu's status and Israel's territory are reported to have significantly diminished (2 Kgs. 10:32–33). In light of this proposal, it is certainly possible that this was the price Jehu paid for Hazael's aid in the murder conspiracy.[11]

The assassination of the two royal families caused abrupt changes in the government of both nations. Jehu took the throne in Israel. Since this was the third coup in Israel's history, they may have been more accustomed to such a

---

9. J. Maxwell Miller and John H. Hayes, *A History of Ancient Israel and Judah*, 2nd ed. (Westminster John Knox, 2006), 325.

10. Schniedewind ("Tel Dan Stela," 84) bases his conclusions on 1 Kgs. 19:15–18 as a non-Deuternomic piece. Stith notes that Hazael did not seem to continue the battle at Ramoth-Gilead after the coup, indicating complicity in the act: "Jehu," in *The New Interpreters Dictionary of the Bible*, ed. K. Sakenfeld et al. (Abingdon, 2008), 3:213.

11. Kyle Greenwood also argues for the alliance, "Late Tenth- and Ninth-Century Issues: Ahab Underplayed? Jehoshaphat Overplayed?," in *Ancient Israel's History: An Introduction to Issues and Sources*, ed. Bill Arnold and Richard Hess (Baker Academic, 2014), 316.

shake-up in the monarchy. Accustomed to peaceful successions, Judah experienced considerable turmoil, as reported in 2 Kings 11.

JUDAH, 839–744 BCE: UNCERTAINTY AND GROWTH

The biblical text states that Athaliah, the mother of the murdered Ahaziah, king of Judah, and an Omride by birth, took the throne in Jerusalem and "arose to destroy all the 'seed of the kingdom'" (2 Kgs. 11:1, my translation).[12] The phrase is odd in that it leaves her intention unclear. Did she intend to destroy David's house and establish the Omride dynasty in Judah? Did she intend to kill all the heirs except hers? Was she a coconspirator with Jehu and Hazael, or did she take the throne to prevent Jehu from moving south once Israel was secure? Her motivation is unknown, and so are the acts themselves. There is no further report that she actually carried out her plans to murder "the seed of the kingdom."

The Bible reports that Ahaziah's sister, Jehosheba/Jehoshabeath, took the young heir apparent, Joash (Ahaziah's son), and hid him from Jehu and Athaliah (2 Kgs. 11:2). Second Chronicles reports Jehosheba/Jehoshabeath was married to one of the priests, Johoiada, and the young heir was hidden in the temple (22:10–12). Was Ahaziah's sister also Athaliah's daughter? Again, this is beyond what the biblical text explains.[13] Their relationship is unknown. Yet, clearly, Queen Athaliah did more than pull off a palace coup: she reigned for six years, says 2 Kings 11:3. Judah was ruled by a non-Davidic queen; despite how the biblical narratives report her reign in a negative light, she must have had the support of others in the ruling class to remain on the throne for six years. Either way, an Omride queen reigned in Judah during this tumultuous time! She was the only woman to rule as monarch of either nation.

However, the hiding of the young heir signals some opposition to her reign and worries about the prince's safety. When Joash, the young heir, was seven, he was made king of Judah in 832 BCE, in a secret covenant by the priest

---

12. As stated in chap. 8, above, Athaliah's relationship to Omri and Ahab is unclear. If the dates for the kings are close to being correct, it is doubtful that she would be a daughter of Omri.

13. As noted above, some consider Athaliah to be Ahab and Jezebel's daughter, even though neither the biblical text nor any other source states that. This leads to problematic assumptions, as in the notes of a study Bible: "After the death of Ahaziah, king of Judah, Athaliah–just as ambitious and cruel as her mother[,] Jezebel–took over the kingdom by killing all remaining male members of the royal family." *The New Interpreter's Study Bible* (Abingdon, 2003), 542.

Jehoiada (2 Kgs. 11:4–12). Jehoiada then instituted a coup against Athaliah, who was then killed by the guards (11:13–16).

Joash's reign is known only from the biblical text, where he is remembered as a good king (12:2), who repaired the temple (12:4–16) and prevented an attack by Hazael of Aram, probably by becoming his vassal (12:17–18). Finally, Joash was killed by his servants (12:19–21), indicating ongoing instability in Jerusalem.

Joash was succeeded by his son Amaziah, who reigned for twenty-nine years, according to 2 Kings 14:1. He waged war on Israel and lost (14:8–14). Later, he was killed by a group plotting against him (14:17–20). The last four Judean monarchs were killed in coups, adding to the instability of Judah.

His son Azariah (Uzziah) succeeded his father and reigned for fifty-two years (15:1). Azariah, for part of his reign, was confined to a different house because he contracted leprosy (i.e., some skin disease; 15:5–6). Jotham served in his father's place when Azariah became ill and then reigned for sixteen years alone: their approximate dates of reign are sometimes shown as overlapping because of their coregency.[14]

As noted above, there are no extrabiblical records of this time in Judah's history. The biblical information for this period is itself slim and focused on the kings and their acts. All in all, the narratives of the kings of Judah and Israel in this period reflect the country's and region's instability under the shadow of Assyria's growing power.

The Assyrian Empire was trying to expand into the region but had not made it as far as Judah by the beginning of Jotham's coregency in 759 BCE. Shalmaneser III, king of the Neo-Assyrian Empire,[15] had attacked Aram (Syria) and the alliance of "twelve kings" earlier in his 849, 848, and 845 campaigns, but whether Israel and/or Judah participated in these battles is unclear. Since the Assyrians were interested in pushing into the region of Canaan, Israel was a prime target because of its control of the trade route, the Way of the Sea. Judah was less of a target since it was more isolated. Going by archaeological evidence, Israel Finkelstein explains that from the mid-ninth to the mid-eighth centuries (BCE), occupation of the hill country south of Jerusalem, the Beersheba Valley, and the Shephelah regions of Judah continued

---

14. See Miller and Hayes, *Ancient Israel and Judah*, 336–38. There is no extrabiblical information to aid in resolving the chronological issues of the Bible. Suffice it to say that son followed father during this period from 839 to 728; yet Judah experienced more instability than in earlier periods.

15. The Assyrian history, like other nations, has periods: The old Assyrian period, 2025–1378 BCE; the Middle period, 1365–934 BCE; and the Neo-Assyrian period, 911–609 BCE. In the Neo-Assyrian period, Assyria became the largest empire known in the Afro-Asiatic region till then.

to expand, and towns grew larger. They were fortified, indicating an expanding government structure.[16] Judah expanded its population and infrastructure despite the internal political instability in the wake of Jehu's murders. This growth and intentional fortification was at least in part in response to the growing threat of Aram and Assyria.

ISRAEL UNDER ATTACK (839–802 BCE)

The biblical account of King Jehu focuses primarily on the assassinations that placed him in power. According to the biblical text, his full reign lasted twenty-eight years (2 Kgs. 10:36), but the country was not wholly independent. As noted above, Shalmaneser III of Assyria fought several campaigns in the area. These campaigns were recorded on one of the best-preserved monuments of this ancient period, the Black Obelisk (fig. 9).[17] One of the reliefs portrays a king bowing in front of Shalmaneser with this inscription, "I received tribute of Jehu, of Bīt Ḫumrî [son of Omri]: silver, gold, a golden bowl, a golden goblet, golden cups, golden buckets, tin, a staff of the king's hand, and javelins."[18] If the obelisk accurately represents Jehu, this is the only known image of an Israelite king. It is unknown if the Black Obelisk was fact or propaganda; either way, Jehu, like Ahab before him, was known in the region as a player in the historical events of the day. The Bible does not record Jehu paying tribute to the Assyrians but states that he lost territory to Hazael of Aram (2 Kgs. 10:32–33).

Which is correct? It could be both. Paying tribute to prevent further attacks from Assyria and losing territory to Hazael are both possible. Shalmaneser III made two more campaigns into the area in 838 and 837. Then the Assyrian threat diminished for the remainder of Jehu's reign.

Jehu was followed by his son Jehoahaz in 821 BCE. The Assyrian threat had diminished, but Israel and Aram continued to battle for territory (2 Kgs. 13:3–4).[19] Then, after a long absence, Assyria reemerged under Adad-nirari III

---

16. Israel Finkelstein, "The Rise of Jerusalem and Judah," in *Jerusalem in the Bible and Archaeology: The First Temple Period*, ed. A. Vaughn and A. Killebrew, Society of Biblical Literature Symposium 18 (Brill, 2003), 92–95.

17. The Black Obelisk is in the British Museum: https://etc.worldhistory.org/photos/black-obelisk-of-shalmaneser-iii-british-museum/.

18. *COS*, 2:270.

19. Recently, Finkelstein and others who argue for the low chronology state that the destruction layers in Tel Rehov, Beth-shean, Taanach, and Megiddo should not be dated in the tenth century but instead attributed to the kingdom of Aram-Damascus during this later period. See Israel Finkelstein and Neil Silberman, *The Bible Unearthed: Archaeology's New Vision*

Figure 9. Depiction of King Jehu of Israel giving tribute to King Shalmaneser III of Assyria, on the Black Obelisk of Shalmaneser III from Nimrud (circa 827 BC) in the British Museum (London). (Courtesy of Steven G. Johnson)

with a campaign in 804–802 BCE, at the end of Jehoahaz's reign.[20] Jehoahaz must have died around the same time as this campaign, for his son Jehoash is listed on the Tel al-Rimah Stela as paying tribute to Adad-nirari III.[21] The strengthening of Assyrian control impacted Aram first because it sat between Assyria and Israel. Assyria needed to gain control of Aram before attacking Israel. Because Aram was busy in fighting Assyria, Israel recovered the land previously lost to it (13:22–25).[22] In summary, this period in Israel saw regional fights for territory, with occasional attempts by Assyria to take over the surrounding regions.

---

of Ancient Israel and the Origin of Its Sacred Texts (Free Press, 2001), 203. His arguments need to be taken seriously; but, as Grabbe notes, there is no doubt that Israel was at war with Aram, as reported in the biblical text; to say more about the extent of Aram's control over the region is unknown. See Lester Grabbe, *Ancient Israel: What Do We Know and How Do We Know It?* (T&T Clark, 2007), 147–48.

20. Assyria is probably "a savior" of Israel from attacks by Aram of 2 Kgs. 13:5.

21. "I received the tribute of Joash, the Samarian," in *COS*, 2:276; https://www.ancient pages.com/2022/02/22/stele-of-tell-al-rimah-and-deeds-of-assyrian-king-adad-nirari-against-rebellious-kings/.

22. Victor Matthews, *A Brief History of Ancient Israel* (Westminster John Knox, 2002), 70.

A PERIOD OF PEACE FOR ISRAEL AND JUDAH (788–750 BCE)

After these hostilities, Israel and Judah entered a stable period under Jeroboam II, son of Joash, in Israel and under Uzziah/Azariah in Judah. Assyria and Aram were weakened by internal political instability. Assyria could not enforce Israel's tribute payments. Aram could not hold the Israelite territory taken earlier. Jeroboam II of Israel retook the regions of the Transjordan and the northern sections of Israel previously lost to Aram (2 Kgs. 14:25). For approximately forty years, Israel and Judah were not troubled by Aram or Assyria.

Israel and Judah continued to grow and gain control of the region as in other periods of relative peace. Artifacts known as the Samaria ostraca confirm this.[23] Ostraca are broken pieces of pottery on which a scribe writes a receipt for goods.[24] Sixty-three wine and olive oil delivery receipts on broken pottery demonstrate vigorous trade in Israel.[25] The book of Amos also confirms the prosperity of Israel during this period. The prophet's primary complaint is the treatment of the poor by the rich (5:10–13). Nothing is known of Judah during this period because 2 Kings provides only the briefest of the formulaic measures of kings, though it is safe to assume it probably paralleled the growth of Israel since there were no outside threats.

ISRAEL AND JUDAH IN THE ASSYRIAN ADVANCE (745–736 BCE)

The fate of Israel and Judah would not rest in their own hands. In Assyria, Tiglath-Pileser III came to power in 745 BCE. He reversed the weakened state of Assyria and began his bid for control of the Afro-Asiatic area. Israel and Judah were spared for a time as Tiglath-Pileser III turned his attention first to the conquest of Babylon and other territories to the east and north.

---

23. A total of 102 ostraca were discovered in Samaria, but only 63 of them are readable. Scott B. Noegel, "The Samaria Ostraca," in *The Ancient Near East: Historical Sources in Translation*, ed. Mark W. Chavalas (Blackwell, 2006), 396–99.

24. George Andrew Reisner, *Israelite Ostraca from Samaria* (Harvard University Press, 1951), available on the Harvard Library Viewer, http://iiif.lib.harvard.edu/manifests/view/drs:13110600$39i.

25. Amihai Mazar, *Archaeology of the Land of the Bible: 10,000–586 B.C.E.* (Doubleday, 1990), 409–10. These ostraca contain theophoric names, with both the *-yw* and *-baal* suffixes, demonstrating that despite the report of Jehu's removal of the Baal cults, worship of this deity clearly continued.

CHART 5: KINGS OF ISRAEL AND JUDAH (788–722 BCE)

Kings of Israel	Kings of Judah
Jeroboam II 788–750	Uzziah/Azariah 785–742
Zechariah 750 (reigned six months)	
murdered by	
Shallum 749 (reigned one month)	
murdered by	
Menahem 749–737	
Pekahiah 736–735	Jotham 742–735
murdered by	
Pekah 735–731	Jehoahaz/Ahaz I 735–728
Hoshea 730–722	
Fall of Israel	

At the same time when Assyria was rising, Israel was experiencing its own political turmoil, possibly caused by disagreements about addressing the Assyrian threat.[26] Ahab had stood with the other countries in the region against Assyria. Jehu, Jehoahaz, and Joash of Israel solved the Assyrian issue by being loyal to the growing Assyrian Empire. The question was what Jeroboam's heirs would do in the face of another Assyrian threat.

Upon the death of Jeroboam II of Israel in 750 BCE, the monarchy of Israel descended into turmoil. Jeroboam's son Zechariah lasted only six months, being murdered by Shallum, son of Jabesh (2 Kgs. 15:10). Shallum was not a royal, so he likely was an army officer. He held the throne for one month, only to be killed by Menahem, who then became king. Menahem was listed in 2 Kings only as the son of Gadi, indicating that he was not a royal. King Menahem reigned until 737 BCE.

Tiglath-Pileser III returned to Aram and Israel in 738–737 BCE. His annals record tribute collections from Rezin of Damascus and Menahem of Israel.[27] So 2 Kings 15:19 reports, "King Pul of Assyria came against the land; Menahem

---

26. This was also noted by John Bright in *A History of Israel*, 3rd ed. (Westminster, 1981), 273.
27. *COS*, 2:285, The Annals; and 2:287, The Iran Stele: https://armstronginstitute.org/114-iran-stele-a-warning-to-biblical-samaria, 2018.

gave Pul a thousand talents of silver, so that he might help him confirm his hold on the royal power."[28] Thus Menahem adopted the approach taken by the Jehu dynasty and paid heavy tribute to prevent military action and secure his kingship. Shortly after that, he was succeeded by his son, Pekahiah. Two years later, according to 2 Kings 15:23–25, Pekahiah was assassinated by Pekah. He also was not a royal.[29] The kingdom of Israel was facing instability from the inside and, at the same time, the external threat from Assyria.

JUDAH ATTACKED BY ISRAEL AND ARAM (736–732 BCE)

Pekah of Israel joined Rezin of Damascus (Aram) in a plan to defeat or at least repel Assyria. In preparation, the two pressed Judah to join them. Jotham of Judah did not want to participate. Pekah and Rezin decided to attack Judah and remove Jotham from the throne (2 Kgs. 16:5, Isa. 7:6). By the time of the attack, Jotham of Judah had died, and his son Jehoahaz/Ahaz I had ascended to the throne. This was the first time in the long history of Israel and Judah that one turned on the other and attempted a full-blown attack. Several biblical accounts of this period tell a different story about the reasons for the attack and the ensuing events in Judah (2 Kgs. 16:5–9; Isa. 6:1–12:6; 2 Chr. 28:5–21). The 2 Kings account states that Pekah and Rezin were unsuccessful in their attempt to capture Jerusalem and the king (2 Kgs. 16:5–7). But 2 Chronicles states that Judah *was* defeated and thousands were killed or taken captive (28:5–7). The book of Isaiah reflects the prophet's advice to the king (7:1–15). At least it is clear that Israel and Aram staged an attack, threatening Judah and the current king. All the texts report this as a significant attack on Judah.

With few options, Ahaz of Judah appealed to Tiglath-Pileser of Assyria and sent tribute in exchange for help. Tiglath-Pileser's annals report that "Jehoahaz [Ahaz] of Judea paid tribute," but the timing of the tribute is unknown (cf. 2 Kgs. 16:8; 2 Chr. 28:16–21).[30] It would seem likely the tribute paid for Assyria's help when Israel and Aram attacked Judah (ca. 736–732 BCE).

---

28. The "he" here is "Pul, king of Assyria," presumably a shortened name for Tiglath-Pileser III.

29. The chronology listed in the biblical text is difficult to reconcile: 2 Kgs. 15:32 states that in the second year of Pekah, Jotham became king of Judah. The period after the reign of Jeroboam II to the end of Israel's existence was a tumultuous time, but it is doubtful that Pekah became king any earlier than 735 BCE. Either the Israelite king or the regnal year listed here is incorrect. Other events and sources have contributed to the determination of the order of the kings by scholars. See H. J. Cook, "Pekah," *VT* 14 (1964): 124.

30. *COS*, 2:289. Since this is a summary inscription, it is not clear when the tribute was paid. It could have been during the Syro-Ephraimite crisis (ca. 736–732 BCE) or after the destruction of Aram and the attacks on Israel.

The response of the Assyrians permanently changed the course of all three nations—Israel, Judah, and Aram. According to 2 Kings, the Assyrian king destroyed Aram and killed Rezin, the king of Aram (2 Kgs. 16:9). Pekah of Israel was forced to become an involuntary vassal of Assyria. Since Aram was destroyed, Israel now shared a border with Assyria. Ahaz of Judah became a voluntary vassal of Assyria. As 2 Kings reports, Ahaz then traveled to Damascus to meet the Assyrian king; he returned and built an altar presumably to Anu, or another one of the Assyrian gods, in the temple in Jerusalem. Ahaz moved the altar to *Adoni* to the side of the temple and ordered the priests to sacrifice on the altar he built to the Assyrian gods (16:15–18).

The 2 Chronicles' account of Ahaz is even worse, portraying him as despicable. It contradicts the 2 Kings record. Ahaz is portrayed as a Baal worshiper even before the coalition threat and someone who "sacrificed his children to the fire," a reference to child sacrifice (2 Chr. 28:2–4). The book also states that Judah lost to Pekah and Rezin, and some citizens were deported to Damascus and Samaria. Others were murdered (2 Chr. 28:5–7). At the same time, Edom and Philistia also attacked Judah (2 Chr. 28:16–18). Ahaz asked for help, but in the 2 Chronicles account, Tiglath-Pileser refused, even after Ahaz gave him the temple treasures (2 Chr. 28:20–21).

In contrast, Isaiah 7–8 portrays Ahaz as a frightened king, unsure of what to do. There is no indication in Isaiah that the king either sought the aid of Assyria or built an altar to an Assyrian god. Indeed, he acted like the newly crowned monarch. Ahaz lacked experience and was unsure what action to take. Isaiah advised the young king not to join the coalition with Israel and Aram and not to reach out to the Assyrians for help.

Which of the narratives about Ahaz is accurate? A ruling principle of historical writing is to rule out the most extreme sources and prioritize the accounts written closest to the time of the events. Using these criteria, the account of the Chronicler is extreme and written during the Persian period (539–330 BCE). On both criteria, the Chronicler is easier to discount. The report in 2 Kings matches biblical and extrabiblical information about the destruction of Aram. This account would also match Isaiah's advice and the young king's reaction to ignore Isaiah and instead to reach out to Assyria. Both these accounts were probably written in some form close to the events. As to Ahaz's visit to Assyria, there is no additional evidence to confirm this event, nor were visits of conquered kings required as part of the usual Assyrian policy.

Simply put, we do not know the reason for the joint Israel and Aram attack on Jerusalem or even all the nations involved. One reasonable explanation was that if Judah was loyal to Assyria, Israel and Aram did not want Judah to attack from the south while Assyria approached from the north. Clearly, the attack by Israel and Aram was a serious threat to Judah and marked the end of any alliance between Judah and Israel. But the whole incident remains shrouded in mystery. In the wake of growing Assyrian power, the countries of Canaan tried to strengthen their positions for the coming wars and failed.

THE END OF THE NORTHERN KINGDOM OF ISRAEL (732–722 BCE)

The next move belonged to Tiglath-Pileser, and it came quickly. In the 734–732 BCE campaign, he conquered all of Aram and annexed it into the growing Assyrian Empire.[31] He then moved on to Israel. His annals state:

> The land of Bit-Humria [House of Omri, Israel]; [. . . its] "auxiliary army," [.] all of its people, [. . .] [I/they killed] Peqah, their king, and I installed Hoshea [as king] over them. I received from them 10 talents of gold, [1,000?] talents of silver, [with] their [possessions,] and [I car]ried them [to Assyria].[32]

He also attacked some Philistine cities, thus controlling the Way of the Sea trade route and any access these countries might have to Egypt. The biblical account is slightly different from the annals of Tiglath-Pileser, claiming the Assyrian king captured "Ijon, Abel-beth-maacah, Janoah, Kedesh, Hazor, Gilead, and Galilee, all the land of Naphtali, and he carried the people captive to Assyria" (2 Kgs. 15:29).[33] It also states it was Hoshea who killed Pekah and then became king of Israel (15:30), but there is no mention that the Assyrian king was involved.

Exile was how Tiglath-Pileser punished the leaders of captured territories and ensured that they caused no more trouble. Indeed, Aram (Syria) received the brunt of Tiglath-Pileser's actions in this campaign, but Israel also lost territory.

Hoshea would remain king of a smaller Israel for nine years. Tiglath-Pileser III died in 728 BCE and was succeeded by Shalmaneser V, who lived

---

31. *COS*, 2:286. Calah [Nimrod] Annal [year] 23: line 1–line 18.

32. *COS*, 2:286 and 2:288; both are fragmentary. Miller and Hayes (*Ancient Israel and Judah*, 383) suggest that the inscription reads "they" instead of "I"; this implies that the people of Israel killed their king.

33. K. Younger argues that Tiglath-pileser III took over and deported citizens from Galilee to other parts of Assyria and took part of the Israelite army to fight for him. Younger, "The Deportations of the Israelites," *JBL* 117, no. 2 (1998): 214.

for five years, until 722. His short reign may account for the poor record of his campaigns. Babylonian sources credited him with ravaging Israel (Samaria) once and for all, but no additional information exists.[34] His son, Sargon II, also claimed to have been the one to take Samaria at the beginning of his reign, vanquishing Israel for good and becoming king of Samaria in approximately 721–720 BCE.[35]

> [The inhabitants of Sa]merina who agreed [and plotted] with a king [hostile to] me, not to do service and not to bring tribute and who did battle, I fought against them with the power of the great gods, my lords. I counted as spoil 27,280 people together with their chariots, and gods, in which they trusted. I formed a unit of 200 of [their] chariots for my royal force. I settled the rest of them in the midst of Assyria. I repopulated Samerina [Samaria] more than before. I brought into it people from countries conquered at my hands. I appointed my eunuch over them. And I counted them as Assyrians.[36]

The dual claims from the two kings sparked debate over the number of campaigns the Assyrians waged against Israel.[37] Second Kings 17:4 reports that Hoshea of Israel tried to align with the Pharaoh while a vassal of Shalmaneser. The Assyrian king then took Hoshea captive, possibly in 725 BCE (cf. Hos.7:11).[38] This information fits the above inscription attributed to Sargon II, where the "inhabitants of Samaria plotted with a king hostile to me [and] . . . not to bring tribute." There is no easy resolution to which Assyrian ruler struck the final blow that brought about the fall of Israel. Either way, the Assyrian rulers were determined to control the entire region. They waged several campaigns, each involving the annexing of territory and the deportation of part of the population of Aram (Syria) and Israel (Samaria).[39] The biblical account states that the king of Assyria, Shalmaneser, besieged Samaria for three years (2 Kgs. 17:5). The entire area north of Judah was part of the

---

34. A. K. Grayson, *ABC*, 73.

35. *COS*, 2:293. This text from the annals of Sargon II, on the walls of his palace, is debated because it is broken. "[the Samar]ians . . . . . . who c]ause my victory. [. . .] carried off as spoil. 50 chariots for my royal force [I . . .]. The remainder is conjecture based on 2 Kgs. 17:6.

36. *COS*, 2:295–96. This is a translation of the fragmentary Nimrud Prisms D & E.

37. Several scholars argue for two campaigns: Bob Becking, *The Fall of Samaria: A Historical and Archaeological Study* (Brill, 1985), 38; and Ron Tappy, *The Archaeology of Israelite Samaria*, vol. 2, *The Eighth Century B.C.E.*, Harvard Semitic Studies 50 (Scholars Press, 2001), 558–75. Christine Tetley argues for one campaign, "The Date of Samaria's Fall as a Reason for Rejecting the Hypothesis of Two Conquests," *Catholic Biblical Quarterly* 64 (2002): 62.

38. Miller and Hayes, *Ancient Israel and Judah*, 386.

39. At this point, names assigned by an empire such as Syria (Aram) and Samaria will appear more often in the literature. But in the late Persian period, the names given by the empire are supplanting the older names.

Assyrian Empire by 720 BCE. The northern kingdom of Israel was taken in 722 BCE and became part of the Assyrian Empire.

THE LASTING IMPACT OF THE ASSYRIAN EMPIRE (745–609 BCE)

At its height, the Assyrian Empire controlled most of the Afro-Asiatic region, from the Persian Gulf to the Nile (map 9). Assyrian policy was to deport captives from a single nation to multiple places throughout the empire. This was done for several reasons. First, dividing the people made it harder for them to organize and pose a threat of rebellion. Second, people were sent to rebuild lands destroyed in the conquest and to provide farm labor to support the empire. Third, people were needed to bolster border-city populations and thus to protect the most vulnerable places from attack.[40] Finally, some captives were conscripted into the Assyrian army.[41] The annals of the Assyrian kings indicate that the people taken from conquered nations were treated not as prisoners but as Assyrian citizens.[42] This act was designed to destroy former national loyalty and obliterate memory of the country of one's origin. The Bible reports that the citizens of Israel were sent to Halah, Gozan, and cities of the Medes (2 Kgs. 17:6). The Assyrian records do not record where the people of Israel were taken. However, Bob Becking notes that letters from all of these regions contain West Semitic personal names, indicating a wide dispersion of the people of Aram (Syria) and Israel.[43] Second Kings 17:24–41 and various Assyrian records also report that others from across the empire were brought to settle in Samaria.[44] The biblical text says little about the people brought to Samaria except for their worship of their own gods along with *Adoni* (2 Kgs. 17:24–34). This behavior would make sense for people resettled from other areas.

One additional policy of the Assyrians deserves note here. One way the Assyrians built a world empire was to adopt a single language for communication: Aramaic.[45] In an inscription discovered in the fortress of Sargon II, this feat is relayed in Sargon's voice:

---

40. B. Oded, *Mass Deportations and Deportees in the Neo-Assyrian Empire* (Reichert, 1979), 67–74.

41. Younger, "Deportations of the Israelites," 219. The annals of Sargon II also state that some were conscripted.

42. Oded, *Mass Deportations and Deportees*, 81–85. See the inscription of Sargon above.

43. Becking, *Fall of Samaria*, 61–73.

44. N. Na'aman and R. Zadock, "Sargon II's Deportations to Israel and Philistia (716–708 B.C.E.)," *Journal of Cuneiform Studies* 40, no. 1 (1988): 36–46; and R. Steiner, "The Aramaic Text in Demotic Script: The Liturgy of a New Year's Festival Imported from Bethel to Syene by Exiles from Rash," *Journal of the American Oriental Society* 111, no. 2 (1991): 362–63.

45. William Schniedewind, *How the Bible Became a Book* (Cambridge University Press, 2004), 45.

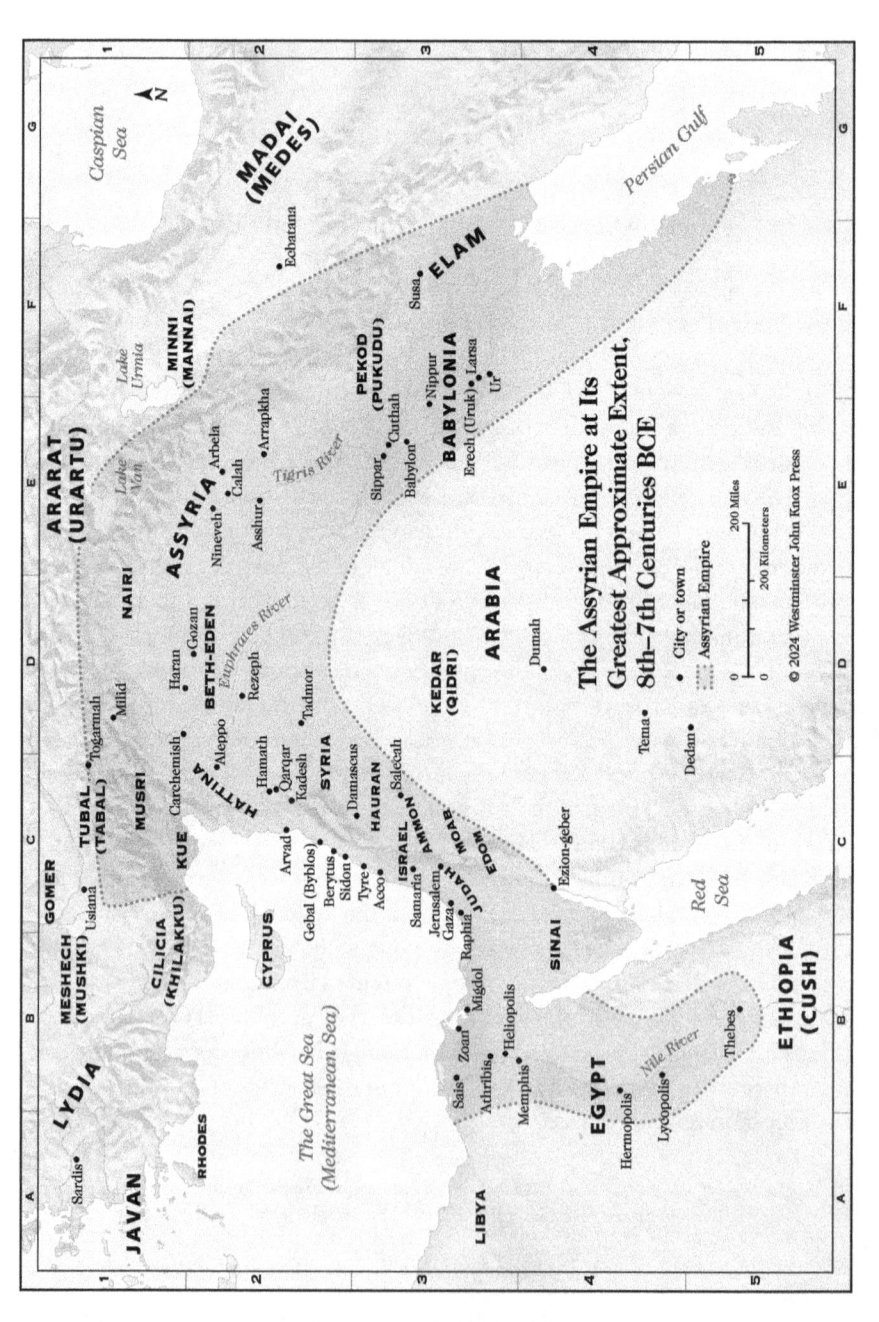

Map 9. The Assyrian Empire at its greatest approximate extent. (Courtesy of Westminster John Knox Press)

> Peoples of the four regions of the world, of foreign tongue and divergent speech, dwellers of mountain and lowland, all that were ruled by the light of the gods, the lord of all, I carried off at Assur, my lord's, command, by the might of my scepter. I (made them of one mouth) and settled them therein. Assyrians, fully competent to teach them how to fear god and the king, I dispatched to them as scribes and sheriffs (superintendents). (*ARAB* 2:65–66; cf. 2:44)[46]

This act spread writing throughout the empire, including in Israel and Judah. The forced settlers learned a common language, at least for commerce and military functions. These changes impacted the region by making Aramaic, an Afro-Asiatic language that shared much in common with Hebrew, the language of the larger empire.[47]

The Assyrian attacks ended the kingdom of Israel in the north forever. Judah alone remained. Yet the name "Israel" did not cease with the demise of the country. After losing the northern kingdom of Israel, the name "Israel" was used in multiple ways. It references the former Northern Kingdom (2 Kgs. 21:2; 2 Chr. 30:6; Ezek. 9:9; Jer. 3:18). It is also a synonym for the southern kingdom of Judah after the fall of the Northern Kingdom in 722 BCE (2 Chr. 35:25; Isa. 1:3), as well as for both the kingdoms, as in Ezekiel. 37:16. Isaiah and Jeremiah used the phrase "God of Israel" to refer to God more than fifty times. To further add to the confusion, Isaiah 40–66 and Ezekiel sometimes used the word "Israel" to refer to the deportees from both Israel and the later ones from Judah. Finally, the book of Ezra uses "Israel" exclusively for the Judeans exiled to Babylon in the sixth century BCE and "Judeans" for those not deported. Two things are clear from these observations. The name "Israel" did not disappear with the loss of the northern territory. Second, from 722 BCE forward, it is more challenging to discern the meaning of "Israel" in the later texts.

The physical nation of Israel ceased in the ancient period. While the nation of Judah survived the Assyrians, and communities who worship *Adoni* persisted for centuries in the region of Canaan after 722 BCE, there was no independent Israel after 722 BCE (until 1948).[48] However, the name never ceased to be used. Modern Israel was established as a country in 1948, almost 2,700 years later, using the ancient name. So, the name "Israel" is not monolithic.

---

46. Sargon II, in *Ancient Records of Assyria and Babylonia*, vol. 2, *Ancient Records of Assyria from Sargon to the End*, ed. Daniel David Luckenbill (University of Chicago Press, 1926–27), #122 on 2:65–66; cf. #86 on 2:44, https://isac.uchicago.edu/sites/default/files/uploads/shared/docs/ancient_records_assyria2.pdf.

47. Schniedewind, *Bible Became a Book*, 65.

48. First Maccabees 13:41 adds to this confusion by naming the nation they established as Israel, but it is located in the Judean territory.

It has as many meanings as the person or groups who use it. Preachers and teachers should be careful to precisely define what is meant when using the term "Israel" in teaching and preaching.

SUMMARY

There was a lot of change from 840 to 722 BCE. The early period saw local fights over land and times of peace and prosperity. But by 722, Aram (Syria) and Israel were destroyed, subsumed by Assyria. This period also marks the first scattering of the people who worship *Adoni* beyond their borders. In 722, Assyria was in firm control of the Way of the Sea, at least to the Philistine border. Judah was a voluntary vassal, with Assyria as its closest neighbor to the north. The northern kingdom of Israel was now part of Assyria. Israel and Judah went from prosperity to control by an outside empire, ending in Israel's destruction. For Judah, this would be the first but not the last time the nation would tilt from stability to subjugation.

10

Judah under Assyrian Domination (722–639 BCE)

The previous chapter ended with Aram (Syria) and Israel destroyed and Judah under the control of Assyria. The Israelites either became hostages, refugees, or, if they remained in their homes, citizens of the Assyrian Empire. Judah now shared a northern border with Assyria and was flooded with refugees from the areas in the north.[1] During this time, Judah had three kings.

CHART 6: KINGS OF JUDAH (727–642 BCE)

Hezekiah	727–699
Manasseh	698–644
Amon	643–642

JUDAH UNDER HEZEKIAH (727–699 BCE)

Hezekiah came to the throne in Judah at a difficult time. According to Assyrian records, Sargon II campaigned twice in the region (719–718 and 712–711 BCE).[2] Judah may have been part of these military actions, but it is not

---

1. Megen Broshi, "The Expansion of Jerusalem in the Reigns of Hezekiah and Manasseh," *IEJ* 26 (1976): 21–26; Israel Finkelstein and Neil Silberman, "Temple and Dynasty: Hezekiah and the Remaking of Judah and the Rise of Pan-Israelite Ideology," *JSOT* 30, no. 3 (2006): 266.
2. Some scholars, such as Miller and Hayes, argue for two attacks against Judah, the first in 712–11; then in 701 BCE, against Hezekiah; see J. Maxwell Miller and John H. Hayes, *A History of Ancient Israel and Judah*, 2nd ed. (Westminster John Knox, 2006), 404–6. Evidence

definitive. Sargon remained in control of Judah and the entire region until he died in 705 BCE. Despite the Assyrian threat, Judah entered a period of growth after the fall of Israel in 722 BCE.

Archaeologists note that Jerusalem grew by almost 200 percent to a population of ten to twelve thousand, and the city gained new "suburbs" on a second hill, fortified by a new broad wall, in the years after the fall of Israel (map 10).[3] The Siloam (Hezekiah's) tunnel was constructed to provide a secure water source inside the city during a siege.[4] Monumental inscriptions show King Hezekiah's success and give archaeologists more information than in the prior periods.[5] In the region of Judah, archaeologists have found many carved seals and seal impressions (bullae) from this time period. These were used for letters and were impressed in wet clay jars to indicate the owner of the food stores.[6] These discoveries indicate a successful and growing Judah. One of those impressions in clay was inscribed, "Belonging to Hezekiah, [son of Ahaz,] king of Judah," and was discovered in the royal section of Jerusalem called the Ophel, or city of David.[7] This important finding is the first verifiable evidence of Hezekiah and confirms his existence and position as king.[8]

Besides seals, the appearance of inscriptions and ostraca also increased significantly during this period, all indicating growth in Judah's culture, literacy, and status. The seals and seal impressions have varying degrees of artistry, suggesting that the wealthy and merchant classes used them. Also, seals of previous periods in the region often used symbols, but these have only letters, indicating that more of the population understood the alphabet.[9] This suggests increased functional literacy rates among the people in the area.[10] In

---

clearly shows a campaign against the Philistine Ashdod in 712–11, but Judah is not mentioned, so no clear support has been found for this point.

3. Hillel Geva, "Western Jerusalem at the End of the First Temple Period," in *Jerusalem in Bible and Archaeology: The First Temple Period*, ed. Andrew Vaughn and Ann Killebrew (SBL Press, 2003), 202–4.

4. Megalim Institute, "Hezekiah's Tunnel," video, 2014, https://www.youtube.com/watch?v=RI3t80ZSg6M.

5. Finkelstein and Silberman, "Temple and Dynasty," 264.

6. N. Avigad, "The Contribution of Hebrew Seals to an Understanding of Israelite Religion and Society," in *Ancient Israelite Religion*, ed. P. Miller et al. (Fortress, 1987), 195–208.

7. Robin Ngo, "King Hezekiah in the Bible: Royal Seal of Hezekiah Comes to Light," *Bible History Daily*, 2025, https://www.biblicalarchaeology.org/daily/news/king-hezekiah-in-the-bible-royal-seal-of-hezekiah-comes-to-light/.

8. Two other seals with the name of Hezekiah are known but came from private collections. Seals in private collections carry a high probability of being forgeries so are not usually recognized for historical verification. Ngo, "King Hezekiah."

9. William Schniedewind, *How the Bible Became a Book* (Cambridge University Press, 2004), 70–73.

10. Richard Hess, "Questions of Reading and Writing in Ancient Israel," *BBR* 19 (2009): 1–9.

other words, there were a few fully literate scribes, but other people, probably for commercial purposes, had a rudimentary understanding of reading and possibly writing. This was a significant change from the past, when any form of writing belonged to the learned scribes.

It was not only the capital of Jerusalem that grew. Israel Finkelstein reports, "There is good reason to suggest that in the years before Sennacherib's campaign (701 BCE), Judah obtained its maximal territorial expansion and unprecedented population density."[11] Royal agricultural production grew. The proof was the discovery of mass-produced pottery with the seal impression "[belonging] to the king" in several Judean towns. These jars are evidence of national stores of supplies. There was also large-scale olive production in Tell Beit Mirsim and Beth-Shemesh.[12] Judah went from being the smaller sister of Israel to becoming a regional state, with more fortifications and a national distribution system for agricultural products.

The country's growth is apparent. What is not as clear is what caused this rapid expansion. Megen Broshi, followed many years later by Israel Finkelstein and Neil Silberman, argued that the growth resulted from the influx of refugees from Israel, escaping to Judah. This event not only changed the size of Judah but also changed religious practices and the shape of the biblical text.[13] William M. Schneidewind adds, "Undoubtedly, many of the refugees from the north were elites, who most reflected the region's cultural diversity and economic prosperity. They invaded the culturally isolated, rural south and brought with them the social values of the 'city.'"[14] Other scholars refute this explanation, stating the lack of written mention of refugees in the biblical text or Assyrian documents. They argue that the growth was more gradual, possibly because Judah was now part of the Assyrian Empire, and the empire facilitated trade among nations. Hence, the growth was the result of Assyrian orders.[15] Given the evidence at this time, it is impossible to pinpoint the growth to a single period or factor. All these factors probably contributed to the nation's growth.

---

11. Finkelstein and Silberman, "Temple and Dynasty," 264.
12. Israel Finkelstein and N. Na'aman, "The Judahite Shephelah in the Late 8th and Early 7th Centuries BCE," *Tel Aviv* 31 (2004): 74.
13. Broshi, "Expansion of Jerusalem," 21–26; Finkelstein and Silberman, "Temple and Dynasty," 266.
14. William Schniedewind, *Bible Became a Book*, 107.
15. N. Na'aman, "When and How Did Jerusalem Become a Great City? The Rise of Jerusalem as Judah's Premier City in the Eighth-Seventh Centuries B.C.E.," *BASOR* 347 (2007): 47. Israel Finkelstein directly disputes the claims of Na'aman, "The Settlement History of Jerusalem in the Eighth and Seventh Centuries BCE," *Revue biblique* 115, no. 4 (2008): 499–515. Guillaume argues that the growth was even later, after 701; Philippe Guillaume, "Jerusalem 720–705 BCE: No Flood of Israelite Refugees," *Scandinavian Journal of the Old Testament* 22, no. 2 (2008): 207.

It is also challenging to assess Hezekiah's allegiances during the early part of his reign. The Assyrian ruler, Sargon II, campaigned in the area often (720–719, 716–715, and 712–711 BCE). The Bible does not mention these campaigns. James Maxwell Miller and John H. Hayes believe that during the early years of his reign, Hezekiah was cooperating with Assyria, possibly lending military aid in the 720–719 campaign, and after that, was probably "nominally in control of the entire Philistine region, minus Ashkelon."[16] One interpretation of this expansion is that Hezekiah was rewarded for his loyalty with more territory.

Second Chronicles 32 says that Hezekiah rebuilt the walls damaged years earlier and provided secure access to water inside the cities of Judah (32:2–8). These construction projects took years of planning and work and were confirmed by archaeological discoveries in the city of David area of Jerusalem (map 10).[17] It would have been almost impossible to fortify more of Jerusalem and secure this water source without the Assyrian Empire's approval. These acts would have been seen as open rebellion without such approval. The discovery of "*lmlk*," "[belonging] to the king," on storage jars may indicate a stockpiling of supplies.[18] Most scholars argue that these actions demonstrate Hezekiah's preparation for war against Assyria.

The motivation for Hezekiah's early cooperation with the empire is unknown, but it allowed Judah to amass wealth and fortify its cities without interference from the Assyrians (2 Chr. 32:5–6, 28–29). Was Hezekiah secretly preparing for a revolt against Assyria? Or was he a loyal vassal king to the Assyrians as he oversaw the growth in his part of the empire? Some scholars have proposed that Hezekiah was part of a multicountry secret revolt.[19] Were he and other leaders working with Assyria and at the same time planning their exit?

One possible clue is the visit of the envoys of King Merodach-baladan II of Babylon described in 2 Kings (20:12–19; cf. Isa. 39:1–8). He was king of Babylon in 721–710 BCE, was driven from his throne, then regained the throne for 703–702 BCE. Jimmy J. M. Roberts argues the visit was during Merodach-baladan's second reign and that the "underlying goal was probably to confirm his [Hezekiah's] continued participation in the anti-Assyrian league that included Babylonia, the Aramaean and Chaldean tribes, the Arabs, and the Elamites to the east and south of Assyria, and the Syrian

---

16. Miller and Hayes, *Ancient Israel and Judah*, 405.

17. Amihai Mazar, *Archaeology of the Land of the Bible: 10,000–586 B.C.E.* (Doubleday, 1990), 418.

18. Miller and Hayes, *Ancient Israel and Judah*, 413; Finkelstein and Silberman, "Temple and Dynasty," 264. Both works express similar doubts about the exact conclusions that can be drawn from the existence of these jars.

19. Victor Matthews, *A Brief History of Ancient Israel* (Westminster John Knox, 2002), 80–81, for instance.

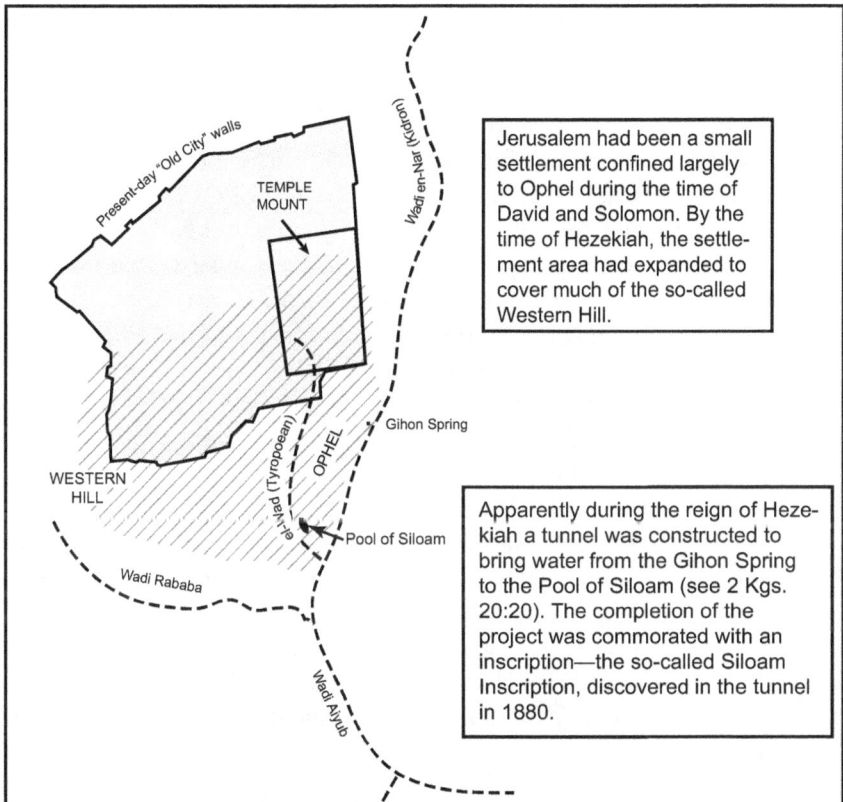

Map 10. Jerusalem at the time of Hezekiah. (Courtesy of Westminster John Knox Press)

[Aramaean]-Palestinian states and Nubian Egypt in the west."[20] According to Roberts's theory, these countries held by the Assyrians worked together to overthrow their overlord. Lester L. Grabbe argues against this theory, saying this alliance was too large, and the distance from Babylon to Jerusalem makes the envoys' visit improbable.[21] This may be the case. However, Miller and Hayes do note that several Philistine city-states worked with Hezekiah, as did Egypt.[22] Thus, all evidence points to King Hezekiah as being, at least, in a coalition with these closer neighbors. Whether the alliance included the

---

20. J. J. M. Roberts, *First Isaiah*, Hermeneia (Fortress, 2015), 488–89.
21. Lester Grabbe, *Ancient Israel: What Do We Know and How Do We Know It?* (T&T Clark, 2007), 198. He could be right; I am not arguing for the historicity of the visit, only that it indicates collusion among the nations held in the grip of Assyria.
22. Miller and Hayes, *Ancient Israel and Judah*, 415.

eastern countries like Babylon is unknown. What is undeniably clear was the growth and fortification of Judah and the amassing of supplies throughout the nation.

From the biblical perspective, the kingdom's growth was secondary to Hezekiah's religious reforms. Both 2 Kings and 2 Chronicles speak of these reforms as the first acts of Hezekiah (2 Kgs. 18:1–4; 2 Chr. 29:1–36). If Hezekiah was preparing for battle against the Assyrians, these cultic reforms and a return to God may have been part of that preparation, a pattern that appears in the book of Judges. In Judges, a new leader called a judge would then judge the people and bring them back to God before going into battle against the enemy. The biblical writers remembered Hezekiah as one who "removed the high places, broke down the pillars, and cut down the sacred pole" (forbidden worship outside the temple) (2 Kgs. 18:4).

Judah grew in population, agricultural production, and economic power during the reign of Hezekiah. While the cause can't be definitively identified, this growth was likely the result of the influx of refugees from Israel and of Judah's participation in the commercial opportunities of the Assyrian Empire. This growth perhaps took place with Assyrian approval in the early years, but later, it may have become preparation for a revolt without Assyrian knowledge. The religious reforms of Hezekiah could have been part of this preparation, following the earlier pattern in Israel and Judah of religious reform and revival before war.

THE ASSYRIAN ATTACK ON JUDAH IN 701 BCE

The Assyrian king, Sargon II, died in Anatolia in 705 BCE. The monarchs of territories conquered by the Assyrians, including Hezekiah, saw it as an opportunity to rebel and probably stopped paying tribute and taxes. Sennacherib came to the throne in 705 BCE. Unfortunately for them, he was as powerful as his father. He first turned his attention to Babylon, quickly regaining control and replacing the king with one he chose.[23] In 701 BCE, he turned westward to Judah and Egypt. The 2 Kings account states, "King Sennacherib of Assyria came up against all the fortified cities of Judah and captured them" (18:13). King Hezekiah tried to appease Sennacherib:

> King Hezekiah of Judah sent to the king of Assyria at Lachish, saying, "I have done wrong; withdraw from me; whatever you impose on me I will bear." The king of Assyria demanded of King Hezekiah of

---

23. *COS*, 2:300.

Judah three hundred talents of silver and thirty talents of gold. Hezekiah gave him all the silver that was found in the house of [*Adoni*] and in the treasuries of the king's house. At that time Hezekiah stripped the gold from the doors of the temple of [*Adoni*] and from the doorposts that King Hezekiah of Judah had overlaid and gave it to the king of Assyria. (18:14–16)[24]

However, this did not satisfy the Assyrian king. Sennacherib's officials appeared in Jerusalem and refused to negotiate with the Judean king (18:17–36).

The Assyrian records also cover the regional attack in 701 BCE. They first tell of the fate of the cities in Philistia, most of which surrendered to head off an attack.[25] Then the kings of Egypt and Ethiopia came to the aid of the countries of Canaan (Syria [Aram]-Palestine) and were defeated at Eltekeh in western Judah, confirming a coalition among the nations.[26] Turning to Judah, the records of Sennacherib claim to have "besieged forty-six fortified walled cities and the surrounding smaller towns[,] which were without number."[27] Even if that is an exaggeration, Judah was severely damaged. Archaeological evidence indicates destruction in numerous Judean sites in this time period, including major cities. The destruction conforms to Sennacherib's Annals, which describe the Assyrians as "Using packed-down ramps and applying battering rams, infantry, attacks by mines, breaches and siege machines."[28] Sennacherib's attack on the fortified Judean city of Lachish is depicted on a wall in Sennacherib's palace in Nineveh.[29] Lachish was not easy to take. It was elevated and heavily fortified. The art reliefs on the wall in the palace are gruesome, showing some of the inhabitants led in chains as prisoners and others impaled and murdered. As to the fate of Jerusalem, Sennacherib's annals report,

> He [Hezekiah], himself, I locked up within Jerusalem, his royal city, like a bird in a cage. I surrounded him with earthworks and made it unthinkable for him to exit by the city gate. His cities[,] which I had despoiled myself, I cut off from his land and gave them to Mitinti, king

---

24. Temples served as ancient banks in many Mesopotamian cultures, so much of the wealth of the nation may have been stored there: https://epichistoryfacts.com/the-ancient-temples-that-doubled-as-banks/. Weights in the ancient world varied from region to region; using Scott's average of 30 kg (66 lbs.) for a talent, the equivalent of 9,000 kg (19,800 lbs.) of silver and 900 kg (1,984 lbs.) of gold—that would be a vast sum indeed. Robert Scott, "Weights and Measures in the Bible," *BA* 22 (1959): 34.
25. *COS*, 2:302–3.
26. *COS*, 2:303.
27. *COS*, 2:303.
28. *COS*, 2:303.
29. See J. M. Russell, *Sennacherib's Palace without Rival at Nineveh* (University of Chicago Press, 1991). Also Osama Amin, "Siege of Lachish Reliefs at the British Museum," 2017, http://etc.worldhistory.org/photos/siege-lachish-reliefs-british-museum/.

of Ashdod[;] Padi, king of Ekron[;] and Sillibel, king of Gaza, and thus diminished his land. I imposed duties and gifts from my lordship upon him, in addition to the former tribute, their yearly payment.[30]

The Assyrian record and the biblical text agree that Jerusalem was surrounded but not ravaged. Why did Sennacherib spare Jerusalem? The answer is unknown, although scholars have suggested several possibilities. One option is for Hezekiah to capitulate and pay. The biblical account and the annals both demonstrate that he paid heavy tribute to the point of stripping the temple treasures.[31] However, even if this is the case, why was Hezekiah left on the throne when other leaders were removed? Margaret Barker argues that a plague swept through the Assyrian army and inflicted heavy casualties.[32] She bases this on an analysis of 2 Kgs. 19:35–36 (NIV): "That night the angel of [*Adoni*][33] went out and put to death a hundred and eighty-five thousand in the Assyrian camp." The deaths are described as causing Sennacherib to break camp and withdraw. Olmstead points to other possible plague outbreaks within the Assyrian military.[34] Another potential factor was the threat of the army of Egypt (known as Cush) moving toward the area (2 Kgs. 19:9). They were reported as defeated earlier, but this does not mean they did not return to Judah as part of the coalition of nations formed to destroy Assyria.[35] Whatever the combination of factors, Hezekiah paid heavy tribute, becoming a vassal of Assyria again, but Jerusalem was spared. Afterward, Hezekiah disappeared from politics. He was forced to step away from day-to-day governance, either by Sennacherib or by the debilitating effects of an illness, as reported in 2 Kings 20:1–21.

---

30. *COS*, 2:303.
31. Miller and Hayes, *Ancient Israel and Judah*, 419.
32. Margaret Barker, "Hezekiah's Boil," *JSOT* 26, no. 1 (2001): 31–42. She uses three pieces of evidence: the illness of Hezekiah involved a boil, as does bubonic plague; in mass graves at Lachish dated to this period, the men, women, and children do not show signs of violence, but the bodies were burned as done when an infection invades a population; and the account of the plague that attacked the Assyrians (Flavius Josephus, *The Antiquities of the Jews* 10.1.5, trans. William Whiston, https://penelope.uchicago.edu/josephus/ant-10.html).
33. The Hebrew words translated as "angel of [*Adoni*]" in English actually say "messenger of [*Adoni*]" in Hebrew. The term "messenger" opens up the interpretation to involve other entities, such as plagues (see Exod. 9:1–7).
34. A. T. Olmstead, *History of the Assyrians* (University of Chicago Press, 1923), 164, 169. As in the biblical account, the plague was not a certainty but a possibility. Plagues were known to impact armies in the ancient world; Richard Duncan-Jones, "The Antonine Plague Revisited," *Arctos* 52 (2018): 41–72, https://anaskafh.arsakeio.gr/wp-content/uploads/2020/07/the_antonine_plague_revisited.pdf.
35. Mark Chavalas, "An Historian's Approach to Understanding the Accounts of Sennacherib's Invasion of Judah," *Fides et Historia* 27, no. 2 (1995): 5–22.

The damage inflicted on Judah was catastrophic. Finkelstein writes that before 701 BCE, there were approximately 276 cities or villages in Judah in the late eighth century (750–701 BCE), and only 38 remained after 700 BCE.[36] In his annals, Sennacherib declares that he "took out 200,150 people."[37] This was probably an exaggeration since Finkelstein estimates the population of Judah was 120,000 people in 701 BCE.[38] Regardless of the exact number of people killed or captured, much of the land of southern Judah, including the Shephelah, was handed over to another ruler. This territory was never regained. Hezekiah had wagered that Sennacherib would not be as powerful as his father Sargon II. From a political and historical perspective, Hezekiah revolted against Assyria and paid a high price, including the destruction of much of Judah. Despite these facts, the biblical text remembers him differently. With the only measure of a good king being faithfulness to God and devotion to worship in Solomon's Temple, Hezekiah was remembered as good and faithful. His actions in the revolt were not considered significant, even though he lost temple treasures. It is another reminder that the biblical writers presented kings by using the single criterion of right worship. They were not focused on the political and military decisions of the king. Hezekiah was a successful king who built parts of Jerusalem that still exist and managed a quickly growing population. Assyrian control of the area was inevitable, and Hezekiah's revolt did result in the loss of territory and the further scattering of the people to other areas.

MANASSEH (698–644 BCE) AND AMON (643–642 BCE) OF JUDAH

Second Kings 21:1 states that Manasseh became king when he was twelve years old and reigned for fifty-five years, the longest-reigning king of Judah. Little is known historically about this period. Early in his reign, Sennacherib's campaigns decreased in Judah, although there were some additional campaigns in Egypt.[39] In the annals of the next two Assyrian monarchs, Manasseh is only mentioned in lists of kings, probably reflecting Judah's reduced territory and

---

36. Israel Finkelstein, "The Archaeology of the Days of Manasseh," in *Scripture and Other Artifacts: Essays on the Bible and Archaeology in Honor of Philip J. King*, ed. M. Coogan, C. Exum, and L. Stager (Westminster/John Knox, 1994), 173.
37. *COS*, 2:303.
38. Finkelstein, "Days of Manasseh," 177.
39. Miller and Hayes, *Ancient Israel and Judah*, 420–37.

status.⁴⁰ From all appearances, Judah was a loyal vassal of Assyria during the long reign of Manasseh. Finkelstein notes some gains during Manasseh's reign. The population that retreated from the territories lost by Hezekiah moved to the Judean hills and more arid regions, such as the Judean wilderness and the Beersheba Valley, allowing access to the trade route, the Transjordanian Route, that ran east of the Jordan River and connected westward to Egypt.⁴¹ This expansion into new territory resulted in some economic recovery.⁴²

The biblical account of Manasseh is harsh and reflects none of these recovery efforts. It states he did more evil than any previous king and misled the people "to do more evil than the nations had done that [*Adoni*] destroyed before the people of Israel" (2 Kgs. 21:9), with "nations" meaning the previous Canaanites. Manasseh is accused of every cultic violation possible: rebuilding the high places, making altars to Baal, worshiping the host of heaven, making his son pass through fire, using soothsayers, mediums, and divinators ("wizards" in v. 6 NRSVue), and setting up a carved image of Asherah in the temple, a gross desecration. Second Chronicles gives a similar account and then adds an additional incident. In this narrative, the king is captured and taken to Assyria, where he prays to *Adoni* for deliverance,⁴³ returns a changed man, restores temple worship, and builds new fortification walls in Jerusalem (2 Chr. 33:10–17). This account rehabilitates Manasseh. The forced trip to Assyria or rebuilding the walls cannot be verified independently, so it is uncertain where the narrative originated. It would also have been unlikely that Manasseh could have built new fortifications without Assyrian permission.

According to 2 Kings 21, Amon, Manasseh's son, reigned for only two years and was just as evil as his father. He was murdered by his servants (21:23). Then "the people of the land" killed those who attacked the king, and they placed Manasseh's son Josiah on the throne (21:24). There are no other records of these events, so it is difficult to determine exactly what happened and why.

SUMMARY

Judah remained under Assyrian control for almost one hundred years (722 to 609 BCE). The attack in 701 BCE inflicted heavy damage on Judah and cost

---

40. Manasseh appears in the annals of Sennacherib's son Esarhaddon as one of the kings required to provide people to transport building materials to Nineveh: *ANET*, 291. Ashurbanipal, Sennacherib's son, reports that Manasseh sent Judean forces to fight with the Assyrians against Egypt; *ANET*, 294–95.
    41. Finkelstein, "Days of Manasseh," 178.
    42. Finkelstein, "Days of Manasseh," 178.
    43. The prayer is recorded in the deuterocanonical book The Prayer of Manasseh.

Hezekiah and the country much of their wealth. Under Manasseh, some of the residents migrated eastward toward the Jordan River.

Early in Hezekiah's reign, the country achieved prosperity and expansion. This all ended with the attack by the Assyrians. In addition to the losses in battle, the country had to pay heavy tribute, which sapped their already reduced resources. The nation was primarily agricultural, and this work allowed it to survive.[44] Judah managed to rebound but remained under the control of Assyria. Even with this modest growth, Judah, after Hezekiah, was a much-reduced nation.

---

44. Leo Perdue and Warren Carter, *Israel and Empire: A Postcolonial History of Israel and Early Judaism*, ed. C. Baker (Bloomsbury T&T Clark, 2015), 65.

11

Battle for Control of the Afro-Asiatic Region (639–539 BCE)

While Judah remained a vassal, King Ashurbanipal of Assyria remained firmly in control of the Afro-Asiatic area, just as his father and grandfather before him.[1] Judah was one small country in that empire. Since being overtaken by Sennacherib, Egypt continued to revolt against the empire. When Psamtik I came to the throne of Egypt, he made an agreement with the Assyrians for Egypt's independence in 640 BCE. Ashurbanipal probably agreed because he was dealing with several revolts in the northern and eastern territories, keeping him occupied elsewhere. With a more powerful Egypt, Judah was caught between Egypt and Assyria. Each wanted control of the region and the vital Way of the Sea.[2] This placed the nation of Judah in an even more precarious position.

CHART 7: LAST KINGS OF JUDAH (641–586 BCE)

Josiah	641–609
Jehoahaz II	609 (reigned three months)
Jehoiakim	608–598
Jehoiachin	598 (reigned three months)
Zedekiah	598–586
Destruction of Jerusalem and End of the Monarchy	

1. Nadav Na'aman, "The Kingdom of Judah under Josiah," *Tel Aviv* 18 (1991): 53–55.
2. J. Maxwell Miller and John H. Hayes, *A History of Ancient Israel and Judah*, 2nd ed. (Westminster John Knox, 2006), 448.

JOSIAH (641–609 BCE)

According to both 2 Kings 22:1 and 2 Chronicles 34:1, Josiah was only eight years old when he was crowned king of Judah after the murder of his father, Amon. During his early years, young Josiah was a king in name only. An unnamed co-regent ran the nation. Josiah never appeared in the records of Assyria, Babylon, and Egypt, leaving the biblical account as the only record.

Josiah was seen as a great king and reformer in the biblical texts of Kings and Chronicles: "He [Josiah] did what was right in the sight of [*Adoni*] and walked in all the ways of his father David; he did not turn aside to the right or to the left" (2 Kgs. 22:2). He was remembered as one who destroyed all the worship places and vessels of the other gods, including places like Bethel in the old northern kingdom of Israel (23:4–20).

Second Kings states that in his eighteenth year, Josiah authorized an audit of the temple monies for needed repairs (22:3–7). During the restoration, "the book [*scroll* in Hebrew] of the law" was discovered and brought to Josiah (22:8–10), prompting the king to enact religious reforms. One of those reforms, according to 2 Kings, was to institute a Passover because "no such Passover has been kept since the days of the judges who judged Israel, even during all the days of the kings of Israel and . . . Judah" (23:22).[3] Was it possible that the Passover, which is so central to faith after the exile, had not been practiced since the period of the judges? The answer is unclear. Except for 2 Chronicles 30, where Hezekiah invites "all Israel and Judah" (v. 6) to keep the Passover in the temple, there are no other narratives of Judean or Israelite kings participating in the Passover. Second Chronicles 35 is where Josiah's Passover is narrated. Both of these are large celebrations in the Jerusalem temple.

The Passover instructions in Exodus 12–13 were composed for a household celebration; the narratives in 2 Chronicles are longer, written much later, and narrated a public ceremony at the Jerusalem temple. Does this signal an addition to the Exodus traditions of Passover as a celebration in the home that was added during the time of Hezekiah and Josiah, or is this a later addition reflecting practices of the Persian or Hellenistic period (539–64 BCE)? Another biblical witness, the book of Jeremiah, does not mention any religious reforms of the Passover celebrations under Josiah. Indeed, Jeremiah 4:6–10 is an oracle from the days of King Josiah that condemns Judah for false worship. Jeremiah's lack of mentioning these reforms is puzzling since the need for such reforms was precisely what Jeremiah focused on in many of his oracles.[4] These

---

3. This conflicts with 2 Chr. 30:2, which speaks of a Passover celebration during the reign of Hezekiah.

4. Lester Grabbe, *Ancient Israel: What Do We Know and How Do We Know It?* (T&T Clark, 2007), 206.

discrepancies make it impossible to say much about the reforms and when or where they took place, especially since there is no archaeological evidence of changes to the temple or other reforms.

Historically, it is impossible to know why Josiah is credited with these reforms and why he occupied such an exalted place in the biblical text. Indeed, even though his actions during his reign probably set the Babylonian destruction of Jerusalem in motion, Josiah is not blamed for this in the biblical text. The blame is placed instead on the acts of Manasseh, his grandfather (2 Kgs. 23:26–27).[5] By contrast, 2 Chronicles does not blame any king for the loss. It blames the people for Jerusalem's destruction: "All the leading priests and the people also were exceedingly unfaithful, following all the abominations of the nations, and they polluted the house of [*Adoni*] that he had consecrated in Jerusalem" (2 Chr. 36:14).

The case of Josiah also serves as a cautionary tale in biblical scholarship. For the past two hundred years, scholars have focused on Josiah's actions as described in the text, taking much of the biblical claims at face value. Scholars claimed that under Josiah, Judah became an independent state and recaptured much of the territory from the former northern Israel and part of the seacoast.[6] However, the archaeological record does not support this assessment. Judah remained under the control of the Assyrians and then, following Assyria's decline, the Egyptians. The population probably did not exceed seventy-five thousand, with 20 percent living in Jerusalem.[7] The biblical text claims that Josiah's reforms were far-reaching, including the old Northern Kingdom and "all the shrines of the high places . . . in the towns of Samaria that kings of Israel had made" (2 Kgs. 23:19). These actions were more of a theological wish than a historical reality. Reforms outside Judah would have been difficult since these northern areas were now in Assyrian territory.

Assumptions about the historical truth of Josiah's territorial claims were not the only problematic issue in biblical scholarship of this period. The scholar John Bright states that the book of the law discovered in the temple during Josiah's reign "was, as is generally agreed today, some form of the book of Deuteronomy."[8] This assumption, made by generations of scholars, led to the

---

5. Halpern notes that this indicates how the biblical tradition changed from the time of Josiah until the later writing in the postexilic period. Baruch Halpern, "Why Manasseh Is Blamed for the Babylonian Exile: The Evolution of a Biblical Tradition," *VT* 48 (1998): 473–514.

6. John Bright, *A History of Israel*, 3rd ed. (Westminster, 1981), 316–17; Alberto Soggin, *A History of Israel: From Beginnings to the Bar Kochba Revolt, AD 135*, trans. J. Bowden (SCM, 1985), 257.

7. Israel Finkelstein and Neil Silberman, *The Bible Unearthed: Archaeology's New Vision of Ancient Israel and the Origin of Its Sacred Texts* (Free Press, 2001), 289.

8. Bright, *A History*, 319. Finkelstein and Silberman (*Bible Unearthed*, 281) also claim that the scroll was "an original version of Deuteronomy," but written during this period rather than "found."

further assumption that the Deuteronomic History was compiled and edited during this period of Josiah's reign, making the first form of Joshua–Kings.[9] It would certainly explain why Josiah received such high praise in the biblical text and by generations of scholars.

During this period, indeed, literacy grew in the population outside the scribal schools as multiple epigraphic finds attest.[10] As William Schniedewind states, "With the emergence of literacy and the flourishing of literature, a textual revolution arose in the days of King Josiah. This was one of the most profound cultural revolutions in human history: the assertion of the orthodoxy of texts."[11] This evidence of writing and increasing literacy were indeed important sociological occurrences, but to go further and claim that these reforms led to a developed form of the narrative portions of the first five books of the Hebrew Bible and the historical books of Joshua–2 Kings is going beyond what we can know. Studies in the past few years have demonstrated that the balance between oral tradition and written text is complex, as was the lengthy editing process of the texts that would eventually become the Hebrew Bible. Susan Niditch notes, "Recognition of Israelite attitudes to orality and literacy and the complex interplay between the two forces us to question long-respected theories about the development of the Israelite literary traditions preserved in the Bible."[12] Without further evidence, it is difficult, if not impossible, to claim that the Torah and the historical books were codified during Josiah's reign.

Just when the texts were available also raises questions about the scroll discovered by Josiah. For example, why would a law code of such importance be left somewhere in the temple and forgotten for an extended period? The biblical texts of this period of Judah's history, the so-called historical books and the prophets' oracles, tell little about how people worshiped, the festivals they held annually, or even their daily devotional life. The laws outlined in Leviticus are from a much later period; it is impossible to say which were centuries old and which were from the later postexilic periods. In other words, earlier scholars claimed to know much more about this period and its writings than can be

---

9. Noll reports, "In fact, an entire historical hypothesis has been spun from this tale, a hypothesis that, in some scholarly circles, is no longer even spoken of as a 'hypothesis.' It is treated as though the hypothesis were inscribed in an ancient and trustworthy text, not merely in modern textbooks." K. L. Noll, *Canaan and Israel in Antiquity: A Textbook on History and Religion*, 2nd ed. (Bloomsbury T&T Clark, 2013), 230–31.

10. Lachish Ostracon 3 is written from a soldier to his superior and is dated around 600 BCE; *COS*, 3:78. The Mesad Hashavyahu ostracon is a plea for a hearing from a worker to an official for the return of his garment from another. The ostracon was written before the destruction of the tower in 609 BCE; *COS*, 3:77. Likewise, 200 inscribed ostraca were discovered in Arad. These are administrative texts; *COS*, 3:81–85.

11. William Schniedewind, *How the Bible Became a Book* (Cambridge University Press, 2004), 91.

12. Susan Niditch, *Oral World and Written Word* (Westminster John Knox, 1996), 134.

verified. The connection of this "book of the law" to a form of Deuteronomy is not a certainty, and the biblical text never makes this connection.[13]

In summary, Josiah was too young to reign for the first decade of his kingship, but once he came of age, he is remembered as a great king who enacted sweeping religious reforms and destroyed many non-*Adoni* places of worship in Judah and the old Israelite territory. Yet there is no evidence of these widespread reforms nor any evidence outside the text concerning King Josiah.

A BATTLE OF EMPIRES AND THE DEATH OF JOSIAH (610–609 BCE)

Ashurbanipal of Assyria remained in control of his vast empire during the early years of Josiah's reign. Still, revolts in his empire's northern and eastern parts kept him away from Canaan, leaving Egypt to advance its influence in the region. Ashurbanipal died in 627 BCE, probably after abdicating the throne in 630.[14] His death prompted a four-year civil war in Assyria (627–623 BCE), with Sin-shar-ishkun, Ashurbanipal's son, finally becoming king. This struggle caused Assyria to weaken geopolitically and allowed nations under its control to revolt.

A new threat appeared in the east as Nabopolassar strengthened Babylon. He attacked Assyria several times between 626 BCE and 615 BCE.[15] In early campaigns, Nabopolassar lost to the Assyrians. However, in 612 BCE, Babylonian forces, in alliance with the Medes, captured the Assyrian capital of Nineveh.[16] The final strike in 610 BCE ended the Neo-Assyria Empire's control of the region.[17] The Assyrian Empire had been the largest to date in the Afro-Asiatic region. Its reign lasted about 135 years.

In preparation for the battle in 610 BCE, Neco II of Egypt rode up the Way of the Sea to join his forces with the Assyrian army.[18] He met Josiah of Judah at Megiddo (Armageddon in Greek = Mountain of Megiddo), probably in the

---

13. See Katherine Stott, "Finding the Lost Book of the Law: Re-reading the Story of 'the Book of the Law' (Deuteronomy–2 Kings) in Light of Classical Literature," *JSOT* 30 (2005): 153–69; and Nadav Na'aman, "The 'Discovered Book' and the Legitimation of Josiah's Reform," *JBL* 130 (2011): 47–62.

14. Miller and Hayes, *Ancient Israel and Judah*, 444.

15. A. K. Grayson, *ABC*, 91.

16. This event is the historical backdrop for the prophetic book of Nahum, which celebrates the fall of Nineveh and the end of Assyrian domination over Judah.

17. We know little about this period that ended the Assyrian Empire because there are no Assyrian or Babylonian records for these final battles; Grabbe, *Ancient Israel*, 187.

18. Na'aman ("The Kingdom of Judah," 51) observes that this mode of travel in and of itself is unusual since Egyptian troops usually sailed to the Lebanon coast on the way to Babylon.

late summer of 610 BCE.[19] What happened then and why is unclear. Second Kings reports that when Josiah arrived at Megiddo, Neco II killed him (23:29). The 2 Chronicles account states that Josiah attacked Neco II for unknown reasons. A battle ensued. Josiah was wounded and taken to Jerusalem, where he died (35:20–27). The 2 Kings account is more reliable and does not speculate as to why this happened. Either way, Josiah was killed during this encounter. Why Josiah met the Egyptians at Megiddo and what his reasons were remain unanswered.[20] It is also unanswered why Neco II acted as he did. Whatever happened between Neco and Josiah at Megiddo led to further action against Judah after the Egyptians returned from their battles in Assyria.

JEHOAHAZ II (609 BCE)

The Bible reports that upon the death of Josiah, his son Jehoahaz II was made king at the age of twenty-three by "the people of the land" (2 Kgs. 23:30). "The people of the land" appears as a term seventy-three times in the Hebrew Bible. During the monarchy, they had a part in the death of Queen Athaliah and were the ones who killed the servants who murdered Josiah's father, Amon. Yet, their identity is difficult to ascertain. It is unexplained in the biblical texts, and scholars are divided on the exact meaning.[21] The title clearly meant something to the ancient audience, but it is impossible to know this group's function without further information. Whoever they were, they had enough power to depose and kill kings.

Jehoahaz remained king for only three months (2 Kgs. 23:31; 2 Chr. 36:1–2). After the Babylonians defeated Egypt and Assyria in 610, Pharoah Neco did not return immediately to Egypt. He stopped in Judah to imprison the new king and demand a tribute of one hundred talents of silver and one of gold (2 Kgs. 23:33). A talent was approximately 30 kilograms, or 66 pounds.[22] Neco also placed Jehoahaz's brother, Eliakim, on the throne and forced Jehoahaz into exile in Egypt (23:34). This act declared that Egypt, not Assyria or Babylon, was the power in the region. It also deepened the mystery concerning the relationship between Judah and Egypt during Josiah's reign and what

---

19. Miller and Hayes, *Ancient Israel and Judah*, 460.

20. The "why" of Josiah's death is also presented in the apocryphal literature and several other ancient sources. While none has a more satisfactory answer, it is clear that the nation continued to grapple with how he had died. See Steve Delamarter, "The Death of Josiah in Scripture and Tradition: Wrestling with the Problem of Evil," *VT* 54, no. 1 (2004): 29–60.

21. Robert Gordis, "Sectional Rivalry in the Kingdom of Judah," *Jewish Quarterly Review* 25 (1925): 237–59; A. Oppenheimer, *The 'Am ha-Aretz: A Study in the Social History of the Jewish People in the Hellenistic-Roman Period* (Brill, 1977); Joseph Healey, "'Am ha-Aretz," *ABD* 1:169.

22. *ABD* 6:905.

happened at Megiddo. The murder of Josiah was not enough for Neco II. The capture and exile of Josiah's son and replacement of the monarch were the acts of a superior king over a rebellious lesser state. Whatever Josiah and Judah did to raise the ire of Egypt, it was disastrous.

ELIAKIM/JEHOIAKIM (608–598 BCE)

Neco renamed Eliakim (meaning "God established") to Jehoiakim ("*Adoni* established") (2 Kgs. 23:34). Changing the general "God" to the specific name of Judah's God in his name may have been a strategy to win the acceptance of this new king, who was forced upon the people. The biblical accounts of his reign are brief and do not speak of international events. The 2 Kings and 2 Chronicles accounts differ, and the book of Jeremiah provides additional information about the internal turmoil within Judah itself.

Judah was clearly in Egyptian hands at the beginning of Jehoiakim's reign. This would change beginning in 605 BCE. The first significant battle between Egypt and Babylon came in 605 BCE at Carchemish, about 650 kilometers (400 miles) north of Jerusalem. Egypt tried to press to the north and Babylon to the south.[23] Crown Prince Nebuchadrezzar (Nebuchadnezzar in 2 Kings 24–25) led the Babylonian army to victory over the Egyptians, who retreated south.[24] The Babylonians attacked again at Hamath, ending Neco's bid to control the region.[25] The defeat of the Egyptians is celebrated in Jeremiah 46:1–12. Egypt's defeat, however, was not exactly a celebratory occasion for Judah: it only signaled a change in the empire controlling the region.

Shortly after this battle, Nabopolassar, the king of Babylon, died, and Nebuchadrezzar returned to Babylon to take the throne. He came to Canaan by 603–602 BCE to complete his campaign. By his fourth year, in about 601, he could claim complete control of the region, which he called Hatti Land.[26] From the annals, it is difficult to know the bounds of Hatti Land, and scholars are unsure, but it is clear that the king and his armies were taking more of the empire in hand. According to 2 Kings 24:1, Jehoiakim remained a loyal vassal of Nebuchadrezzar for three years after his campaign. Later, in 601 or 600 BCE, Nebuchadrezzar tried to capture Egypt, was defeated, and

---

23. Carchemish, near the present Jarabulus in Syria (Aram), is located on the Syrian (Aramaean) and Turkish border, with most of its ruins within Turkey.

24. Riblah is located about 150 km (93 miles) north of Damascus.

25. Grayson, *ABC*, 99. Josephus reports that Judean troops were part of the Egyptian force (*Contra Apion* 1.136–137), but we lack corroboration of this, so Judah's involvement remains a question.

26. Grayson, *ABC*, 100.

retreated to Babylon.[27] This defeat was probably the catalyst for Jehoiakim's subsequent revolt.

JUDAH'S REVOLT AND THE FIRST DEPORTATION (597 BCE)

According to 2 Kings 24 and 2 Chronicles 36 and the Babylonian Chronicles, Jehoiakim staged a revolt with refusal to pay tribute to Babylon, resulting in Babylon's attack on Jerusalem in 598–597 BCE.[28] The Babylonian account is brief: "He [Nebuchadrezzar] encamped against the city of Judah and on the second day of the month of Adar[,] he captured the city (and) seized (its) king."[29] The biblical accounts, however, do not agree on the details of this first attack.

Second Kings 24 reports that Jehoiakim died before the Babylonians arrived. His eighteen-year-old son, Jehoiachin, was then king. Subsequently, the new king was exiled to Babylon along with others, probably all the high state and religious officials and soldiers. Judah also paid a heavy tribute with treasures from the king's house and the temple.[30] The book of Jeremiah states that the deportees numbered 3,023 (2 Kgs. 24:12; Jer. 52:28). Second Chronicles 36 reports two deportations: Jehoiakim was taken to Babylon first, leaving behind his son, Jehoiachin, who was made the king and then taken to Babylon along with the payment of heavy tribute. No additional people were listed as exiled with the two kings in this account. A third source, Josephus, states that Nebuchadrezzar killed Jehoiakim.[31]

Traditionally, the 2 Kings account was accepted by scholars because it is the closest match to the Babylonian Chronicles. However, the Babylonian source omits the Judean king's name, so it could refer to either the father or the son. Jehoiachin is mentioned in a Babylonian tablet at a later but unknown date.[32] Therefore, we can be sure that Jehoiachin, the young king, arrived in Babylon. The tablet has no mention of his father. The biblical

---

27. Grayson, *ABC*, 101.
28. Miller and Hayes, *Ancient Israel and Judah*, 466.
29. Grayson, *ABC*, 102.
30. The king of Babylon also exiled artisans, claims 2 Kgs. 24:14, leaving only the poor of the land. There is no doubt that the leadership was exiled at the time, but the exact number of people is unknown.
31. Flavius Josephus, *The Complete Works of Josephus: Complete and Unabridged*, trans. William Whiston (Delmarva Publications, 2016), 10.96.
32. The tablet is a receipt for supplies needed by the king. This document seems to show that the Babylonian government provided the Judean king with supplies; *ANET*, 308.

variations of this event make it difficult to determine precisely what occurred. It would be reasonable that the rebelling king would be either killed or exiled. If Nebuchadrezzar intended to exile Jehoiakim but arrived and discovered him dead, the exile of Jehoiakim's son, the new king, and the other leadership would make sense. Whatever the version of events, Nebuchadrezzar exiled the leadership, including the high priest, Ezekiel. He then raided the city for its treasures as monetary punishment and placed a new king on the throne. The message was clear: rebellion would not be tolerated. None of the written records reflect resistance to the Babylonians in Judah at this point. Indeed, 2 Kings 24:12 states that King Jehoiachin "gave himself up," and no damage to the capital was reported.

The Babylonian Chronicles provide exact dates for these actions. "Year 7 [598–597 BCE], month of Kislimu [18 December 598–15 January 597]; the king of Akkad moved his troops into Hatti Land. He encamped against the city of Judah[,] and on the second day of the month of Adar [Mar. 15 or 16, 587 BCE] he captured the city (and) seized the king."[33] This record is the first firm date for an event in the Hebrew Bible.

The deportation policies of the Babylonians were different from those of the Assyrians. The Assyrians had spread the exiles randomly throughout their empire so they could not work together to revolt or return home. The Babylonians exiled the people from a single nation into the same place. They were not free to return to their country, but one or more groups remained together. Because of this policy, we have more information about the Judean exiles. Second Kings 25:27–30 states that Jehoiachin was imprisoned until Nebuchadrezzar's son released him after thirty-seven years. An administrative record was discovered stating that Nebuchadrezzar allocated the king of Judah resources during his imprisonment.[34] The book of Ezekiel reported that the exiles were not treated as enslaved people but as citizens. They could practice their religion and have a local government and ethnic identity.[35] This treatment was confirmed by a group of written tablets that detail some of the transactions of the Judean exiles in Babylon.[36]

However, even if the Babylonians had a different policy for the exiles, it does not change the fact that the people exiled were taken as prisoners of war and forced from their homeland, with their king imprisoned for thirty-seven years.

---

33. Grayson, *ABC*, 102. The two dates represent the Babylonian calendar, which measures days from dusk to dusk (as in Gen. 1). Babylonian dates have been changed to reflect modern terminology.

34. *ANET*, 308.

35. Miller and Hayes, *Ancient Israel and Judah*, 494.

36. Laurie Pearce and Cornelia Wunsch, *Documents of Judean Exiles and West Semites in Babylonia in the Collection of David Sofer*, CUSAS 28 (CDL, 2014).

ZEDEKIAH (598–586 BCE)

When Jehoiachin was exiled, Nebuchadrezzar placed Jehoiachin's uncle "Mattaniah" on the throne and "changed his name to Zedekiah" (2 Kgs. 24:17).[37] While Babylon had not destroyed the city, Zedekiah faced a Jerusalem with many leaders, skilled soldiers, and workers exiled. He also inherited a divided country. The book of Jeremiah reports that the prophets were of two camps about the meaning of these calamitous events, each probably representing part of the people (Jer. 28). On one side, the prophet Hananiah assured the people that God would deliver them and the exiles would return soon. This view probably grew from Sennacherib's unsuccessful military campaign and inability to capture Jerusalem in 701 BCE. The memory of that miracle caused the people to believe that God had made Jerusalem invincible.[38] On the other hand, Jeremiah responded by saying that Judah must submit to Babylon to prevent mass slaughter, and he sent a letter to the exiles telling them to settle in Babylon and not to expect to return soon (Jer. 29:1–32).

Little was known of Judah during Zedekiah's early reign. Some scholars read Jeremiah 27:1 as an indication of a summit in Jerusalem where Zedekiah gathered with the leaders of Edom, Moab, Ammon, Tyre, and Sidon.[39] The book of Jeremiah speaks of sending a message from God to the kings via their messengers in Jerusalem, warning them to yield to Babylon, but this is the only reference to this event, so its meaning is unclear. An Egyptian inscription indicates a visit to the land of Palestine by Psammetichus II, son of Necho/Neco, in 591 BCE.[40] Whether this is further evidence for a summit is also uncertain. Even more confusing, Jeremiah was to deliver this message to the gathered leaders:

> Thus says the [*Adoni*] of hosts, the God of Israel: This is what you shall say to your masters: It is I who by my great power and my outstretched arm have made the earth, with the people and animals that are on the earth, and I give it to whomever I please. Now I have given all these lands into the hand of King Nebuchadnezzar of Babylon, my servant, and I have given him even the wild animals of the field to serve him. All the nations shall serve him and his son and his grandson, until the time of his own land comes; then many nations and great kings shall make him their slave. (Jer. 27:4b–7).

---

37. Grayson, *ABC*, 102: "A king of his own choice he appointed in the city [and] taking a vast tribute he brought it to Babylon."

38. O. Lipschits, "Judah, Jerusalem, and the Temple (586–539 B.C.)," *Transeuphratène* 22 (2001): 129.

39. Bright, *A History*, 329; Miller and Hayes, *Ancient Israel and Judah*, 469.

40. Miller and Hayes, *Ancient Israel and Judah*, 473.

Why would the nations gather to hear this word? It simply adds to the mystery of this political summit. Jeremiah 51:59 also reports that Zedekiah traveled to Babylon in his fourth year, but no additional documentation for this trip has been found.

Second Kings is silent concerning Zedekiah during his early reign; then in the ninth year of his reign, he rebelled against Babylon (2 Kgs. 24:20). Second Chronicles 36:13 calls this rebellion an evil act: "He also rebelled against King Nebuchadnezzar, who had made him swear by God; he stiffened his neck and hardened his heart against turning to [*Adoni*], the God of Israel." Ezekiel reports that Zedekiah "rebelled . . . by sending ambassadors to Egypt, that they might give him horses and a large army," and thus broke the covenant he made with Nebuchadrezzar (17:15). An extrabiblical letter discovered at Lachish may describe the same event: "It has been reported to your servant, saying, 'The commander of the army, Koniyahu son of Elnathan, has arrived in order to go down to Egypt.'"[41] Could he be the ambassador mentioned in Ezekiel? It is possible but not definite. All the biblical sources except 2 Kings judge the king's rebellion as ill-fated and unfaithful to God. It is unclear if the accounts in Jeremiah and Ezekiel were recorded during the reign of Zedekiah, but the 2 Chronicles account criticizing the king was recorded long after the events had unfolded, so it cannot be considered a reliable historical source.

THE SECOND DEPORTATION; DESTRUCTION OF JERUSALEM AND THE FIRST TEMPLE (587/586 BCE)

Second Kings 25:1 appears to follow the dating in the Babylonian Chronicles. It reports, "In the ninth year of his reign, in the tenth month, on the tenth day of the month, King Nebuchadnezzar of Babylon came with all his army against Jerusalem and laid siege to it; they built siegeworks against it all around."[42] Most agree that this was the beginning of the siege in early January 587 BCE.[43] The military strategy was simple but cruel: surround the city and starve out the population. During this time, additional forces destroyed other cities in Judah.[44] At some point during the siege of Jerusalem, the Egyptian

---

41. Dennis Pardee, *Handbook of Ancient Hebrew Letters*, SBL Sources for Biblical Studies 15 (Scholars Press, 1982), 84–85.

42. The Babylonian Chronicles break off after the 11th year of Nebuchadrezzar, so there is no corresponding confirmation of the date. Assuming the biblical text is correct, the siege would occur in the 18th year of his reign.

43. Oded Lipschits, *The Fall and Rise of Jerusalem* (Eisenbrauns, 2005), 74.

44. Mazar (*Archaeology*, 459–60) claims that the towns in the Shephelah, the Negev, and the Judean Desert were devastated by the Babylonians; only the area of Benjamin remained

army entered Palestine, causing a reprieve, but the Egyptians withdrew without engaging the Babylonians (Jer. 37:1–10).[45]

It is hard to overstate the dire conditions in the starving city during the eighteen months of Babylon's siege; some of that agony is reflected in Jeremiah and Lamentations. Jerusalem was sealed and could not get additional supplies: it must not have taken long for the population to turn against each other as food grew scarce. Oded Lipschits argues that the Babylonian attack against Jerusalem was part of a plan by Nebuchadrezzar to deal with Egypt and gain control of the region and its trade routes. Jerusalem was the first city taken, but he also attacked Tyre, Sidon, Ammon, Moab, and coastal cities.[46] Nebuchadrezzar used the lengthy attack on Jerusalem to demonstrate his power and perseverance to other rulers. Finally, Babylonians breached the city walls at the end of July 586.[47] According to the biblical text, the food had finally run out (2 Kgs. 25:3–4). This may be why there was no report of resistance. The biblical text states that Zedekiah tried to flee but was captured near Jericho. After being taken to Nebuchadrezzar's compound in Riblah in Aram (ca. 100 miles [160 km] north of Damascus), Zedekiah was forced to watch as his sons were murdered; then he was blinded and carried off to Babylon (2 Kgs. 25:1–7).

The text in 2 Kings further reports that Nebuchadrezzar sent an officer who ordered the destruction of the city walls a month later. The temple and the king's palace were burnt along with the other great houses (2 Kgs. 25:9). The Babylonians also exiled part of the population (2 Kgs. 25:8–21). The archaeological record shows that no section of Jerusalem went unscathed.[48] The city was destroyed and burned.[49] Countless residents of Jerusalem either starved or died during the Babylonian assault. However, the destruction this time was limited to the city and surrounding areas "and caused only minimal damage to other parts of the Kingdom."[50]

Regarding the scope of the deportation, earlier scholars followed the "empty land" theory. They argued that Judah was all but abandoned after the Babylonian attacks.[51] Some contemporary scholars continue to make this claim.[52] Lipschits writes, "The conclusion is that Jerusalem and its environs

---

untouched. The Lachish letters report what was probably the destruction of Azekah because a commander says their fire signals no longer burned (*ANET*, 322).

45. Miller and Hayes, *Ancient Israel and Judah*, 475.
46. Lipschits, "Judah, Jerusalem, and the Temple," 131.
47. Lipschits, *Fall and Rise of Jerusalem*, 74.
48. Finkelstein and Silbermann, *Bible Unearthed*, 295.
49. Mazar, *Archaeology*, 458.
50. Lipschits, *Fall and Rise of Jerusalem*, 84.
51. W. F. Albright, *The Archaeology of Palestine* (Penguin Books, 1949), 142.
52. Ephraim Stern, "The Babylonian Gap," *BAR* 26, no. 6 (2000): 45–51.

took a heavy blow from the Babylonians at the beginning of the sixth century and they were almost entirely depleted of their inhabitants."[53] There is no doubt that Judah lost a lot of its population through the deaths during the Babylonian siege and attack, the forced exile, and the ones who chose to leave Judah and move further south. It is impossible to state how many were exiled or killed.

The written documents for this period are scant. The books of 2 Kings and 2 Chronicles report the attack and deportation in 586 BCE, but little after that point. The book of Jeremiah provides some information but is far from a clear record (chaps. 39–43). The book of Lamentations, a psalter rather than history, reflects the mourning of the people over the loss of Jerusalem. It contains five city laments and tells of the sorrow and pain of this event and the people's anger and sorrow toward God, who allowed such a thing to happen. While traditionally attributed to Jeremiah, these laments are close relatives to the lament psalms and the city laments of other Afro-Asiatic countries. No doubt the grief expressed in these poetic songs added to the belief that Jerusalem and Judah were completely destroyed. Other sources, such as the Babylonian Chronicles, break off in 594–593 BCE and mention nothing about this period. However, the Babylonians appointed a governor, Gedaliah, over Judah (2 Kgs. 25:22). If the land were empty, a governor would be unnecessary.

The archaeological record for this period is also difficult to decipher. First, later excavations in Jerusalem and other cities removed or covered the remains from this period. Second, it is hard to distinguish the Assyrian destruction from the Babylonian one since the two attacks happened within 125 years of each other, and the sites were not completely rebuilt between these occupations.[54]

As always, we know less than we wish, but some information does exist. First, many towns in Judah were not touched. Nebuchadrezzar attacked the major fortified cities, so the destruction was focused on areas with the greatest population density. But most of the people in Judah did not live in these fortified cities.[55] The cities north of Jerusalem in the traditional territory of Benjamin were spared. Even in Jerusalem, the damage did not mean the residents abandoned it completely. Gabriel Barkay excavated areas in Jerusalem and discovered burial caves from this period. He notes, "The evidence from the burial caves of Ketef Hinnom points to continuous settlement in Jerusalem throughout the 6th century B.C.E. and until the return to Zion and the days

---

53. Lipschits, "Judah, Jerusalem, and the Temple," 133.
54. As stated earlier, the range in carbon 14 dating makes it difficult to distinguish between dates that are closer than 200–300 years.
55. Joseph Blenkinsopp, "The Bible, Archaeology, and Politics; or, The Empty Land Revisited," *JSOT* 27, no. 2 (2002): 180.

of Persian overlordship."[56] Israel Finkelstein estimates that Judah contained 75,000 people before the destruction. If, for example, 40,000 were exiled or killed in the attack, that still left almost 50 percent of the population living in a war-ravaged country.[57] According to Jeremiah 41:5 and the book of Lamentations, the people continued to worship both at Mizpah and Jerusalem, even if all that happened at the temple ruins were prayers of lamentation over the loss. As in other periods, we do not know as much as we would like about how they survived and worshiped, but sociological studies of groups torn by war suggest that those who remained in Judah settled and moved forward as they slowly rebuilt their lives and countries.

JUDAH IN THE POSTEXILIC PERIOD OF BABYLONIAN CONTROL (587 BCE–539 BCE)

The people who worshiped *Adoni* were now scattered and were now part of the Babylonian Empire. They no longer had a king. The Babylonians set a governor over Judah: "He [Nebuchadrezzar] appointed Gedaliah son of Ahikam son of Shaphan as governor over the people who remained in the land of Judah, whom King Nebuchadnezzar of Babylon had left" (2 Kgs. 25:22). In Hebrew, the word "governor" does not appear. The text reads, "[Nebuchadrezzar] appointed Gedaliah over them" (25:22).[58] Gedaliah's actual title and purpose are unclear. Because the elite were exiled, he was probably not a member of the house of David. Joel Weinberg argues he did not formally serve as a governor since this title was only used for an official of the Babylonian king, but as "an officially installed representative of the Jewish remnant before the Babylonian authorities in Judah."[59]

Gedaliah made his home at Mizpah, in the old territory of Benjamin, about eight miles north of Jerusalem. Whether he moved there because Jerusalem was uninhabitable or because this was a region of support for him is uncertain. He was either an elite who sided with Babylon against David's house or was among "the poorest people of the land" (2 Kgs. 25:12).[60] A seal impression found at Lachish states, "Belonging to Gedaliah, who is over the royal

---

56. Gabriel Barkay, "A Burial Cave of the Late First Temple Period on the Slope of Mount Zion," in *Ancient Jerusalem Revealed*, ed. G. Hillel (Israel Exploration Society, 1994), 106.

57. Finkelstein and Silberman, *Bible Unearthed*, 306. They account for those exiled but not for those killed in the war. I added the additional 20,000 based on the destruction of Judah's major cities.

58. My translation.

59. Joel Weinberg, "Gedaliah the Son of Ahikam in Mizpah: His Status and Role, Supporters and Opponents," *ZAW* 119, no. 3 (2007): 359.

60. Weinberg, "Gedaliah," 360.

house."[61] If this is the same person, he was an official before the exile.[62] But we cannot be sure the seal is from the same person.

The book of Jeremiah offers the only report of Gedaliah's work. His first act was to tell the people not to be afraid to work for the Chaldeans (Babylonians) and to go out and harvest the "wine and summer fruits and oil" (Jer. 40:10) and live in the Judean towns. Gedaliah appears to be on the same political side as Jeremiah: settle in, make yourselves at home, live, and wait out the Babylonian regime.

The Babylonians did not build their own military centers. Nebuchadrezzar took over the fortifications of the Assyrian military. So we have no way to distinguish archaeologically between the Assyrian and Babylonian occupations.[63] Finally, Nebuchadrezzar appointed local people, as he did in the case of Gedaliah, to oversee the multiple regions of his empire instead of placing Babylonians in these regions. Again, this means no unique items were left of the Babylonians in Judah. Besides the destruction, the Babylonians left almost no trace of their control of Judah.

From here forward, it is hard to say much more. Jeremiah 40 reports that Ishmael, supposedly a member of the Davidic royal family, attempted to murder Gedaliah. James Maxwell Miller and John H. Hayes suggest that this was an attempt by the house of David to retake the throne.[64] After the murder of Gedaliah (41:1–3), a group of Judeans attacked Ishmael, and he fled to Ammon (41:10–15). The group then took Jeremiah and fled to Egypt, fearing the wrath of the Babylonians (43:5–7). Jeremiah (52:30) mentions a third deportation by the Babylonians in about 581BCE, but it is unknown whether this deportation was connected to the murder of Gedaliah.

THE DIASPORA

Diaspora is a word that describes a people once united in one land who later migrated to multiple places. It is a term often used by biblical scholars and sociologists. It comes from the Greek (verb: *diaspeirein*; noun: *diaspora*) and

---

61. Peter Hooke, "A Scarab and Sealing from Tell Duweir," *PEQ* 67 (1935): 195–97. It is not certain that this is the seal of the same Gedaliah, but it shows that the name was used in this period.

62. Miller and Hayes, *Ancient Israel and Judah*, 484.

63. Miller and Hayes, *Ancient Israel and Judah*, 482. Some scholars disagree with this position, arguing that the Babylonians had their own separate administration that, curiously, "did not leave any clear traces in the country's archaeological record." Ephraim Stern, *The Assyrian, Babylonian, and Persian Periods (732–332 BCE)*, vol. 2 of *Archaeology of the Land of the Bible*, by A. Mazar et al. (Doubleday, 2001), 308.

64. Miller and Hayes, *Ancient Israel and Judah*, 485.

means "scattering" or "dispersion." A people may migrate for various reasons, including forced removal by an empire; escape from warfare; fleeing conditions caused by climate change such as flooding, drought (famine), swarms of pests (locusts, mosquitoes); or seeking economic opportunity. The extent of the Diaspora communities originating from northern Israel and southern Judah is not known. The first of these communities began during the Assyrian Empire by those forced into exile when Israel was defeated in 722 BCE. Others escaped the coming attacks by self-relocation. The years of turmoil between 722 BCE and 587 BCE resulted in forced and voluntary relocation for the people of the former Israel and Judah. Much of the "voluntary" relocation directly resulted from wars. Later, during the Persian, Greek, and Roman Empires, Jews scattered for economic opportunity. By the time of the apostle Paul in the first century CE, Jewish communities were spread throughout the Mediterranean region, including North Africa and possibly Spain. This scattering would require a change in how the people of Israel and Judah practiced their faith. Their theology was of a God with a fixed home in Jerusalem, so they had to adapt their faith to accommodate the Diaspora. Also, they needed to codify and institutionalize their lives, worship, and culture so such could be replicated in different regions within different cultures.

The People in Babylon

By the time the second group of deportees arrived from Judah after 587/586 BCE, the first group had lived in Babylon for over a decade. Some royals may have been imprisoned after the first deportation in 597, but the lives of the others are unknown. Forced enculturation of the deportees was not a Babylonian policy, so the exiled Judeans could form their own organizations. For example, Ezekiel refers to "the elders of Judah/Israel" among the exiles, indicating that these elder leaders remained an ongoing group (Ezek. 8:1; 14:1; 20:1, 3).[65] Eventually, Aramaic became the lingua franca of the people in Judah and those who lived throughout the empire.[66] This meant that exiles could communicate with others, so they were better able to work and live in a community with Babylonians and other exiles.

---

65. Israel Eph'al, "The Western Minorities in Babylonia in the 6th–5th Centuries B.C.: Maintenance and Cohesion," *Orientalia* 47, no. 1 (1978): 74–90. He notices reports of similar treatment among exiled Philistines and Phoenicians, indicating a state policy.

66. Efrem Yildiz recognizes it as the language of commerce as early as the Neo-Assyrian period, in "The Aramaic Language and Its Classification," *Journal of Assyrian Academic Studies* 14, no. 1 (2000): 26.

Little is known about the daily lives of these exiles or their worship practices. Some remained faithful to *Adoni* for generations.[67] Jon Berquist writes of multiple communities of exiles in Babylon. It is uncertain if these are different groups from the two exiles or if people were moved, or chose to move, after they arrived in Babylon. He notes, "Ezekiel depicts exile as a mostly rural event" while, by contrast, "Deutero-Isaiah focuses on the religious practices of the exiles and their Babylonian captors and depicts the sort of temple life that indicates the city of Babylon itself as the locale."[68] The exiles' presence is confirmed by Babylonian tablets that contain Hebrew names in commercial and land-leasing documents.[69] The use of Hebrew names indicates that the people maintained the culture and religious practices of their former land. Jews settled in Babylon and established permanent communities.[70]

The People in Egypt

War always causes refugees to move to try and escape the fighting. Especially after Sennacherib attacked Judah in 701 BCE to the Babylonian attacks in 597–587, exiles were pushed further south to Egypt. Irina Levinskaya notes that "Egypt was, perhaps, the most important Jewish center" in the whole region until after 100 CE.[71] Jews flourished in North Africa for hundreds of years. Jeremiah himself was taken to Egypt (Jer. 42–43). Very likely, multiple Jewish communities existed in Egypt from different times.

One of those places with a significant Jewish community was in Elephantine. Elephantine was an island in the Nile and had a military fortress to protect Egypt from the south. The beginnings of the Elephantine community are uncertain, but a letter in the Jewish archives, called the Elephantine papyri, states that it was before 525 BCE.[72] It appears that the Jews were free to form communities in Egyptian cities and worship and live as they pleased. Just as with the Babylonians, the region's lingua franca at the time was Aramaic, which facilitated communication with other Jewish colonies here and there.

---

67. Miller and Hayes, *Ancient Israel and Judah*, 495.
68. Jon Berquist, *Judaism in Persia's Shadow: A Social and Historical Approach* (Fortress, 1995), 15. Not all agree with this reading of Second Isaiah.
69. Miller and Hayes, *Ancient Israel and Judah*, 492; Pearce and Wunsch, *Documents of Judean Exiles*, 16–29. Documents found in both the Babylonian and Persian periods indicate that these communities continued to believe in *Adoni* for generations.
70. "Ancient Jewish History: The Babylonian Jewish Community," 1998–2025, https://www.jewishvirtuallibrary.org/the-babylonian-jewish-community.
71. Irina Levinskaya, "Diaspora," in *New Interpreter's Dictionary of the Bible*, 2:121.
72. *ANET*, 492.

THE LASTING TRAUMA OF EXILE AND THE SCATTERING OF REFUGEES AND EXILES

According to Daniel Smith-Christopher, modern scholars have downplayed the destructive and traumatizing impact of exile on the people of Israel and Judah.[73] He argues that these are seen especially in the books of Ezekiel and Lamentations. Passages such as Lamentations 4:4–10 use graphic terms to tell the story of the siege on Jerusalem, leading to its destruction and exile for many:

> The tongue of the infant sticks
>   to the roof of its mouth for thirst;
> the children beg for food,
>   but there is nothing for them.
>
> Those who feasted on delicacies
>   perish in the streets;
> those who were brought up in purple
>   cling to ash heaps.
>
> For the chastisement of my people has been greater
>   than the punishment of Sodom,
> which was overthrown in a moment,
>   though no hand was laid on it.
>
> Her princes were purer than snow,
>   whiter than milk;
> their bodies were more ruddy than coral,
>   their form cut like sapphire.
>
> Now their visage is blacker than soot;
>   they are not recognized in the streets.
> Their skin has shriveled on their bones;
>   it has become as dry as wood.
>
> Happier were those pierced by the sword
>   than those pierced by hunger,
> whose life drains away, deprived
>   of the produce of the field.
>
> The hands of compassionate women
>   have boiled their own children;
> they became their food
>   in the destruction of my people.

---

73. Daniel Smith-Christopher, *A Biblical Theology of Exile* (Fortress, 2002), 30–31.

Battle for Control of the Afro-Asiatic Region

Scholars have tended to see these words as metaphorical instead of a poem that tells truths too painful for prose. The pain of the people is also embedded in Psalms. For example, Psalm 44 is a national lament that cries (in vv. 9–11),

> Yet you have rejected us and shamed us
>   and have not gone out with our armies.
> You made us turn back from the foe,
>   and our enemies have gotten spoil.
> You have made us like sheep for slaughter
>   and have scattered us among the nations.
> You have sold your people for a trifle,
>   demanding no high price for them.

The Suffering Servant song in Isaiah 52:13–53:12 may be another metaphorical representation of the experiences of exile. These words represent both the trauma of the people who remained and those exiled, who were now refugees. The history of Judah and Israel is often divided into the preexilic and postexilic periods, a division demonstrating how this event—the loss of the temple and the scattering of the people—remained and remains a central cataclysmic event in the memory of the people.

THE END OF THE BABYLONIAN EMPIRE (561–539 BCE)

Nebuchadrezzar of Babylon was a fierce warrior and held the empire together until he died in 561 BCE. After him, the leadership of Babylon was unstable, causing the empire to totter. His son, Amelmarduk, reigned for only two years (561–560 BCE). He is the "King Evil-Merodach" of the Bible (2 Kgs. 25:27; Jer. 52:31). Unexpectedly, he was killed in a coup by Neriglissar, his brother-in-law, who then reigned in 559–556 BCE. Neriglissar's young son was king briefly until another coup replaced him. Finally, Nabonidus took the throne from 556 BCE to 539 BCE. He was a nobleman from Haran,[74] but his reign caused more internal instability. He worshiped the moon god, Sin, and tried to unify the empire by making Sin the primary god of Babylon instead of Marduk.[75] The powerful priests of Marduk opposed him and worked for his

---

74. Miller and Hayes, *Ancient Israel and Judah*, 489. Much of the biographical information comes from a stela he erected to his mother, Adad-guppi, in Ekhulkhul temple to the Moon God of Harran; *ANET*, 560–62.

75. P. Beaulieu, "King Nabonidus and the Neo-Babylonian Empire," in *Civilizations of the Ancient Near East*, ed. J. Sasson et al. (Scribner's Sons, 1995), 2:975.

removal. This opposition may be the reason he fled the capital. He lived in the Arabian Desert for over a decade, leaving his son Bel-shar-usar ("Belshazzar" of Dan. 5:22) in charge.[76]

Meanwhile, Cyrus II was the son of Cambyses I, king of Anshan, and Princess Mandane, daughter of Astyages the last king of the Median Empire. After defeating the Medes in Lydia, Cyrus II proclaimed himself the king of Persia in 559 BCE, overthrew his grandfather, and became Cyrus the Great. His reign began the Achaemenid, or Persian, Empire (550–323 BCE). This distant king would soon control a vast empire.

Nabonidus returned from the desert to Babylon in October 543 BCE to prepare for an attack from the ever-more-powerful Cyrus.[77] The Babylonian Empire had been left in the hands of his son, who was not ready for the threat. Cyrus first met the Babylonian army at "Opis on the banks of the Tigris [River]," and the Babylonians retreated.[78] On October 12, 539 BCE, Babylon capitulated quickly and was taken without a fight.[79] The empire changed hands without a whimper from the last Babylonian king, Nabonidus, and the Babylonian Empire became part of the Persian Empire. Judah's fate was decided far from its country and people.

The biblical books of Kings and Chronicles end with the Babylonian destruction of Jerusalem. Other books continue to tell the story and record the postexilic period. But these books take a different form and do not provide a continuous narrative after the Babylonian attack. The books that narrate the two nations end with the exile (Joshua–2 Kings). Because Judah is a small part of the vast Persian Empire, the empire's chronicles do not help much in understanding what was happening in Judah during the time of the exile from 587/586 to 529 BCE.

SUMMARY

This transition from Assyrian to Egyptian to Babylonian control of the region of Canaan resulted in destruction and warfare for Judah. The Assyrian Empire was Judah's overlord for 135 years after destroying Israel, exiling their elite, and taking over their lands. Next, the Egyptians were in control of Judah for a few years, killing Josiah at Meggido and exiling his son to Egypt. The Babylonians conquered the Assyrians and gained control of the whole region.

---

76. Miller and Hayes, *Ancient Israel and Judah*, 490.
77. Miller and Hayes, *Ancient Israel and Judah*, 503.
78. Grayson, *ABC*, 109.
79. Grayson, *ABC*, 109–10.

In response to Hezekiah's revolt, the Babylonians destroyed many of the fortified cities in Judah in 701 BCE. In response to Zechariah's revolt, Judah was trampled down, Jerusalem was surrounded and starved, then sacked and burned in 587/586 BCE.

Judeans were a small, insignificant group of people living amid vast empires. The exiles of both nations formed permanent communities throughout the Afro-Asiatic region in the wake of Assyrian and Babylonian destructions. These successive exiles combined with the forced migration of Israelites and Judeans looked like the end of their culture and faith.

12

The Persian Empire (539–330 BCE)

The territory taken by Cyrus was vast, stretching from the Indus River in the east (present-day Pakistan) to the border of Egypt and parts of Greece in the west and north to the Caspian and Black Seas. A few years later, his son Darius would add Egypt to their holdings. Cyrus's territory far surpassed the size of the Assyrian or Babylonian Empires. It was known as the Achaemenid Empire, named after an ancestor of Cyrus and founder of the empire. Cyrus and his family were from what would be modern-day Iran. The Afro-Asiatic region was now part of an even larger empire.

Written extrabiblical sources concerning Judah disappeared during the Persian period. The biblical books of Kings and Chronicles break off when the Babylonians destroyed Jerusalem. The biblical narratives do not resume until the return of some of the exiles in the books of Ezra and Nehemiah, and these do not provide a wealth of traceable information. Judah was a small part of the vast Persian Empire, whose records do not include them. This means that the source materials for understanding the history of Judah during this period are scant. While historians can tell the larger history of the empire, specific information about Judah is limited. The biblical sources contain information about the concerns, context, and cultural changes that occurred during this period, even if these cannot be explicitly dated.

THE BEGINNINGS OF THE PERSIAN EMPIRE: CYRUS II AND DARIUS I (539–486 BCE)

Cyrus II (the Great) now held an extensive territory that could not be effectively held by force alone.[1] He decided that the best way to preserve his rule was to ingratiate himself and his empire in the people's hearts. He would not be seen as a ruthless overlord but as a generous benefactor.[2] According to the book of Ezra, Cyrus issued a decree for the people to return to Jerusalem because the God of heaven "charged me to build him a house at Jerusalem." The decree was probably issued within the first year of his reign (1:1–2). The exiles could also go "with silver and gold, with goods, and with livestock, besides freewill offerings for the house of God in Jerusalem" (1:4). The Ezra text promises a return and orders the rebuilding but hedges on the resources, indicating that much of them would come from the exiles. This fits with other edicts attributed to Cyrus, such as one found in Babylon. It reads in part

> By his exalted [word], all the kings who sit upon thrones throughout the world, from the Upper to the Lower Sea, who live in the dis[tricts far-off], . . . I returned the [images of] the gods to the sacred centers [on the other side of] the Tigris[,] whose sanctuaries had been abandoned for a long time, and I let them dwell in eternal abodes. I gathered all their inhabitants and returned [to them] their dwellings.[3]

Isaiah 45:1–7 declares that Cyrus was *Adoni*'s anointed one. Even though Cyrus does not know *Adoni*, God is directing Cyrus's actions for the sake of "my servant Jacob" (45:4). Scholars debate how the word "anointed," or *messiah*, was to be understood here. John Watts notes, "YHWH [*Adoni*] introduces him [Cyrus] to Israel as his 'shepherd' and 'anointed one,' the royal titles of Israel's kings."[4] Joseph Blenkinsopp agrees but sees this as a temporary title, meant to initiate the exiles' return and the temple's rebuilding, not to replace Judah's Davidic line.[5] Either way, Cyrus was remembered as God's instrument for restoring Judah. Notably, this is the first time the biblical text assigns Judean royal titles to the king of a controlling empire. It could indicate that people now accepted imperial rule as a regular part of life.

This portrayal of Cyrus as a benevolent ruler sounds almost too good to be true. Cyrus's treatment of people was not uniform, which was evident in

---

1. Pierre Briant, *From Cyrus to Alexander: A History of the Persian Empire* (Eisenbrauns, 2002), 79.
2. Briant, *Cyrus to Alexander*, 79.
3. *COS*, 2:315.
4. John Watts, *Isaiah 34–66*, 2nd ed., Word Biblical Commentary (Nelson, 2005), 702.
5. Joseph Blenkinsopp, *Isaiah 40–55* (Doubleday, 2002), 248–49.

Babylon and Judah.[6] Pierre Briant explains, "The maintenance of [the controlled nations'] socioeconomic privileges depended on their unreserved allegiance to the victors and accepting the reality of the newly imposed imperial structures."[7] Revolt was met with the same brutal measures as in the previous empires. Also, the acts of graciousness represented by the Persian leader may have been less in actuality than the propaganda claims.[8] Ezra 1:4 supports this observation, stating that the exiles provided "freewill offerings for the house of God" to support rebuilding the temple. In other words, some of the sacred treasures were returned, but Cyrus did not pay for the return or rebuilding.

After Cyrus died in battle in 530 BCE, Cambyses II became king of the Persian Empire. His reign was only eight years long and troubled. Cambyses spent most of his reign fighting on the western front with Egypt and was killed in Syria (Aram).[9] What happened next is much debated.[10] It appears that Bardiya, Cambyses's brother, took the throne while Cambyses was on the Egyptian campaign. Darius I challenged Bardiya for the throne and eventually emerged as the king in 522 BCE.[11]

His reign was lengthy, but he did not gain much additional territory.[12] Darius was credited with organizing the vast empire that his predecessors took. He created twenty regional governorships, or satrapies, which were further divided into *medinahs*, or provinces.[13] Each administrative satrapy had a governor called a satrap. These governors were either members of the king's family or high-ranking Persian officials.[14] Judah and Samaria were part of the satrap of *Abri-Nari*, which means "Beyond the River."[15] Its territory stretched from the Euphrates River to the Sinai Peninsula, plus the island of Cyprus.[16] Under Darius's rule, the empire continued to develop its infrastructure, organize its administration, and develop its economic resources. There were occasional

---

6. Amélie Kuhrt, "Ancient Near Eastern History: The Case of Cyrus the Great of Persia," in *Understanding the History of Ancient Israel*, ed. H. Williamson (Oxford University Press, 2007), 117.
7. Briant, *Cyrus to Alexander*, 80.
8. Kuhrt, "Cyrus the Great of Persia," 117.
9. Briant, *Cyrus to Alexander*, 61.
10. See Briant for all the theories, in *Cyrus to Alexander*, 97–106.
11. Mark Leuchter argues that Darius was not a relative but a usurper: *An Empire Far and Wide: The Achaemenid Dynastic Myth and Jewish Scribes in the Late Persian Period* (Oxford University Press, 2024), 18.
12. Briant, *Cyrus to Alexander*, 139.
13. Briant, *Cyrus to Alexander*, 467; cf., e.g., Esth. 1:1.
14. Lester Grabbe, *A History of the Jews and Judaism in the Second Temple Period* (T&T Clark, 2004), 1:132.
15. This is the Semitic title; the Persians called it "Athura." A. F. Rainey, "The Satrapy 'Beyond the River,'" *Australian Journal of Biblical Archaeology* 1 (1969): 45.
16. J. Maxwell Miller and John H. Hayes, *A History of Ancient Israel and Judah*, 2nd ed. (Westminster John Knox, 2006), 523.

uprisings that were quelled successfully, including one in Egypt that must have involved Judah to some extent.[17] Darius turned Persia into an effective and profitable empire and passed an economic powerhouse to subsequent generations.

In 512 BCE, Darius captured more territory in the west, using his naval fleet to extend his empire into Europe from the Bosporus Strait and up the Danube River into what now is Ukraine.[18] By 499 BCE, the Ionian (Greek) cities of Aeolis, Doris, Cyprus, and Caria rebelled against Darius. Darius was successful in ending the rebellion in 494 BCE. Then, he decided to attack Athens and other powerful city-states and was defeated in the famous Battle of Marathon (490 BCE). This was the beginning of the Greco-Persian wars, which would play a large part in the rest of the Persian Empire. Darius did not take the defeat well and planned another attack. That was interrupted by a revolt in Egypt in 486 BCE. Before he could deal with it, Darius became ill and died in November 486.[19]

When he died, the Achaemenid Empire was at its largest, holding territory from the Iaxartes River in central Asia (modern-day Kyrgyzstan) to the Persian Gulf and from the Danube River (modern-day Ukraine) to the Indus River (modern-day India) (map 11).[20] In addition, he organized the Persian Empire into an efficient governmental structure and focused on economic growth.

JUDAH UNDER CYRUS II AND DARIUS I (539–486 BCE)

Judah became a *medinah* in the Persian Empire, and the Diaspora resulted in the people who descended from Judah being spread throughout the empire. Most of the Diaspora were from communities formed in the periods of Assyrian and Babylonian control. The people of Judah relocated in the Persian period for economic reasons. With people spread throughout the empire, they and their faith needed a name. Like the Assyrians and the Babylonians, the Persian Empire continued using Aramaic as the official commercial language. Aramaic would remain the common language of the region until the fourth century CE.[21] Aramaic and Hebrew were related Afro-Asiatic languages and

---

17. Lester Grabbe, *Judaism from Cyrus to Hadrian*, vol. 1, *The Persian and Greek Periods* (Fortress, 1992), 126.
18. Miller and Hayes, *Ancient Israel and Judah*, 524.
19. Briant, *Cyrus to Alexander*, 161.
20. Briant, *Cyrus to Alexander*, 161.
21. Efrem Yildiz, "The Aramaic Language and Its Classification," *Journal of Assyrian Academic Studies* 14, no. 1 (2000): 32. Persia was not the first empire to adopt Aramaic. It was first used widely during the Neo-Assyrian period (26). After 323 BCE, Greek was also a commonly used language in Judah.

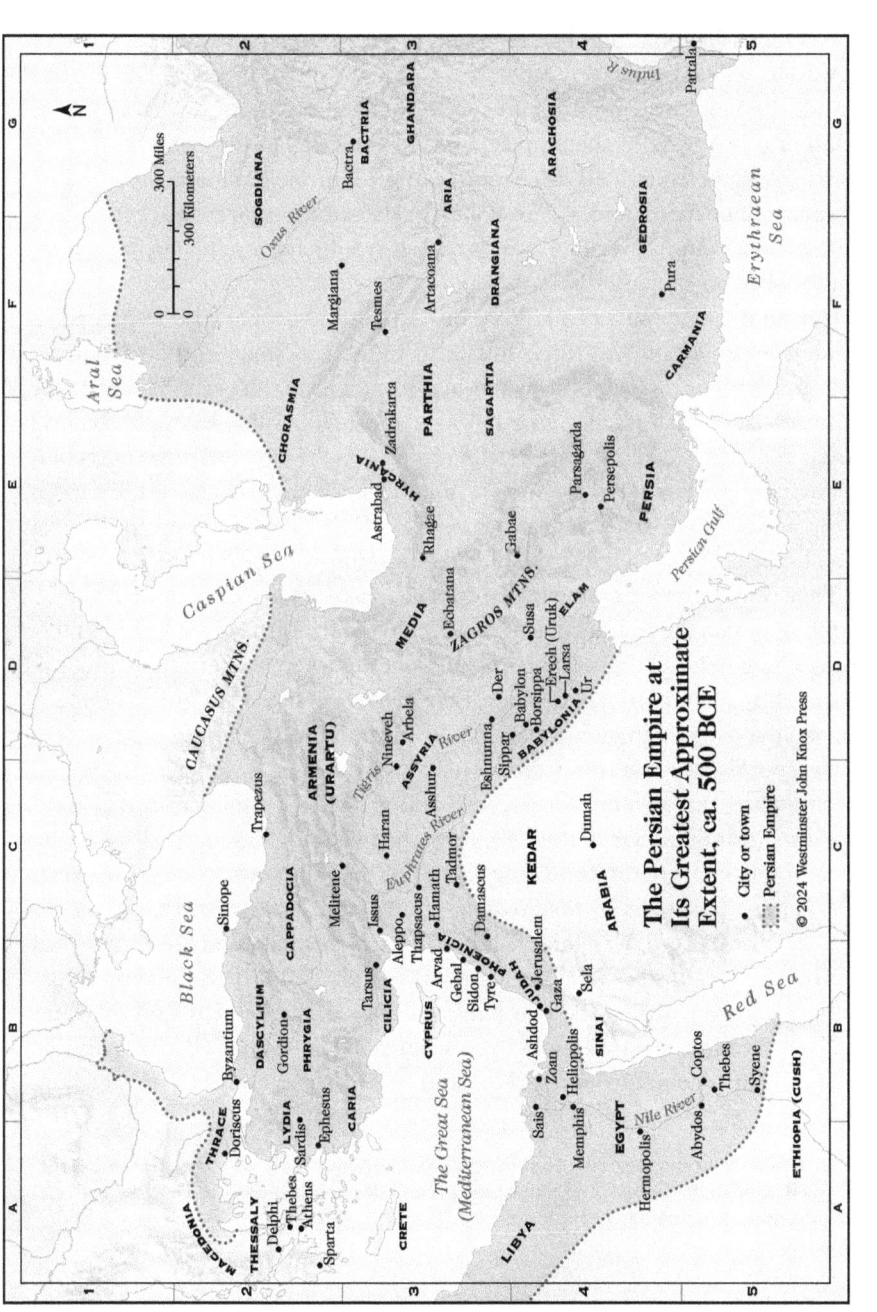

Map 11. The Persian Empire at its greatest approximate extent. (Courtesy of Westminster John Knox Press)

shared much in common. The kingdom of *Yudah*, in Hebrew, became *Yahud* in Aramaic. The people were called *Yehudim*,[22] the plural of *Yahud*. During this period, the name was used for the *Yahud medinah*, for those descended from Judah in other parts of the empire, and for the religion they practiced. The words would be translated later into multiple European languages with the necessary phonetic changes. For example, the substitution of the letter *J* for the *Y* comes from its German translation. It would eventually become "Jew" and "Jewish" in English.[23]

During the early part of the Persian Empire, the people who remained in Judah were going on with their lives, but Judah was small and far from the main trade routes. Much of its economy was agrarian, just as it had been for centuries. In Jerusalem, monumental structures such as the walls, palace, and temple remained in ruins. Some residents lived in the city, but how much of it was rebuilt or occupied at the time is unknown. Mizpah remained the capital of the *medinah* until the reign of Artaxerxes.[24] The Persians were not interested in the central hill region of Judah except for its crops.

They were more interested in the coastal areas. Trade and commerce grew, and the cities on the coast provided the conduit for the growing shipping enterprise. The coastal plain was repopulated with cities in Samaria and Philistia occupied by Samaritans, Philistines, Phoenicians, and traders and merchants from all the seagoing regions (map 12). It was trade and commerce dependent on transport by sea that drove the growth. From then on, trading by sea would become an essential source of income and growth for the coastal regions.[25] This also meant that, while still necessary, the two trade routes (the Way of the Sea and the Transjordanian Route) were not the only ways to travel between Africa and Asia. Travel by boat was faster and often less expensive.

The books of Ezra, Haggai, Zechariah 1–8, Nehemiah, and the apocryphal 1 Esdras 2–9 tell of the return of some of the exiles and the rebuilding of the Jerusalem temple during the two hundred years of the Persian Empire. Ezra and Nehemiah are the two books that narrate the Persian period in an episodic fashion. Esdras functions much like 1 and 2 Chronicles and is a later retelling

---

22. This is the beginning of the names "Jew," "Judah," and "Judeans." However, the word continued through the Greek and Latin languages and various European languages to arrive at the words used in English. The substitution of the letter *J* for the *Y* comes from its German translation.

23. Elon Gilad, "Why Are Jews Called Jews?," *Haaretz*, 2017, https://www.haaretz.com/archaeology/2017-02-15/ty-article/why-are-jews-called-jews/0000017f-dbeb-d856-a37f-ffeb3f760000.

24. Diana Edelman, Philip Davies, Christophe Nihan, and Thomas Romer, *Opening the Books of Moses* (Routledge, 2014), 61.

25. Andrea Berlin, "Between Large Forces: Palestine in the Hellenistic Period," *BA* 60, no. 1 (March 1997): 3–4.

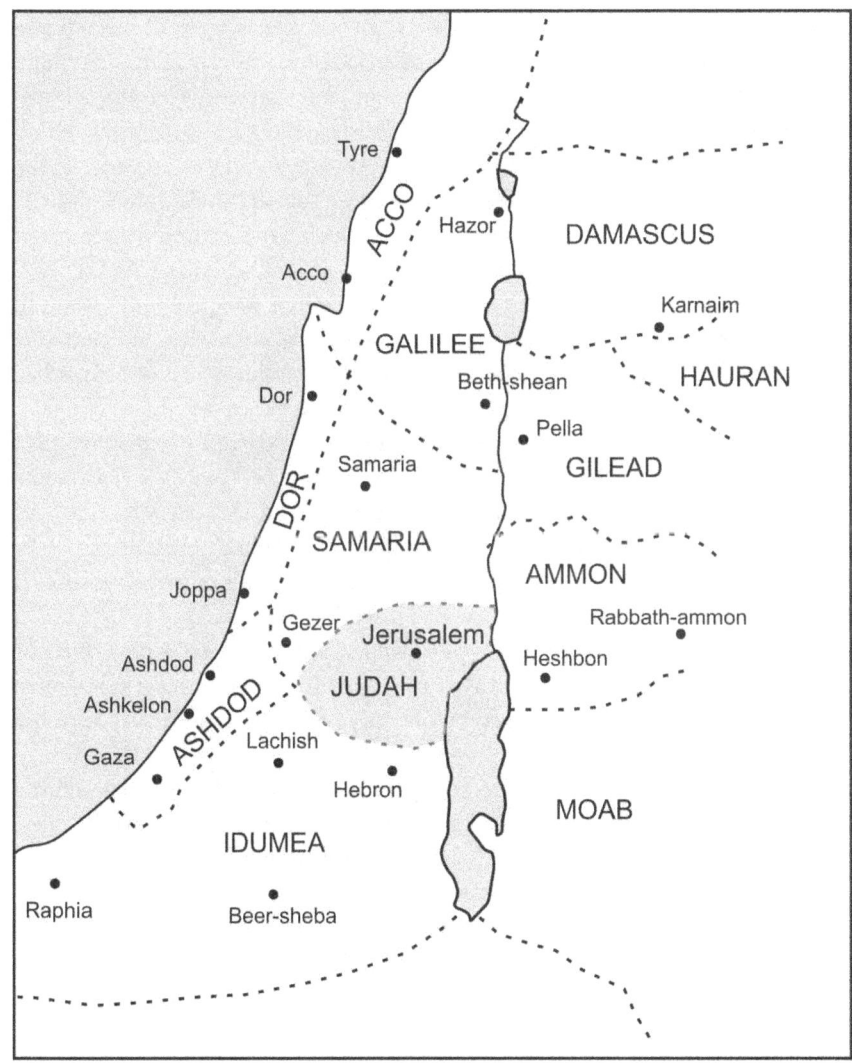

Map 12. Persian Province of Judah among other provinces "Beyond the River." (Courtesy of Westminster John Knox Press)

of the material in Ezra and Nehemiah. Haggai, a short book, was written in about 520 BCE and focuses only on the rebuilding of the temple. Zechariah 1–8 are also focused on the temple rebuilding, and chapters 9–14 are probably from the later Hellenistic period. Isaiah 40–66 was also composed in the postexilic period, but the time frame is more difficult to determine. They are the prophetic voices of the period. Like all biblical books, these scrolls tell only part of the story. They focus on the return of some exiles, the rebuilding of the temple and Jerusalem, and tensions among the leadership in the region. However, the texts are not straightforward, and internal textual conflicts make organizing them into a timeline difficult. Also, as noted above, since Judah was a small and isolated *medinah*, it does not appear in Persian records, so the Bible is the only source of information about the region at this time.

The first chapter of Ezra recounts Cyrus's decree mandating the return of "everyone whose spirit God had stirred" (Ezra 1:5). The exiles were allowed to return and rebuild the house of *Adoni*. The decree was probably issued in either 539 or 538 BCE. Ezra then describes several groups who returned: one led by Sheshbazzar (1:1–11), one by Zerubbabel, Jeshua, and other leaders (Ezra 2), and a later group during the reign of Artaxerxes led by Ezra (chap. 7). Why the different groups? We do not know for sure and cannot assign an exact date for these returns. Based on the multiple reports in Ezra, it is reasonable to presume that the biblical narrative preserved memories of several waves of return by groups of persons who relocated from Babylon to Jerusalem.

The first return in the book of Ezra is led by Sheshbazzar, a "prince of Judah" (1:8), possibly referring to a tribal leader. Sheshbazzar is listed as a governor in Ezra 5:14 in a letter supposedly penned by Tattenai, the governor of the satrapy called "Beyond the River" (5:2). This was the satrapy of which Judah was a member. As discussed below, there are significant issues with the letter and its origins.

The report of Sheshbazzar and the returnees is brief. The return focused on the treasure that "Sheshbazzar brought up when the exiles were brought up from Babylonia to Jerusalem" (1:11b). It also states the neighbors of the Judeans gave them valuable gifts and livestock (1:6), and Cyrus returned the temple treasures taken by Nebuchadrezzar (1:7–11a). According to this account, the exiles left Babylon with a staggering 5,400 "gold and silver vessels" (1:11a). Without independent sources, the biblical text is the only witness.

The second return narrated in Ezra was led by Zerubbabel and other leaders (Ezra 2–5). Zerubbabel does not have a title in Ezra but is called a governor in the book of Haggai (1:1, 14; 2:2, 21). The report of the second return is more extensive than the one led by Sheshbazzar, including a list of returnees (Ezra 2:4–70). The list is long, with laypersons and temple personnel, including priests, Levites, singers, and other temple workers. The list includes the number of people. There is a similar list in Nehemiah 7. Closer analysis shows that the list is a composite developed by multiple editors, so the account is too fragmented to be of historical value.[26] Several scholars believe Zerubbabel was Jehoiachin's

---

26. H. G. M. Williamson, *Ezra-Nehemiah*, Word Biblical Commentary, vol. 16 (Word Books, 1985), 28.

grandson, which would make him an heir to the Davidic line. Jehoiachin was the Davidic king exiled to Babylon and released from captivity in the thirty-seventh year of his captivity.[27] Could this have been an attempt by the Davidic line to reclaim the throne? The book of Haggai supports this claim:

> The word of [*Adoni*] came a second time to Haggai on the twenty-fourth day of the month:
> "Speak to Zerubbabel, governor of Judah, saying: I am about to shake the heavens and the earth and to overthrow the throne of kingdoms; I am about to destroy the strength of the kingdoms of the nations and overthrow the chariots and their riders, and the horses and their riders shall fall, every one by the sword of a comrade. On that day, says [*Adoni*] of hosts, I will take you, O Zerubbabel my servant, son of Shealtiel, says [*Adoni*], and make you like a signet ring; for I have chosen you, says [*Adoni*] of hosts." (2:20–23)

This appears to be a prophecy that Zerubbabel would be restored to the kingship, which makes his disappearance in Ezra after laying the foundation of the temple all the more puzzling. Were the Persians concerned, so they removed him? Or did he return to his life in Babylon? The biblical text is silent on the matter. However, the Davidic royal line disappears from the Hebrew Bible at this point.[28]

The book of Ezra neither explains why there are two returns thus far nor discusses the chronology. Sheshbazzar and Zerubbabel are remembered as leaders of the exiles, but it is unknown if they were officials appointed by the Persian Empire.[29] The point of the returns was to rebuild the temple in Jerusalem (Ezra 1:2; 3:10). Both Sheshbazzar (5:16, in the letter from Tattenai) and Zerubbabel (3:10) were credited with laying the foundation, presumably shortly after they arrived. There is no way to know if the foundation was laid twice by different leaders, a single foundation by one or the other, or both together. Sara Japhet argues that Sheshbazzar was given the temple vessels to transport to Jerusalem, and he then laid the foundations for the temple, but it was not completed at the time.[30] Then, during Darius's reign, Zerubbabel returned to complete the temple, inspired by the prophets Haggai and Zechariah.[31] This scenario is plausible but remains a theory.

---

27. For example, Marvin Sweeney, *I & II Kings*, Old Testament Library (Westminster John Knox, 2007), 465; and William Schniedewind, *How the Bible Became a Book* (Cambridge University Press, 2004), 162–63.

28. Schniedewind, *Bible Became a Book*, 163.

29. Ralph Klein, "Ezra-Nehemiah, Books of," in *ABD* 2:735.

30. Sara Japhet, "Sheshbazzar and Zerubbabel—against the Background of the Historical and Religious Tendencies of Ezra-Nehemiah," *ZAW* 94 (1982): 93.

31. Japhet, "Sheshbazzar and Zerubbabel," 93. Miller and Hayes follow this construction in *Ancient Israel and Judah*, 513.

What is apparent in the text is that the return of the exiles resulted in conflicts with the people who remained in the land. The conflicts were significant enough that the temple building ceased until at least Cyrus died, and Darius began his reign in 522 BCE.

The first conflict is narrated in Ezra 4:4–5. It contains no details, just that "then the people of the land discouraged the people of Judah and made them afraid to build [the temple], and they bribed officials to frustrate their plan."

Another conflict is described in Ezra 4:6–24. It is in the form of a letter from unknown leaders who oppose the refortification of the city of Jerusalem and its walls, not just the temple. However, its placement here is puzzling. The focus of Ezra overall is on building the temple, the resumption of worship, and the purity of the citizens. The rebuilding of the walls of Jerusalem was the focus of Nehemiah's later mission (445–443 BCE). Was the letter quoted in this passage mistakenly placed here rather than in Nehemiah?[32] Is the letter a historical artifact?

Ezra 4:6 sets the letter in the ascension year (485 BCE) of an "Ahasuerus." Williamson and others agree that the person behind this name is actually Xerxes, who followed Darius I in 486 BCE.[33] If this is true, the letter belongs at a later time. Also, Ezra and Nehemiah were originally a single book, and biblical narratives are not necessarily in chronological order.[34] This discrepancy is difficult to resolve. Scholars presume that the letter originated in Samaria because of Sanballat's opposition to Nehemiah's mission (Neh. 4:1–23).[35] Sanballet was the leader of Samaria, the name for the old northern kingdom of Israel. It is possible that just as all the laws developed over time were eventually gathered in the same place in the Torah, this passage indicates that opposition to rebuilding Jerusalem's walls and temple came from all sides. That could be the reason for the narrative's placement here, even though it comes from a later time.

Ezra 5:3–17 returns to the issue of the temple. Tattenai, governor of the satrapy Beyond the River, and Shethar-bosenai, an envoy of the king, write a letter to Darius asking if permission was granted by Cyrus to the Judeans to rebuild the Jerusalem temple (5:6–17). To resolve the issue, Ezra 6:1–5 says that Darius ordered a search of the royal archives. A "second" copy of Cyrus's edict was discovered. However, this copy differs from the one in Ezra 1:1. It does

---

32. Sara Japhet, "The Temple in the Restoration Period: Reality and Ideology," *Union Seminary Quarterly Review* 44 (1991): 205; J. M. Myers, *Ezra, Nehemiah*, Anchor Bible (Doubleday, 1965), xxxii; J. Blenkinsopp, *Ezra-Nehemiah*, Old Testament Library (Westminster, 1988), 113–15, 203–4.
33. Williamson, *Ezra-Nehemiah*, 52. NIV translates *Ahasuerus* as "Xerxes" in the biblical text.
34. Williamson, *Ezra-Nehemiah*, xxi.
35. Williamson, *Ezra-Nehemiah*, 61.

not specify a return of the exiles but focuses on the rebuilding of the temple, complete with its dimensions and the restoration of the temple vessels. It also states that the Royal Persian Treasury would pay for the construction (6:3–14).

Is the edict (6:3–14) a historical artifact? Scholars are divided on the issue. The coauthor, Tattenai, was a governor of Beyond the River in 502 BCE.[36] Lester Grabbe notes that the permission to rebuild the temple would have come from a local governor such as Tattenai, not the Persian King Cyrus or Darius.[37] The reason the king appointed local governors was to deal with regional issues. Also, the Persian government would not ordinarily pay for the temple's construction in an occupied area. There is also the issue of the two differing decrees (1:1–4 and 6:3–14).[38] Grabbe believes the second "found" document is suspect.[39] Other scholars disagree and claim the second decree as authentic,[40] noting how it resembles other royal Persian documents.[41] Because the document cannot be authenticated, there is no definitive proof. It illustrates one of the problems in untangling ancient conflicting sources.

Yet, even after the way is cleared for the temple to be built, it is delayed. What were the issues that hindered the building of the temple? According to Ezra and Haggai, building the temple was a long process with at least two identifiable problems. Ezra identifies the problem as the conflict between the returning exiles and "the people of the land." This reason is further narrated in Ezra and Haggai. The prophet Haggai says the problem is the exiles, who built their own houses and lives and neglected the building of the temple (Hag. 1:1–6), a reason that appears only in this prophetic book. Whatever the exact cause, the construction of the temple did not proceed until the second year of Darius, in about 520 BCE, or about eighteen years after the first possible time of return.

The Bible speaks of various conflicts between the groups vying for control of Judah. Ezra records discord between the returning exiles and the "people of the land" as the cause for the temple-construction delays (Ezra 4–5). Who were the "people of the land" wanting to help the exiles rebuild the temple? Most probably, they were descendants of the very people left in Judah when the exiles were taken to Babylon, as well as some of the exiles who moved

---

36. Rainey, "Satrapy," 53.
37. Lester Grabbe, "The 'Persian Documents,' in the Book of Ezra: Are They Authentic?," in *Judah and the Judeans in the Persian Period*, ed. O. Lipschits and M. Oeming (Eisenbrauns, 2006), 548.
38. Grabbe, "The 'Persian Documents,'" 548.
39. Grabbe, "The 'Persian Documents,'" 548.
40. Miller and Hayes, *Ancient Israel and Judah*, 509; Japhet, "Temple in the Restoration," 211–12.
41. Japhet, "Temple in the Restoration," 211–12.

from Israel to Judah in the Assyrian movement of peoples (Ezra 4:2).[42] Also included in the "people of the land" (Ezra 3:3; 4:4) was a third group, the Samaritans, who were the residents of the area occupied by the old northern kingdom of Israel and the Assyrian exiles who adopted the faith of Israel.[43] The center of the conflict was the relationship between all these groups.

Before the exile, full citizenship came from being Judean. After the exile, the returning exiles, the remnant, saw themselves as "God's true Israel congregation."[44] The return was more than seventy years later, so the returning groups were probably the grandchildren and great-grandchildren of those first taken into exile. These exiled people were the descendants of Judah's priests, princes, and power brokers. The exiles returned, probably expecting to resume the leading places and status occupied by their ancestors.

The people of the land were the ones the Babylonians left in the destroyed Jerusalem and surrounding area. They rebuilt their lives and homes, some took on leadership roles, and some married women from surrounding countries. They did just as Gedaliah, the overseer appointed by Babylon, stated in 2 Kings 25:24, "'Do not be afraid because of the Chaldean officials; live in the land, serve the king of Babylon, and it shall be well with you.'" The people of the land saw no reason to give up the land and leadership to the returning ones. In the intervening time, the people remaining in Judah had created leaders, rebuilt some of the city, and run the country without the exiles.

Inevitably, there would be tension and disagreements between these two groups. For example, Ezra 3 states that worship was restored in Jerusalem (3:1–6). This demonstrates that the exiles thought of themselves as the true leaders: only after they arrived could worship resume. However, as noted above, the people who lived in Judah during the exiles' time in Babylon had been worshiping at the temple site all along. This is one example of the tension between the two groups.

---

42. This is not to be confused with the "people of the land" during preexilic Judah, from the reign of Athaliah through the exile. This postexilic "people of the land" was a specific identified class associated with other leaders; Joseph Healey, "'Am ha-Aretz," *ABD* 1:68.

43. Gary Knoppers, *Jews and Samaritans: The Origins and History and Their Early Relations* (Oxford University Press, 2013), 137. Other scholars disagree. Provan, Long, and Longman argue that the '*Am ha-Aretz* was composed of native Judeans/Israelites, people whose ancestors were exiled by the Assyrians and now were the opposition; see Iain Provan, V. Philips Long, and Tremper Longman III, *A Biblical History of Israel* (Westminster John Knox, 2003), 294. Others claim they were the Samaritans, as does Herbert Ryle in *The Books of Ezra and Nehemiah* (Cambridge University Press, 1901).

44. A. H. J. Gunneweg, "'*Am ha-Aretz*—A Semantic Revolution," *ZAW* 95 (1983): 439. Also, Aharon Oppenheimer, *The 'Am ha-Aretz: A Study of the Social History of the Jewish People in the Hellenistic-Roman Period*, trans. I. Levine (Brill, 1977), 11.

Conflict among the two groups was one reason for the delay in building the temple. Yet another reason was given by the prophet Haggai: the people themselves were neglecting the temple. According to Haggai 1:1, the prophet was active in the second year of Darius, or 521 BCE. This prophetic book calls out the people living in Jerusalem, both the exiles and those who remained, for abandoning the building of the temple (1:2–11).

With his urging and the work of Zerubbabel, labor on the temple resumed. Then, according to Ezra, the temple was completed in the "sixth year of the reign of King Darius" (6:15). That would place the temple's completion in either 516 or 515 BCE, or about four to five years after Haggai and twenty-four years after Cyrus's decree of return. Historically, these dates are estimates. The grand vision of a return to rebuild the temple was a dream long delayed. Archaeologically, no remains of this Second Temple exist. Most argue that "this important shrine was modeled on a plan somewhat similar to the original Solomonic form but probably smaller and without much finery."[45] Why are there no remains of the Second Temple? Herod, a Jew who rose to be a minor king in the Roman Empire and would appear in the Gospels, expanded and rebuilt the temple in the first century CE. The smaller temple was incorporated into Herod's larger building project.

The postexilic temple, like Jerusalem, was rebuilt by the locals and the returning exiles despite their disagreements. It is also significant to recognize that the rebuilt temple was regionally important, but it was no longer the only place for worship by the Jewish people. The temple was for those in close proximity to Jerusalem and would remain the central place for public religious ceremonies. Those in the Diaspora would not be able to travel to the temple often.

The main activity of the temple was always blood sacrifice, and everything centered on this activity.[46] Grabbe notes the different reasons for sacrifices: "There were required sacrifices on a daily, weekly, and monthly basis and also at major religious festivals."[47] This practice may seem gross or wrong to the modern reader, but this had been the practice of the temple throughout the Hebrew Bible. While details are slim, the sacrifices were accompanied by worship, including singing psalms and prayer. Each Judean male required sacrifices for sin, blessing, or thanksgiving, and most men in or near Jerusalem attended the temple regularly. Temple sacrifice also provided a social and

---

45. John Betlyon, "A People Transformed: Palestine in the Persian Period," *NEA* 68 (2005): 39.

46. Lester Grabbe, *An Introduction to Second Temple Judaism: History and Religion of the Jews in the Time of Nehemiah, the Maccabees, Hillel and Jesus* (T&T Clark, 2010), 40.

47. Grabbe, *Second Temple Judaism*, 40.

family function. Only part of the animal was burned in the sacrifice or given to the priest; the rest provided a meal for family and friends.[48]

Without a monarchy, the temple and its leadership gained importance during the Persian period. It became the center of cultural life in Judah.[49] This transition to temple leadership began when the temple was completed and grew into the central power in Judah by the end of the Persian Empire. The position of high priest was already one of power and privilege before the exile. The priests were responsible for maintaining the religious cult on behalf of the people and were also keepers and expounders of Jewish law. Priests were also well compensated for their work, receiving part of the offering, tithes, and land (Lev. 6:16–18; 7:28–36; Num. 18:8–13, 21–23a). As the Persian period continued, the position of high priest gained political power. As Grabbe explains: "In some cases, the high priest may have been the official governor; at other times, the ruling power looked to the high priest as the main representative of the Jewish people."[50] So, an additional change in this period was the growing role of the high priest in Jewish society.

THE SAMARITANS: ORIGIN AND RELATIONSHIP TO JUDAH

After the exile, the focus of the biblical text is on Judah. However, while the monarchy of Israel was destroyed, many of the people of Israel remained there. There are no known written sources from Israel after 722 BCE. The text of 2 Kings states, "[*Adoni*] removed Israel out of his sight, as he had foretold through all his servants the prophets. So Israel was exiled from their own land to Assyria until this day" (17:23). Second Chronicles, however, speaks of Israelite tribes after 722. Hezekiah of Judah invites the Ephraimites and the Manassites for the Passover (2 Chr. 30:1; 31:1). During the restorations under Judah's King Josiah, part of the money for the temple repairs comes from Manasseh, Ephraim, and of all the remnant of Israel (2 Chr. 34:9). Granted, the people who were part of these tribes may have resided in Judah at this point. Still, the text does identify them using northern tribe names.

According to archaeological surveys, Assyria did not ravage the Israelite countryside, and the Israelites deported by the Assyrians were only part of the

---

48. Grabbe, *Second Temple Judaism*, 40.
49. Jon Berquist, *Judaism in Persia's Shadow: A Social and Historical Approach* (Fortress, 1995), 147.
50. Grabbe, *Second Temple Judaism*, 46.

society's elite.[51] At the same time, the existence of a northern Hebrew dialect in some parts of the Hebrew Bible, sometimes called Israelian Hebrew, adds to the evidence that the culture of the previous nation endured.[52] Samaria site surveys demonstrate that some areas in Israel had a population decline in and around 722 while others remained constant, proving that the Assyrian destruction was incomplete. In addition, since material items such as pottery and home construction remained the same, the population before and after 722 BCE was substantially the same.[53]

To summarize, Israelite culture continued in the northern territory. Gary Knoppers also asserts, "Whatever exiles from foreign states were forcibly imported into the Samarian highlands [by Assyria], most seem to have been gradually absorbed into the local population."[54] At some point, the old kingdom of Israel became known as Samaria, after its capital. It was not a population change but a name change. The Samaritans of the New Testament are the descendants of the Israelites of the Northern Kingdom.

Israelite culture also continued throughout the Assyrian, Babylonian, and Persian control of the region. The northern region, especially the northern Samaritan hills and the area surrounding the city of Samaria, grew at an unprecedented rate.[55] The Persian period mirrored the period after the death of Solomon when there was a large, rich Samaria and an impoverished and diminished Judah.[56] Religiously, the area does not show a significant influence from the Assyrian exiles who were imported into the region. Knoppers summarizes, "If the use of personal names is any indication, the area of Samaria became more Yahwistic, not less so, in the Persian period than in the time of the Israelite monarchy."[57] He also assesses the leadership of Samaria as more cosmopolitan and wealthy than in Judah, but that, overall, the two cultures "shared striking and significant cultural and religious features in spite of their differences."[58] In other words, there was no break in the worship of *Adoni* in the northern area following the Assyrian exile in 722. The people of Samaria and

---

51. Nathan Schur, *History of the Samaritans* (Peter Lang, 1989), 20–21.
52. Knoppers, *Jews and Samaritans*, 29.
53. Knoppers, *Jews and Samaritans*, 38.
54. Knoppers, *Jews and Samaritans*, 43. Some of the southern regions were slower to grow; Israel Finkelstein, Z. Ledermann, and S. Bunimovitz, *Highlands of Many Cultures: The Southern Samaria Survey* (Institute of Archaeology, 1997).
55. Knoppers, *Jews and Samaritans*, 105.
56. Yitzak Magen, "The Dating of the First Phase of the Samaritan Temple at Mount Gerizim in Light of the Archaeological Evidence," in *Judah and Judeans in the Fourth Century B.C.E.*, ed. O. Lipschits, G. Knoppers, and R. Albertz (Eisenbrauns, 2007), 187.
57. Knoppers, *Jews and Samaritans*, 117.
58. Knoppers, *Jews and Samaritans*, 119.

Judah had a similar culture and followed the same God. It makes the ongoing tensions between the two during the Persian period and after even more mysterious.

It appears that the Samaritans tried to aid the Judeans in rebuilding their temple. Ezra 4:1–5 contains the first appearance of the tensions between the exiles and the Samaritans. The Samaritans are not overtly mentioned. The text calls them "adversaries of Judah and Benjamin" (4:1) who approached Zerubbabel and others and said, "Let us build with you, for we worship your God as you do, and we have been sacrificing to him ever since the days of King Esar-haddon of Assyria, who brought us here" (4:2). This is a reference to those who lived in Samaria after 722 BCE. Zerubbabel promptly rejected their offer of assistance. Yet there was no reason to see this offer of help as adversarial. Indeed, the Samaritans were proposing the very things needed to complete the project: aid and money! The Judeans characterized the people of Samaria as exiles from other places (Ezra 4:2 and 2 Kgs. 17:19–28). Even though, as noted above, Samaria was not depopulated of Israelites. The people were either born into a family that worshiped the same God or were exiled there and joined the Israelites in their worship.

The Samaritans probably decided to build their own worship space for *Adoni* after the Judean rejection. A smaller space was built during the Persian period and expanded during the Hellenistic period. The Persian period temple in Samaria on Mount Gerizim was built in the mid-fifth century (440–460 BCE), about seventy-five years after the Second Temple in Jerusalem.[59] The temple in Jerusalem was the model for the temple on Mount Gerizim.[60] Archaeological excavations "yielded thousands of pottery vessels and burned bones of sacrifices—of sheep, goats, cattle, and doves."[61] According to archaeological evidence, this smaller temple was used for approximately 250 years until the larger one was completed.[62]

The causes of the tensions between Judah and Samaria may never be known. Knoppers reminds modern readers that because of their shared culture, worship of the same God, and proximity, the Jews and Samaritans, like it or not, were connected, and their fates were intertwined.[63] Despite the animosity reflected in the biblical text and other sources, the two provinces continued in the same fraught sibling relationship that had been the norm since the split after Solomon's death.

---

59. Magen, "Samaritan Temple," 162–164. This estimate comes from carbon 14 dating on the bones from the sacrifices.
60. Magen, "Samaritan Temple," 161.
61. Magen, "Samaritan Temple," 161.
62. Magen, "Samaritan Temple," 164.
63. Knoppers, *Jews and Samaritans*, 222.

THE NEXT PHASE OF THE PERSIAN EMPIRE: XERXES, ARTAXERXES I, DARIUS II, ARTAXERXES II (486–358 BCE)

The next period of Persian domination involved little change in territory but multiple revolts. Right before Darius I's death in 486, Egypt revolted. Xerxes, one of Darius's sons, handled the rebellion in 485/484 BCE and, by that act, became the heir apparent.[64] Xerxes ruled until 465 BCE, when conspirators murdered him. Artaxerxes, his youngest son, killed his older brother Darius and became the king.[65] Artaxerxes I had a long, turbulent reign. The Egyptians rebelled again at the beginning of his reign, and the Greeks caused trouble throughout.[66] Artaxerxes died in 424, leaving one son, Xerxes II, who reigned for only forty-five days. He was assassinated by his half brother, who seized the throne. But that half brother was also killed by another half brother, Ochus, who took the name Darius II. He ruled for twenty years until 404 BCE, when Persia subdued Greek cities in Asia Minor.[67] The last reign of this period was a peaceful succession of father-to-son. Artaxerxes II succeeded his father in 404 BCE and reigned until 359 BCE. The Greeks continued to revolt. Egypt also used this opportunity to rebel and join forces with some Greek city-states so that Artaxerxes II and his holdings were under constant attack. Asia Minor kept causing trouble, and most governors maintained their own armies independent of the Persian Empire to control their assigned regions.[68] This period in the Persian Empire was full of conflict in the royal house, and some areas were constantly revolting.

JUDAH AND SAMARIA (486–358 BCE)

Judah remained a tiny province in the great Persian Empire during this time. There were several lingering questions concerning the relationship between Judah and Samaria. Were Judah and Samaria considered two provinces or one? If they were separate, did one receive preferential treatment from the empire? These unanswered questions come to the forefront in the conflicts narrated by Ezra and Nehemiah concerning the building of the wall in Jerusalem.

---

64. Lester Grabbe, *Judaism from Cyrus to Hadrian* (Fortress, 1992), 1:130.
65. Briant, *Cyrus to Alexander*, 564.
66. Grabbe, *Cyrus to Hadrian*, 131.
67. Miller and Hayes, *Ancient Israel and Judah*, 502.
68. Grabbe, *Cyrus to Hadrian*, 140.

THE WORK OF NEHEMIAH (445–433 BCE)

Ezra 7:1–10:44 narrates the return of Ezra and company to Jerusalem. This return occurred in the seventh year of Artaxerxes, but 7:7 does not specify if the king was Artaxerxes I (465–424), II (405–359), or III (359–337).[69] Likewise of uncertain date, Nehemiah's return is reported in the twentieth year of Artaxerxes (Neh. 2:1). Some scholars argue that Ezra appeared in approximately 458 BCE, with Nehemiah thirteen years later, in 445 BCE. Others question this assumption, arguing that the initial date of Nehemiah (2:1) is between 445 BCE and 433 BCE, during the reign of Artaxerxes I, with Ezra in 398 BCE, fifty years later, in the reign of Artaxerxes II.[70]

Which date for Ezra is correct? Jon Berquist points out that the biblical texts are unclear and do not state that Ezra arrived before Nehemiah.[71] Ezra is the subject of Nehemiah chapters 8–10, but scholars see this section as an independent piece placed in the text during the editing process.[72] The two men are also mentioned together (Neh. 12:26), but again, this is believed to be the work of an editor.[73] Other than these examples of editorial insertion, Nehemiah never discusses Ezra, and vice versa. Nehemiah and Ezra appear to be independent traditions but combined later, in the editing process. The topic has been endlessly debated, and neither argument wins the day. Little is known about the Persian period in Judah and Samaria; this is just one example of that reality.

Because it can be verified with other historical documents, the book of Nehemiah is considered a more reliable source than Ezra. Some scholars believe that Nehemiah himself wrote part of the book of Nehemiah.[74] Grabbe sees Ezra as less historically reliable, noting, "Our analysis has unearthed a great many problems with the Ezra story. Whatever historical core there might have been has been heavily overladen with literary and theological invention and elaboration."[75] Moreover, Ezra's confusing order of events thwarts attempts to understand its historical progression. Grabbe's comments are

---

69. Briant notes this as also a problem in Babylonian and Aramaic sources; *Cyrus to Alexander*, 569.

70. Miller and Hayes tentatively agree with the second suggestion and place Nehemiah first; *Ancient Israel and Judah*, 528–30.

71. Berquist, *Judaism in Persia's Shadow*, 110. Reading the two texts chronologically because of their order is a Western way of reading.

72. Williamson, *Ezra-Nehemiah*, 276. One major reason is the change from the first-person narration by Nehemiah (1:1–7:4), which returns in chap. 11, after chaps. 8–10 in a third-person point of view.

73. Williamson, *Ezra-Nehemiah*, 365.

74. Grabbe, *Jews and Judaism*, 1:294–95.

75. Grabbe, *Jews and Judaism*, 1:329.

convincing, whether one dates Ezra early or late. Nehemiah provides more verifiable information. For example, Nehemiah's association with Sanballat, the leader of Samaria, also appears in other sources, such as the Elephantine papyri. Thus, we will explore Nehemiah's account of the postexilic time in the fifth century, not because it was chronologically first but because it is the most reliable. However, the biblical account cannot be independently verified so its historical accuracy is unknown.

Most scholars place Nehemiah's return in the reign of Artaxerxes I (465–424 BCE). Nehemiah 1:1; 2:1, 5 state that in Artaxerxes's twentieth year, Nehemiah requested to return to Jerusalem. He was the "cupbearer to the king" (1:11). A cupbearer was educated in court etiquette, had a lucrative position, and had the trust of and constant access to the king.[76] The king granted this permission and sent Nehemiah with letters to the governors of Beyond the River, granting him passage to Judah (2:1–8). Nehemiah returned to King Artaxerxes twelve years later (13:6), making his time in Jerusalem approximately 445–433 BCE.[77] The last chapter of Nehemiah reports that he returned to Jerusalem again, but the exact time is unknown.

Events in the Afro-Asiatic region may have impacted Artaxerxes's actions and explain why Nehemiah returned with "officers of the army and cavalry" (Neh. 2:9). From 464 to 454 BCE, Egypt openly revolted against Artaxerxes I.[78] Around the same time, the satrap of Babylon also revolted.[79] With Syria (Aram), Samaria, and Judah between Egypt and Babylon, Artaxerxes may have wished to place someone trustworthy in the region to provide stability.[80]

What caused Nehemiah to return to Jerusalem? He was an official close to the king, living in Susa (Neh. 1:1). Susa is about 950 miles (1,500 km) from Jerusalem. According to the text, Nehemiah's brother Hanani and companions arrived in Susa and reported to him, "The remnant there in the province who escaped captivity are in great trouble and shame; the wall of Jerusalem is broken down, and its gates have been destroyed by fire" (1:3). The report implies that these events and the ensuing degradation were recent and not a reference to the destruction by the Babylonians 140 years or so earlier. The temple was completed in 520 BCE, some seventy-five years before Nehemiah's

---

76. Edwin M. Yamauchi, "Was Nehemiah the Cupbearer a Eunuch?," *ZAW* 92 (1980): 134.

77. André Lemaire, "Fifth- and Fourth-Century Issues: Governorship and Priesthood in Jerusalem," in *Ancient Israel's History: An Introduction to Issues and Sources*, ed. Bill Arnold and Richard Hess (Baker Academic, 2014), 409; also Grabbe, *Jews and Judaism*, 1:295; and Miller and Hayes, *Ancient Israel and Judah*, 530. Other scholars placing Ezra chronologically before Nehemiah argue for a later date, between 430 and 424 BCE; Williamson, *Ezra-Nehemiah*, xxxvi.

78. Briant, *Cyrus to Alexander*, 573.

79. Miller and Hayes, *Ancient Israel and Judah*, 530.

80. Miller and Hayes, *Ancient Israel and Judah*, 530.

mission, meaning the city and the temple had already experienced years of reconstruction. Was Hanani reporting Jerusalem's recent destruction, after the temple had been rebuilt?

Evidence points to another attack on the area. According to archaeological discoveries, around 475 BCE, cities in Benjamin and southern Samaria were destroyed.[81] This destruction is not reported in the Bible and was unknown until modern-era excavations.[82] The level of destruction was significant, demonstrating that the biblical text does not reflect all the events that transpired in Judah. There is no known evidence of destruction in Jerusalem around 475, but this is unsurprising since much of this layer was destroyed by later building projects. It is possible, then, that Nehemiah's brother was reporting a recent attack in Jerusalem around 475, probably related to the other revolts in the area. No reliable information on Judah outside the biblical text was available during this time. Grabbe notes, "It would not be surprising if there was an event, interpreted by the Persians as a revolt in Judah during the long decades between 500 and 445."[83] Whatever prompted Hanani's visit to his brother moved Nehemiah to ask the king's permission to return to address the situation. Nehemiah asked the king, "Send me to Judah, to the city of my ancestors' graves, so that I may rebuild it" (2:5). His first act was to rebuild Jerusalem's walls: "Then [Nehemiah] said to them, 'You see the trouble we are in, how Jerusalem lies in ruins with its gates burned. Come, let us rebuild the wall of Jerusalem, so that we may no longer suffer disgrace'" (Neh. 2:17).

Nehemiah's plea was to rebuild Jerusalem as a whole. However, the reconstruction of the walls was what especially caused tension with other leaders in the region. Nehemiah's arrival and rebuilding projects did not please them. Refortifying Jerusalem was seen as a threat to other local leaders, specifically Sanballat the Horonite (governor of Samaria), Tobiah the Ammonite, and Geshem the Arab.[84] The three leaders mentioned are the ones who surround Judah: Sanballat to the north, Tobiah to the east, and Geshem to the south, with the sea, of course, to the west. Knoppers notes, "From Nehemiah's vantage point, Judah is surrounded by adversaries."[85] Sanballat, the governor during the building of the Samaritan temple, and Geshem are the main antagonists in the text (Neh. 6:2–6). Another indication of regional tensions is the

---

81. Ephraim Stern, *The Assyrian, Babylonian, and Persian Periods (732–332 BCE)*, vol. 2 of *Archaeology of the Land of the Bible*, by A. Mazar et al. (Doubleday, 2001), 431–34, 577. The date comes from Attic pottery and thus is approximate. Destruction levels were found in Shechem, Tel en-Naṣbeh, Bethel, Tel el-Ful, and Gibeon, among others.

82. Stern, *Archaeology*, 2:577.

83. Grabbe, *Jews and Judaism*, 1:293.

84. A papyrus from Elephantine (Egypt, 407 BCE) to a later governor of Judah mentions Sanballat of Samaria, confirming the name in the Nehemiah account; *ANET*, 492.

85. Knoppers, *Jews and Samaritans*, 145.

way Sanballat is addressed. The text does not use Sanballat's title of governor. Instead, it refers to him as "the Horonite," which probably refers to his home area (likely Horonaim, in Moab), not his position.[86] Second, Nehemiah makes it clear that Judeans and only Judeans have a place in Judah: "The God of heaven is the one who will give us success, and we his servants are going to start building; but you [pl.] have no share or claim or memorial [historic right] in Jerusalem" (Neh. 2:20).

Nehemiah's position could not be more explicit: there is no place for others, even if they worship the same God. However, Grabbe notes, "Nehemiah gives *a* perspective, not *the* perspective."[87] Nehemiah presents a pro-Judean isolationist position.

The text also demonstrates substantial connections between Judah and their neighbors, including culture, treaties, and business relationships. This reality is reflected in Nehemiah's polemic about Tobiah from Ammon:

> Moreover, in those days the nobles of Judah sent many letters to Tobiah, and Tobiah's letters came to them. For many in Judah were bound by oath to him, because he was the son-in-law of Shecaniah son of Arah, and his son Jehohanan had married the daughter of Meshullam son of Berechiah. Also they spoke of his good deeds in my presence and reported my words to him. And Tobiah sent letters to intimidate me. (Neh. 6:17–19)

Shecaniah is possibly one of the wall builders, as in 3:29, and Meshullam is named in 3:30. These Judean elders, then, had an ongoing relationship with Tobiah. This relationship would outlast Nehemiah's decade-long governorship. Tobiah is given a room in the courts of the Jerusalem temple, sanctioned by the priest (13:4–9), and Sanballat's daughter marries the son of the high priest (13:28). It appears, then, that the other leadership did not support Nehemiah's program of isolationism. Internal tension is reflected in the text regarding this isolationist policy.

How much of Jerusalem did Nehemiah rebuild? Unfortunately, few archaeological remains come from this period in Jerusalem, partly because it was destroyed by later Hasmonean and Herodian construction.[88] However, multiple archaeological digs over several decades found that evidence of the Persian period remains only in the central part of the city of David, which is closest to the Temple Mount.[89] The city during Nehemiah's time was significantly

---

86. Knoppers, *Jews and Samaritans*, 147.
87. Grabbe, *Jews and Judaism*, 1:294.
88. Stern, *Archaeology*, 2:435.
89. Israel Finkelstein, "Jerusalem in the Persian (and Early Hellenistic) Period and the Wall of Nehemiah," *JSOT* 34 (2008): 506.

reduced from its zenith during Hezekiah's time. Israel Finkelstein estimates the number of persons living in Jerusalem during this period to be approximately 400–500 persons.[90] This archaeological evidence fits with the biblical accounts of a smaller city and temple (Neh. 7:4; 11:1–2). Despite the efforts of the people of the land and the exiles, Jerusalem was barely a city, and most people lived in the outlying regions (11:1–2). Over the decades, several archaeologists have argued that they have identified the walls built in the Persian period at Nehemiah's direction.[91] Others disagreed with these findings, stating that no Persian evidence was found in the debated walls.[92] This debate shows no definitive evidence for the refortification of Jerusalem as presented in Nehemiah. At this time, however, Jerusalem appears to be just as Nehemiah described it: a small, sparsely populated city, with most of the population occupying the rural centers of Judah near Jerusalem.[93]

THE WORK OF EZRA

The exact time frame of Ezra's mission is unclear. Ezra 8:31–35 states that the temple was already built when Ezra arrived in Jerusalem, and "those who had come from captivity, the returned exiles, offered burnt offerings to the God of Israel." However, that reference is the only verse that aids in dating his mission to after 515 BCE. The Hebrew Bible is the only source of information about Ezra, so its chronology cannot be resolved. Ezra 7:1 states he went to Jerusalem in the reign of Artaxerxes, but there is no indication of which Artaxerxes.

In addition, Ezra is a mysterious character. There is no indication of his function in Persia or why the king was aware of a Jewish priest in Babylon and would offer him such broad powers and resources, as recounted in Ezra 7:12–26. He is described only as going up from Babylon as "a scribe skilled in the law of Moses" (7:6). His genealogy places him as a descendant of Aaron (7:1–5), an association with the Jerusalem temple. However, such a genealogical

---

90. Finkelstein, "Jerusalem in the Persian . . . Period," 507.
91. K. M. Kenyon, *Digging Up Jerusalem* (Benn, 1974), 183–87; Y. Shiloh, *Excavations at the City of David: I. 1978–1982 Interim Report of the First Five Seasons*, Qedem [vol.] 19 (Hebrew University, 1984), 29.
92. Finkelstein, "Jerusalem in the Persian . . . Period," 508; David Ussishkin, "On Nehemiah's Wall and the Size of Jerusalem during the Persian Period: An Archaeologist's View," in *New Perspectives on Ezra-Nehemiah: History, Historiography, Text, Literature, and Interpretation*, ed. I. Kalimi (Eisenbrauns, 2012), 117.
93. Finkelstein notes that the archaeological confirmation of Jerusalem's condition is another piece of evidence against scholars who argue that much of the biblical text was written in the Persian and Hellenistic periods; "Jerusalem in the Persian . . . Period," 514.

claim cannot be verified. Most scholars claim that Nehemiah 8 and 9 were inserted into Nehemiah and probably belonged between Ezra chapters 8 and 9, based on the theory presented by Charles Torrey.[94] His argument centers on Ezra's stated purpose "to study the law of [*Adoni*] and to do it and to teach the statutes and ordinances in Israel" (Ezra 7:10). Yet, this very act of teaching the law is missing in the book of Ezra. Ezra teaching the law is precisely what is described in Nehemiah 8–10. It is certainly possible that those chapters would fit better in the book of Ezra than in the book of Nehemiah.

The book of Ezra contains a letter said to be from Artaxerxes (7:12–26). The letter was written in Aramaic, with pieces verified as original and written by Persian authorities with significant additions.[95] The extent of the editing makes these two elements impossible to separate clearly. The letter authorizes a return of the exiles and gifts of gold and silver from the king for the temple. The letter also authorizes the return of the temple vessels, which is problematic since the earlier mission *also* carried the temple vessels (1:7–11). In other words, an additional return could make sense; however, the gifts of gold and silver and the return of vessels are questionable.

The letter gave Ezra broad powers: "All who will not obey the law of your God and the law of the king, let judgment be strictly executed on them, whether for death or for banishment or for confiscation of their goods or for imprisonment" (7:26). Ezra shared a concern with Nehemiah over the purity of the people and the presence of foreign wives. According to the narrative, he went further than Nehemiah and pushed the people to "make a covenant with our God to send away all these wives and their children, according to the counsel of my lord and of those who tremble at the commandment of our God" (Ezra 10:3). This action was taken because "the holy seed has mixed itself with the peoples of the lands" (9:2). This narrative of Ezra's return and work makes him seem unyielding, cruel, sexist, and isolationist.[96] Some scholars explain the reasons behind these acts as concern for religious purity and identity concerns.[97] Others believe they were motivated by a desire for cultural viability in a growing Persian Empire.[98] As explained in discussing the earlier chapters of Ezra, tension arose between the returning exiles, or "Israel,"

---

94. Charles Torrey, *Ezra Studies* (University of Chicago Press, 1910).

95. Grabbe, "The 'Persian Documents,'" 557; Williamson, *Ezra-Nehemiah*, 98.

96. This observation does not make a sweeping assessment of Judaism's treatment of women but deals with this text in Ezra.

97. F. C. Fensham, *The Books of Ezra and Nehemiah* (Eerdmans, 1982), 124; and Blenkinsopp, *Ezra-Nehemiah*, 176.

98. Daniel Smith-Christopher, "The Mixed[-]Marriage Crisis in Ezra 9–10 and Nehemiah 13: A Study of the Sociology of the Post-Exilic Judaean Community," in *Second Temple Studies*, vol. 2, *Temple and Community in the Persian Period*, ed. T. Eskenazi and K. Richards (JSOT Press, 1994), 243–65.

and the people(s) of the land, who included those of other nations along with Samaritans and the people of Judah who remained behind during the exile.[99] Also, just as in Nehemiah, some objected to such a radical plan (Ezra 10:15). This was not the first time an isolationist view was stated as the rule of law (Josh. 6:17–18). What is clear in all these examples is a concern that Judah might become like other nations in the empire or that others would lead them away from their faith.

The most important developments we can take away from Ezra's mission are religious and sociological. In preexilic Judah, the focus of religious practice was centered in the temple. The people defined themselves as people of one place, a singular culture, and shared religious practice. This was no longer the case. The people of Judah struggled to rebuild the temple and were still struggling to rebuild Judah. Jews were now living throughout much of the known world, so their theology and view of what it means to be Jewish was changing. One major change is marked here by Ezra's reading and interpretation of the law.

In Nehemiah 8:1, the people ask Ezra to read "the book of the law of Moses, which [*Adoni*] had given to Israel." What was the content of the "book" used by Ezra? Was the Pentateuch, or at least the laws from Exodus and Leviticus, the book Ezra read? The content of the book Ezra read is heavily debated, and no one argument wins the day.[100] What is clear is that an early form of the laws was circulating at this time, even if we cannot verify the exact content. Judaism was much in flux during this long Persian period. However, since the ancient Judeans' idea of Scripture differed from ours, the text could still be authoritative even as it was adaptable.[101] This reading of the law is the first indication of the Torah's importance in later Judaism. The people who worshiped one God and who lived in Jerusalem were changing how they practiced their faith. At some point, what came to be called "the Book," later "the Tanakh," all of the Hebrew Bible, would replace the Jerusalem temple as the unifying element of Judaism worldwide. Ezra's reading of "the book of the law of Moses" demonstrates one of the steps along the way. One other essential step in the future of the faith emerged during the Persian period. This is the approximate time period determined when figurines of other gods ceased to be discovered in archaeological digs.[102] This indicates that monotheism and the prohibitions against graven images were being practiced.

---

99. Harold Washington, "Israel's Holy Seed and the Foreign Women of Ezra-Nehemiah: A Kristevan Reading," *Biblical Interpretation* 11 (2003): 430.

100. Cornelius Houtman, "Ezra and the Law," in *Remembering All the Way: A Collection of Old Testament Studies*, by B. Albrektson et al. (Brill, 1981), 91–115.

101. Houtman, "Ezra and the Law," 111.

102. Philip King and Lawrence Stager, *Life in Biblical Israel*, ed. D. Knight (Westminster John Knox, 2001), 348.

This change in religious practice, emphasizing the importance of the religious text, was further indicated by the decades-long struggle to build the temple. While still culturally significant, the temple's status in the Persian period was complicated. First, the plural must be used now. There were temples in Jerusalem, Mount Gerizim, and Elephantine, Egypt, by 410 BCE and possibly in other places.[103] In Jerusalem, the temple was still crucial for the Judean worshiping community.[104] At the same time, Isaiah 66:1–2 sees the heavens, not the temple, as God's home.[105] The people were beginning to understand that God is everywhere, not just in Jerusalem. The God who traveled with the enslaved in the exodus became mobile again, only this time in multiple places at once. The faithful now envisioned God and themselves in a larger world, and this larger worldview required changes in their theology.

Part of history telling is reporting on a period's cultural and sociological issues. While there is little historical knowledge about Judah during this period, the biblical accounts provide information on cultural and religious change. These changes proved a crucial link between the practices before the exile and how Judah, Samaria, and Judaism developed after the return from exile.

LIFE IN THE DIASPORA

By this point in history, the world had drastically changed, and a specific geographical place no longer defined Jews. It is unknown how many Jewish communities existed during the Persian period. We can assemble clues about some of them.

There is no historical record of the Diaspora community in Susa, the Persian capital. According to Nehemiah 1:1, Nehemiah lived there in service to the king.[106] This is the first evidence of how far into Asia some Jewish communities may have existed during the Persian period. Susa is almost 1,000 miles (1,610 km) from Jerusalem.

The Jewish community in Babylon remained active and viable for centuries. While there is no narrative of their lives or how their community functioned, business records during the Persian period demonstrate their presence.[107]

---

103. Stephan Rosenberg, "The Jewish Temple at Elephantine," *NEA* 67 (2004): 6.

104. The building of the temple is central in Ezra 1–6 and in the prophets Haggai, Zechariah, Malachi, and Ezekiel.

105. Japhet, "Temple in the Restoration," 233.

106. The Persian capital is mentioned in Dan. 8:2 in a vision. The Book of Esther is set in Susa, but it does not provide any reliable historical information.

107. There are currently three sets of documents. First, a group of from 521–487 BCE: Kathleen Abraham, *Business and Politics under the Persian Empire: The Financial Dealings of Marduk-nāṣir-apli of the House of Egibi (521–487 B.C.E.)* (Eisenbrauns, 2004). Second, a group of texts

The Muršu collection of documents are business transactions from the Nippur region from approximately 450–400 BCE.[108] Laurie Pearce and Cornelia Wunsch have identified the names of several cities—Ālu-ša-Našar (Našar town, sometimes town of Našar's house), Āl-Yāḫdu (Judahtown), and Bīt-Abī-râm (Town of Abraham's House)—as towns where Jews were transacting business.[109] Unfortunately, none of the locations of these towns can be established.[110] Besides the cities, the only information gleaned from these texts are Judean names and evidence of thriving Jewish communities.[111] The Bible reports that Ezra came from Babylon (Ezra 7:6) but gives no other information about life there during the Persian period. There may be no surviving narratives, but the records reflect an ongoing Jewish presence.

More information about the Jewish communities in Egypt is available. Jeremiah reports that Jews fled to Tahpanhes, Egypt, during the Babylonian occupation (Jer. 43:1–7) and says the prophet lived out his days there. Archaeologically, no clear evidence of Jewish life in Tahpanhes exists, making Jeremiah its only witness. However, Tahpanhes was on the Sinai border, making it a logical stop for Jews fleeing Judah.

A second Jewish community in Egypt was established at Elephantine. Elephantine is located on an island in the upper Nile River. The establishment of the community was for military protection from nations further south. Jews made up part of this military garrison. It is unknown when Jews arrived, although one letter places them there when Cyrus's son, Cambyses, arrived in 525 BCE.[112] More is known about this community because of the discovery of 175 documents aptly named the Elephantine papyri.[113] These documents are primarily judicial and family documents.

One religious document was found here, the Passover Papyrus, dated 419 BCE, which clearly indicates the practice of the Jewish Feast of Passover.[114] The papyrus was heavily damaged, so it only reports a small part of

---

from 572–477 BCE: Laurie Pearce and Cornelia Wunsch, *Documents of Judean Exiles and West Semites in Babylonia in the Collection of David Sofer* (CDL, 2014). Third, H. V. Hilprecht and A. T. Clay, *Business Documents of Murashû Sons of Nippur: Dated in the Reign of Artaxerxes I (464–424 B.C.)* (University of Pennsylvania Press, 1898); and A. T. Clay, . . . *Dated in the Reign of Darius II (424–404 B.C.)* (1904).

108. Hilprecht and Clay, *Business Documents*.
109. Pearce and Wunsch, *Documents of Judean Exiles*, 6.
110. Pearce and Wunsch, *Documents of Judean Exiles*, 6.
111. Laurie Pearce, "New Evidence for Judeans in Babylonia," in *Judah and Judeans in the Persian Period*, ed. O.Lipschits and M. Oeming (Eisenbrauns, 2006), 400.
112. Sami Ahmed, "The Jewish Community at Elephantine," *Iliff Review* 22 (1965): 11.
113. Bezalel Porten et al., *The Elephantine Papyri in English: Three Millennia of Cross-Cultural Continuity and Change*, 2nd ed. (Society of Biblical Literature, 2011); its table of contents, https://www.sbl-site.org/assets/pdfs/pubs/069552P.front.pdf.
114. Rosenberg, "The Jewish Temple at Elephantine," 4.

the instructions, such as the date of the seven-day observance, the prohibition against work during the observation, and the removal of leavened products from the home.[115]

The community also had a temple patterned after the one in Jerusalem.[116] They participated in Sabbath and Passover observances, but how closely they conformed to the practices in Jerusalem is unknown.[117] These insights are some of the only pictures of worship life outside of Jerusalem during the Persian period. The Elephantine Temple was destroyed in 410 BCE following tensions with other religious leaders.[118] In 407 BCE, Jedaniah, the leader of the Elephantine Jewish community, wrote to Bagohi, the governor of the Beyond the River province.[119] The letter requests permission to rebuild the temple because the community tried to get permission from the Jerusalem priesthood but did not receive a reply.[120] It further promises "meal-offerings and the incense and the burnt-offering they will offer on the altar of YHW [*Adoni*] the God in your name and we shall pray for you at all times—we and our wives and our children and the Jews, all [of them] who are here."[121] The letter also states that a similar letter was sent to the sons of the governor of Samaria. Does this mean the Elephantine community required permission from the governors of both Judah and Samaria? The letter does not say that, but the two letters may indicate that Judah and Samaria were two distinct provinces during this time. It also suggests that Elephantine was under the direction of the officials and priests in Jerusalem and possibly in Samaria. The documents do not contain a reply, but the temple must have been rebuilt since it is mentioned in a real estate receipt from 402 BCE.[122]

The Jewish communities in the Diaspora continued to grow during the long period of the Persian Empire, but there is little concrete information about them until the conquest of Alexander the Great in 323 BCE. The Persian Empire provided economic opportunities, probably prompting Jews to leave Judah and relocate to other areas of the empire.

---

115. Tamara Cohn Eskenazi, "The Passover Papyrus Orders a Religious Furlough for Judean Soldiers," *The Torah.com*, 2020, https://www.thetorah.com/article/the-passover-papyrus-order-a-religious-furlough-for-judean-soldiers.
116. Miller and Hayes, *Ancient Israel and Judah*, 496.
117. Gard Granerød, "The Former and the Future Temple of YHW in Elephantine: A Traditio-Historical Case Study of Ancient Near Eastern Antiquarianism," *ZAW* 127 (2015): 63.
118. Leuchter, *Empire Far and Wide*, 41.
119. Bezalel Porten, "Dear Jerusalem: Priests [at Elephantine] Petition to Rebuild Their Temple," *BAR* Library, https://library.biblicalarchaeology.org/sidebar/dear-jerusalem-priests-petition-to-rebuild-their-temple/.
120. Leuchter, *Empire Far and Wide*, 41.
121. Porten, "Dear Jerusalem."
122. Rosenberg, "The Jewish Temple at Elephantine," 9.

THE END OF THE PERSIAN EMPIRE: ARTAXERXES III (OCHUS), ARSES, AND DARIUS III (359–330 BCE)

There is little Persian information for this period and no specific Judean or Samaritan information. After the longest reign of any Persian king, Artaxerxes II died forty-five years after he became king, in 359. During his reign, he managed multiple revolts but did not manage to retake Egypt. His youngest son, Ochus (named after his grandfather Darius II), was already a satrap and army commander.[123]

Ochus came to the throne in 359 BCE and took the name Artaxerxes III. His reign saw a continuation of the revolts and a growing outside threat from Philip of Macedon. He moved to retake Egypt, and the campaign took a decade.[124] There were also revolts in Phoenicia and Cyprus from 351 to 345 BCE.[125] The Persians retook Egypt in 342 BCE, with Ochus leading the army. These revolts were in the adjacent areas, so they may have involved Judah and Samaria, but there is no evidence of their participation. After the victory, the king returned home, and the empire remained quiet for the rest of his reign. In 338 BCE, Bagoas, a member of the king's court, supposedly poisoned the king.[126] Artaxerxes III's son, Arses, became king for a short period; supposedly, Bagoas poisoned him as well.[127] Darius III was a distant relative and became king in 336 BCE. In the spring of 334 BCE, Alexander the Great invaded Persian territory, and by 330 BCE, the Persian Empire was no more.

SUMMARY

The Persian Empire was more extensive than any previously known empire in this region. Unlike the Assyrians and Babylonians, its policies moved from conquest to empire development, except for the ongoing conflicts with the Greek peoples and occasional revolts elsewhere. Because the empire held power for two centuries, there were times of more and less oversight. They also developed an extensive maritime presence in the Mediterranean for trade and military purposes. The Persians added royal roads that made both military movement and commerce easier. The empire was organized into twenty satrapies, each part of the empire and ruled by a satrap. The Persians replaced

---

123. Briant, *Cyrus to Alexander*, 680.
124. Grabbe, *Jews and Judaism*, 1:323.
125. Briant, *Cyrus to Alexander*, 682.
126. Grabbe, *Jews and Judaism*, 1:324.
127. Grabbe, *Jews and Judaism*, 1:324.

the system of conquered countries that paid tribute and taxes to the king and his empire. Residents of each satrapy paid taxes, and each satrapy benefited from these shared taxes. The Persians did not force their culture or religion on others. They also introduced the widespread use of coinage, making the movement of both persons and resources across longer distances easier. At the same time, smaller cultures and economies disappeared or were forever changed. The hold of the empire caused these cultures to redefine themselves and often resulted in the people moving throughout the empire for purely economic reasons. In other words, all the people of Canaan were more scattered throughout the territory now encompassed by the Persian Empire than ever before, and many slowly assimilated into it. Unfortunately, there is no information from the rest of the nations of Canaan besides Judah and Samaria, so it is unknown how they fared.[128]

Little is known concerning the treatment of Jews during this period. The business and family documents of the Diaspora show successful work with little persecution. At Elephantine, the Jews lived in a defined geographical area, but this was probably by choice rather than because they were forced to do so.[129] The documents from Elephantine provide insights into the worship practices of Jews outside Jerusalem. With twenty different satrapies, Jews were perhaps treated in various ways depending on the leadership of the region. Regardless, this long period of the Persian Empire had a permanent impact on Judaism. During this and the subsequent Greek and Roman empires, Judaism grew into a religion centered on its texts. The New Testament Gospels continue to reflect the importance of both the temple and the book because they are set in Judah. The book of Acts and the Epistles relay the ways Judaism and Christianity were changing in other places in the empire in the first and second centuries CE.

The Persian period also closed with the split between the Judeans and the Samaritans well entrenched. This rift—which officially began with the death of Solomon and the division of the monarchy into Judah and Israel—continued into the time of the New Testament and beyond.

---

128. Briant, *Cyrus to Alexander*, 685.
129. Ahmed, "Jewish Community at Elephantine," 13.

13

The Early Hellenistic Period (330–168 BCE)

ALEXANDER THE GREAT (336–323 BCE)

Alexander moved into Asia Minor in 334 BCE, first taking the Mediterranean Coast in what now is Turkey. In 333 BCE, his army met the Persians for the first time in what is now Turkey, at Issus, a strategic bottleneck between mountains and coast, near Syria/Aram.[1] Alexander and his army won the contest, and Darius III fled, but his family was captured.[2] Alexander moved southward along the Mediterranean coast instead of pursuing Darius inland. It was a strategically important move. He took Phoenicia after a six-month siege, ending their naval domination of this region, and cut their naval fleet off from being used by Darius III. In 332 BCE, he traveled further south, on the Way of the Sea along the Mediterranean coast, heading for Egypt.

Flavius Josephus reported that during Alexander's travels toward Egypt, he went to Jerusalem, entered the Jerusalem temple, and offered sacrifices to the God of Israel.[3] Modern historians have dismissed this account, attributing it to a legend, one of the many tales written about Alexander over the years.[4] Several Greek historians narrated Alexander's travels during this time, and none reported a visit to Jerusalem.[5] Historically, we know nothing about

---

1. Robin Waterfield, *Creators, Conquerors, and Citizens: A History of Ancient Greece* (Oxford University Press, 2018), 334.
2. Lester Grabbe, *A History of the Jews and Judaism in the Second Temple Period* (T&T Clark, 2008), 2:270.
3. Flavius Josephus *The Antiquities of the Jews*, trans. William Whiston, 11.8.4–5, https://www.gutenberg.org/files/2848/2848-h/2848-h.htm.
4. Grabbe, *History of the Jews*, 2:270.
5. Victor Tcherikover, *Hellenistic Civilization and the Jews*, trans. S. Applebaum (Atheneum, 1959), 41.

Judah during Alexander's trip through the area. However, Alexander was in Samaria in 332 BCE, or at least directly imposed new leadership. On his way to take control of Egypt, he appointed a new governor. Before his return, that governor was murdered.[6]

Alexander met resistance in Gaza, the gateway to Egypt, but prevailed after a prolonged engagement. Egypt capitulated without a fight in late 332 BCE.[7] After the winter rains, Alexander took his troops northward along the Mediterranean coast again. On his way back, he returned to Samaria in 331 BCE to assign a second governor and deal with those who had killed the first one.[8]

In the autumn of 331 BCE, he met Darius III and his army a second time, at Guagamala, in what now is the Kurdistan Region of northern Iraq. Darius III lost to Alexander again and fled east to Media. Alexander moved on and claimed Babylon and Susa without a fight. The governor of Persepolis, the capital of the Persian Empire, put up a fight but was defeated. Alexander and his troops looted the city and burned down the palace of King Xerxes.[9]

Alexander turned eastward to find Darius III, who was trying to muster a new army in his home region. However, some of his men, presumably led by Bessus, a noble and governor, killed Darius before Alexander arrived. They then left the king's body by the roadside to delay Alexander and allow Bessus and others to escape.[10] Alexander gave Darius a royal funeral, probably to ingratiate himself with the local leaders.

Persia's control of the regions to the west ended with Darius III's death in 330 BCE, and Alexander proclaimed himself king of the Achaemenid Empire, taking Darius's signet ring for himself.[11] Alexander was the king of the Macedonian Empire before this act, and while the kingdom would become the Greek Empire, it is unclear that Alexander called it by that name. Indeed, he adopted Persia's crown and many of its customs, despite the disapproval among the Greeks who saw it as "orientalizing" of the kingdom.[12] Alexander also allowed many Persian governors to stay as leaders, further angering some Greek nobles who thought every governor should be Greek.[13]

---

6. Grabbe, *History of the Jews*, 2:276.
7. Grabbe, *History of the Jews*, 2:270.
8. Andrea Berlin, "Between Large Forces: Palestine in the Hellenistic Period," *BA* 60, no. 1 (March 1997): 3–4.
9. Lester Grabbe, *Judaism from Cyrus to Hadrian*, vol. 1 (Fortress, 1992), 207. Xerxes's palace was larger than Darius's home. Torching that palace may have been part of the Greeks' revenge for Xerxes's invasion of Greece years earlier.
10. Waldemar Heckel, *In the Path of Conquest: Resistance to Alexander the Great* (Oxford University Press, 2020), 164.
11. Grabbe, *From Cyrus to Hadrian*, 1:207.
12. Grabbe, *From Cyrus to Hadrian*, 1:208.
13. Grabbe, *From Cyrus to Hadrian*, 1:208.

In 329 BCE, Alexander and the Greek forces moved east to subdue or make peace with the satraps in the Persian Empire's furthest eastern regions. By 327 BCE, the Greek troops were tired after nine years of fighting and began to doubt Alexander's leadership.[14] In India in 326 BCE, Alexander's army revolted after months of marching in the monsoon rains.[15] Alexander decided to turn back. He returned to Susa in 324 BCE and then to Babylon.[16] Alexander the Great died there on June 11, 323, before his thirty-third birthday. Scholars debate whether he died of natural causes such as malaria or was murdered. He left no male heir or succession plan, so the empire's future was up for grabs.

THE DIADOCHI AND THEIR WARS FOR CONTROL (322 BCE–281 BCE)

The Greek Empire engaged in fifty years of warfare with no clear successor. Unfortunately, there are not a lot of records of the period, so details are sketchy. Revolts began in the empire almost immediately after Alexander's death.[17] The senior officers met to decide what to do. These senior officers were called the Diadochi, which means "successors" in Greek. They were divided. They could wait for Alexander's wife to give birth in the hope that the baby was a boy or crown Alexander's half brother as king, naming him King Philip III.[18] Alexander's brother had some developmental challenges and would never be able to serve on his own. Either Philip or the baby would require a regent to rule for the foreseeable future. The officers compromised, planning to make them joint kings if the baby was a boy. The baby boy was born a few months later and named Alexander IV. In the meantime, senior officers close to Alexander divided the empire into regions, with each region awarded to one of the officers, presumably to protect it until the baby was old enough to rule. Rebellions were common, especially among the Greek states, so a close eye on the regions was needed.[19]

At some point during this period, the leaders of the Hellenistic Empire renamed some of the areas. In the centuries before, the two regions overlapping with or near Judah and Israel had the ancient names Canaan and Aram (Syria). Those regional names changed during the Hellenistic period. The

---

14. Heckel, *In the Path of Conquest*, 249–50.
15. Waterfield, *History of Ancient Greece*, 341.
16. Waterfield, *History of Ancient Greece*, 345.
17. Grabbe, *History of the Jews*, 2:271.
18. Waterfield, *History of Ancient Greece*, 355.
19. Waterfield, *History of Ancient Greece*, 355–59.

region of Canaan was now named Palestine, from a Greek word for Philistia. However, "Palestine" represents not just Philistia but the entire area from Phoenicia to Egypt, roughly the same region as Canaan.[20] Another name for this region, Coele-Syria, encompasses both Palestine and Syria (Aram). These last chapters will use these two names since they were widely adopted.

As noted, there were years of war for the empire, each officer wanting a piece of the empire. The first division in 321 BCE gave Babylon to Seleucus and Egypt to Ptolemy, with Coele-Syria between them.[21] In the next period, 321–317 BCE, Cassander held Greece and Macedonia, in addition to the lands controlled by Seleucus and Ptolemy.[22] After the Treaty of Gaza in 311 BCE, Ptolemy was given control over Egypt, Palestine, and Syria (Aram). Seleucus was to rule the old Assyrian and Babylonian Kingdoms. Palestine and Syria (Aram), or Coele-Syria, belonged to Ptolemy, but both leaders wanted it. There were several battles for Palestine and Syria (Aram) between the two. While we do not have any direct information about how Judah was affected, with this much conflict in the region, there must have been impacts on the Judeans.[23] Josephus reports that Ptolemy took captives from Judah and Samaria and sent them to Egypt. Other Jews immigrated to Egypt voluntarily, possibly because of the unrest in the area.[24] Lester Grabbe suggests that these battles significantly impacted Syria (Aram), Samaria, and Judah.[25] Even if the fighting was not happening in Judah or Samaria, armies needed supplies, and the local people would have been economically burdened by troops demanding their resources.[26]

In 311 BCE, the nobles continued fighting. Alexander IV was fourteen and getting close to the age at which he could rule without the nobles. But the Diadochi had no intention of allowing him to rule. Cassander poisoned the young king and his mother.[27] By 301 BCE, after the Battle of Ipsus, the regions were divided for the last time. Ptolemy claimed Egypt and the Coastlands of Palestine. Lysimachus took Western Turkey and Greece. Cassander took Macedon. Seleucus was to lead Syria/Aram-Palestine, Babylon, and the Eastern regions.

Ptolemy and Seleucus both still wanted Syria/Aram-Palestine. The 311 BCE agreement had awarded it to Ptolemy. This new agreement in 301 BCE

20. David Jacobson, "When Palestine Meant Israel," *BAR* 27, no. 3 (2001), https://library.biblicalarchaeology.org/article/when-palestine-meant-israel/.
21. Grabbe, *History of the Jews*, 2:272.
22. Grabbe, *History of the Jews*, 2:272.
23. Grabbe, *History of the Jews*, 2:278.
24. Josephus, *Jewish Antiquities* 12.3.23.
25. Grabbe, *From Cyrus to Hadrian*, 1:211.
26. Grabbe, *History of the Jews*, 2:280.
27. Waterfield, *History of Ancient Greece*, 362.

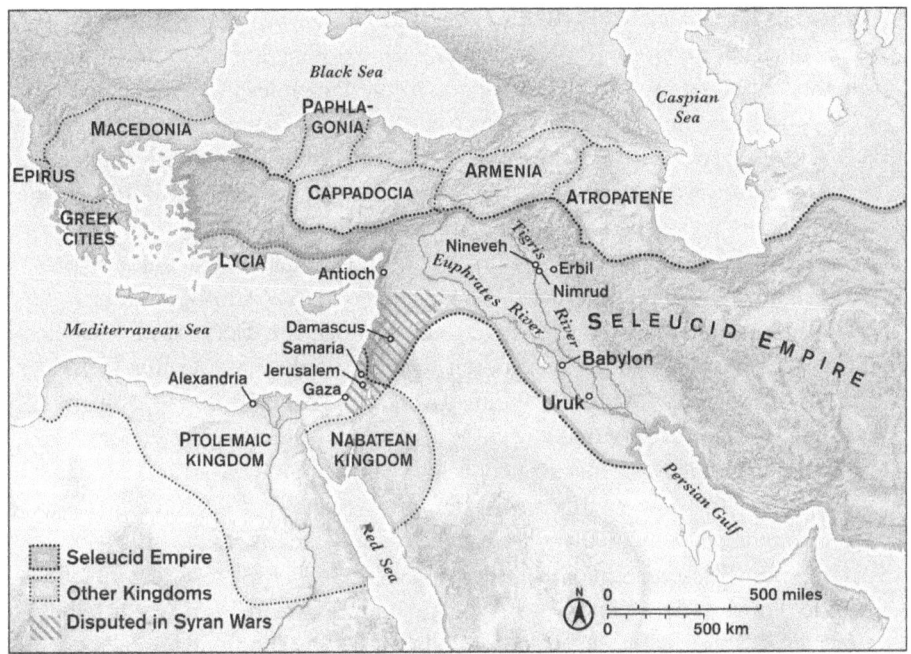

Map 13. The Seleucid Empire. (Courtesy of Ben Pease)

assigned Syria/Aram-Palestine to Seleucus and his heirs. Ptolemy was absent when the deal was penned, and he refused to concede Syria/Aram-Palestine to Seleucus. Judah was again in the crosshairs of warring men. Seleucus owed Ptolemy for his help in capturing Babylon in 312 BCE and decided not to start a war over the area.[28] He did not challenge Ptolemy's claim to Syria/Aram-Palestine. His successors would not feel the same way and would continue trying to take control of the disputed area. Again, the region's pathways were strategically crucial to outside empires, and the people of Judah and Samaria were caught in the middle (map 13).

PTOLEMAIC PERIOD (280 BCE–205 BCE)

The former Greek Empire of Alexander was subdivided among the Hellenistic leaders who served under him and became kings of their regions in their own right. Ptolemy II succeeded his father in 282 BCE and ruled until 246 BCE. Seleucus, king of the Seleucid Empire, was assassinated, and his successor,

---

28. Grabbe, *History of the Jews*, 2:288.

Antiochus I, ruled from 280 BCE to 261 BCE. During this period, the heart of the conflicts between the Ptolemaic and Seleucid Kingdoms continued to be whether Syria/Aram-Palestine belonged to the Ptolemies in Egypt as agreed in 302, or to the Seleucid Empire from the earlier 311 agreement. Each new Seleucid king would try to take Syria/Aram-Palestine. A pattern emerged: at the end of a war over Syria/Aram-Palestine, the two kings would sign a peace treaty that stayed in effect for the rest of their lives—patterned like the first treaty signed in 271 BCE by Ptolemy II and Antiochus I.[29] These Syrian (Aramaean) Wars directly impacted the people of Syria/Aram-Palestine.

In the first war between Ptolemy II and Antiochus I, Egypt won, and the territories remained as they were under the kings' fathers. Antiochus II (261–246 BCE) instigated the Second Syrian (Aramaean) War (260–253 BCE) against Ptolemy II. There are not many details except that the hostilities lasted for seven years. The fighting was concentrated in Asia Minor and Syria (Aram), attempting to reduce the power of Ptolemy II in the Aegean Sea.[30] Like the first, this war was ended by a treaty that was in effect for only the lives of the two rulers.[31] Syria/Aram-Palestine remained in Ptolemy's hands after the second conflict.

The Third Syrian (Aramaean) War, or the Laodicean War, was a family affair. First, Ptolemy III succeeded his father in 246 BCE, nullifying the peace agreement made after the Second Syrian (Aramaean) War. After the death of Antiochus II in Ephesus, also in 246, one son, Seleucus II, was recognized as king of the Seleucid Empire in Asia Minor. Another son, Antiochus, by another wife, was a rival for the throne and was declared the king in Antioch.[32] Antioch was the capital of the Seleucid Empire. Antiochus's uncle was the new Ptolemy III. Ptolemy took an army to support his sister and nephew, but by the time he arrived, Antiochus and his mother had been murdered. Egypt declared war against Seleucus II, starting the Third Syrian (Aramaean) War (246–241 BCE). Another treaty was eventually signed to end the war. The Seleucid Empire had been weakened by infighting. Ptolemy III and his army were in Syria (Aram), but his reason to defend it, to hold it for his nephew, was no longer valid. He could try to hold Syria (Aram) or withdraw with the booty to Egypt.[33] He withdrew and returned home.[34]

In the Seleucid Empire, another brother challenged Seleucus II for the empire. This rivalry concluded when the brother was murdered, and

---

29. John Grainger, *The Syrian Wars*, Mnemosyne, bibliotheca classica Batava, Supplementum 320 (Brill, 2010), 89.
30. Grainger, *Syrian Wars*, 127.
31. Grainger, *Syrian Wars*, 136
32. Grainger, *Syrian Wars*, 155.
33. Grainger, *Syrian Wars*, 164.
34. Grainger, *Syrian Wars*, 164.

Seleucus II died shortly afterward in 226 BCE.[35] Seleucus III followed his father and was himself murdered, serving only three years on the throne (226–223 BCE), further weakening the Seleucid Empire. Antiochus III came to the throne of a much-weakened Seleucid Empire in 223 BCE. He dedicated himself to taking back all the lands lost by other Seleucid kings.

Ptolemy III died in 222 BCE. His son, Ptolemy IV, succeeded him. While the accounts are not detailed, Ptolemy IV was twenty years old when he became king. Most historians agree that his reign was the beginning of a Ptolemaic decline.[36]

The Fourth Syrian (Aramaean) War was begun by Antiochus III, who was determined to place Syria/Aram-Palestine under Seleucid control. He was defeated by a Ptolemaic general, Theodotus, in the first encounter in 219 BCE. Later, Theodotus, now governor of Coele-Syria/Aram, turned on Ptolemy IV and gave his allegiance to Antiochus III.[37] This act resulted in Antiochus III gaining territory, including some cities in Samaria. Seleucid soldiers moved into Samaria to claim it.[38] In 217 BCE, Ptolemy IV and Antiochus III and their armies battled in Raphia, in southern Gaza.[39] The Ptolemaic forces prevailed, and Syria/Aram-Palestine was returned to their control. As was the custom, the two kings agreed on a peace treaty that settled the matter.

Ptolemy IV died in 204 BCE when his son, Ptolemy V, was only six. There was a fight over who would serve as the child's regent.[40] In this process, the rest of the child's family was murdered, leaving only the child Ptolemy V on the throne, with no other heirs.[41] This led to revolts and coup attempts, which damaged the central government and made it unable to respond to external threats.[42]

THE END OF THE PTOLEMAIC EMPIRE (204–199 BCE)

The two empires are set in a repetitive pattern. Antiochus III is now free of the peace treaty since it was made with Ptolemy IV. The Fifth Syrian (Aramaean) War began in 202 BCE, when Antiochus III moved steadily south through

---

35. Grabbe, *History of the Jews*, 2:291.
36. Grabbe, *History of the Jews*, 2:291.
37. Grabbe, *History of the Jews*, 2:298.
38. Grabbe, *History of the Jews*, 2:299.
39. The city of Raphia today is a major border crossing to Egypt from Gaza.
40. Grainger, *Syrian Wars*, 236.
41. Grainger, *Syrian Wars*, 242.
42. Grainger, *Syrian Wars*, 242.

Syria/Aram-Palestine, taking territory as he went. Many of the cities in Syria/Aram-Palestine capitulated and accepted Seleucid rule.[43] Finally, he captured the southern town of Gaza in 201 BCE.[44] After all the years of war, the people of Coele-Syria/Aram were accustomed to being invaded by one or the other, the Ptolemies or the Seleucids. In the winter of 200 BCE, the Ptolemaic army responded from Egypt and reconquered Syria/Aram-Palestine, where most cities capitulated again.[45] This was possible because the Seleucid army had withdrawn, perhaps because they thought the Egyptians were too weak to reassert control.[46] Josephus captures the nation's attitude: "The Jews, as well as the inhabitants of Coele-Syria [Syria/Aram-Palestine], suffered greatly, and their land was sorely harassed. . . . They were very like to a ship in a storm which is tossed on the waves on both sides."[47] Josephus also implies elsewhere that the Jews preferred Seleucid rule, but there is no clear evidence of this.[48]

With the Ptolemies again in control of Palestine-Syria, the Fifth Syrian (Aramaean) War was not over. Antiochus III was determined to take back Syria/Aram-Palestine once and for all. In the autumn of 200 BCE, the two armies met again in the northeast corner of modern-day Israel at Panias (Caesarea Philippi).[49] The Egyptians lost the battle and retreated to the Phoenician city of Sidon, on the Mediterranean coast. Antiochus claimed Syria (Aram) and northern Palestine as Seleucid territory and moved to Sidon to finish the recapture. The siege of Sidon lasted until the summer of 199 BCE, when the Egyptians surrendered.[50] The Ptolemaic control of Syria/Aram-Palestine had come to an end.

These conflicts between the Seleucids and Ptolemies directly involved Judah and Samaria. Since Alexander had initially placed a Ptolemy garrison in Samaria, changing the controlling empire meant damaging or capturing Samaria. Judah also did not survive these regular conflicts unscathed. There were divisions among the residents of Judah, with some favoring Seleucid rule and others supporting Ptolemaic rule.[51] In addition, during the Syrian (Aramaean) Wars, an Egyptian garrison was placed in Jerusalem.[52] During the final Seleucid conquest, Jerusalem was damaged—whether by the infighting of the Jews or an outside force is unclear.[53]

43. Grabbe, *History of the Jews*, 2:320.
44. Grainger, *Syrian Wars*, 251.
45. Grainger, *Syrian Wars*, 255–56.
46. Grainger, *Syrian Wars*, 256.
47. Josephus, *Jewish Antiquities* 12.3.3.
48. Josephus, *Jewish Antiquities* 12.3.3.
49. Grabbe, *History of the Jews*, 2:320–21.
50. Grainger, *Syrian Wars*, 261.
51. Jerome, *Jerome's Commentary on Daniel*, trans. Gleason Archer (Baker, 1958), 125.
52. Grabbe, *History of the Jews*, 2:321.
53. Grabbe, *History of the Jews*, 2:323.

JUDAH AND JEWISH COMMUNITIES DURING THE PTOLEMAIC CONTROL OF SYRIA/ARAM-PALESTINE (301–199 BCE)

The Ptolemaic Empire, with a capital in Alexandria, Egypt, controlled Syria/Aram-Palestine from 301 to 199 BCE. The Greeks had conquered a well-developed Persian Empire with infrastructure, buildings, and existing governmental structures. This means that in most regions, there was no clear cultural or archaeological difference between the Persian and the Greek eras.

The coastal towns of Palestine and Phoenicia continued population growth because of their strategic positions on the Mediterranean Sea for protection and trade. The Greeks further expanded this area, adding more storage facilities in cities on the coast and at strategic locations inland, usually on the trade routes.[54] Commerce continued to be an essential economic engine for the region, indicating the importance of goods and services produced for the entire Greek Empire.[55] Southern areas of the Samarian hills saw increased agricultural activity.[56] Areas north of Samaria were less developed and populated. It appears that the Ptolemies focused more effort on the southern regions of Palestine during their reign.

Some cities were further fortified by the Ptolemies. For example, with its proximity to Egypt, Gaza became a major city and was the entrance to Egypt. It had a large customs house for taxation and commercial trade between Africa and Asia. Other cities in southern Palestine grew because they were road stations between Petra (in the Arabah) and Gaza. These cities supported commerce with products and travel services. This route between Petra and Gaza linked the King's Highway and the Arabic Peninsula to the coast and Egypt.

Palestine and Syria/Aram (Coele-Syria) were also the areas contested and fought over in the multiple Syrian (Aramaean) wars, significantly affecting the region. Battles were often fought on the coastal plain, again demonstrating the ongoing importance of the coastal cities. But in a way, these wars became routine. It was so routine that, scholars explain, after each battle came a quick return to normal business. "Commercial opportunities resumed, afforded by trade in imported goods and products of local agriculture (including wheat and wine) and small industry (e.g., purple dye)."[57] The commercial enterprise of the coastal regions meant a higher standard of living and a more

---

54. Grabbe, *History of the Jews*, 2:47.
55. Grabbe, *History of the Jews*, 2:46–47.
56. Grabbe, *History of the Jews*, 2:46.
57. Berlin, "Between Large Forces," 4.

cosmopolitan life for those who interacted with traders, seamen, and others from throughout the empire.

The interior lands were not as central to Ptolemaic protection and commercial plans.[58] Judah remained rural and thinly populated, with Jerusalem as the only larger settlement. Jerusalem remained small, occupying only the old city of David, and was primarily unfortified.[59] Judah saw few commercial transactions, so the tax structure of the coastal areas would not be effective there. Instead, taxes were based on a simple annual tax collected by the high priest at the temple in Jerusalem and taxes on staples such as oil, wheat, and wine.[60] This made Judah a temple-economy settlement, with its primary function being religious, not commercial.

Samaria became a Greek garrison city in the northern hill country, with added fortifications to the existing structures. It was a strategic location for the garrison. Samaria remained a garrison city for the entire Hellenistic period. Shechem, right below the Samaritan temple on Mount Gerizim, was reoccupied, with new areas for homes and fortifications.[61] The sacred precinct of the town was also expanded.[62] Shechem was also primarily a temple-economy settlement. The economy of northern Palestine (formerly Samaria) was mainly agricultural, with grains, grapes, and olives as the primary crops.[63] Half the wine and oil were exported, and most were transported by sea.[64] The farthest northern regions of Palestine were thinly populated. Andrea Berlin reports that large farm areas in this region were designated as "King's Land." The Ptolemaic government farmed these lands for commerce and military supplies.[65]

Overall, except for the wealthy priests and other officials who lived in the larger towns, hellenization brought no significant changes to Jewish communities in Palestine in the Ptolemaic years. They lived, farmed, and worked as they had done through all the previous empires. They paid taxes to a new group, but that was a slight change. The Syrian (Aramaean) battles were focused on the coast, so even those did not seriously impact populations elsewhere. For most in the interior hill country, life remained as it was.

This does not mean that the Greek political structures did not reach them. Every village was supervised by a Greek administration, primarily for

---

58. Berlin, "Between Large Forces," 4–5.
59. Israel Finkelstein, "Jerusalem in the Persian (and Early Hellenistic) Period and the Wall of Nehemiah," *JSOT* 32, no. 4 (2008): 514.
60. Berlin, "Between Large Forces," 9.
61. Berlin, "Between Large Forces," 11.
62. Gary Knoppers, *Jews and Samaritans: The Origins and History and Their Early Relations* (Oxford University Press, 2013), 171.
63. Grabbe, *History of the Jews*, 2:215.
64. Grabbe, *History of the Jews*, 2:215.
65. Berlin, "Between Large Forces," 12. Others disagree with her assessment.

taxes.[66] International trade and travelers between the continents of Asia and Africa touched all except the most isolated areas. The language of trade and the administration of the cities was Greek, so those interacting with officials or merchants had to have at least some knowledge of the Greek language.[67] Depending on location and employment, a Judean or Samaritan had a variety of interactions with Greek speakers and Greek culture. For their part, the Ptolemy colonizers did not force or even encourage the adoption of Greek culture. They only changed the military, economic, and political systems in Syria/Aram-Palestine to the extent that it benefited them in their ruling capacity.[68]

Moving from the area of Syria/Aram-Palestine, Jews were now living in many communities across the empire because of multiple exiles, forced migration, and economic reasons. One of the dominant professions of Jewish immigrants listed in ancient papyri was military service.[69] This would have been a good option for the sons who did not inherit the land in Judah or Samaria. It provided them with options for the future that were not available at home. Locations like the military garrison at Elephantine, Egypt, showed a significant increase in Jewish residents during this period. Other professions in the Greek Empire perhaps involved trade or skilled labor, which could also provide opportunities for immigrants. Scholars believe that by the third century, probably more Jews were living outside Palestine than in Palestine.

This brings us to the question of who was considered a Jew and how the Jews, both in Palestine and elsewhere in the empire, defined themselves. Initially, the name was tied to the region of Judah, but ancient writings confirm that the Elephantine colony also used the term for generations.[70] Was it an ethnic or religious term? We cannot be sure how the people of this time defined themselves, but it seemed an ethnic designation. It appears a person was a Jew primarily because they were born one, either in Palestine or in other parts of the empire.[71] Yet that ethnic designation could also be religious. In the ancient world, ethnic and religious identity was closely tied together.

One of the changes during this period was in the practice of faith and religion. As noted previously, two changes occurred during the period of the Persian Empire. One was that with the loss of the monarchy, the high priest became the highest office in Judah. The priest was even charged with collecting taxes for the Ptolemies. The second was the growth of Jewish immigrant communities throughout the region. During this period, communities in the

---

66. Grabbe, *History of the Jews*, 2:168.
67. Grabbe, *History of the Jews*, 2:161.
68. Grabbe, *History of the Jews*, 2:140–41.
69. Grabbe, *History of the Jews*, 2:195.
70. Grabbe, *History of the Jews*, 2:154.
71. Grabbe, *History of the Jews*, 2:154.

Jewish Diaspora developed new ways to practice their faith without access to the temple.

During the Hellenistic period, worship in Judah was still primarily practiced at home, and the temple was the center of sacrificial worship, as described in the late Persian period. People would routinely travel to the temple in Jerusalem on festival days or for personal reasons.[72] In other words, worship continued as it had for generations.

Likewise, in Samaria, the temple on Mount Gerizim was the central location for sacrificial worship. With Samaria's population in the country's southern regions, most people could visit the temple for festivals. Interestingly, inscriptions of persons of Samaritan descent living in other parts of the empire indicate that they called themselves "Israelites."[73] This may indicate the Samaritans' desire to be seen as different from their southern Judean neighbors.

Many Jewish communities outside Palestine did not participate in the sacrificial system of temple worship in their communities. The number of people who traveled to Palestine for this ritual is unknown. How did they worship without engaging in this central rite? The most common practice of faith continued in prayer and worship at home. This practice was the center of faith since at least the early monarchy. Several texts confirm that home prayer was a central practice (Dan. 6:11; Tob. 3; Jdt. 8:36–10:2).

However, Egyptian inscriptions in 280 BCE indicate the existence of synagogues in Egypt. For example, a plaque from a synagogue near Alexandria was dedicated to Ptolemy III (fl. 246–221 BCE).[74] The inscription also states that the Jews founded the synagogue as a "House of Prayer."[75] The biblical literature is silent on the issue, but this evidence indicates that synagogues were part of regular Jewish community life in Egypt during this time.[76] Although the synagogue did not provide cultic activities, it partially replaced the temple as a place of prayer, singing, and some liturgical functions, though there is no known liturgy.[77]

The development of synagogues in Egypt should not predispose one to think others developed similarly throughout the Greek Empire. Each community created its own ways of worship. While we have evidence for communities gathering in synagogues in Egypt during the Ptolemaic period, that does not govern or preclude other developments in the rest of the empire.

---

72. Grabbe, *History of the Jews*, 2:235.
73. Knoppers, *Jews and Samaritans*, 171.
74. William Horbury and David Noy, *Jewish Inscriptions of Graeco-Roman Egypt* (Cambridge University Press, 1992), no. 22.
75. J. Gwyn Griffiths, "Egypt and the Rise of the Synagogue," *JTS* 38, no. 1 (1987): 3.
76. Grabbe, *History of the Jews*, 2:236–37.
77. Grabbe, *History of the Jews*, 2:237.

A second significant development during the Ptolemy period is the translation of the Torah into Greek in the early to mid-third century in Alexandria, Egypt.[78] It would be called the Septuagint. In today's world, a new translation of the Bible may seem routine, but in the third century, it was an innovation. Since the beginning of the Assyrian Empire, the common language of business has been Aramaic, and fewer people were speaking Hebrew. After Alexander conquered the region, Greek became the common language of the empire. In Egypt, the Jews spoke Hellenistic Greek.[79] The Septuagint became the first translation of the Hebrew Bible. Because the Hebrew Bible itself was not yet a closed canon, the Septuagint significantly differed from the Hebrew Bible we know today. The first translation of the Hebrew Bible was one of the most significant events of the Ptolemaic Era. Together, these developments forever altered the ways Judaism was practiced.

EARLY SELEUCID CONTROL OF PALESTINE: ANTIOCHUS III (199–187 BCE)

The Ptolemaic Empire ruled the people of Egypt and Syria/Aram-Palestine from 301 BCE to 199 BCE. The area was small, and there was a manageable group of cultures. The people shared much in common. By contrast, the Seleucid Empire now stretched from India in the east to Palestine and parts of Turkey in the west. Its southern border was the Gulf of Oman, and to the north, it stretched almost to the Black Sea and Kyrgyzstan. Its vast territory contained many different people, cultures, and countries. It was a more extensive empire by far and thus required a different way of dealing with its inhabitants. The king of the Seleucid Empire was Antiochus III, and he spent part of his reign ensuring that Syria/Aram-Palestine was firmly under Seleucid rule.

Antiochus III, the Great, moved to Asia Minor after finally taking control of Coele-Syria. There, he encountered conflict with the Romans, who succeeded in several battles. The Seleucids lost the territory north and west of the Taurus Mountains in modern-day Turkey. He was forced into a treaty with Rome that included sending a family member as a hostage to Rome to ensure compliance. Antiochus III sent his oldest son, Demetrius, to Rome. With this humiliating capitulation to the Romans, other areas in his empire saw an opportunity to take advantage of this weakness and began revolting.

---

78. Lee Martin McDonald, *The Biblical Canon: Its Origin, Transmission, and Authority*, rev. 3rd ed. (Hendrickson, 2007), 115.

79. Grabbe, *History of the Jews*, 2:253.

Antiochus was quelling one of those uprisings in Persia when he was killed in 187 BCE.[80]

JUDAH AND JEWISH COMMUNITIES UNDER EARLY SELEUCID RULE (199–187 BCE)

During the first years of Seleucid rule, Antiochus III aided Judah. His decree for Jerusalem was generous, and his edict reports that he was welcomed into Jerusalem with a reception. It appears that most of the residents of the city were pro-Seleucid, at least by the time he arrived. Antiochus provided a small allowance for sacrifices in the temple. He reduced some of the taxes for the temple personnel so the money could be used for repairs to the city. Antiochus also decreased taxes by one-third for the entire population and decreed that those enslaved in the fifth Syrian (Aramaean) war would be freed and their property restored.[81] These policies may represent his goals for the whole of Syria/Aram-Palestine. By his actions, Antiochus ingratiated himself to the people, provided security for the city, and aided the local economy with tax cuts. He wanted a peaceful and prosperous Judah as a functioning part of the empire.[82]

Simon II, the high priest, oversaw all work on the temple in Jerusalem from 219 to 196 BCE. After the Seleucid takeover, he supervised substantial renovations to the temple complex, building a retaining wall and adding Greek architectural features. The Jerusalem temple was expanded into a larger acropolis at the northern edge of the city, "putting it on an equal footing with its Samaritan rival."[83] In addition, Jerusalem's population grew so much that it expanded to the southwestern hill (now the Jewish and Armenian quarters).[84]

All these changes created or continued factions among the Jews in Judah that would have ramifications for its future. Scholars identify three main groups of Jews during this period. The first was the *moderates*, such as Simon II, the high priest. This group was focused on the Torah laws and ensuring that

---

80. Michel Austin, "Antiochus III the Great c. 242–187 BC," in *Encyclopedia of Ancient Greece*, ed. Nigel Wilson (Routledge, 2006), 58–59.

81. Scholars have seen this edict as authentic in most of its allowances, consistent with Antiochus's edicts to others. Grabbe, *History of the Jews*, 2:325–26. But others continue to question the exact specifications of the edicts; Rotem Avneri Meir and Julia Rhyder, "Antiochus III's Decrees for Jerusalem and the Issue of Comparison," *Journal of Ancient Judaism* 15 (2024): 175–80.

82. George Athas, *Bridging the Testaments: The History and the Theology of God's People in the Second Temple Period* (Zondervan Academic, 2023), 278.

83. Athas, *Bridging the Testaments*, 280.

84. Berlin, "Between Large Forces," 16.

the temple had a central religious role in Judah. Culturally, this group was accepting Greek culture and architecture. They were responsible for the Greek elements in the temple and sent their sons to Greek schools.[85] The moderates upheld Jewish religious traditions but had no problem embracing Greek culture as well. The second group, the *progressives*, were even more willing to see the possibility of blending Jewish faith and hellenization. For example, they were open to a generic merging or understanding of *Adoni* as Zeus, and vice versa.[86] The *majority* group was the conservatives, who disapproved of hellenization and still harbored dreams of an independent Judah.[87] They believed in an isolationist approach and abhorred anything Greek. These divisions would play essential roles in Judah's future.

There are no known Seleucid edicts issued for Samaria about the Jews or the temple in this northern region. Still, a Seleucid stela found in Israel does contain a protection order for villagers in Samaria. The military in the area were prohibited from billeting in their homes, taking property, and conscripting the villagers themselves.[88] It is possible that the same tax and infrastructure concessions were offered to the Samaritans. Antiochus III was interested in quelling revolts by ingratiating the Seleucids with the local people throughout the empire. Offering Judah and Samaria the same concessions and tax breaks would make sense.

SELEUCID CONTROL OF PALESTINE: SELEUCUS IV (187–175 BCE) AND ANTIOCHUS IV (175–170 BCE)

Antiochus III was succeeded by his son Seleucus IV Philopater. Seleucus IV's reign was a period of quiet without war. This king was murdered, supposedly by Heliodorus.[89] Other scholars doubt this account and believe that Antiochus IV, who would then become king, was behind the assassination.[90] With his death, the succession gets complicated.

Seleucus IV Philopater's oldest son, Demetrius, was held hostage in Rome, per the earlier treaty.[91] His younger son, Antiochus, was only five. If appointed king, Antiochus would need a regent. Demetrius could not become king

---

85. Athas, *Bridging the Testaments*, 281.
86. Athas, *Bridging the Testaments*, 283.
87. Athas, *Bridging the Testaments*, 284.
88. Grabbe, *History of the Jews*, 2:325.
89. Dov Gera, *Judaea and Mediterranean Politics* (Brill, 1998), 108.
90. John D. Grainger, *The Fall of the Seleukid Empire, 187–75 BCE* (Pen & Sword, 2016), 29.
91. Gera, *Judaea*, 110.

because of his captivity. Heliodorus took control of the kingdom supposedly as regent.[92] Heliodorus was then removed, and the king's brother, Antiochus IV, declared himself co-king.[93] A few years later, in 170 BCE, the young king died at the hands of his uncle Antiochus IV.[94]

Antiochus IV then became the sole king. He was ruthless and ambitious, intending to add Egypt to his empire. At the same time, the Ptolemies were plotting to return Syria/Aram-Palestine to their control. Judah, Samaria, and the rest of Palestine were again caught between the two empires. Antiochus IV began his reign by ensuring that he had good relationships in Rome and paid some back payments due from his brother Antiochus III for the Roman-Seleucid War. Then his interests quickly turned to Syria/Aram, Palestine, and Egypt.

JUDAH AND JEWISH COMMUNITIES UNDER SELEUCUS IV (187–175 BCE) AND ANTIOCHUS IV (175–170 BCE)

The sources are silent concerning Judah and the Jewish communities during the reign of Seleucus IV. As noted, his reign was quiet, with few military actions. It appears that Judah and the Jewish communities continued without any intervention, except for a financial dispute.

Second Maccabees 3 tells of a financial quarrel that may have occurred with Judah. The Seleucid tax collector Heliodorus, who later killed the king, was sent to Jerusalem to inspect the treasury and take the "untold sums" he heard were there. According to 2 Maccabees 3, a miraculous intervention saved the funds. There is no historical evidence for this event. Other than this incident, it appears that Judah was undisturbed until Seleucus IV died in 175 BCE.

First and Second Maccabees do not indicate any change in policy or treatment of the Jews early in Antiochus IV's reign. The high priest in Jerusalem, Simon II, was a moderate and was succeeded by his son, Onias III. Onias III is remembered in 2 Maccabees as one who brought "unbroken peace" and ensured that "the laws were strictly observed" (3:1). The high priest was the top official in the land of Judah. He was responsible for maintaining the religious traditions on the one hand and working with the Seleucids politically on the other. Until this point, everything was running as it had in the past.

---

92. Gera, *Judaea*, 110.
93. Gera, *Judaea*, 113.
94. Grainger, *Syrian Wars*, 293.

The next event is crucial to what happened in Jerusalem. The deuterocanonical account is the only reliable source, so we depend on it. There were also two different accounts from Josephus, but scholars are skeptical of these and do not believe they are accurate.[95]

As noted, Onias III was the high priest. According to 2 Maccabees 4:7–10, Jason, Onias III's brother, visited Antiochus IV soon after he was crowned as the Seleucid king. He offered the king a total of 440 talents of silver as a bribe to be appointed the high priest. This was possible because the office was religious *and* governmental. He also provided 150 talents more to build a gymnasium (a Greek cultural and educational center) in Jerusalem and "enroll the people of Jerusalem as" citizens of Antioch, the capital of the Seleucid Empire (2 Macc. 4:9). Second Maccabees sees this as intentional hellenization and abandonment of Jewish law and tradition (4:7–17).

Seen another way, building a gymnasium and taking a Greek name would allow Jerusalem to become a Greek *polis*, just as Samaria was. Recognizing the city as a *polis* would provide a pathway to Greek citizenship for Jerusalem's wealthy and influential residents, entitle them to additional privileges, and set them on an equal footing with Samaria and other capitals in the region.[96] It would move Jerusalem from an insignificant town to a Greek city-state in the Seleucid Empire, with all the benefits of this designation. This was not a religious designation and would not change Jewish worship practices. Judaism was still recognized as an ethos and religion in the Seleucid Empire.[97] It was a political designation that would open the city to an installed garrison and a multicultural population. Becoming a *polis* placed the power of the empire directly in Jerusalem. It brought new people with new beliefs and cultures to Jerusalem. It was an economic and status boom for the priests and the wealthy.

Antiochus IV accepted Jason's proposal and appointed him the high priest in place of his brother Onias III. Under Jason, Jerusalem became a *polis*. Second Maccabees interprets this as the wrong move, claiming that the city became hellenized (i.e., culturally more Greek) and the priests began ignoring their duties (4:13–17). However, a careful reading of the text notes that no specific breaches of Jewish law are listed.[98] In addition, there was no significant outcry to the changes among other leaders in Jerusalem. Apparently enough people were in favor of Jason's plan for Jerusalem to prevent others from stopping him.

Did these acts by Jason cause Jerusalem to become hellenized? Historically, it was not this single act that brought hellenization to Judah. Hellenization,

---

95. Grabbe, *History of the Jews* (2020), 3:316–18.
96. Grabbe, *History of the Jews*, 3:320–21.
97. Athas, *Bridging the Testaments*, 314.
98. Grabbe, *History of the Jews*, 3:330.

the introduction of Greek culture and language, had occurred since Alexander's takeover of Judah in 323 BCE. As George Atlas declares, by the time Jason replaced his brother as high priest,

> Hellenism had renovated the thought structures of Judaism, even in the most conservative Jewish circles. Greek philosophical ideas had irreversibly entered Jewish theological discourse and become mainstream. These ideas did not enter Jewish thought *de novo*; they found purchase in prior theological and cultural notions within Judaism. Thus, they did not hijack Jewish thought but developed it along prior trajectories. These ideas would persist into the first century, such as the quasi-platonic metaphysic of spiritual reality lying behind the structures of the mundane, physical world and its institutions; that the body and the soul could, in theory, be distinguished; that life might be possible beyond death; that thought was an important practice; and that the individual was as important as the corporate.[99]

As noted, hellenization had been coming for generations. Indeed, the Maccabean books themselves were written in Greek, not the traditional Hebrew. This was because Greek was replacing Aramaic as the area's lingua franca. Jason's changes did not begin hellenization; they simply extended what had been happening since 323 BCE (Alexander's death).

Jason remained the high priest for three years. What occurred next is a sordid tale reported only in 1 and 2 Maccabees. Jason was replaced by Menelaus, who, according to 2 Maccabees, also went to Antiochus IV and offered more money than Jason had for the post (4:23–24). Antiochus had no loyalty to Jason and granted the post to Menelaus, who returned to Jerusalem to assume the role of high priest (4:25–26). Then, he had to make good on his promise of 300 talents of silver more than Jason's agreement of 440 talents (4:8, 24). This burdened him and the people. Menelaus fell behind on the payments and was summoned to explain why he was not keeping up with the money due. When Menelaus arrived, Antiochus IV had left the capital to handle a revolt and appointed Andronicus as his deputy. Menelaus took some of the golden sacred temple vessels with him and used them to bribe Andronicus. Menelaus had appointed Lysimachus, his brother, in his place as he traveled (2 Macc. 4:27–32).

Meanwhile, Onias III, the priest displaced by Jason, publicly exposed the bribe. He then fled Jerusalem to a Greek sanctuary at Daphne, near Antioch. He could not be touched if he remained in the sanctuary. Menelaus and Andronicus plotted to kill Onias III by convincing him to leave the sanctuary: as soon as he did, he was murdered (2 Macc. 4:28–34). When Antiochus IV

---

99. Athas, *Bridging the Testaments*, 306.

returned, the Jews appealed to him to address the murder. The king was "grieved at heart and filled with pity and wept because of the moderation and good conduct of the deceased" (4:37). The king killed Andronicus for the murder of the former high priest.

Meanwhile, in Jerusalem, news of the stolen vessels resulted in riots. Lysimachus, left in charge as high priest, sent three thousand armed men against the crowds. The crowds counterattacked and killed Lysimachus (2 Macc. 4:39–42). The people brought charges against Menelaus, and "three men sent by the senate presented the case before him [the king]" (4:44).

Here is the first textual indication in the Bible of the group that would be called the Sanhedrin in the New Testament. The text in 2 Maccabees calls them the *gerousia*, council of elders, translated as "senate" (4:44). Since this appears to be something other than a group formed for only the purpose of accusing Menelaus, scholars understand this council or senate to be an advisory council to the high priest.[100] The *gerousia*, or senate, thus sent three men to Antiochus IV to argue for Menelaus's impeachment.

Menelaus reached out to the king through one of his officials and offered even more money to spare himself (4:45). Antiochus was about to invade Egypt and needed all the funds he could get. He agreed to the bribe, acquitted Menelaus, and had the three members of the *gerousia* murdered. Menelaus returned to Jerusalem to take up his post as the high priest against the wishes of the Jewish people.

More significant regional concerns overshadowed the tensions in Jerusalem. While dating can be difficult, in 169 or early 170 BCE, Antiochus IV and Ptolemy VI began the sixth Syrian (Aramaean) War. This war was more complicated than the others, mainly because of the involvement of Rome. Rome had its eye on the area and had been behind several wars waged around the Mediterranean Sea. Its power was growing in the region, and it would be the controlling empire within a hundred years.

It is unclear who attacked first, but Antiochus IV won the first round in November 170 BCE.[101] Antiochus was the first Greek king since Alexander the Great to invade Egypt.[102] Then Antiochus IV may have declared himself king of Egypt.[103] After a peace treaty failed, Antiochus IV blockaded Alexandria, a major port.[104] The Ptolemys appealed to Rome for intervention, but Antiochus IV withdrew to return north.[105] In the spring, Antiochus IV

---

100. Grabbe, *History of the Jews*, 3:337.
101. Grainger, *Syrian Wars*, 296.
102. Grainger, *Syrian Wars*, 296.
103. Athas, *Bridging the Testaments*, 327.
104. Grainger, *Syrian Wars*, 301.
105. Grainger, *Syrian Wars*, 301.

attacked Egypt again and offered terms for a treaty that was rejected, so he moved to take Egypt again.[106] The Roman Senate demanded that Antiochus IV withdraw from Egypt,[107] removing the threat of further war. The Romans did not want the Seleucid king to have greater power.[108] Ptolemy VI in Egypt was ordered to stay out of Antiochus's territory in Palestine, and Antiochus IV would not try to take Egypt again.[109]

According to the biblical text, while Antiochus IV was in Egypt, Jason raised an army to attack Menelaus and retake the position of high priest. Jason retook the city, and Menelaus fled to the citadel (2 Macc. 5:5). The citadel was probably the old fortification built by the Ptolemies in Jerusalem and then taken and refortified as the Seleucid garrison by Antiochus III.[110] According to 2 Maccabees, Jason and his army slaughtered citizens of Jerusalem unnecessarily (5:6). Antiochus heard of the revolt in Jerusalem and decided to intervene. What happened next is not clear. Second Maccabees reports that the Seleucid reaction was fierce. "He [Antiochus IV] commanded his soldiers to cut down relentlessly everyone they met and to kill those who went into their houses. Then there was a massacre of young and old, destruction of boys, women, and children, and the slaughter of young girls and infants" (5:12–13).

Menelaus returned from the citadel and resumed his position as the high priest. Parts of the city were destroyed (1 Macc. 1:33–35). The text also reports that the Seleucids built a citadel (1:33), but as noted, there was already a citadel with a garrison since Jerusalem was a *polis*. It may indicate a heavier presence of Seleucid soldiers.

According to historical records outside the Bible, it is unclear whether Antiochus IV visited Jerusalem after this attack or before the invasion of Egypt.[111] Second Maccabees states that Menelaus gave Antiochus IV a temple tour (5:15–16). This act violated Jewish law since only priests were allowed in the holy places.[112] To make matters worse, Antiochus helped himself to the eighteen hundred talents in the temple treasury (5:21) and the golden altar, the lampstand, the table for the bread of Presence, the cups for drink offerings, the

---

106. Grainger, *Syrian Wars*, 397.
107. Grabbe, *History of the Jews*, 3:343.
108. Grainger, *Syrian Wars*, 307.
109. Grainger, *Syrian Wars*, 307.
110. Robin Ngo, "The Seleucid Akra: 2,200-Year-Old Jerusalem Fortress Uncovered?," Bible and Archaeology News, September 21, 2019, https://www.biblicalarchaeology.org/daily/news/the-seleucid-akra/. It is still unclear if this discovery can be definitively linked with the citadel of 2 Maccabees.
111. Grabbe, *History of the Jews*, 3:345. Grabbe holds that the visit to the Jerusalem temple may have occurred before the attack on Egypt. The reports in 1 and 2 Maccabees are confusing.
112. Grabbe, *History of the Jews*, 3:343.

bowls, the golden censers, the curtain, the crowns, and the golden decoration on the temples (1 Macc. 1:21–23). The text does not state if this was a payment for what was owed by Menelaus or not, but the stripping of the temple was an abomination to the Jews.

Antiochus appointed two *epistatai*: Phrygian Philip over Jerusalem and Andronicus at Gerizim. The *epistatai* were royal representatives appointed over a city, responsible for legislation, tax collection, and enrolling citizens as Greek citizens.[113] These official roles were political, not religious, indicating that Jason's revolt may have been more significant than described in the biblical text. Since oversight was ordered over Samaria also, this could indicate that the Samaritans were also involved, or at least the Seleucids thought they were.[114] Whatever happened was significant enough to station Seleucid officials in the two cities, with direct oversight over Jerusalem and Samaria.

According to 1 Maccabees 1:41–50, Antiochus IV issued an edict that "they should be one people and that all should give up their particular customs. . . . The king sent letters . . . to forbid burnt offerings and sacrifices and drink offerings in the sanctuary, . . . to build altars and sacred precincts and shrines for idols; to sacrifice pigs and other unclean animals, and to leave their sons uncircumcised." This edict resulted in the Torah laws being declared illegal, and their observance was punishable by death. Some scholars argue that the temple in Jerusalem was rededicated to Zeus Olympios / Baal Shamin and that Menelaus was reappointed as a high priest.[115] Most scholars believe this edict occurred in 168 or 167 BCE.[116]

We wonder, Why? Antiochus IV was not a religious zealot, nor did he push the worship of Greek gods in the Seleucid Empire.[117] So why did this Greek Empire become involved in Jewish religious concerns? It may have been simply the fact of the revolts centered on the temple and the office of the high priest. Jewish religious culture and the divisions among groups of Jews were dividing the people and causing unrest. Excavations on Mount Gerizim bolster this argument. It does not appear that these same restrictions were placed on the Samaritan temple, even though an *epistatēs* (official) was assigned.[118] In addition, there was no indication that Antiochius's decree was for Jews outside of Judah.[119] It appears to have been specific to Jerusalem.[120] This Judean edict

---

113. Vasile Babota, *The Institution of the Hasmonean High Priesthood* (Brill, 2013), 59.
114. Grabbe, *History of the Jews*, 3:348.
115. Seth Schwartz, *The Ancient Jews from Alexander to Muhammad* (Cambridge University Press, 2012), 42.
116. Grabbe, *History of the Jews*, 3:356.
117. Grabbe, *History of the Jews*, 3:352–56.
118. Babota, *High Priesthood*, 60.
119. Grabbe, *History of the Jews*, 3:349.
120. Athas, *Bridging the Testaments*, 331.

came with teeth, threatening the punishment of death; the Jewish people were forced to allow these changes and, indeed, to alter the ways they worshiped. Those who did not comply were persecuted. It was a dark time: many of the conservative Jewish groups escaped Jerusalem and hid elsewhere in Judah or escaped to other regions to avoid persecution. Jerusalem was left to those Jews who were comfortable with Greek worship in the temple.

SUMMARY

The Persian Empire ended when Alexander the Great defeated it in 330 BCE. After his death in 323 BCE, his empire was divided by the leadership under Alexander. Syria (Aram) and Palestine sat between two empires, the Ptolemies in Egypt and the Seleucids in Mesopotamia. The Ptolemies controlled Palestine from 280 to 205 BCE. However, during that time, there were multiple wars over the territory of Palestine, with both empires believing they should control it and its valuable seaports. Samaria again grew in this period and had a Greek garrison in it. Judah remained thinly populated. Throughout this period, both nations were slowly being introduced to Hellenistic culture. The language of business transactions and politics switched from Aramaic to Greek.

The Seleucids gained control of Syria (Aram) and Palestine in 199 BCE. During the reign of Antiochus III, Judah was relieved of some of the Ptolemies' taxes and began to rebuild after the damage of the most recent Syrian (Aramaean) war. Everything was quiet for a time; however, factions developed in Jerusalem over the amount of hellenization in the culture and religion.

Changes happened when Antiochus IV became king. Jason went to him and bought the high priest position in Jerusalem. He was a moderate and sought to build a gymnasium (a Greek cultural and education center) and create Jerusalem as a Greek *polis*. This was hailed by some and hated by others in Jerusalem, causing the factions to entrench themselves deeper. After three years, Menelaus went to the king and paid a higher price for the position of high priest, replacing Jason. At about the same time, the sixth Syrian (Aramaean) war broke out. Antiochus IV appeared to be winning when Rome intervened and forced a peace treaty between the Seleucids and Ptolemies. Meanwhile, Jason attacked Menelaus and his troops to retake the priesthood. Antiochus IV heard of it and sent in his troops.

Antiochus's administration imposed rules on the inhabitants of Judah, specifically Jerusalem. This resulted in a permanent Greek presence. Jewish worship and even household rituals were banned. It also allowed the multiethnic population in Jerusalem to worship other gods in the temple.[121] The temple complex no longer belonged exclusively to Jews. Some scholars argue that this resulted in the Jews in Judah losing the empire's recognition as a protected ethnic class.[122] The addition of Seleucid oversight in Samaria may also indicate that region, too, losing its protected status.[123] However, this is not certain because there were Jews throughout the Seleucid Empire who did not appear to be affected, and the temple in Samaria did not indicate a significant change in religious practices. The Jerusalem temple was now supposedly dedicated to Zeus, and there were sacrifices made to multiple gods. Some Jews saw this as a growth of Judaism into a multicultural religion. Others, such as those writing 1 and 2 Maccabees, saw this as an abomination and an affront to their religious practices. These actions set the stage for the Maccabean revolt against the Seleucid Empire.

---

121. Babota, *High Priesthood*, 62.
122. Athas, *Bridging the Testaments*, 331.
123. Athas, *Bridging the Testaments*, 337.

14

The Maccabean Revolt and the Hasmonean Dynasty (168–63 BCE)

As noted in the preceding chapter, the Jews who disagreed with the new worship restrictions escaped Jerusalem and fled into the Judean hills and other places in the empire. This was not a single religious group, but various groups holding different theological positions. The writers of 2 Maccabees 6 described what they saw happening in response to the order of Antiochus IV: "Harsh and utterly grievous was the onslaught of evil" (6:3); Gentiles were using the altar for profane sacrifices (6:3–5); "People could neither keep the Sabbath nor observe the festivals of their ancestors nor so much as confess themselves to be Jews" (6:6); and persecution and death came for those circumcising their children or practicing their faith (6:10–11). The official decree also encouraged other Greek cities in Palestine to persecute the Jews (6:8).

The historical sources for this time period of Palestine are not plentiful, so we must depend on deuterocanonical accounts and Josephus's writings. First Maccabees covers the period from 175 to 134 BCE and centers on the actions of the Maccabean family. Second Maccabees covers the issues surrounding the office of the high priest before the revolt began and the revolt up to 131 BCE.[1] Neither book is in strictly chronological order. Josephus pulled his information from multiple sources, and the content is not always historically accurate. The surviving sources limit our knowledge of this time.

---

1. Daniel Harrington, *First and Second Maccabees* (Liturgical Press, 2012), ix.

RESISTERS UNITE UNDER THE
HASMONEAN FAMILY (167–163 BCE)

Although the number of resistance groups to the Greek takeover of Jerusalem is unknown, the texts do tell of two that banded together: the Hasmonean family and the Hasideans (1 Macc. 2:42). These groups eventually organized around the Hasmonean family from the village of Modein, in the Judean hills.[2] Their leader was Judas Maccabeus, one of five sons. Their early actions were centered on fellow Jews they believed were not practicing a strict faith. They "organized an army," attacked and killed "renegades, . . . tore down the altars" to gods other than *Adoni*, and "forcibly circumcised . . . boys" (1 Macc. 2:42–48). Second Maccabees reports that Judas and others also visited villages and enlisted others who "continued in the Jewish faith" and "gathered about six thousand" (8:1–4). They also began raids on local Seleucid troops and supplies.

Eventually the local Seleucid leaders decided there was enough of a threat to intervene (1 Macc. 3:10–24; *Ant.* 12.6.4–7.2). The report that Antiochus IV Epiphanes heard about the battles with Seleucid leaders and turned all the empire's resources toward defeating Judas and his troops is undoubtedly exaggerated. Still, Judas Maccabeus and his followers were making trouble for the local authorities (1 Macc. 3:27–31).[3] Antiochus IV was busy elsewhere and left on an extended campaign to the eastern portion of the Seleucid Empire. He left Lysias in charge, the governor of Syria (Aram) and the western portions of the empire, including Samaria and Judah.

Judas Maccabeus was a good commander and took full advantage of the rugged mountain terrain of southern Judah for attacks and escapes.[4] Multiple sources portray one battle demonstrating the Hasmonean commando tactics (1 Macc. 3:27–4:25; 2 Macc. 8:8–36; *Ant.* 12.7.2–4). Seleucid forces had established an encampment near Emmaus in 165 BCE. They were there to deal with Judas and his rebels once and for all. Judas Maccabeus was encamped in Mizpah, fourteen miles away, and lured some of the Seleucid army there for a "surprise" attack on his forces. Judas Maccabeus was informed that the Greek commander, Gorgias, and his troops were on the way. Then he took three thousand men and cut through the mountain passes to the main camp in Emmaus. Judas and his men attacked the unprepared main camp at

---

2. Seth Schwartz, *The Ancient Jews from Alexander to Muhammad* (Cambridge University Press, 2012), 45.

3. Lester Grabbe, *A History of the Jews and Judaism in the Second Temple Period* (T&T Clark, 2020), 3:363–64.

4. Bezalel Bar-Kochva, *Judas Maccabaeus: The Jewish Struggle against the Seleucids* (Cambridge University Press, 1989), 138.

dawn the next day. At the same time, Gorgias and his men searched in vain for the rebels in Mizpah. Judas Maccabeus's men raided the Emmaus camp quickly and left before the troops could return. Gorgias and the Seleucids withdrew to the coastal plain and lost the camp. The Jewish forces then plundered the remaining camp for weapons and resources. Lester Grabbe reflects on the events, "In that way, the Maccabees made themselves champions of the people, and their victory at Emmaus began to unite more Jews behind their cause" (cf. 2 Macc. 8:25–29).[5]

The order of the following events is difficult to sort out, and most scholars think the chapters recounting events in 2 Maccabees are out of order.[6] After the defeat of the Seleucid troops, the Maccabean rebels controlled much of the countryside north of Jerusalem. The Seleucid forces tried to gain the upper hand, but the rebel attacks continued (2 Macc. 10:14–17). These defeats frustrated Antiochus IV. He urged Lysias to negotiate with the rebels, and negotiations began in the fall of 165 BCE. These negotiations are reflected in letters included in 2 Maccabees, but they appear out of order.[7] The first letter was from Lysias to the Jews (2 Macc. 11:16–21), which Bezalel Bar-Kochva dates to late October 165 BCE.[8] He believes this was accompanied by a letter in which the Romans offer to help negotiate (2 Macc. 11:34–38).[9] The rebels demanded that worship in Jerusalem return to its former state and that all persecution cease. Antiochus IV rejected these terms in early 164 BCE.[10] At some point, Menelaus, the current high priest of Jerusalem, became involved in the negotiations, and Lysias sent a third letter in March 164 BCE, promising limited immunity to those who would cease the revolt.[11] Some probably accepted this proposal and ended their fighting. However, the overall response from the Maccabees was to increase the number of attacks.[12]

The Seleucid Empire decided its only option was a full-scale assault on Judah led by Lysias. This attack was with a reduced army since Antiochus IV and much of his military were still occupied in the east. Lysias, however, had a superior strategy for his campaign. He did not follow the previous unsuccessful idea of building a camp in the Judean highlands north of Jerusalem. In October 164 BCE, he settled his encampment to the south in a fortress at Beth-Zur (1 Macc. 4:28–35; 2 Macc. 11:1–21). Lysias had the high ground

---

5. Grabbe, *History of the Jews*, 3:357.
6. Grabbe, *History of the Jews*, 3:366.
7. Bar-Kochva, *Judas Maccabaeus*, 516–18, 541.
8. Bar-Kochva, *Judas Maccabaeus*, 516–18, 541.
9. Bar-Kochva, *Judas Maccabaeus*, 516–18, 541.
10. Bar-Kochva, *Judas Maccabaeus*, 541.
11. Bar-Kochva, *Judas Maccabaeus*, 516–18, 541.
12. Grabbe, *History of the Jews*, 3:359.

and could view and attack the region at will. Most scholars agree that this location and the number of troops quartered there meant a serious threat and probably would have ended in Judah's defeat if not for an unexpected turn of events.[13] What ended Lysias's staging for attacks on Judah happened far away.

Antiochus IV had been fighting in the eastern part of the Seleucid Empire for a year. While in Persia, he became ill and died in November 164 BCE.[14] Lysias was informed of the death before it became widely known; he withdrew and returned to Antioch, to secure the succession of the king's young son.[15] With Lysias and his troops withdrawing, Judah was left on its own. Both 1 and 2 Maccabees claim this as a Maccabean triumph, ascribing it to divine intervention (1 Macc. 4:28–35; 2 Macc. 11:6–15).[16]

The Maccabees took Beth-Zur and proceeded to retake Jerusalem and purify the temple. Menelaus and others controlling Jerusalem moved to the citadel (*acra/akra*). The citadel was a military stronghold area for the Seleucid troops in Jerusalem. The Maccabees and other followers took over the rest of the city, and the Seleucids controlled the citadel. Jerusalem became a partitioned and divided city for the first time, but not the last time.[17]

The temple was rededicated in December 164 BCE or January 163 BCE. The purification and rededication lasted eight days.[18] Judas Maccabeus and his brothers "rose and offered sacrifice, as the law directs, on the new altar of burnt offerings that they had built" (1 Macc. 4:53). The commemoration of this event became the Festival of Hanukkah (1 Macc. 4:36–59; 2 Macc. 10:1–9; *Ant.* 12.7.6–7).[19] After the rededication, the Hasmoneans continued in their quest to retake Judah. First, they focused on rebuilding and fortifying their areas in Jerusalem, even as the Greek garrisons remained in the

---

13. Grabbe, *History of the Jews*, 3:266; George Athas, *Bridging the Testaments: The History and the Theology of God's People in the Second Temple Period* (Zondervan Academic, 2023), 359; Bar-Kochva, *Judas Maccabaeus*, 366.

14. Second Maccabees 9:1–29 has a gruesome account of the death of Antiochus IV, including a deathbed vow to free Judah from persecution and let worship be restored as in the past. There is no historical information to validate this account.

15. Athas, *Bridging the Testaments*, 360.

16. Bar-Kochva, *Judas Maccabaeus*, 368.

17. Athas, *Bridging the Testaments*, 361.

18. Some have assigned a date of December 25, 164 BCE, for the rededication of the temple, but Bar Kochva explains this as a miscalculation of the calendars used (*Judas Maccabaeus*, 280–82). Grabbe believes that Antiochus died *after* the temple was retaken, so he dates the temple's rededication to November–December 165 BCE (*History of the Jews*, 3:371). John 10:22 notes the Festival of Dedication was in the winter, reaffirming the winter timing.

19. The legend about a small amount of oil lasting eight days appears to be just that and does not appear in 1 and 2 Maccabees. That legend is how the celebration became known as the Festival of Lights or *Hanukkah*. It is the continuation of the celebration of this event.

Jerusalem citadel (1 Macc. 4:60–61). The Maccabees also attacked Gentiles who oppressed Jews in the outlying regions (1 Macc. 5; 2 Macc. 10:10–38).

THE SELEUCIDS FIGHT TO TAKE BACK CONTROL (163–161 BCE)

Back in Antioch, Antiochus V was made king. Since he was only nine years old, Lysias was appointed as regent. While the Seleucids were busy with the transition, Judas Maccabeus attacked the citadel in Jerusalem to remove the Seleucids once and for all (1 Macc. 6:18–27). This act prompted Lysias to respond with significant force in the late spring of 162 BCE (1 Macc. 6:28–47; 2 Macc. 13).[20] Lysias took the same route as the last campaign and set up camp at Beth-Zur. The Seleucid forces engaged the Maccabees at Beth-zechariah and defeated them. Then, the Seleucids, with the young king in attendance, marched on Jerusalem, took control of the city, and surrounded the temple.[21] The Maccabees were either scattered or sequestered in the temple. The temple complex had been fortified, so it would take time to breach it.

While Lysias was besieging Jerusalem, he received news that Philip, the general who had been with Antiochus IV in the east, had taken Antioch in a move to become king (2 Macc. 13:23). Lysias had no choice but to withdraw a second time and return with the young king to challenge Philip in the summer of 162 BCE.

Lysias decided the best course of action for Judah was a diplomatic solution. First, he repealed Antiochus IV's original edict against the religious practices of the Jews. In the name of the young king Antiochus V, this decree to rescind the edict is recorded in 2 Maccabees 11:22–26. Also, at some point during Lysias's campaign in Judah, the high priest Menelaus was executed.[22] Lysias appointed Alcimus, another priest serving the temple, to take the office. He seemed to be a choice others could support, and the Hasideans gave up fighting as part of the Maccabean revolt and accepted Alcimus as the high priest (1 Macc. 7:12–14). The Maccabees, however, were not happy with the choice and did not settle with the new king.

---

20. Bar-Kochva, *Judas Maccabaeus*, 291.
21. Grabbe, *History of the Jews*, 3:374. Sources report that the young king was with the army when it attacked Jerusalem.
22. Second Maccabees says he was executed at the beginning of the campaign (13:1–8). From a different source, Josephus states he was executed to appease the rebels as part of the peace. The Maccabees and other conservatives would not tolerate Menelaus as the high priest (*Ant.* 12.9.7 [383–385]). Most scholars agree that the Josephus account is the most probable. The Jews would not trust Menelaus to return the temple to an exclusive place for Jews.

Lysias returned to Antioch with Antiochus V and killed Philip, securing the throne.[23] While the Maccabees were fighting for control of Jerusalem, Jewish life in places other than Judah continued as it had. Samaria did not appear to have the same conflicts with the Seleucids and continued worship on Mount Gerizim. Alexandria was the center of worship life for Jews in Egypt, even for some of the conservatives who left Judah and immigrated to Egypt during the persecution under Antiochus IV. Onias IV, the hereditary Zadokite priest and son of the murdered high priest Onias III, was exiled to Egypt, where he tried to set up a rival temple in Leontopolis, complete with an altar for sacrifices. It was not adopted by other Jews in Egypt who still prayed toward Jerusalem and sent their portion of the annual temple tax to Jerusalem.[24]

Demetrius, the uncle of the current Seleucid king Antiochus V, had been held in Rome as a hostage to guarantee that the Seleucids would not attack the Romans. In the fall of 162 BCE, he was twenty-three and requested that the Roman Senate allow him to return to Antioch and take the throne, but he was denied.[25] He escaped Rome and returned to Antioch to take the throne anyhow, where he successfully ordered the young king and Lysias to be murdered (1 Macc. 7:1–4). At this point, Alcimus, Lysias's appointed high priest, fled Jerusalem and went to Antioch to appeal to Demetrius to establish him just as Lysias had done and to punish Judas and the Maccabeans (2 Macc. 14:3–13). Demetrius appointed Bacchides as commander and sent him, with troops, to deal with the Maccabees and establish Alcimus as high priest once and for all (1 Macc. 7:5–25). Bacchides took Jerusalem while the Maccabees stayed in the northern hills. He reinstalled Alcimus as the high priest, then returned to Antioch, leaving Alcimus with some forces in Jerusalem.

After Bacchides returned, Nicanor was appointed governor of the region to deal with Judas and his fighters. Surprisingly, he offered peace to Judas (1 Macc. 7:28). Here, the sources are split. First Maccabees states that Judas *did not* accept Nicanor's proposal (7:29–31). A battle ensued, and five hundred Seleucids were killed. Second Maccabees and Josephus state that Judas *did* accept his offer of peace, and Nicanor "kept Judas always in his presence; he was warmly attached to the man" (2 Macc. 14:24 and *Ant* 12.10.4).[26] According to the version in 2 Maccabees and Josephus, at this point, Alcimus returned to Antioch and told King Demetrius of the events in Jerusalem. Demetrius ordered Nicanor to arrest Judas (2 Macc. 14:26–28). Nicanor knew he could

---

23. Grabbe, *History of the Jews*, 3:374.
24. Athas, *Bridging the Testaments*, 384–88.
25. Bar-Kochva, *Judas Maccabaeus*, 376.
26. Babota states that he was not appointed the high priest in place of Alcimus. Instead, he was appointed as "deputy" high priest to try to settle the conflict. Vasile Babota, *The Institution of the Hasmonean High Priesthood* (Brill, 2013), 101.

not defy the king, and he prepared to take Judas, who figured out the plan and fled. Both sources agree that Nicanor threatened to destroy the temple if Judas was not captured and brought to him (1 Macc. 7:33–38; 2 Macc. 14:31–36). Another battle in 161 BCE resulted in Nicanor's death at the hands of the rebels. Judas supposedly took his head and arm and displayed them in Jerusalem. The Maccabees again controlled Jerusalem.

At some point after Demetrius became the king of the Seleucids, Judas and/or other leaders in Jerusalem sent envoys to Rome "to establish friendship and alliance and to free themselves from the yoke; for they saw that the kingdom of the Greeks was enslaving Israel completely" (1 Macc. 8:17–18). The timing of this visit to Rome is uncertain, but it was during this tense period. The Romans entered a friendship treaty with Judah but with no explicit promises of support against the Seleucids (8:31–32). Judah was on its own.[27]

Demetrius immediately responded to Nicanor's death and sent Bacchides back to Judah with a large force, which arrived in 161 BCE. The Seleucids met the Maccabees at Elasa, about 10 miles (15 km) north of Jerusalem, and Judas Maccabeus was killed (9:1–22). At this point, the Maccabean resistance ended. Judah was firmly in Seleucid's hands. The remainder of the Maccabean brothers hid in the Judean hills and were pursued by Seleucid troops (9:25–26). A Nabatean chef killed one brother (9:35–36), and the youngest brother, Jonathan, became the leader of what was left of the Maccabean fighters (9:28–31).

In summary, the conservative Jewish groups coalesced around the Hasmonean brothers, and this group became the Maccabees. They proved to be effective commando fighters. However, they also benefited from other events in the empire involving succession to the throne that caused Lysias and the Seleucid troops to withdraw at two opportune times. In the end, the draconian decree of Antiochus IV was reversed. But the Maccabees were defeated, and the temple remained in the hands of Jews who accepted both Judaism and Hellenistic culture. But the Maccabees' victories over the Seleucid Empire proved that resistance was possible.

THEOLOGICAL AND POLITICAL JEWISH SECTS DURING GREEK CONTROL

During the Maccabean resistance, diverse Jewish groups with varied beliefs and political ideas were present in Judah. As with most religious groups, it is

---

27. Lester Grabbe notes the Romans would make treaties with small nations, but the meaning was symbolic. The treaty reported in 1 Macc. 8 required Judah to respond to an attack on Rome, but if Demetrius continued his attacks, Judah could appeal to Rome again seeking support; *History of the Jews*, 3:379.

impossible to pinpoint the exact time when they formed. They formed over the long periods of Persian and Greek rule over Judah, but around this period, they were active and provided various theological and political views. The first mention of Sadducees, Pharisees, and Essenes was around 100 BCE.[28]

The Maccabees were conservative theologically and also wanted an independent Judah. However, not all Jews agreed with their views. It is often overlooked that they attacked and killed Jews who did not follow their theological and political beliefs. Their beliefs were uncompromising, and they went as far as forcibly circumcising fellow Jews.

One group mentioned in 1 and 2 Maccabees was the Hasideans, the pious in Hebrew. They initially fought with the Maccabees. They opposed Menelaus as the high priest but were willing to accept Alcimus and put down their arms. Indeed, many Jews were willing to accept Alcimus as the high priest. The reversal of Antiochus IV's decrees meant religious freedom and a temple for Jews alone. It is unclear if they were an actual sect or a group of warriors. The Hasideans joined the larger majority group of Jews who were content with hellenization if they were free to worship as they pleased and in an exclusive space.[29] Most Jews in Jerusalem were probably part of this large group and not affiliated with any sects. The Hasideans disappeared into this larger majority.

The Essenes were an ultraconservative group that formed at some point in this period and withdrew into the Judean hills. They abhorred all things Hellenistic. The Essenes were an isolated group with strict community rules, including celibacy and communal living.[30] They thought they were the heirs of the sons of Zadok, and only the sons of Zadok could serve as high priests, which meant that all the high priests after Onias were illegitimate.[31] The Essenes believed in the soul's immortality and resurrection of the body.[32] They developed an apocalyptic eschatology and expected God's intervention to remove the controlling empire and set right Jewish society through proper temple worship and cultural reform.[33] Their historical leader was the Teacher of Righteousness, whose name is unknown. They penned the Dead Sea Scrolls, discovered between 1946 and 1956, yet with fragments found even up to 2021. The Essenes produced the scrolls, including biblical, apocryphal,

---

28. Grabbe, *History of the Jews*, 3:173.
29. Grabbe, *History of the Jews*, 3:381.
30. John Collins, "Essenes," *ABD* 2:619. Ancient sources, including Josephus and Philo of Alexandria, stated the Essenes were celibate. Other documents, such as the Damascus Document, speak about women and children. It is possible that different communities of Essenes had different rules. Hershel Shanks, "First Person: Was the Dead Sea Scroll Community Celibate?" *BAR* 43, no. 3 (May-June 2017): 6.
31. Athas, *Bridging the Testaments*, 401–2.
32. Collins, "Essenes," 619.
33. Athas, *Bridging the Testaments*, 401.

and community manuscripts. These scrolls have provided insights into early biblical manuscripts and clues about the mix of ancient Jewish-Christian traditions. It is unknown if they fought with the Maccabees.

The Pharisees were another ultraconservative group that opposed hellenization. Unlike the Essenes, they were politically active, remaining active in Jerusalem. They believed in an oral Torah, which included further interpretation and extension of the laws in the written Torah. They were concerned with the laws governing the temple and everyday life, especially purity concerns. This dedication to the law is why they have a reputation for being legalistic.[34] The Pharisees also believed in apocalyptic eschatology, God's direct intervention in the world, predestination, resurrection after death, and the immortality of the soul.[35] They figure prominently in the later history of Judah.

The Sadducees were probably not a sect in the traditional sense of a group formed because they were against something. They were intellectuals who saw the written Torah as divine authority, not the extrapolation of the laws. It is difficult to know what the Sadducees believed because the existing sources represent them negatively.[36] They did not believe in the afterlife or resurrection and were not apocalyptic.[37] The Sadducees did not oppose hellenization and often had Greek education. They were politically active and associated with some of the high priests. The Pharisees and the Sadducees will have a prominent role in the Gospels.

These Judean groups represent some theological diversity during this period that Judean leaders and the high priest needed to account for or react to. There was no unified Judaism in Judah during this time, and these descriptions don't even consider Jews in other areas of the empire who attended synagogue where study and prayer, not sacrifices, defined their faith.

JUDAH UNDER SELEUCID POWER (161–152 BCE)

The Maccabean rebels were decimated. With their few followers left, the brothers hid in the Judean desert hills (1 Macc. 9:33). But Bacchides, determined to destroy them once and for all, continued to pursue them (9:43–53). He did not manage to eliminate the remaining brothers but successfully drove them from Judah; they escaped by swimming across the Jordan River. Bacchides also moved to fortify strongholds across Judah (9:50). Using the Roman

---

34. Anthony Saldarini, "Pharisees," *ABD* 5:302–3.
35. Athas, *Bridging the Testaments*, 403.
36. Josephus, the New Testament, and a few rabbinic sources all portray them in a negative light; see Grabbe, *History of the Jews*, 3:138.
37. Gary Porton, "Sadducees," *ABD* 5:892.

playbook, he took the sons of high-ranking Jewish families as hostages to guarantee Seleucid control (9:53).

At this point, the series of events becomes murky. Alcimus was made high priest again after the defeat of Judas (who was briefly installed as high priest, according to some sources), but he died in either 159 or 160 BCE.[38] At some point, Bacchides returned to Antioch (9:57), but with the enhanced fortifications, the Seleucids remained in control of Judah. This was followed by a few years of uncertainty. After the death of Alcimus came a seven-year gap without mention of another high priest being appointed. The next record of a high priest's appointment is in 152 BCE. There is a lot of scholarly speculation about what happened in the intervening years, but few answers. There may or may not have been a high priest. What is certain is that the youngest Maccabean brother, Jonathan, used this time without direct conflict with the Seleucids to rebuild his rebel forces, kill his Jewish enemies (9:58–61), and fortify his stronghold at Bethbasi (9:62–63).

Meanwhile, there were problems in the Seleucid Empire. Alexander Balas appeared and claimed to be a son of Antiochus IV; in 154 BCE, the Roman Senate acknowledged him as such.[39] At about the same time, Demetrius attempted unsuccessfully to take Cyprus from the Ptolemies of Egypt. Ptolemy VI then acknowledged Alexander Balas as his cousin and aligned with him against Demetrius. The politics of empire would take center stage for the next few years and would impact Judah and Samaria.

At the same time, Bacchides had to respond to the escalation of fighting in Judah (1 Macc. 9:63–64). He returned to Judah in 154 BCE and engaged the rebels, probably with fewer forces, because of the military engagement in Cyprus (9:63–69).[40] The battle was lengthy, with significant losses on each side. Bacchides decided to withdraw and go back to Antioch. Jonathan sent ambassadors to make offers of peace and obtain the release of the hostages (9:70–73). The text is not specific about who these hostages were: probably prisoners of war from their battles or hostages taken by Bacchides earlier (9:53), or possibly both. Bacchides promised not to attack again and returned to Antioch (9:71–73). At this point, Jonathan did not settle in Jerusalem. He "settled in Michmash [seven miles north of Jerusalem] and began to judge the people, and he destroyed the godless out of Israel" (9:73). After this came a break of a few years without Seleucid attacks in the region.

---

38. Grabbe dates it to 160 BCE (*History of the Jews*, 3:390), and Babota to May 159 (*High Priesthood*, 116); Athas, on the other hand, claims that Alcimus did not die at this time but survived as an invalid until Jonathan was appointed (*Bridging the Testaments*, 413–14).

39. Athas, *Bridging the Testaments*, 408. Two ancient Greek writers state that Alexander Balas was not a royal son (Polybius and Diodorus).

40. Athas, *Bridging the Testaments*, 408.

During the next two years, constant revolts occurred in the Seleucid Empire.[41] In addition, Alexander Balas was gaining friends and power. He and the Ptolemies had allied. The Roman Senate acknowledged him as the heir to rule the Seleucid Empire. In 152 BCE, Alexander Balas landed on the Phoenician coast and settled in Ptolemais. Ptolemais is modern-day Acre, about 100 miles (164 km) north of Jerusalem. Alexander Balas was making an all-out attempt to take the kingdom, beginning in the west. Another Syrian (Aramaean) war for control of the area seemed inevitable.

Demetrius needed friends, especially in Syria/Aram-Palestine. He turned to his enemy, Jonathan. In a letter, Demetrius granted Jonathan a position as a Seleucid general, with the authority to recruit troops.[42] He also agreed to release the young hostages of the Jewish elite (1 Macc. 10:6). Jonathan left Michmash and moved to Jerusalem with the support of the Seleucid throne. The rebel was now a member of the Seleucid military structure. The text reports that Jonathan "rebuilt and restored the city" and refortified the temple walls (10:10–11).

The Seleucid kingdom was now divided, with some supporting Demetrius and others favoring Alexander Balas. With the support of Rome and Egypt, Alexander Balas was a de facto king, even as Demetrius was still the technical king of the entire kingdom. Alexander Balas acted as the king in his own right and countered Demetrius's offer by bestowing on Jonathan the office of high priest and the title of "Friend" of the King. This move placed Jonathan as a counselor and close associate of Alexander.[43] Jonathan accepted Alexander's offer. The title came with the gifts of a purple robe and crown. Jonathan took office and presided at the Feast of Tabernacles in the fall of 152 BCE (10:15–21). Most Jews accepted his role as high priest, except the extremely hellenized Jews on one side and the conservative Essenes on the other.[44] The Hasmoneans had moved from being rebel fighters to serving in the highest office in Judah.

Demetrius then countered Alexander's counteroffer to Jonathan and Judah (1 Macc. 10:22–45). The promises were extravagant, with no taxes to pay and adding part of Samaria to Judah, including Alexander's declared capital, Ptolemais (now Acre, Israel, on the seacoast north of Mount Carmel). These were promises Demetrius probably could not keep. Jonathan and the Jews in Judah remained aligned with Alexander Balas (10:46–47). In 150 BCE, Alexander defeated and killed Demetrius. Now Alexander was the sole king of the Seleucid Empire. Later that year, Alexander married Cleopatra Thea, the daughter

---

41. Babota, *High Priesthood*, 123–24.
42. Athas, *Bridging the Testaments*, 411.
43. Grabbe, *History of the Jews*, 3:393.
44. Athas, *Bridging the Testaments*, 413.

of Egypt's ruler, Ptolemy VI. This act strengthened Alexander's connection to Ptolemy and his empire. He also invited Jonathan to Ptolemais, where he was honored as a first friend, governor, and general (10:59–66). The title "First Friend" meant that Jonathan was one of the men closest to the new king.

This act, however, did not change Judah's status. They were still under the control of the Seleucid Empire, though Jonathan cemented his position in the Seleucid Empire as a warrior priest. After Demetrius's death and the relocation of the empire's capital from Antioch to Ptolemais, the eastern sections of the empire revolted, and Alexander did not respond.[45] By 147 BCE, Alexander lost all the empire east of Mesopotamia.[46]

In 147 BCE, Demetrius's son, Demetrius II, arrived in Syria (Aram) to reclaim the rest of the empire from Alexander Balas, beginning the seventh Syrian (Aramaean) war. Demetrius II also appointed a governor, Apollonius, to Syria/Aram-Palestine. The governor openly challenged Jonathan to engage in battle. In the first round of the battle, Jonathan and his forces took over Joppa (1 Macc. 10:75–76). Next, Apollonius directly engaged Jonathan and his troops. Jonathan defeated Apollonius and then captured Ashdod (10:77–89). With this victory, Jonathan gained control of Philistia on the coast.[47] At this point, Jonathan was not aligned with either Alexander or Demetrius, but Demetrius demanded that Jonathan explain himself.[48]

The next few years were chaotic, with so-called allies changing sides to enhance their positions. Ptolemy wanted Syria/Aram-Palestine back in the Egyptian fold and took over the coastal cities. Alexander fled into Arabia and was killed (1 Macc. 11:1–17). During all this unrest, Jonathan tried to remove the Seleucid garrison at the citadel in Jerusalem (11:20). In 145 BCE, Ptolemy VI died shortly after Alexander died, leaving Demetrius II to be king of the much-diminished Seleucid Empire, unchallenged for the moment. Demetrius II heard about Jonathan's attack on the garrison in Jerusalem and summoned him to Ptolemais (11:20–22). Jonathan told his troops to continue the siege of the garrison as he went to Ptolemais with gifts, gold, and silver (11:24). Thereby Jonathan succeeded and was named a "first friend," kept the position of high priest, gained some territory in Samaria, and was freed from taxation by the empire (11:23–37).[49] However, Jonathan's troops could not breach the citadel, so the Seleucid troops remained in Jerusalem.

---

45. John Grainger, *The Fall of the Seleukid Empire 187–75 BCE* (Pen & Sword, 2016), 110–11.
46. Athas, *Bridging the Testaments*, 416.
47. Grabbe, *History of the Jews*, 3:396.
48. Grabbe, *History of the Jews*, 3:396–97.
49. Grabbe, *History of the Jews*, 3:397.

In 145 BCE, the friendship required action, and three thousand Jewish fighters were sent to Antioch to defend Demetrius II from his troops.[50] At the time, Demetrius II was trying to regain the lost territories in the east. This act demonstrated Jonathan's commitment to keeping the peace. But the empire was about to suffer a leadership crisis again. In the same year, another contender for the throne appeared. Diodotus Tryphon (Trypho), a general under Demetrius I and Alexander Balas, proclaimed the young Antiochus VI the rightful king of the Seleucid Empire (1 Macc. 11:54–59).

A succession battle ensued; Demetrius II lost and fled in late 145 or early 144 BCE. Antiochus VI was declared the new king, Jonathan was made a friend of the new king, and Jonathan's brother Simon was made the "governor from the Ladder of Tyre to the borders of Egypt" (11:57–59). Jonathan also renewed Judah's ties with Rome but received no protection or promises of independent status. Judah was still under Seleucid oversight.[51]

Jonathan had successfully moved from rebel to Seleucid general and survived several regime changes, but his luck was about to run out. He had plans to negotiate for a free and independent Judah. Tryphon, acting on behalf of the young king, Antiochus VI, met Jonathan at Beth-shan in 143 BCE, and offered to give him the city of Ptolemais (1 Macc. 12:40–45). However, Jonathan was tricked and eventually killed.[52] Tryphon then tried to destroy Jonathan's troops in Judah (12:46–53).

SIMON AS HIGH PRIEST (143–134 BCE)

Simon was the only Hasmonean brother left after Jonathan's death. He succeeded Jonathan as the nation's high priest and political leader, but Judah remained under Seleucid control (1 Macc. 13:1–11).[53] The date he was installed is debated: 1 Maccabees and Josephus use different dates. There seems to have been some opposition to his appointment among the Jews, but he was publicly acclaimed by 140 BCE.[54] Simon was a military leader who had fought with his brothers for the Judean cause. He had been a leader of

---

50. Grabbe, *History of the Jews*, 3:397.
51. Grabbe, *History of the Jews*, 3:401.
52. We find conflicting stories of Jonathan's death: 1 Macc. 12:50 implies that Jonathan was killed with his men when he entered the city; the next chapter has Jonathan being held hostage for a time (13:12–19).
53. Kenneth Atkinson, *A History of the Hasmonean State: Josephus and Beyond* (Bloomsbury T&T Clark, 2016), 32. Jonathan did have children who could have inherited the position.
54. Atkinson, *Hasmonean State*, 35.

the rebel forces for several years and had fought alongside the Hasmoneans since the beginning of the revolts. Sometime after Simon's acclamation by the people, Tryphon returned to Judah in yet another attempt to completely control the region. He had several battles with Simon's forces before returning to Ptolemais (13:12–24). Tryphon had made his intentions clear concerning the Jews and could no longer be trusted.[55]

At about the same time, Antiochus VI died or was murdered, leaving Tryphon as the solo king of a tottering empire. In the void of direct Seleucid involvement, Simon reinforced Judah. He stored food to be better prepared for the next war (1 Macc. 13:33). He also sent ambassadors to Demetrius II, the deposed Seleucid king who had fled, asking for tax relief and support. Demetrius II still ruled the coastal cities.[56] Demetrius II granted his request, probably anxious to ally with Simon against Tryphon (13:34–40).

Demetrius II made far-reaching concessions to the Jews in 143–142 BCE. They were freed from paying tribute and the delinquent crown tax. The Jews were awarded all the fortifications in Judah, and past deeds were forgiven (13:37–40). Following his brothers' playbook, Simon also sent envoys to Rome. They were received the same way as the previous two times, with honor but again without an offer of protection (14:40).[57] It is unclear if this is before or after the letter of concessions from Demetrius II.[58]

The concessions of Demetrius II prompted the declaration in 1 Maccabees (13:41–42), "The yoke of the nations was removed from Israel, and the people began to write in their documents and contracts, 'In the first year of Simon the great high priest and commander and leader of the Jews.'" The year 143–142 BCE seemed to be Judah's first time since 736 BCE without direct colonial oversight.[59] This pronouncement would be premature: Tryphon was still in the picture. But for the time being, Judah was left alone while the two kings were busy with other matters and multiple revolts. Simon had blocked off the Acra (citadel), so the garrison was not receiving supplies. The Seleucid troops in the Acra reached out to Simon for a peace treaty. Simon agreed and then expelled them from their fortifications. The Acra had finally fallen (13:49–53).

---

55. Grabbe, *History of the Jews*, 3:403.
56. Grabbe, *History of the Jews*, 3:403.
57. Because of a significant scholarly debate about the timing of this event, we have no way to know, but Simon could be following the playbook of his brother and be using the letter from Rome earlier in his appointment to bolster his positions. For the debate, see Grabbe, *History of the Jews*, 3:405–7.
58. Atkinson says this may be the reason for Demetrius's letter (*Hasmonean State*, 37).
59. King Ahaz appealed to Tiglath-pileser of Assyria for aid during the Syro-Ephraimite crisis in 736 BCE. Since then Judah had been part of larger empires.

Internally, there was debate over how a somewhat free Judah would govern itself. Up to this point, Judah was part of the empire and had limited options. The high priest had religious and political power but had been appointed by and under the authority of the empire. Should the high priest have these same broad powers in a free Judah? Under whose authority? Some believed in restoring the Davidic line of kings as promised in 2 Samuel 7:4–16. Many were writing on official papers, "Simon, the great high priest and commander and leader of the Jews" (1 Macc. 13:42). Should Simon have such powers? The answer was determined and recorded on bronze tablets erected on Mount Zion (14:25–27).[60] The official powers were given by an assembly of "priests and the people and the rulers of the nation and the elders of the country" (14:28).[61] The people were the ones to appoint the high priest and to do so "until a trustworthy prophet should arise" (14:41). Did this mean that the role of the high priest was not to be considered a hereditary position? Simon had succeeded his brother. Did this mean a word from a prophet could cause the removal of the high priest? Would a prophecy allow a return to a monarchy? All these matters remained questions as Judah moved forward in its conditional independence. The declaration on the bronze tablets was recorded in the third year of Simon's tenure in 140 BCE (14:27). The tablets also specified that the high priest should wear purple and gold (14:41–43), copying the colors of the Seleucid monarchy. Judah was now firmly in the hands of the official high priest instead of a monarch.

Simon made some gains during his tenure. As noted above, he finally captured and took control of the Acra (citadel) in Jerusalem and expelled the Seleucid soldiers in 142 BCE. Also, in 142, the Roman Senate formally recognized the Jewish state, giving Judah a protective status from Rome that they had long sought (1 Macc. 14:16–24; 15:15–24). Simon also captured Gazara (Gezer) on the coastal plain and Joppa, a Mediterranean port city, and their lucrative trade economies (13:42–48; 14:5). However, Judah's semi-independent situation was tenuous.

Demetrius II had been fighting in the east to keep control of the empire. But in 141 BCE, the Parthians captured Babylon. The Parthians were an Iranian tribe from the east who rebelled against the Seleucid Empire and would eventually control the Seleucid Empire's eastern part. In the fight, Demetrius II was captured and exiled for the rest of his life.[62] This left Tryphon as the only king of a much-reduced Seleucid Empire. Demetrius II's younger brother, Antiochus VII Sidetes, immediately challenged Tryphon for the throne. The young Antiochus initiated a peace agreement with Simon that affirmed the

---

60. Grabbe claims that the information on the stela is probably genuine because the text and the tablets were contemporaneous; *History of the Jews*, 3:404.

61. Grabbe, *History of the Jews*, 3:404.

62. Athas, *Bridging the Testaments*, 430.

terms offered by his late brother (1 Macc. 15:1–9). In 138 BCE, Antiochus VII attacked Tryphon at Dor, on the coast south of Haifa and Mount Carmel. Simon sent troops to aid him (15:26). Tryphon escaped but was killed later in Turkey, where he fled (*Ant.* 13.7.2 [223–224]).

After the death of Tryphon, Antiochus VII was the sole ruler and had no need for the alliances and peace treaties he had agreed to earlier (1 Macc. 15:25–27). He believed that Judah was still a Seleucid territory and demanded that Joppa, Gazara (Gezer), and the Jerusalem Acra (citadel) be given up to the Seleucids, as well as back tribute of one thousand talents paid to avoid war (15:28–31). Antiochus VII then ordered an attack on Judah (15:38–16:10). Simon was now sixty and sent his sons, Judas, John Hyrcanus, Mattathias, and one unnamed son, into battle because he was too old to fight. They and the Judean army attacked and defeated the Seleucid troops (16:1–10). Simon and the Judeans do not bend to the new Seleucid king.

Simon also had at least one daughter, who was married to Ptolemy (son of) Abubus. Simon appointed him as the governor of Jericho and the Jordan Valley (16:11–12). Since Simon appointed him, he would have been Jewish, despite the Ptolemaic name.[63] This is his only reference in ancient documents. He could have been from Egypt or given the name for other reasons.

In 134 BCE, Simon and his family were invited to Jericho by Ptolemy. While they were enjoying dinner, he murdered Simon and captured or murdered the rest of the family. It is not clear if two of Simon's sons died at the same time or were held captive with their mother and killed later. Ptolemy planned to take over Judah (1 Macc. 16:13–17). John Hyrcanus, one of Simon's remaining sons, was not with the rest of the family. Simon had left his son John as general of the Hasmonean troops in Gezer.[64] Ptolemy sent troops to kill John Hyrcanus in his plot to take over as high priest (16:19–20). John Hyrcanus received advance word of his father's death and the death plot and escaped by killing the assassins who came after him (16:20–21).

The account in 1 Maccabees ends with Simon's death. Moving forward, Josephus's two works are the primary source of material for this time; as before, this limits the integrity of the historical record.

JOHN HYRCANUS I (135–104 BCE)

John Hyrcanus was determined to defend his family's position and become high priest. He faced some significant obstacles. First, based on Josephus,

---

63. Grabbe, *History of the Jews*, 3:409.
64. Atkinson, *Hasmonean State*, 49.

scholars say he had not obtained the age of thirty, the age required to become a high priest.[65] Second, it was unknown at the time whether his mother and two brothers, one of which was older, were still alive and held captive by Ptolemy. Third, it had not been settled whether the office was to remain hereditary. But all these issues would need to wait. There was a crisis, and decisions were immediately required because Judah was threatened.

John Hyrcanus did not wait for these questions to be resolved and led a military campaign to attack Ptolemy at his fortress near Jericho. It was a long siege, lasting until the autumn, when John Hyrcanus was forced to withdraw. At some point, the remainder of his imprisoned family was tortured and murdered by Ptolemy.[66] Then Ptolemy fled to Philadelphia (now called Amman), east of the Jordan River.[67]

John Hyrcanus had to return to Jerusalem because Antiochus VII attacked it in the fall of 135 BCE and seized it for almost a year.[68] John Hyrcanus ended the siege by paying tribute for the capture of Joppa and Gezer, tearing down the defensive wall in Jerusalem, and providing family members as hostages to guarantee compliance.[69] This agreement brought peace between Antiochus VII and Judah, but Judah was again a vassal state of the Seleucid Empire. John Hyrcanus even fought with Antiochus VII Sidetes against the Parthians in 130 or 129 BCE. Antiochus VII was killed in the conflict, and in an odd twist, Demetrius II became the king of the Seleucids again after being released by the Parthians. After Demetrius II returned to the throne, he was busy elsewhere in the kingdom. Others who claimed their right to the Seleucid throne besieged the kingdom, and the empire was weakened by internal fighting and a failed attempt to conquer Egypt.

In this power vacuum, John Hyrcanus began conquering the surrounding lands. He retook Joppa, Gezer, and part of the Transjordan. These strategic cities provided significant income through taxes on goods. Other than the taking of these lands, what happened over the next few decades is unknown. John Hyrcanus then turned to Samaria in 111 BCE and took it after a long siege.[70] He destroyed Shechem and the temple on Mount Gerizim, and the Hasmoneans did not allow the Samaritans to rebuild it.[71] This act by John Hyrcanus was a decisive point in the animosity between the Jews and the Samaritans, resulting in the permanent religious split reflected in the New

---

65. Atkinson, *Hasmonean State*, 48.
66. Atkinson, *Hasmonean State*, 55.
67. Atkinson, *Hasmonean State*, 55.
68. Atkinson, *Hasmonean State*, 55.
69. Grabbe, *History of the Jews*, 3:411.
70. Josephus, *Ant.* 13.10.2.
71. Knoppers, *Jews and Samaritans*, 218–19.

Testament.⁷² Why he decided to destroy the temple is also unknown. Then he tried to take the Greek *polis* of Samaria, but the attempt failed. His two sons succeeded in about 108 BCE.⁷³

The rest of John Hyrcanus's life was a prosperous time for Judah. They reaped the additional territories' benefits and even began minting their own coins.⁷⁴ John Hyrcanus served as high priest for thirty-one years before he died in 104 BCE.

JUDAH ARISTOBULUS (104–103 BCE)

Before his death, John Hyrcanus named his wife, not one of his sons, to be his political successor.⁷⁵ This was an unprecedented act. Unfortunately, sources do not record her name. Jewish law forbade her from serving as a high priest, which presented a succession problem since John Hyrcanus had four sons. Was she to rule and appoint one of the sons as the high priest? The documents do not preserve the reason, but one of the sons did not wait to find out. The eldest son, Judah Aristobulus, led a coup and imprisoned his mother and his three brothers. Later, his mother starved to death in captivity.⁷⁶ He also appointed one brother, Antigonus, as a military leader.

After Judah Aristobulus became the high priest, Josephus reports that he placed the crown on his own head and declared himself king of the Jews.⁷⁷ He would have been the first king since 586 BCE in Judah, but it is uncertain whether he became the king, especially since he minted coins with the phrase "Judah the High Priest and the Congregation of the Jews."⁷⁸ His tenure was brief, lasting only ten months. He, or his brother Antigonus, captured part of Galilee and forced the population to adopt circumcision and live by Jewish law. This was his only accomplishment.⁷⁹ According to Josephus, Judah Aristobulus fell ill shortly after the first time he presided as high priest. His brother, Antigonus, replaced him at the temple for the rest of the Festival of Tabernacles. This infuriated Judah Aristobulus, and he ordered his brother to be murdered. A few days later, Judah Aristobulus also died. His time as the high priest was short and violent.

---

72. Knoppers, *Jews and Samaritans*, 219; Atkinson, *Hasmonean State*, 77.
73. Grabbe, *History of the Jews*, 3:414.
74. Grabbe, *History of the Jews*, 3:415.
75. Atkinson, *Hasmonean State*, 82.
76. Grabbe, *History of the Jews*, 3:417.
77. Josephus, *Ant.* 13.11.1 (13.301–302).
78. Atkinson, *Hasmonean State*, 81.
79. Josephus, *Ant.* 9.3. Grabbe, *History of the Jews*, 3:418. Yet Atkinson declares that archaeological evidence for this takeover and forced religious conversion is not evident; *Hasmonean State*, 94–95.

ALEXANDER JANNAEUS (103–76 BCE)

After Aristobulus's death, his widow, Alexandra, released the remaining brothers and appointed Alexander Jannaeus, often called Jannaeus, as the new ruler and high priest. It is unknown whether this was before or after she married Alexander Jannaeus.[80] One of his first acts was to ensure his succession to the office; one brother disappeared, and the other one was murdered.[81] He came to the position at an opportune time: the Seleucid Empire was weakened by infighting and revolts. Jannaeus took full advantage of this situation to expand Judah's territory.

Unfortunately, his first attempts to capture cities on the coast found him embroiled in a Ptolemy-succession fight. Jannaeus decided to invade the city of Ptolemais. The people of Ptolemais called on Ptolemy IX, the king of Cyprus, for help. Ptolemy IX responded with troops, and Jannaeus had no choice but to make a treaty with him. Jannaeus, not trusting Ptolemy IX, also contacted Ptolemy's estranged mother, Cleopatra III of Egypt, for support.[82] The two estranged family members were fighting for control of the region. Ptolemy IX had lost early contests and was limited to the island of Cyprus. Alexander Jannaeus was playing both sides in this so-called Egyptian War of the Scepters. When Ptolemy IX discovered his double cross, he attacked Jannaeus and his troops in Galilee, destroying towns and defeating Jannaeus.[83] Jannaeus's problems grew when the other party in this war, Cleopatra III, arrived on the coast, led by Jewish generals. Now there were two warring armies in Judah, both unhappy with Jannaeus. The conflicts caused significant damage. Ptolemy IX decided to withdraw from Galilee and try to capture Egypt while Cleopatra III was busy in Judah, but he was defeated and returned to Cyprus. Cleopatra III then planned to capture Judah. Jannaeus approached her and provided gifts for a peace treaty.[84] With the conflict settled, Cleopatra III returned to Egypt.

Another brother entered the fight for control in Egypt, bogging down the Ptolemies in another succession fight. At the same time, there was a fight for the throne of the Seleucid Empire. Jannaeus took full advantage of both empires' inability to intercede in Judah. In approximately 100 BCE, he took Gaza after a long siege. Then, he turned to the Transjordan, aiming to recapture it. He

---

80. Scholars debate whether Alexander married his brother's wife or two women had similar names. Most scholars believe she was the widow of the late Aristobulus; see Grabbe, *History of the Jews*, 3:419; Athas, *Bridging the Testaments*, 481–82.
81. Atkinson, *Hasmonean State*, 107.
82. Atkinson, *Hasmonean State*, 109.
83. Atkinson, *Hasmonean State*, 112–14. Archaeological evidence supports invasion.
84. Grabbe, *History of the Jews*, 3:420.

was successful early on, but then, in 94 BCE, he and his troops were trapped in the ravines of the Golan region, where the locals killed many of his soldiers.[85]

In 95/94 BCE, there was an internal revolt against Jannaeus. Josephus states that Jannaeus had been at war for six years, with fifty thousand Jews killed in battle. This loss was one of the reasons for the revolt. Like his brother, Jannaeus also announced himself as a king. Any or all of these reasons could have prompted the dissatisfaction. The revolt openly started during the Festival of Tabernacles and may also have been prompted by disagreements between the Pharisees and the Sadducees.[86] The crowd demonstrated their anger by pelting Jannaeus with lemons during the festival.

The response from Jannaeus was quick. Josephus's numbers are probably exaggerated at six thousand dead due to Jannaeus's suppression of the revolt, but it does indicate a harsh response. He then walled off the temple courtyard and the altar with a wooden fence, limiting it to priests only. Before Jannaeus's act, all Jewish men could access the courtyard of the temple and watch sacrificial ceremonies at the altar. According to Josephus, the high priest's actions caused a civil war that lasted six years.[87]

In the meantime, the fight for the Seleucid throne had finally been settled. It was divided between two brothers. One brother, Philip I, ruled in Antioch; the other, Demetrius III, ruled in Damascus.[88] Jannaeus's opponents in Judah appealed to Demetrius III in 88–90 BCE for assistance.[89] Demetrius had lost the northern portion of his territory, and the addition of Samaria and Judah was attractive. Demetrius and Jannaeus battled near Shechem. Jannaeus had Jewish troops and mercenaries.[90] The Samaritans and Jannaeus's opponents in Judah fought alongside Demetrius III. This was indeed a civil war, yet with an outside party involved. Demetrius III and his forces were winning the battle, and Jannaeus fled to the mountains.[91] But at this point, Demetrius III gave up the fight and returned to Damascus because his brother Philip threatened to invade his capital.[92]

---

85. Atkinson, *Hasmonean State*, 123.
86. Scholars, following Josephus, see this as a theological battle between the Sadducees and the conservative Pharisees and Essenes; see Atkinson, *Hasmonean State*, 123–24.
87. Josephus, *Ant.* 13.13.5.
88. Grabbe, *History of the Jews*, 3:421.
89. The date is uncertain, see Grabbe, *History of the Jews*, 3:422; or Atkinson, *Hasmonean State*, 126.
90. Grabbe, *History of the Jews*, 3:422.
91. Josephus, *Ant.* 13.14.
92. Grabbe, *History of the Jews*, 3:422. Grabbe notes that, according to Josephus, Demetrius retreats because the Jews joined Alexander in the middle of the battle. That is possible but unlikely, especially based on what happens next.

Jannaeus pursued the Jews and Samaritans who fought with Demetrius near the Samaritan capital.[93] According to Josephus, he captured eight hundred men with their families and took them back to Jerusalem, where he crucified the men and, while they were being crucified, forced them to witness the slaughter of their wives and children. Jannaeus watched this gruesome execution while feasting with his concubines.[94] The numbers may be an exaggeration, but it was a shocking way to deal with the opposition. The people were appalled by the vile nature of this act. It was made worse because he was the high priest.

In 87 BCE, the Seleucid king Demetrius III was defeated by Philip and exiled. Antiochus XII Dionysus, another brother of Philip I and Demetrius III, claimed the throne in Damascus and then battled with the tribes in the Transjordan.[95] Judah was between the two warring armies. What happened next is unclear. It is safe to say that all the parties continued to fight for the areas formerly under firm Seleucid control. Jannaeus died while in battle in the Transjordan in 76 BCE. He left the disputed crown to his wife, Shelamzion (Salome) Alexandra.[96] She would serve as ruler and appoint the next high priest.

SHELAMZION (SALOME) ALEXANDRA (76–67 BCE)

Alexandra appointed her oldest son, John Hyrcanus II, the high priest, but she retained civil rule. It appears that both she and her eldest son were Pharisees. Under her reign, the Pharisees gained theological and political power, including restoring the Pharisaic regulations abolished by John Hyrcanus I.[97] Her younger son, Aristobulus II, was a Sadducee, like his recently deceased father.[98] These differences caused tensions in the family. Alexandra placed Aristobulus II as a military commander. This act settled the tension between the two brothers and the two religious groups. Each had a role in the leadership of Judah.

Her rule was prosperous and peaceful. Alexandra was a good administrator and doubled the size of the military, seeing an opportunity to advance the fortunes of Judah.[99] She had a peace treaty with Tigranes of Armenia, the only

---

93. Atkinson, *Hasmonean State*, 127. The city is uncertain, but it was in Samaria.
94. Josephus, *Ant.* 13.13.2; and Nahum Pesher 4Q169 3–4, I, 1–7.
95. Josephus, *Ant.* 13.15.1.
96. Atkinson, *Hasmonean State*, 134–35. Atkinson notes that Josephus does not indicate her Hebrew name, but it is found in the Dead Sea Scrolls 4QpapHistorical Text C (4Q331 1 ii 7).
97. Atkinson, *Hasmonean State*, 136; *Ant.* 13.16.1–2.
98. Atkinson, *Hasmonean State*, 136.
99. Grabbe, *History of the Jews*, 3:425.

power in the region. The Seleucid Empire was dying and was finally brought to an end in 64 BCE.

Alexandra also raised the profile of the Pharisees, and many returned from their self-imposed exile in Alexandria. When she became ill, Hyrcanus II was made coregent in 70–69 BCE.[100] But her youngest son, Aristobulus II, occupied twenty-two Judean fortresses and declared himself king.[101] He controlled much of the military, and Alexandra responded by imprisoning his family. She died before she could continue to fight her youngest son. Alexandra led Judah for nine years and was successful and skillful.[102] Her service marks the end of the Hasmonean rule. Her sons' fighting would cause their failure and the loss of Judah at the hands of the Romans.

END OF THE HASMONEAN KINGDOM (67–63 BCE)

What happened here is especially difficult to untangle since the two sources by Josephus conflict.[103] This is an approximate recital of events. When Alexandra died, Hyrcanus II assumed solo power. Aristobulus II immediately declared war against his brother. The armies met near Jericho. Hyrcanus II lost and fled to Jerusalem, joined his wife and children, and abdicated his throne and position as high priest.[104] Thus Hyrcanus II became a private citizen. Josephus framed this war between the brothers as between the Pharisees (Hyrcanus II) and the Sadducees (Aristobulus).[105] The theological and political differences between these sects would remain on display for many years as Jews navigated the events that followed.

Sometime later, Antipater, whom Josephus calls an "Idumean," went to Hyrcanus II. Antipater was the father of King Herod the Great, known via the New Testament. He was from the Edomite area. Josephus states that Antipater convinced Hyrcanus he was in danger from his brother, and Hyrcanus needed to flee to Petra. Then, Antipater convinced Hyrcanus to remove his brother and resume power with the help of Aretas, a leader in Petra. In exchange, Aretas would receive the land east of the Jordan River that Jannaeus had taken earlier with a group of Judeans.[106] With Aretas's army, Hyrcanus II attacked

---

100. Josephus, *Ant.* 14.1.2.
101. Grabbe, *History of the Jews*, 3:425.
102. Josephus presents two different perspectives on Alexandra: in *Jewish War*, he portrays her as a successful leader; in *Antiquities*, however, he describes her as a pawn of the Pharisees. The reason is known only to Josephus.
103. Atkinson, *Hasmonean State*, 147.
104. Josephus, *Ant.* 14.6.1.
105. Atkinson, *Hasmonean State*, 149.
106. Josephus, *Ant.* 14.1.4.

and ultimately defeated Aristobulus II, who was barricaded in the temple. Josephus states that it was Passover 65 BCE, so the fighting paused while the sacrifices were offered.[107] The brotherly fight over the throne kept the Judeans occupied with internal issues.

In the meantime, the Romans had been overtaking much of the old Seleucid Empire. Pompey was fighting the Armenians. He sent his lieutenant, Scaurus, to investigate the sibling civil war in Judah, and he arrived while the two were battling over Jerusalem. Both brothers, trying to get Scaurus on his own side, sent gifts.[108] The Romans accepted Aristobulus II's offer. Their reason is unclear because Josephus's account is slanted toward Aristobulus.[109] Scaurus returned to Damascus, and Aristobulus II attacked his brother with the help of troops lent by the Romans, defeated him, and retook the throne and high priest's position.[110]

Pompey then came to Judah in the spring of 63 BCE.[111] He met the two brothers near Jericho. Both brothers and a group of Judeans who wished to end the Hasmonean monarchy sent emissaries on their behalf.[112] Each emissary offered their reasons and tributes. Pompey stated that he needed longer to decide. Aristobulus II did not want to wait and set out to return to Jerusalem. Pompey took it as an insult. Eventually, Aristobulus barricaded himself and his followers again on the Temple Mount. With the help of Hyrcanus, Pompey entered Jerusalem and besieged them for three months before the Romans took the city and killed many. Pompey finally entered the temple and the Holy of Holies but did not defile the temple or take its treasures. Pompey allowed Hyrcanus II to remain as the high priest, but not as king, and he took Aristobulus II to Rome. Judah's independence had ended. The Judeans continued to fight occasionally, but Judah was now under Roman rule and would remain so for many years to come.

SUMMARY

This period saw the end of the Seleucid Hellenistic Empire. It was not conquered at its full power but collapsed from within due to internal fights over the throne. Throughout this period, the Romans were gaining strength and

---

107. Josephus, *Ant.* 14.2.1–2. Grabbe, *History of the Jews*, 3:433.
108. Grabbe, *History of the Jews*, 3:432.
109. Josephus, *Ant.* 14.2.3.
110. Josephus, *Ant.* 14.2.3.
111. Atkinson, *Hasmonean State*, 150.
112. Atkinson, *Hasmonean State*, 150.

power. They began to take the western territories of the Seleucid Empire, and the Seleucids were too weak to retaliate.

The Hasmonean family rose from a rebel group of conservatives and managed to control Judah through the office of high priest. Two of them also declared themselves kings, but there did not appear to be a popular acclamation of their kingship. During the time of the Hasmoneans, Judah had brief periods of self-rule, but always in the shadows of the larger empires. The Hasmoneans were effective fighters, but occasionally their brutality and family violence were shocking. This period also saw a change in the work of the high priest and questions concerning kingship. Hellenization also changed the theology of the Jews. The influence of the Persian and Greek Empires introduced new philosophical and theological questions. Theological groups in Judah were now arguing about the immortality of the soul, the resurrection of the dead, and how God was active in the world. These issues are a large part of the theological debates that occur in the New Testament.

15

How the Hebrew Bible Became a Book

The prior chapters discussed the history of Israel and Judah from their beginnings to the arrival of Romans in 63 BCE. While this history was unfolding, the books of the Hebrew Bible were taking shape. Now that the history has been told, it is time to revisit the topic first discussed in chapter 1.

Unfortunately, just as with the history of the people, we know a lot less than we wish we knew about the development of the Hebrew Bible. In addition, the way scholars date the texts of the Hebrew Bible divides along theological lines. Maximalists argue for the early formation and adoption of biblical books, with most of the Hebrew Bible completed in the preexilic and early Persian periods. The most conservative argue that Moses wrote the Pentateuch, which was not edited after that. Another camp adopts the minimalist approach, believing the books were entirely written in the later Persian and Hellenistic periods. As with other scholarly arguments in this book, I will take a middle approach and, even in doing that, admit that what we know is much less than we must surmise from a preponderance of the evidence. In this investigation, the Bible and extrabiblical documents offer little assistance. There are no comprehensive ancient discussions of how and when the biblical narratives were compiled and added to the various ancient religious canons or why the books we now have were chosen and not others. There are some hints and reports but nothing that gives us a full picture of the process.

First, we need to define what is meant by the Hebrew Bible. Chapter 1 discussed how different religious traditions have different canons of Scripture. The Orthodox and Catholic traditions have an expanded list of books in their Old Testaments. The Jews and the Protestants use the same books but in different order. Here we are dealing with the books in the order presented in the Tanakh, or Hebrew Bible, including its divisions into three sections: Torah, Prophets, and Writings. The chapter is divided into three periods of the development of the Hebrew Bible: (1) earliest narratives, (2) official narratives during state formation, and finally, (3) postexilic edits and additions.

The history of biblical literature is complex because the Hebrew Bible is not a book by a single author but a composite work constructed over hundreds of years. It repeats narratives and tells and retells the stories; for example, 1 and 2 Chronicles retells 1 Samuel to 2 Kings. Some books are collections of smaller pieces produced over time, such as Psalms or Proverbs. The Hebrew Bible also contains conflicting theologies, such as the expansive visions of God as a God for all people in Isaiah, and the exclusive theology presented in Ezra.

THE EARLIEST NARRATIVES (BEFORE 1000 BCE)

As noted in the early chapters of this book, writing was first used during the beginning of the Bronze Age, 3200 BCE. For thousands of years before that invention, humans told stories and eventually began to collect those stories in their oral traditions. Cultures were built, traditions were passed on, and societies were connected through stories long before writing was created. Once writing was invented, it was used by a small group of scribes associated with royal circles. Writing was used for state business. The traditions of the people were still shared in spoken stories, poems, and songs.

To us, storytelling may seem like something from the distant past. However, despite our dependence on the written word, oral tradition is not a thing of the ancient past. An expert in oral traditions, John Foley, reports, "Numerous studies—conducted on six continents—have illustrated that oral tradition remains the dominant mode of communication in the 21st century, despite increasing rates of literacy."[1] Just like our ancient ancestors, we are still people who share stories. We should not underestimate its importance, then or now.

The stories that would become the narratives of the Bible were shared in small and large circles. They were not the creation of an individual "author." They were community stories and songs, refined by the community and edited over time. Songs are also poems. There is evidence of early song sharing in texts such as Exodus 15, where Moses (15:1–18) and Miriam (15:21) shared the story of deliverance with song. Songs allowed the community to be involved in telling the stories by joining their voices together. For our purposes, discussing oral tradition will encompass both storytelling and singing.

---

1. John Miles Foley, "Oral Tradition and Communication," *Britannica*, 2025, https://www.britannica.com/topic/oral-tradition.

Since this practice of oral tradition left no archaeological trace, it cannot be historically documented. However, comparative studies of other nations in the region confirm that the practice of sharing stories orally was widespread.[2] Initially, the study of oral tradition was called form criticism, pioneered by Gerhard von Rad and Martin Noth. They compared individual narratives to determine when they were written. To do this, they were comparing cultural practices to demonstrate that the sections were written at different times. Later, linguistic studies added how the language used in the narratives varied over time. This allowed them to postulate how stories were written and/or edited throughout this early period.

How did smaller stories become larger ones? For example, looking at Exodus 1–15, we see smaller stories within the larger narrative: the stories of Shiprah and Puah (1:8–22), Moses's birth and rescue (2:1–10), his killing an Egyptian and fleeing (2:11–22), and so on. Biblical scholars believe that, at some point, Exodus 1–15 was joined together. Gerhard von Rad argues that this happened when the stories were first written down.[3] However, in oral cultures in the ancient world, designated storytellers held the traditions of the community secure and had memorized multiple stories and songs. Storytellers could have known their own community's version of the exodus story or about the matriarchs and patriarchs. As noted in earlier chapters, smaller groups would join together for protection and worship and share stories and songs. Many scholars believe this story sharing was essential to refining and editing the narratives and songs and placing them in longer episodic narratives.

Were the stories written down during the centuries when oral traditions were prominent? Again, there is no way to know definitively. It is possible, but writing before the establishment of the monarchy was rare (around 1000 BCE). Storytellers could have scribbled notes or prompts on ostraca (broken pottery pieces). David Carr explains that the notes would have "help[ed] students accurately internalize the textual tradition, check their accuracy, correct it, and/or as an aid in the oral presentation of a text."[4] These notes could have contained alphabetic scripts or a sequence of pictures to aid in memorization. However, other than general time frames, there is no way to estimate how long the narratives of the Hebrew Bible were shared before they were first written down. It is also impossible to state when they were first written down or by whom.

---

2. David Carr, "Torah on the Heart: Literary Jewish Textuality within Its Ancient Near Eastern Context," *Oral Tradition* 25, no. 1 (2010): 24.

3. Gerhard von Rad, *The Problem with the Hexateuch and Other Essays*, trans. E. W. Dicken (McGraw Hill, 1966).

4. Carr, "Torah on the Heart," 18–19.

OFFICIAL NARRATIVES AND STATE FORMATION (1000–586 BCE)

The next major step in the development of the Hebrew Bible would be writing down an official version of these oral narratives. "Official" sounds as though the resulting text would become The Text or The Book, not to be changed or altered. But that was not the case: texts were edited, removed from, and added to the Hebrew Bible for centuries. These texts were in flux and were, at the same time, documents of the state.

Why write down a text? This essential question gets to the heart of the purpose of official narratives. It also opens up additional questions concerning literacy rates, who the writers were, when the narratives and poems of oral tradition were written down, and their purpose for preserving these texts.

Literacy rates impact who can access a text and for what reasons. Literacy rates rose throughout the history of Israel and Judah. They were higher in the late monarchy and the Babylonian Empire (700–539 BCE).[5] Literacy continued to grow in the following Persian and early Hellenistic Empires (539–300 BCE), aided by the nearly universal use of Aramaic and then Greek in the area under study. This increase in literacy was empire-wide, not only in Judah and Samaria. But how was literacy defined in the ancient world?

Simply put, it was functional literacy. Reading was not a leisure activity. For example, the epigraphic evidence (inscriptions on durable materials) demonstrates that in other than royal and priestly circles, "the vast majority of texts and letters are pragmatic and brief—military, military-commercial, or commercial in nature."[6] Writing was done for a specific purpose, such as for a deed (Jer. 32:9–15), formerly done orally, before witnesses (Gen. 23:17–18; Ruth 4). For most people in Israel and Judah, it was a tool for commerce. A laborer could read what was needed to do his job but probably did not write since it was not a function of his work. Others, such as clerks or middle-level bureaucrats, could read and write, but only the receipts and other documents required for processing. A military leader or his scribe could read and write within the parameters of the messages sent back and forth on military business. It was not the level of literacy needed to create and copy the narratives and poems that would become the Hebrew Bible. This higher level of literacy was reserved for only a few, such as the scribes.

Who had access to written material depended on the purpose of the document. As noted above, writing for ordinary commerce became more common

---

5. Susan Niditch, *Oral World and Written Word: Ancient Israelite Literature* (Westminster John Knox, 1996), 58.
6. Niditch, *Oral World and Written Word*, 58.

after about 700 BCE. Several collections of epigraphic material discovered confirmed this type of communication, including the Samaria ostraca (850–750 BCE) and the Lachish letters (around 609–587 BCE). These items were discovered together in a protected place, indicating the existence of local archives for storing business and military records.

Other larger empires made depositories for literature, such as Asshur, the early Assyrian capital (6th c. BCE),[7] and the great library in Nineveh, the later capital of Assyria (7th c. BCE).[8] The Bible refers to archival extrabiblical documents such as the Annals of the Kings of Israel or the Annals of the Kings of Judah, which would have been kept in a similar depository by the monarchies of Israel and Judah. There is no report of a library for the sacred documents in the Hebrew Bible, but one must have existed.[9]

What type of expertise and materials did writing require? Business and military receipts and letters were often written on ostraca, usually a shard of broken pottery. The ostraca were portable, readily available, and lasting. Narratives, laws, and poems could not fit on a potsherd, so other materials were needed. The most probable materials available for longer items were papyrus (from Africa, as in the Nile Delta, near Lake Tiberias, and via the Seleucids in Babylonia), mud or baked-clay tablets (esp. Babylonia), or leather scrolls (mentioned by Herodotus, 5th c. BCE), called parchment by the Hellenistic period. Evidence of writing surfaces prepared from papyrus and leather has been found in Israel and Judah. Both could be stitched together to form longer scrolls. It is unknown which was preferred when. Papyrus was mostly imported from Egypt, but the raw material used to make leather was readily available to scribes in Jerusalem because of the sacrifices made in the temple.[10] However, writing on either material, especially with line after line of uniform letters, required specialized training and years of practice. Scrolls are portable, but they are also large and cumbersome. They were also expensive and labor-intensive to make. After the scrolls were made, writing the narratives required more time and expense. Nations, not individual families, commissioned and owned them.

Recording narratives, poems, and longer works of literature was reserved for specialists or scribes. Scribes were common in all Afro-Asiatic nations and had held positions of power and responsibility since the third millennium

---

7. Olaf Perersén, *Archives and Libraries in the City of Assur: A Survey from the German Excavations*, Part II, *Neo-Assyrian Period, Later Periods, General Trends* (Uppsala University / Almqvist & Wiksell, 1989).

8. William Schniedewind, *How the Bible Became a Book* (Cambridge University Press, 2004), 174–75.

9. Niditch, *Oral World and Written Word*, 63.

10. Aaron Demsky, "Writing," *Encylopedia Judaica* 16 (1971): 664.

BCE.[11] They were highly educated specialists who wrote for the crown and government. In Judah and Israel, scribes were active from the early monarchic period in the tenth century.[12] The late monarchial period had different scribal groups: those connected to the royal court, priestly scribes in the Jerusalem temple, and Levite scribes who worked in multiple settings.[13]

One of the most challenging questions to answer is when the narratives and poems of oral tradition were recorded on these scrolls. Unfortunately, here we enter into centuries of dark ages. The evidence in the Hebrew Bible for written documents is scant (cf. Exod. 17:14). We do read of the tablets with the Ten Words (or Ten Commandments) inscribed by God and then by Moses (Exod. 24:4, 12; 31:18; 32:15–19; 34:1–4, 27–29). The second is when Moses wrote the "words of the law" (Deut. 31:24–26). Neither of these passages references the written story of Israel and Judah nor the scrolls of the biblical books. Also, in the time before 1000 BCE, writing was exceedingly rare. Neither of these narratives can be linked with a specific time frame, and both were recorded as part of the national story long after the events described in those stories.

The second challenging question is *how* these oral traditions were written down. Did the scribe record the words of a single storyteller, or did he listen to several of them as part of making these documents? Here, we are entirely in the dark because there is no hint of how these documents were created. However, the narratives and songs of Genesis to Judges have all the hallmarks of multiple traditions combined into a single document. For example, the narratives have various names for God and places (e.g., the mountain is Sinai in Exodus, but Horeb in Deuteronomy). Narratives do not always indicate that the characters know what happened in previous narratives (e.g., David played for Saul in 1 Sam. 16:14–23, but in the next chapter, Saul does not know who David is: 17:55, 58). These are examples of multiple inconsistencies found in the texts of the Hebrew Bible. This so-called textual bumpiness suggests that the written narrative came from numerous sources.

Older theories argue that this process began with Solomon and David when they commissioned the narratives of the Pentateuch from earlier oral traditions to be penned in scrolls.[14] Later, scholars questioned these assumptions. For example, William Schniedewind explains, based on the evidence, that writing extended narratives was not a hallmark of the early monarchical period. Scribes during the early monarchy would have done "accounting,

---

11. *ABD* 5:1012. 2 Kings 22:8–12 tells of the scroll found in the Jerusalem temple. This suggests a storage place in the temple, but it does not speak of a library for sacred documents.
12. Mark Leuchter, *An Empire Far and Wide: The Achaemenid Dynastic Myth and Jewish Scribes in the Late Persian Period* (Oxford University Press, 2024), 36.
13. Leuchter, *Empire Far and Wide*, 37.
14. John van Seters, *The Yahwist: A Historian of Israelite Origins* (Eisenbrauns, 2013), 6.

written letters, and overseen the writing on public monuments."[15] We do not know when or by whom the stories in the Hebrew Bible were committed to writing. It would make sense if the collection of stories and poems first happened during the monarchy. However, whether that process started during the monarchy's early, middle, or late period is unknown.

The first national documents were the tablets from Sinai, protected by the ark of the covenant (Exod. 25). Carried through the wilderness and brought by David to Jerusalem (2 Sam. 6), the tablets were set in the Holy of Holies when the temple was dedicated under Solomon (1 Kgs. 8). After this, information on the ark and its contents disappears. It is not known what happened to it or when. It is not listed in the items taken by the Babylonians (2 Kgs. 25:13–17). It is also not known how the information on the stone tablets was copied to the later scrolls of the Torah.

The next reference to what might be national scrolls connected to the Hebrew Bible was during the reign of King Josiah (641–610 BCE), when officials discovered a "book of the law" in the temple (2 Kgs. 22:8–13). Was this "book" the five scrolls of the Torah, both the law and the stories? The simple answer is that we do not know. Scholars have long thought that what is described as "the law" in this story of Josiah was the book of Deuteronomy, or at least an early form of it.[16] Strictly speaking, the book of Deuteronomy conveyed the words of Moses to a new generation—but what generation? The whole book of Deuteronomy is sermonic and implores the people to uphold and follow the law so they do not end up like the wilderness generation (28:15–68; 31:16–18). Was this episode in 2 Kings 22 the first public reading of what would become the book of Deuteronomy? Possibly.

But when was it written? Most scholars still think much of Genesis to 2 Kings (up to King Hezekiah) was probably available during the time of King Hezekiah, who predated Josiah, reigning from 715 to 687 BCE.[17] There is no direct evidence of this, but some significant occurrences make this time the most probable. What gives the time of King Hezekiah the edge for collecting, editing, and creating a set of national stories, laws, and songs? At the time, Judah was part of the Assyrian Empire, an empire with legendary libraries. The Assyrians also valued writing, which "became an increasingly important tool in administrating the empire."[18] So first, writing became more common, and second, Judah's leaders were exposed to an empire that emphasized

---

15. Schniedewind, *Bible Became a Book*, 63.
16. Lee Martin McDonald, *The Biblical Canon: Its Origin, Transmission, and Authority* (Baker Academic, 2011), 73.
17. This does not mean the narratives at this point contained everything we read today. These texts were still undergoing editing, additions, and so on.
18. Schniedewind, *Bible Became a Book*, 65.

collecting national stories in libraries. This could have influenced the Judeans to do the same.

At the same time, there was a significant increase in urbanization in Judah and especially Jerusalem. In part, this resulted from Assyria's destruction of the northern kingdom of Israel in 722 BCE and the influx of refugees into Judah. Judah was growing but was still under Assyrian control. So, even as the nation thrived, they were not free. Scholars surmise that, based on the way it is written, Deuteronomy was initially produced during religious, political, and social crises.[19] Thus, this period in Judah, under Assyrian domination but also planning a revolt, would have been a good time for religious leaders to reimagine Moses's words to this generation. Especially since Deuteronomy tells the people to remain faithful and follow the law, the book reminds them of the consequences of failure and encourages the care of the stranger (Israelite refugees). It fits well with this time frame. The rest of the Torah may have been recorded or edited during this time.[20]

Did the Israelite refugees from the northern kingdom have their own groups of stories and songs? Again, scholars have argued that they did. The original argument is that they used a different name for God, preferring *Elohim*. Thus, based on the name of God in the text, one could discern which stories originated with the Northern Kingdom. This distinction did not hold up to further academic scrutiny. Still, the period under Hezekiah would have been the logical time to incorporate those Israelite narratives and poems into a broader national narrative. Indeed, this combination of the two traditions could account for some of the text's duplicate narratives and would have functioned to bind Israelites with the Judeans as a single nation with a single story. At the same time, Hezekiah's reign would have been a logical time to record, gather, and/or edit the stories and songs. Yet, this remains an educated guess. Were they priests, or did the king employ them? The collectors and editors were unknown but were in either royal or priestly circles or both.

Hezekiah's reign is also the time of the prophets Micah and Isaiah, and most believe the initial writing of their words was contemporaneous with the events they describe. Isaiah refers to historical events during the reigns of Ahab and Hezekiah. From this time forward, writing had a more prominent place in Israel's culture, and that was reflected in biblical texts. However, this

---

19. Richard Nelson, "Deuteronomy," in *The Access Bible*, ed. Gail O'Day and David Peterson (Oxford University Press, 1999), 219.

20. The book of Leviticus was the possible exception. Parts of the book are older, but the laws of Leviticus became important as the Diaspora communities developed in postexilic times. Yet an early form of Leviticus may have been existing at this time. Erhard Gerstenberger, *Leviticus* (Westminster John Knox, 1996), 3–10.

does not mean that stories and poems were now transferred to written form only. The storytelling tradition continued and was still the primary way people knew the ancestral, exodus, and other stories. At the same time, the written form was taking shape and becoming a more important resource.

The nation was heavily damaged after Sennacherib attacked Judah during Hezekiah's revolt in 701 BCE, although Jerusalem was spared. Prosperity and growth suffered, probably impacting the national writing projects. The next significant opportunity for the composition of the Hebrew Bible to continue was during the time of King Josiah. Again, no explicit evidence exists that texts were produced during this time. However, King Josiah's reign was the first time the biblical text notes the importance of the written national texts.

The narrative in 2 Kings tells of the discovery of "the book of the law," as translated into English (2 Kgs. 22:8). However, in Hebrew, the phrase is more accurately translated as "the writings or scroll of the Torah." Torah does not mean strictly "law" in Hebrew: it means "instruction." Also, the Hebrew word for scroll or book in 2 Kings is singular, not plural. So, did "the writings or scroll of the *Torah*" mean all five books? The truth is that we do not know. Many scholars believe the book was the book of Deuteronomy because the biblical text uses the singular term, not the plural.[21]

Was this national scroll simply forgotten somewhere in the temple after the reign of Hezekiah? It is hard to say, but this is improbable, considering the time and money required to produce it. This discovery was probably a commentary on the two kings who reigned between Hezekiah and Josiah. Manasseh and Amon were judged evil by the biblical text, and Manasseh was singled out as an incredibly evil king. At any rate, what is of interest for the development of the Hebrew Bible was what happened next: "The king stood by the pillar and made a covenant before [*Adoni*], to follow [*Adoni*], keeping his commandments, his decrees, and his statutes, with all his heart and all his soul, to perform the words of this covenant that were written in this book. All the people joined in the covenant" (2 Kgs. 23:3).

As Schniedewind notes, for the first time reforms were undertaken not by the king's command but by the words of the scroll.[22] Earlier, Hezekiah was responsible for the reforms (2 Kgs. 18:3–6): he "kept the commandments that [*Adoni*] had commanded Moses," with no mention of the written Torah. Clearly, this demonstrates a rise in status for the written Torah. While the texts cannot yet be called Scripture, Josiah's adherence to a written Torah illustrates that the written texts were becoming authoritative for the Jerusalem community.

---

21. McDonald, *Biblical Canon*, 74.
22. Schniedewind, *Bible Became a Book*, 108.

Most scholars believe that by the sixth or fifth century BCE, around the time of Babylonian exile and afterward, a series of scrolls included the five books of the Torah, Joshua, Judges, 1 and 2 Samuel, and most of 1 and 2 Kings.[23] This would consist of material added to 2 Kings for the time between Hezekiah and Josiah. As noted above, these texts were authoritative but not yet considered Scripture.

The other sections of the Hebrew Bible were also beginning to be written down between the time of King Hezekiah and the exile. While there were probably copies of the preexilic prophets (Amos, Hosea, Micah, and first Isaiah), they were not authoritative in the ways the Genesis to 2 Kings texts were. The Writings are also taking shape, but like the Prophets, they do not seem to have the status of Genesis–2 Kings. The book of Psalms is difficult to date, but it includes poems from before the monarchy to the late exile.[24] Likewise, the proverbs in the book of Proverbs are a collection of collections, with six units that appear to be from both the preexilic and postexilic periods.[25] Both these books were probably shaped during the sixth and fifth centuries BCE, as well.

The narratives of the nations (Joshua, Judges, 1 and 2 Samuel, and 1 and 2 Kings) became part of the prophets in Jewish tradition and the "historical" books in Christian traditions. The question is, when were they separated from the first five books of the Torah? This question is more difficult since the term *Torah* was used to describe the entire set of books in the Hebrew Bible well into the New Testament period.[26] The Torah is mentioned in Ezra and Nehemiah. However, the Prophets are not mentioned as a separate group of texts until the book of Sirach's Prologue in the apocryphal/deuterocanonical books, around 180 BCE.[27] The Writings were not listed separately until the second century CE.[28]

POSTEXILIC EDITING AND ADDITIONS: BABYLONIAN CONTROL AND EXILE (586–539 BCE)

What happened during the exile? Did these texts remain in Jerusalem? Were any texts taken to Babylon? Did they make more than one copy of these

---

23. McDonald, *Biblical Canon*, 77.
24. Peter C. Craigie and Marvin Tate, *Psalms 1–50*, 2nd ed., Word Biblical Commentary, vol. 19 (Nelson, 2004), 31.
25. Roland Murphy, *Proverbs*, Word Biblical Commentary, vol. 22 (Nelson, 1998), xxi.
26. McDonald, *Biblical Canon*, 76.
27. McDonald, *Biblical Canon*, 79–80.
28. McDonald, *Biblical Canon*, 81.

national scrolls? The biblical text does not tell us, and no extrabiblical material has been found to help. However, the scrolls were not as portable as yet-to-be-created books.[29] They were heavy and awkward to handle. Perhaps they were transported to Babylon, but if they were taken with the exiles, Ezekiel does not tell us he knows anything about that.

On the other hand, Jerusalem sustained significant damage, with the temple burned, looted, and damaged. If the scrolls had been in the temple, they likely would have been destroyed, though hiding them somewhere protected in the city during Babylon's siege of Jerusalem would have been possible. But we do not know what happened. What is clear is that the narratives and songs survived the destruction in Jerusalem. During the early exilic period, specific texts provide additional information about the formation of the Hebrew Bible.

The Two Versions of the Book of Jeremiah

The book of Jeremiah witnesses Judah's last days, including the Babylonian siege of Jerusalem and the two deportations from Jerusalem (597 and 586 BCE). According to Jeremiah 43:6–7, the prophet was taken to Egypt, but not voluntarily, during a third revolt against the Babylonians while Gedaliah was governor. After Jeremiah arrived in Egypt, he continued to prophesy to the people (43:8–44:30). Did he take the scroll containing his prophecies? It is uncertain, but a second version of Jeremiah was the basis for the Greek Septuagint translation undertaken by Jews in Egypt some years later. This "Egyptian" version was shorter and in a different order than the Hebrew version. Chart 8 illustrates the differences.

The first twenty-five chapters are identical in the Hebrew and Greek versions, suggesting that the order for these sections was set before Jeremiah was taken to Egypt. These two diverging versions are the first evidence of multiple texts of the same book of the Hebrew Bible. This means that individual communities continued editing texts after the exile in communities outside of Judah. Since Jeremiah was reportedly in Egypt, it was assumed that those edits occurred with his blessing, although it could have happened after his death. The Hebrew text of Jeremiah appears to be edited also, whether in Jerusalem or Babylon is unknown.

---

29. The book form, first called a codex, gained popularity with the Romans and then with Christians, achieving equal popularity with scrolls in 300 CE. They completely replaced scrolls in Christian circles by the 6th century CE. Colin Roberts and T. C. Skeat, *The Birth of the Codex* (Oxford University Press, 1983), 38–75.

CHART 8: DIFFERENCES IN THE HEBREW AND THE GREEK TEXTS OF THE BOOK OF JEREMIAH*

Hebrew (MT) text	Greek (LXX)
1:1–25:14	1:1–25:14
25:15–38	32:1–24
26	33
27:2–22	34:1–18
28–30	35–37
31:1–34, 37, 35, 36, 38–40	38:1–34, 35–37, 38–40
32–43	39–50
44:1–30; 45:1–5	51:1–30, 31–35
46:2–28	26:2–28
47:1–7	29:1–7
48	31
49:1–5, 28–33, 23–27	30:1–5, 6–11, 12–27
49:7–22	29:8–23
49:34a–39	25:14–19
49:36b	26:1
50–51	27–28

* Entire chapters unless otherwise listed.

Second Kings 24–25

Just as Jeremiah witnesses key moments of the Babylonian conquest of Jerusalem, 2 Kings 24–25 complete the theological history of the exile, telling of the two deportations from Jerusalem and their aftermath. The text tells us that after the deportation in 597 BCE, King Jehoiachin was released in "the thirty-seventh year" of his exile, approximately 560 BCE. Most scholars state that 2 Kings 24–25 were, therefore, a postexilic addition but do not speculate beyond that statement on when or where these updates and edits occurred or who undertook them.[30] Schniedewind, however, argues that these additions to the text

---

30. Marvin Sweeney, *I & II Kings*, Old Testament Library (Westminster John Knox, 2007).

of 2 Kings and a similar closing section to Jeremiah 52 were made under the direction of King Jehoiachin in Babylon. He comes to this conclusion because the last chapters of both books carefully absolve the king of responsibility for the sacking and burning of Jerusalem.[31] This is possible but is not provable. What can be said is that these final sections, telling the latest story of the Judean monarchy, were added at some point after Jehoiachin was released in Babylon.

The Books of Ezekiel and Lamentations

The prophet Ezekiel was taken to Babylon in the first deportation from Jerusalem (597 BCE). He is not thought to have been imprisoned with the royal house but exiled to a community by the Chebar canal outside the city of Babylon.[32] Because the book of Ezekiel does not reflect knowledge of Cyrus and the rise of the Persian Empire, we know it was composed during the Babylonian exile. Its context of Babylon is also reflected in Ezekiel's use of many Babylonian loanwords.[33] In addition, Abraham Winitzer reports, "The book shows an intimate familiarity with the tenets of the Babylonian worldview."[34] Indeed, some of Ezekiel's visions resemble the Babylonian cosmology or understanding of the universe. Were these Babylonian influences purposeful or accidental? We do not know, but it does mark a change. Ezekiel is one of several biblical books reflecting a worldview of the controlling empire.[35]

One other book describes the fall of Jerusalem: the book of Lamentations, which consists of poems and funeral dirges for the city and its people. Jewish tradition associated Lamentations with Jeremiah. However, we cannot identify the author (or authors). The subject is clearly the sorrow and pain of losing the nation and the temple. The book was probably written during the Babylonian period because, like Ezekiel, it also does not mention the Persian defeat of Babylon. Given its close association with Jerusalem, it was perhaps written in Judah at some point after or even during the destruction of Jerusalem.

The Babylonian exile left a lasting mark on the shape of the Hebrew Bible. The biblical books of theological history, Joshua to 2 Kings, were separated

---

31. Schniedewind, *Bible Became a Book*, 149–57.
32. Schniedewind (*Bible Became a Book*, 157) believes it was a work camp.
33. David S. Vanderhooft, *The Neo-Babylonian Empire and Babylon in the Later Prophets*, Harvard Semitic Monographs 59 (Scholars Press, 1999), chap. 6.
34. Abraham Winitzer, "Assyriology and Jewish Studies in Tel Aviv: Ezekiel among the Babylonian *Literati*," ed. Uri Gabbay and Shai Secunda, in *Encounters by the Rivers of Babylon: Scholarly Conversations between Jews, Iranians, and Babylonians in Antiquity* (Mohr Siebeck, 2014), 93.
35. Ecclesiastes was more philosophical than other books, reflecting exposure to ideas such as grappling with the purpose of life and work. The book of Daniel, while set in Babylon, was reacting to the persecutions of the late Hellenistic period. The book of Esther was set in Susa, the capital of Persia.

from the five books of the Torah. They were combined with the prophetic books that warned of what would happen if the people ignored the teachings of the Torah. This realignment of sections resulted in the Prophets portion of the Hebrew Bible being shaped as a lesson: if we ignore God and God's Torah, ignore the requirements to love God and humans, we lose the land promised in the Torah. It is unclear when this realignment occurred, but it definitely was a result of the events involving the exile.

POSTEXILIC EDITING AND ADDITIONS: PERSIAN CONTROL (539–323 BCE)

With the rise of the Persian Empire, Babylonian control gave way to Persian dominance by 539 BCE. The Persians installed governors over the region, assuring a permanent end to the Judean monarchy. Evidence shows that the Babylonians had heavily damaged Judah and Jerusalem. As noted in chapter 11 (above), not everyone in Judah became an exile or refugee during the Babylonian attacks. The severe damage resulted in a significant depopulation of Judah from its zenith during King Hezekiah's time. The Persian period saw modest population growth, but the region was still significantly smaller and poorer.[36] During Persian control, Jerusalem was a small, unfortified city with a few hundred residents, meaning about one hundred adult men.[37] This small size would not support a large literate priestly class. This was confirmed in the book of Nehemiah, where the priests and the temple singers were not being paid, so they were farming to survive (13:10–11). With a reduced Judah and a struggling priestly class, a period of robust text production is doubtful.[38]

Another concern was the changing language patterns. Aramaic was replacing Hebrew as the spoken and written language of the people.[39] Aramaic had been the language of both the Assyrian and Babylonian Empires. Indeed, even in the time of King Hezekiah, the people request the messenger from the king of Assyria to "please speak to your servants in the Aramaic language, for

---

36. Charles Carter, *The Emergence of Yehud in the Persian Period: A Social and Demographic Study*, ed. David Clines and Philip Davies, JSOTSup 294 (Sheffield Academic, 1999), 76.

37. Israel Finkelstein, "Jerusalem in the Persian (and Early Hellenistic) Period and the Wall of Nehemiah," *JSOT* 32, no. 4 (2008): 514.

38. With little supporting evidence, some scholars have long argued that the Persian period was a time of literary flourishing. Giovanni Garbini notes that the Persian period is the golden age of Hebrew literature: "Hebrew Literature in the Persian Period," in *Second Temple Studies*, vol. 2, *Temple and Community in the Persian Period*, ed. T. Eskenazi and K. Richards, JSOTSup 175 (Sheffield Academic, 1994), 188.

39. Schniedewind, *Bible Became a Book*, 174–76.

we understand it" (2 Kgs. 18:26). Aramaic became the dominant language in the larger area in view, including Egypt. One reason was simple: with each generation learning Aramaic as children, the use of Hebrew declined. The second was the Persian Empire, which focused on economic growth; common reading and writing activities grew to facilitate transactions, further reinforcing the use of Aramaic as the lingua franca. This change meant that fewer people could understand the national texts. Nehemiah has a likely reference to translating the text for the people: "So they read from the book, from the law of God, *with interpretation*. They gave the sense, so that the people understood the reading" (8:8, emphasis added). Does this verse mean the people required a translation to Aramaic, or is this the first example of scriptural midrash or providing an interpretive meaning? Scholars are divided on what is intended here.[40] Another text in Nehemiah clearly refers to language, "In those days also I saw Jews who had married women of Ashdod, Ammon, and Moab, and half of their children spoke the language of Ashdod, and they could not speak the language of Judah but spoke the language of various peoples" (Neh. 13:23–24). The nations listed here spoke Aramaic, meaning the children did not know Hebrew. This was confirmed by archaeological research that found few inscriptions with Hebrew writing during the Persian period.[41] Hebrew was becoming the language of priests, but not of the people. Ironically, the very book criticizing the people for not speaking Hebrew, Nehemiah, was not written in the classic Hebrew of the earlier books of the Bible but in late Biblical Hebrew. Likewise, the book of Ezra was primarily written in late Hebrew, and two sections, 4:8–6:18 and 7:12–26, were written in Aramaic. This exemplifies the inevitable cultural changes in Judah, even as attempts were made to maintain the old linguistic traditions.

A third issue that makes it difficult to discern what was happening with text production during this time frame is that there is almost no information, artifacts, or written materials about Judah in the postexilic period. Information about the sixth to the second centuries BCE is paltry. Ezra and Nehemiah are the only written records, each spanning a short time. In addition, there are no historical records of this region, not even from other sources. It was a dark age for information until the time of the Maccabees, who came on the scene in 167 BCE. During these changing cultural conditions, Ezra, Nehemiah, and possibly 1 and 2 Chronicles were the only books from this period. All four books were written in late Biblical Hebrew. Other books, such as the Psalms,

---

40. F. Charles Fensham sees the event as a translation into Aramaic, in *The Books of Ezra and Nehemiah* (Eerdmans, 1982), 171. Schniedewind concurs in *Bible Became a Book*, 179. Joseph Blenkinsopp argues that it is an instance of biblical interpretation, in *Ezra-Nehemiah* (Westminster, 1988), 288.

41. Schniedewind, *Bible Became a Book*, 174.

Proverbs, and the Prophets, were probably being edited and added to, but there is no definitive evidence for this activity.

The historical events recorded in Ezra and Nehemiah were discussed in chapter 12 (above). The focus here is on what can be learned about the status of the scrolls that would become the Hebrew Bible. Nehemiah 8 tells of Ezra presenting the Torah to the people:

> He [Ezra] read from it facing the square before the Water Gate from early morning until midday, in the presence of the men and the women and those who could understand, and the ears of all the people were attentive to the book of the law. Ezra the scribe stood on a wooden platform that had been made for the purpose. . . . And Ezra opened the book in the sight of all the people, for he was standing above all the people, and when he opened it, all the people stood up. (8:3–5)

Several things in this passage point to the growing authority of the Torah of Moses in this postexilic period. First, it was read to all the people, men and women. The reading was in the city, not the temple, which was reserved only for men. It was a public reading at festival time, probably the New Year Festival, Rosh Hashanah.[42] There was a specially constructed platform for Ezra and the Torah scroll. When Ezra began, the people responded and stood for the reading. This process suggests that the written Torah was now a revered and central part of religious and public life. What exactly was read to the people? The text reports that the reading went from early morning to midday but doesn't say what was read.

Nehemiah goes on to say, "On the second day the heads of ancestral houses of all the people, with the priests and the Levites, came together to Ezra the scribe in order to study the words of the law" (8:13). This is the first time the Hebrew Bible documents leaders engaged in the study of the Torah.[43] This act of studying the Torah will soon become one of the cornerstones of Judaism, as seen in the New Testament.

The only other books possibly produced during the Persian period are 1 and 2 Chronicles. These books retell 1–2 Samuel and 1–2 Kings, omitting many narratives about the northern kingdom of Israel and adding theological commentary. The last chapter of 2 Chronicles mimics 2 Kings 25 and adds two verses about Cyrus's promise to rebuild the temple, thus indicating that it

---

42. Fensham, *Ezra and Nehemiah*, 170.
43. Deuteronomy 17:18–20 tells the king to write himself a copy of the law and "read in it all the days of his life." This is not a historical reference but more evidence for the growth of reading the texts.

was written or edited after he took Babylon in 539 BCE. The books also have no sign of Hellenistic (Greek) influence, meaning they were written before the third century BCE.[44]

These books are not of much value for historical information since they are heavily dependent on the other earlier scrolls. However, 1 and 2 Chronicles demonstrate the growing importance of sacred writings and the centrality of priests in the Persian period by retrojecting these elements into the earlier history of Judah. For example, 2 Chronicles 15 records, "For a long time Israel was without the true God and without a teaching priest and without law" (15:3). Verses 1 to 15 were added to a paraphrase of the story of King Asa of Judah in 1 Kings 15:9–14. King Asa was king from 906 to 878 BCE. It was a time when neither the written Torah nor the teaching functions of the priests were recorded in 1 and 2 Kings. This is an example of the editors of Chronicles inserting mention of the written Torah and the study of it into earlier periods.

The book of Esther, set during the Persian Empire, was written in the late Persian or early Hellenistic period. It is focused on the Persian court at Susa, but there are enough historical inaccuracies to question its creation exclusively in the Persian period.[45] Possibly it was first recorded in Susa, the capital of Persia, and edited/expanded later. It is hard to date other than between 400 and 200 BCE.[46] Like many books written in the later periods, it has two related versions: one in Hebrew and the other in Greek.[47]

The prophetic books and the Writings are not mentioned as part of the sacred texts by Ezra or Nehemiah. This omission does not mean the Writings and Prophets were unimportant. They existed in some form before the Persian period. Most books that would become the Hebrew Bible were already in authoritative scrolls by this time. The Jewish canon would not be stated officially for hundreds of years, but the collection of books was becoming less fluid.

The Persian period saw fewer sacred writings produced and edited than during the late monarchy. Instead, it was a time when the importance of written texts grew. Another central development was the teaching of the Torah by the priests and the study of the texts by the leadership in Judah. These practices would continue to grow and be reflected in more complete form in the Gospel texts.

---

44. Sara Japhet, *I & II Chronicles* (Westminster John Knox, 1993), 26.
45. Jon Levenson, *Esther: A Commentary* (Westminster John Knox, 1997), 27.
46. Levenson, *Esther*, 26.
47. Levenson believes the Septuagint was not using an older Greek manuscript, but a different Hebrew manuscript than the one used for the Hebrew Bible. Levenson, *Esther*, 27.

EDITING AND ADDITIONS: GREEK CONTROL AND HASMONEAN LIBERATION (323–64 BCE)

After Alexander the Great and the Greeks defeated the Persian Empire, Judah entered a time of revitalization under the Ptolemies of Egypt. From a textual perspective, things happened fast, especially in the third century BCE. This was when several new books of the Hebrew Bible were produced, more editing was undertaken, and multiple communities copied and translated scrolls into other languages.

One of the latest books in the Hebrew Bible was finished in the Hellenistic period. The book of Daniel combined older hero narratives in Aramaic (1–6) with later accounts of visions in late Biblical Hebrew. There is also a book of Daniel written in Greek. It is longer and contains the Prayer of Azariah, the Song of the Three Jews, and narratives of Bel and the Dragon. The Greek version was used in the Septuagint.[48] The writer(s) of the visions in Daniel 8–14 were aware of the laws passed by Antiochus IV in 167 BCE and the desecration of the temple, making it perhaps the book with the latest completion date in the Hebrew Bible.[49] However, the authors of both sections of the book are unknown.

The book of Psalms demonstrates the breadth of Israel and Judah's history with psalms from the early monarchy to the postexilic periods. It was also one of the last books to be stabilized. Psalms 1–89 show no differences in content or order in the book between the Hebrew text and the Dead Sea Scrolls.[50] However, Psalms 90–150 have multiple differences in the content of individual psalms and the order of the psalms within the book of Psalms.[51] With the Dead Sea Scrolls dating from 300 to 100 BCE, the book of Psalms was one of the latest books to undergo editing, remaining in flux well into the first century CE.[52]

The production of new books that became the Hebrew Bible seems to have reached a point of completion during the Hellenistic period. The prophetic books and the Writings become authoritative in written form. The five books of the Torah were translated into Greek in Alexandria early in the third century BCE, the beginning of what would be called the Septuagint. During the third century, copies of biblical books that would later be found among the Dead Sea Scrolls were written. In the second or first century, the

---

48. Carol Newsom, *Daniel: A Commentary* (Westminster John Knox, 2014), 82.
49. Newsom, *Daniel*, 90–91.
50. Peter Flint, *Dead Sea Scrolls and the Book of Psalms* (Brill, 1997), 141.
51. Flint, *Scrolls and the Book of Psalms*, 141.
52. Flint, *Scrolls and the Book of Psalms*, 146.

Samaritans adopted the five books of the Torah, with their additions, as their only Scriptures.[53]

The Maccabean period (165–64 BCE) saw a significant increase in literary production, but these books would not become part of the Hebrew Bible. It appears that the selection of books in the Hebrew Bible was fixed by this time, though still not understood as Scripture or sacred canon despite their later high profile in the New Testament period: John 13:18 refers to the Hebrew Bible as "scripture," Matthew 7:12 has Jesus citing "the Law and the Prophets," and Luke 24:44 says he is fulfilling "the law of Moses, the prophets, and the psalms." The existing Jewish documents did not have an official list of books in the Hebrew Bible or a date after which no other books were added. However, excluding books from the Maccabean period suggests that the Hebrew Bible was effectively decided before 164 BCE, except for Daniel and the book of Psalms.

Athanasius listed the books of the Old Testament and New Testament for Christians in 367 CE. Thirty years later, the Third Council of Carthage acknowledged the same books. These would become the books of the Roman Catholic and Orthodox traditions. They remained the books of the Old Testament for Christians until the Protestant Reformation excluded the books of the Apocrypha (see the list in chap. 1).

The making and canonization of the biblical books is shrouded in mystery. Thus the explanation above is often based on circumstantial evidence and educated suppositions, but it is our best guess about the process. What is clear is that by the New Testament period, the books of the Hebrew Bible were authoritative and studied in the Jerusalem temple, even if they had not yet achieved the level of Scripture that would come during the first four centuries CE.

---

53. Gary Knoppers, *Jews and Samaritans: The Origins and History of Their Early Relations* (Oxford University Press, 2013), 177.

Glossary of Terms

Achaemenid Empire: Another name for the Persian Empire (539–323 BCE).
acra: The Greek term for "ends/tops." The term for a Seleucid fortress, or citadel (likely on high ground, for security; 1 Macc. 1:36) in Jerusalem to protect Greek leaders and the military. Its location in Jerusalem has possibly been identified, but further research is needed.
Adoni: The name this book substitutes for the divine name of God represented by the Hebrew consonants *yod-he-vav-he* [יהוה].
Afro-Asiatic region: Formerly known as the Middle East, but that name is from a Western perspective. The region encompasses Mesopotamia, Canaan, and Sinai. It is the land that connects Africa and Asia. It also connects to Europe in the north.
Ammon: Small country east of the Jordan River. It borders Israel to the west and Aram (Syria) to the north. It is now modern-day Jordan.
apocryphal or deuterocanonical literature: Books written in the biblical period that were included in the Catholic Bible and the Orthodox Bible but not the Hebrew Bible or Protestant Bible. Some of these books are unique (Tobit, Judith, 1–4 Maccabees), and others contain variant forms of books in the Hebrew Bible (Esther and Daniel). See the table of contents in a study Bible for a complete list of these works.
Aram: An ancient nation directly north of Israel. Its capital is Damascus. It is also called the Kingdom of Damascus or Syria (Aram). Hadad is the throne name of its kings. It is modern-day Syria.
archaeologist: A scientist trained in the work of discovering ancient cultures. The work usually involves excavation of ancient sites buried in the ground.
archivist: Archivists are responsible for collecting and cataloging the discoveries of others. These collections could be the letters of Benjamin Franklin or the items discovered in an archaeological dig in Jerusalem.

artifact: Anything discovered in an archaeological excavation: cooking pots, scrolls, figurines, and so on.

Asherah: The consort (wife) of the Canaanite god El. Often worshiped as a fertility goddess.

ashlar stone: Or dressed stone. These chiseled stones usually indicate an official building or residence when located in an archaeological site.

Babylon: An ancient nation centered between the Tigris and the Euphrates Rivers. The residents are called Babylonians or Chaldeans. Controlled Canaan from 605 to 539 BCE during the Neo-Babylonian Empire.

BCE: Before the Common Era. This term has replaced the old Western term BC, which meant before Christ.

Ben-Hadad: The throne name of the king of Aram. The name means son of the God, Hadad. Aram will later be called Syria.

Canaan: An area within the Afro-Asiatic region. It encompasses ancient Aram, Phoenicia, Israel, Judah, and the Transjordan area. This is an ancient name for the region.

canon: A collection of sacred scriptures, for example, the Hebrew Bible, the New Testament, or the Qur'an.

clan: Early Israelite "family" organization. The clan serves as an extended family and many include more than one village. Local elders govern clans.

comparative studies: An academic study that compares the biblical text with the documents of other Afro-Asiatic nations.

cult: A system of religious beliefs and rituals. The religious practice of the people.

cultic activity: The rituals a people perform in private and public worship.

cultic site: The places where people worship both in their homes and in larger groups.

culture: The totality of how a people live, including thinking, feeling, and believing; the communal storehouse of pooled learning; the standardized lens through which they see the world; and the social legacy of a people, including material items.

cuneiform: An early system of writing using wedged signs (drawn on clay or incised into stone) instead of an alphabet, originating in the Early Bronze Age in ancient Mesopotamia.

Dead Sea Scrolls: A collection of religious texts including copies of biblical books from the Second Temple period (515 BCE–70 CE) discovered in the Qumran Caves in the Judean wilderness. The scrolls provide valuable information about how the biblical texts were understood and edited during this period, including the three languages used: Hebrew, Aramaic, and Greek.

Deuteronomistic source: A group of unknown editors that collected and edited the narratives of Israel and Judah's rise and fall. They shaped the narratives to explain why the two nations were attacked and then controlled by other empires. The books involved are Joshua, Judges, 1–2 Samuel, and 1–2 Kings. This source has a distinctive theology that focuses on worshiping God's presence in the temple in Jerusalem.

Diaspora: The word means "scattering" in Greek. It is a term for the believers of *Adoni* who were scattered as exiles in the empires that controlled the region.

Edom: A small country southeast of Judah in the desert. It is now part of modern-day Jordan.

Epic of Gilgamesh: A Mesopotamian epic poem from about 2100 BCE, it is thought to be one of the earliest works of literature.

epigrapher: An expert who identifies and analyzes epigraphic (written) artifacts and provides translations of these ancient resources.

epigraphic artifacts: Ancient discoveries with writing on them, such as monuments with inscribed writing, business receipts, documents, buildings with inscriptions, and letters.

exegesis: From the Greek *exēgeomai*, meaning "to interpret." It names the process of interpreting a biblical text, which typically involves academic research.

Fertile Crescent: Also known as a land bridge, a swath of cultivatable land—stretching around the desert, from the Persian Gulf in the east, northwestward through Aram (Syria), then southwestward through the land of Canaan (thereby linking with the Nile valley in Egypt)—that was most habitable by humans, the most populated, and the most desired.

four-pillared or Israelite house: This was the plan of houses in Canaan, not just in Israel. It was the basic design for family houses. Some have more than four pillars supporting the second floor. This type of house was common during the Hebrew Bible period for both rural and urban dwellers.

genre: Literary category based on the structure and purpose of a written text.

gymnasium: A community building in Greek culture, an important marker of a hellenized city and society. It was used for training young men both physically and mentally.

Hammurabi: A Babylonian king who wrote and published a law code around 1750 BCE. This law code shares similarities with the Ten Commandments.

Hebrew Bible: Scholars and some churches use this term for the Hebrew Scriptures. These are the scriptures in the Tanakh and in the Protestant

Old Testament. The term reminds readers that two religions share these sacred texts.

Hellenistic Empire: Also known as the Greek Empire. It existed from 323 BCE (death of Alexander the Great) to 30 BCE (Roman conquest of Ptolemaic Egypt). This was a period of dominance for the Greek nation and culture.

henotheism: Worship of one particular god out of a group or council of gods. This was the type of worship often practiced in Israel and Judah prior to the exile.

historiography: The act of an academic historian who investigates primary sources of a specific time period. The end product is a history.

history: A book or article produced in the academic work of historiography, "history writing." The past is investigated by using multiple primary sources, and a context is created for those events based on all available information.

house of the father: The name of a family that includes parents and children, often also grown, young married children, grandparents, and widowed aunts or sisters. The smallest family structure in a system where the family provides all needed social services for the members.

land bridge: *See* Fertile Crescent

legend: A narrative of the past that was often popularly regarded as historical but is usually not verifiable and may contain supernatural elements. It includes both ordinary and extraordinary explanations and stories.

longue durée: A French term for the idea that to study history, one must be concerned with the immediate event placed in a longer context, including multiple extended factors, such as world history leading to the event and geographical and climate concerns, among other influences, to gain a full understanding of a people and their history. Nothing is isolated from the world around it.

Masseboth (maṣṣēbôt): Large sacred standing stones that indicate a Canaanite or Israelite worship (cultic) site.

Medes: A nation in western and northern present-day Iran. They aided Babylon in defeating the Assyrians. One of the first nation-states captured by Cyrus of Persia.

medinah: The province of a Persian satrap. Judah was a *medinah* of the Persian Empire.

Mesopotamia: A smaller section of the Afro-Asiatic region. Specifically, the land between the Tigris and Euphrates Rivers. Babylon was a nation in the southern section of region. Assyria was a nation in the northern part.

Moab: A small country east of the Dead Sea, bordering Judah. It is the setting for the beginning of the book of Ruth and now is in modern-day Jordan.

monotheism: The religious belief in a single god and that there is but one.

myth: A genre of literature, usually a traditional story concerning the early history of a people or explaining some natural or social phenomenon. Myths often involve supernatural beings or events.

Neo-Assyrian Empire: Final period of the Assyrian Empire (911–609 BCE). The Assyrians controlled the Afro-Asiatic region and destroyed Israel in 722 BCE.

oral tradition: Few ancient people were literate even after the invention of writing. A community storyteller told stories such as those in the Hebrew Bible. The stories of the Bible were shared this way for centuries.

ostraca: Shards of broken pots used as writing surfaces. Some ostraca contain drawings and doodles; others serve as practice for writing and as receipts for business transactions.

Palestine: The word derives from a Greek word for Philistia. During the Greek and Roman periods, it indicated the area that covers present-day Israel and Palestine (the West Bank, including East Jerusalem and the Gaza Strip).

peer-reviewed: The standard in academic publishing. An author's work is reviewed by others in the field and deemed to adhere to the profession's standards. Peer review means a student can trust that the work adheres to the field's academic standards.

Pentateuch: The name for the first five books of the Bible. It is a Greek term meaning five scrolls.

pericope: From the Greek for "cutting," it means a section of a text such as an individual story or parable.

Philistia: The nation along the Mediterranean coast, southwest of Judah. Founders were not native to the Afro-Asiatic region and probably from Greek islands. It fought with Judah over land during the early monarchy.

Phoenicia: A small country on the east end of the Mediterranean Sea. It was a seagoing nation. Today it is in northwestern Israel and coastal Lebanon.

physical artifacts: Items such as buildings, monuments, art objects, cooking pots, and other items used by ancient people.

polis: The term used for the Greek (also Ionian) city-states, which fought against the Persian Empire.

polytheism: The belief in multiple gods. The most common ancient form of religion in the Afro-Asiatic region.

primary sources: Ancient documents, artifacts, art, village and city remains. All these were (and are being) discovered by archaeologists and used to better understand the ancient history, culture, and lifestyle of ancient people.

Qumran: A community of a Jewish sect, probably called the Essenes, likely formed during the Maccabean period. Its members were the authors of the Dead Sea Scrolls.

reception history: Academic research of all the intervening cultures between now and the biblical text, consisting of all the traditions of interpreting a text throughout its history as scripture. Also called the history of tradition.

saga: An intuitive and poetic story of a prehistoric reality that communicates truths about the ultimate origins of things.

Samaria: Another name for ancient Israel, in the Northern Kingdom. It was used exclusively after the Persian Empire and in the New Testament.

satrapy: Persian word for a section of the Persian Empire. Darius divided the empire into twenty satrapies. The ruler of the area was a satrap.

Scripture: A document or documents considered sacred and authoritative by a community. This can be a large religious community such as Christians, Jews, or Muslims; or smaller communities such as the Church of Jesus Christ of Latter-day Saints. A community can share the same sacred scriptures but not agree on the interpretation of those scriptures.

TaNaKh: Tanakh, also written TaNaKh, is a Hebrew abbreviation for the three major sections of the Hebrew scriptures. *Ta* represents Torah, the first five books of the collection. *Na* stands for the Hebrew word for prophets. *Kh* refers to the Hebrew word for the Writings.

tel: Sometimes spelled *tell*—a human-made elevated city. The tel grows higher over time as humans discard building materials and trash or purposely build the city's ground higher for better defense.

theocracy: A form of government by divine guidance, where the officials are divinely guided. The king is under the guidance and direction of God.

theophany: An appearance of God to humanity, such as at Mount Sinai.

Torah: This term has multiple meanings. The first, Torah, is the Hebrew word for the first five books of the Bible (Genesis, Exodus, Leviticus, Numbers, and Deuteronomy). In Christian contexts, the word is used interchangeably with Pentateuch (Greek for five scrolls, the first five books of the Bible). The second version of the term, torah (not capitalized), has multiple meanings: God's law, teaching, and instruction.

traditional site: This site is designated as a place in Jewish and/or Christian tradition that represents where an event in the Bible occurred, though there may be no archaeological or historical basis for its identification.

Transjordanian Route: A north-south road through Canaan, east of the Jordan River and on the edge of the desert, called the King's Highway in Num. 20:17; 21:22. One of the two important trade routes that ran north to south.

tribe: Larger social organizations consisting of several clans. Tradition identifies twelve tribes of Israel.

vassal: A lesser nation that an empire controls. A volunteer vassal pays tribute in return for protection. An involuntary vassal is forced to pay the greater nation or be destroyed. Tribute is usually in the form of precious metals, jewels, agricultural products, and men for military service.

Way of the Sea: A preferred trade route that connected Asia and Africa. It ran along the eastern coast of the Mediterranean Sea, southward past Lebanon and the Sidonians, through Israel (around Mount Carmel) and Philistia, and finally into Egypt.

Index of Scripture and Other Ancient Sources

OLD TESTAMENT
295–96

Genesis
1	24, 76–78, 181n33
1–2	66, 78, 80
1–4	81
1–11	27, 76–81
1:1	78
1:1–2:41	76
1:27	76, 76n1
1:31	76
2:4	78–79
2:4b–3:24	76
2:15	22
2:21	77
3–11	80–81
3:1–6	28
3:6	21
4	24
4–11	76
4:1	77n2
4:1–16	22n20
4:3–5	21–22
4:14–16	38
5:27	28
6–9	81
8:20–22	64
10	105
11:10–32	105
11:31	39
12	28
12–25	87
12–50	28, 81–83
12:1–3	83
12:4	40
12:7–8	64
12:16	82
13:18	64
16	20, 83n16
21:32	82
22:1–19	64
23:17–18	276
25–26	115n8
26	82
29	28
29:2	59
30:43	82
32:22	40
32:23	40
35	64
35:1–15	70
41	82
Genesis–Deuteronomy	176, 290–91
Genesis–Malachi	4–6

Exodus
	28, 53, 69
1	85
1–15	83–89, 275
1:8	83
1:8–9	87
1:8–22	275
1:11	84, 84n20
1:13–14	85
1:15–22	83–84
2:11–22	275
3:13–15	67
3:13–22	78
5–15	88
9:1–7	168n32
12–13	174
12:37	87
12:38	88, 104
15–20	89–91
15:1–18	274
15:21	274
16:35	115n8
17:14	278
19–24	90
19:1	89, 91
19:1–25	70
19:20	278
20:1–17	53–54
20:7	66–67
20:22–23:19	53, 54n10, 55
21:12–26	54
21:35–36	54
22–23	53
22:14	28
24:4	278
24:12	278
25	279
31:18	278
32:1–34:35	91
32:15–19	278
34:1–4	278
34:27–29	278
35–40	91

Index of Scripture and Other Ancient Sources

Leviticus 28, 54n10, 64, 176, 280n20
1–16 91
1:3 22
6:16–18 208
11:7–8 103
17–26 91
18:8–13 208
18:21–23a 208
19:34 72
22:20–22 22
25:29–34 91

Numbers 91–92
1 92
1:1–4:49 105
7:1–89 70
10:11 91
14:33 115n8
20:17 44, 298
21:22 44, 298
22:1–40 28
33 92
Numbers–Deuteronomy 69

Deuteronomy 28, 54n10, 175–76, 176n11, 279, 281, 286, 297–98
1:6 278
10:18–19 280
10:19 72
14:8 103
17:18–20 288n43
26:5 39, 40
28:15–68 279
31:16–18 279
31:24–26 278
34:1–5 42

Joshua 110
1:8 98
2:6 58
3:10 103
5:2–15 105
5:6 91
6 100
6:17–18 218
8:30–35 105
10:12–14 28
10:42 98
12:2 40
12:7–24 98
13:2–6 103
14:7 115n8
15–25 106
15:1–12 111
23:2 125n38
24 72, 105
24:1–28 70
24:14 140n37
24:29 98
Joshua–1 Samuel 98–99
Joshua–2 Kings 131, 176, 192, 282, 285, 295
Joshua–2 Chronicles 29

Judges 110
1:1 99
1:21 98
2:6–8 98
3:1–6 103
8:22–23 108
17:1–6 66
17:6 109–110
19:1–21 109

Ruth
1 296
1:1 42
4 276
4:1 61

1 Samuel 107
1:1–19 70
2:9 107, 107n32
3:1 107, 113
3:19–21 107
5:1–5 111
7:6 107
7:15 107
8:6–18 108
9:12 70
10:1 107, 109
10:8 70
10:17–27 109
11:5–11 111
11:8 124
12:12 108
12:14 109
12:17–20 108
13:1 107–8, 108n36, 115
13:8–15 108
13:19–22 96
15:1–23 108
15:10–33 112
16 112
16–17 108
16:11 58
16:14 108
16:14–23 278
17 28
17:52 111
17:55 278
17:58 278
18:1–5 112
18:10–11 108
18:10–16 112
18:20–30 112
19:1–17 112
21:10 112
22:1–5 112
22:3–5 112
23:1–6 112
24:24 22
25:30 109
27:1–4 112
1–2 Samuel 124
1 Samuel–2 Kings 64, 274, 288

2 Samuel
1:19 70
2:1–5 124
2:1–11 111
2:8–11 124
3:1 112
5:1–5 111, 115, 128n2
5:4 91
5:5 125n38

Index of Scripture and Other Ancient Sources

5:6–10	112	15	131–32	15:29–30	155
5:9	118	15:9	24	15:32	153n29
5:11	116	15:9–14	289	16	262n59
6	279	16:8–21	133	16:5–9	153
6:1–23	112	16:18	134	16:9	154
7:4–16	263	16:21–28	134	16:15–18	154
8:14	42	16:31	135 16:31–32	17:5	156
12:31	40	140		17:6	156n35, 157
20:24	127	16:31–34	68	17:19–28	210
2 Samuel–1 Kings		19:15–18	146n10	17:23	208
	125, 131	22	137, 137n27	17:24–41	157
		1–2 Kings	68, 128,	18:1–4	166
1 Kings	137		131, 140,	18:3–4	71
1:35	124		195, 289	18:3–6	281
3:2	70			18:4	166
3:4	124, 128n2	**2 Kings**	91, 136, 151,	18:13	166
4:24 (5:4 Hebrew)	123,		185, 279,	18:14–16	166–67
	123n32		281–83	18:17–36	167
5	98	1:17–18	138	18:26	286–87
5:11–18	127	3	136n25	19:9	168
5:13–18	124	3:4–27	137	19:35–36	168
5:16–6:38	118	8:18	138n32	20:1–21	168
6:1	87, 91,	8:26	138	20:12–19	164
	124–25	8:28–29	143	21	170
6:1–38	112	9:2–3	144	21:1	169
7:1–12	118	9:6–10	144	21:2	159
8	279	10:18–27	144	21:9	170
9:15–25	119	10:28–36	144	21:23–24	170
9:19	119	10:32–33	146, 149	22	279
10:1–13	113	10:36	149	22:1–2	174
11	140	11	147	22:3–10	174
11:42	91, 115, 125	11:1–3	147	22:8	281
11:43	128, 128n2	11:4–16	148	22:8–12	278n11
12	128n2	12	148, 178	22:8–13	279
12:1–2	128	13:3–4	149	23:3	281
12:1–11	125	13:5	250n20	23:4–20	174
12:4	128	13:22–25	150	23:11	118
12:16	128	14:1	148	23:19	175
12:16–2 Kgs:17:41	128	14:8–14	148	23:23	174
12:20	125n38, 128	14:17–20	148	23:26–27	175
12:26–33	70	14:25	151	23:29	178
12:29	131	15:1	148	23:30	178
12:31	131	15:5–6	148	23:31	178
14:19	128	15:10	152	23:33	178, 179n24
14:22	131	15:19	152–53,	23:34	178–79
14:25–27	115		153n28	24	180
14:29	128	15:23–25	153	24–25	179, 284–85

Index of Scripture and Other Ancient Sources

2 Kings (*continued*)
24:1	179
24:12	180–81
24:20	183
25	192, 288
25:1–7	184
25:8–21	184
25:12	186
25:13–17	279
25:22	185–86
25:24	206
25:27	191
25:27–30	181

1 Chronicles 200
9:11	109
13:1	109
15:1	116
1–2 Chronicles	131, 195, 274, 287–89

2 Chronicles 137, 185, 200
15:1–15	289
15:3	289
18	136, 137n27
22:2	136
22:10–12	147
28:2–7	154
28:5–7	153
28:5–21	153
28:16–18	154
28:16–21	153
28:20–21	154
29:1–36	166
29:3–31:21	69
30	174
30:1	208
30:2	174n3
31:1	208
32:2–8	164
32:5–6	164
32:28–29	164
33:10–17	170
34:1	174
34:9	208
35	174
35:20–27	178
35:25	159
36	180, 192, 288
36:1–2	178
36:13	183
36:14	175
36:22–23	288–89

Ezra 159, 195, 200, 274
1–6	219n104
1:1	204
1:1–2	196
1:1–4	205
1:1–11	202
1:2	203
1:4	196–97
1:5	202
1:6–11a	202
1:7–11	217
1:8	202
1:11b	202
2	202
2–5	202
2:4–70	202
3:1–6	206
3:3	206
3:10	203
4–5	205
4:2	206
4:4	206
4:4–5	204
4:6	204
4:6–24	204
5:2	202
5:3–17	204
5:14	202
5:16	203
6:1–5	204
6:3–14	205
6:15	207
7	202
7:1–6	216
7:1–10:44	212
7:6	220
7:10	217
7:12–26	216–26
8–9	217
8:31–35	216
9:2	217
10:3	217
10:15	218
Ezra–Nehemiah	287–89

Nehemiah 195–200
1:1	213, 219
1:1–7:4	212n72
1:3	213
1:11	213
2:1	212–13
2:1–8	213
2:5	213–14
2:9	213
2:17	214
2:19–20	215
3:29–30	215
4:1–23	204
4:8–6:18	287
6:2–6	214
6:17–19	215
7	202
7:4	216
7:12–26	287
8–9	217
8–10	212, 217
8–11	212n72
8:1	218
8:3–5	288
8:8	287, 287n40
8:13	288
11:1–2	216
12:26	212
13	217n98
13:4–9	215
13:6	213
13:10–11	286
13:23–24	287
13:28	215

Esther 219n106, 285n35, 289, 293

Job 6, 282, 289–90

Psalms 111, 166, 274, 282, 287, 290–91
1–89	290

Index of Scripture and Other Ancient Sources

2	109, 130	9:1	25	**Hosea**	282
20	109	27:1	182	1:3–4	144
28:1	29	27:1–10	183–84	7:11	156
44:9–11	191	28	182	10:1–8	68
72	109, 130	29:1–32	182	**Joel**	
72:1–3	23	32:9–15	276	24:17	182, 182n37
82	68, 140	39–43	185	25:1	183
82:6	66	40	187		
90–150	290	40:10	187	**Amos**	282
93–99	130	41:10–15	187	5:10–13	151
104	76	41:1–3	187	5:15	61
137	42	41:5	186	9:7	42
		42–43	189	**Jonah**	
Proverbs	111, 274, 282, 288	43:1–7	220	4:1–5	210
		43:5–7	187	**Micah**	280, 282
8:22–31	76	43:6–7	283	**Nahum**	177n16
10:11	29	43:8–44:30	283	**Haggai**	200–201
15:4–5	29	44:15–25	68	1:1	202
		46:1–12	179	1:1–6	205
Ecclesiastes	111, 285n35	51:59	183	1:1–11	207
		52	285	1:14	202
Song of Songs	111	52:28	180	2:2	202
		52:30	187	2:20–23	203
Isaiah	274, 280	52:31	191	2:21	202
1–39	282			Haggai–Malachi	
1:3	159	**Lamentations**	184, 186, 285		219n104
6:1–12:6	153			**Zechariah**	
7–8	154	4:4–10	190	1–8	200–201
7:1–15	153			9–14	201
7:6	153	**Ezekiel**	159, 181, 183, 189–90, 219n104, 285		
9:2–7	109			**ANCIENT NEAR EASTERN TEXTS**	
11:1–16	109				
24:13	23	1:28	25		
39:1–8	164	8:1	188	**Papyri, Ostraca, and Epigrapichial Citations**	
40–66	159, 189, 189n68, 201	9:9	159		
		14:1	188	Aleppo Fragment	145n5
42:17	68	17:15	183	Amarna letters/tablets	85–87
44:9–17	68	20:1	188		
45:1–7	196	20:3	188	Babylon Chronicles	179–81, 183n42, 185
52:13–53:12	191	37:16	159		
66:1–2	219			bronze tablets, stela, papers re Simon	263, 263n60
Isaiah–Malachi	128, 282, 288–90	**Daniel**	285n35, 291, 293		
		1–6	290	Elephantine Papyri	189, 220
Jeremiah	183–84, 284	5:11	236		
2:4b–7	182	5:22	192	Sanballat on	214n84
3:18	159	7–12	290		
4:6–10	174	8–14 (Greek)	290		
6:9	29	8:2	219n106		

Papyri, Ostraca, and Epigrapichial Citations (*continued*)
Hezekiah inscription 162
inscriptions
  in Egyptian synagogues 236
  regarding "Israelites" 236
Kurkh Monolith 135–36
Lachish letters 183, 183–84n44, 277
letter by Tattenai 202
Merenptah Stela 82, 86–87, 100n11, 101, 113
Mesha Stela/Moabite Stone 135–37
Nimrud Prisms D & E 156n36
Passover Papyri 220–21, 221n115
Psammetichus II inscription 182
Samaria ostraca 151, 277
Shalmaneser III texts 145nn5–6
Shishak/Sheshonq/Shoshenq Megiddo fragment 115–16
Siloam Inscription 165
Stela 113–14, 127, 135n21, 145
tablets 180, 180n32
  Hebrew names in 189
  on exiles 181
Tel al-Rimah Stela 150
tribute inscription 153n30

Annals/Reports of Kings 277
Assyrian 157, 169
Black Obelisk 52, 137n26, 145, 149–50, 149n17
Josiah 175
Kurba'il Statue 145n5
Persian/Greek eras 233
Sargon II 156, 157n41, 159
Sennacherib annals 167–68, 170n40
  decimates population 169
  destroys cities 169
  mural re Lachish 167, 167n29
Tiglath-Pileser III 152–53, 155
Sennacherib 167–68, 170n40
Ur-Nammu of Ur, law code 90

Literature
Enuma Elish 78
Epic of Gilgamesh 33, 295
Hammurabi's Code 31, 33, 53, 90, 295
Lipit-Istar of Ur law code 90

DEUTERO-CANONICAL BOOKS

Tobit 293
3 236

Judith 293
8:36–10:2 236

Sirach
Prologue 282

1 Maccabees 249, 262n19
1 144n111
1–4 238–40
1:19–20 246
1:21–23 244–45
1:33–35 244
1:41–50 245
1:53 246
1:54–55 246–47
2:29–43 246
2:42–48 250
3:27–31 250
3:27–4:25 250–51
4:28–35 251–52
4:36–59 252
4:53 252
4:60–61 253
5 253
6:18–27 253
6:28–47 253
7:1–4 254
7:5–25 254
7:12–14 253
7:28–31 254
7:33–38 255
8 255n27
8:17–18 255
8:31–32 255
9:1–22 255
9:25–26 255
9:28–31 255
9:33 257
9:43–53 257–58
9:57–73 258
10:6 259
10:10–11 259
10:15–47 259
10:59–66 260
10:77–89 260
11:1–37 260
11:54–59 261
12:40–53 261
12:50 261n52
13:1–11 261
13:12–19 261n52
13:12–24 262
13:34–40 262
13:41 159n48
13:42 263
13:42–48 263
13:49–53 262
14:5 263
14:16–24 263
14:25–28 263
14:40–42 262
14:41–43 263
15:1–9 264
15:15–24 263
15:26 264
15:28–31 264
15:38–16:10 264

Index of Scripture and Other Ancient Sources

16:1–10	264	**Prayer of Manasseh**		14.1.2	270, 270n100
16:11–12	264–65		170n43	14.1.4	270, 270n106
16:13–17	264	**3 Maccabees**	242	14.2.1–2	271n107
16:19–20	264–65			14.2.3	271nn109–110
1–2 Maccabees	242, 256, 287, 293	**4 Maccabees**	242	14.6.1	270, 270n104
1–4 Maccabees	293	**DEAD SEA SCROLLS**		16	270n106
2 Maccabees	249, 262n19	256–57, 294, 297		*Jewish War*	270n102
1–6	238–40	Damascus Document	256n30	**PHILO OF ALEXANDRIA**	256, 256n30
3	240	4QpapHistorical Text C			
3:1	240	(4Q331 1 ii 7)	269n96	**NEW TESTAMENT**	
3:10–24	250	Nahum Pesher 4Q169		**Matthew**	
4:7–17	241–42	3–4, I, 1–7	269n94	2	270
4:8	242	Teacher of		7:12	291
4:23–34	242	Righteousness	256	Matthew–John	223
4:37–45	243			Matthew–Acts	289
5:1 14	243–44	**ANCIENT JEWISH**		Matthew Revelation	188
5:5	244n110	**WRITERS**		**Luke**	
5:9	246			24:44	291
5:15–16	244	**Josephus**	256, 256n30	**John**	
5:15–21	144n111			10:22	252n18
5:21	244	*Contra Apion*		13:18	291
5:27	246		264–65	**Acts**	
6:1–6	247	1:136–137	179n25	13:21	108n36
6:3–11	249	*Jewish Antiquities*		Acts–Jude	223
8:1–4	250		249, 261, 264–65		
8:8–36	250–51	9.3	266n79	**2 Timothy**	
9:1–29	252n14	10.1.5	168n32	3:16–17	133
10:1–9	252	10.6.3	180, 180n31		
10:10–38	253	11.8.4–5	225, 225n3	**Hebrews**	
10:14–17	251	12.3.3	232n47–48	11:4	22
11:1–21	251	12.3.23	228, 228n24		
11:6–15	252	12.6.4–7.2	250	**RABBINIC WORKS**	
11:16–21	251	12.7.2–4	250–51	**TALMUD**	79
11:22–26	253	12.7.6–7	252	**MIDRASH**	79
11:34–38	251	12.9.7	253n22		
13	253	12.10.4	254	**GRECO-ROMAN**	
13:1–8	253n22	13.7.2	264	**LITERATURE**	
13:23	253	13.10.2	265n70		
14:3–13	254	13.11.1	266, 266n77	Antiochus III, edicts of	238
14:24	254	13.13.2	269n94		
14:26–28	254	13.13.5	268, 268n87	Antiochus IV, records of	244
14:31–36	255	13.14	268nn91–92		
1 Esdras	200–201	13.15.1	269n95		
2–9	200	13.16.1–2	269n97		

Index of Subjects

Note: Page numbers in italics indicate illustrative material.

Abner, king of Israel, 124
Abram/Abraham (biblical figure), 39
Achaemenid Empire. *See* Persian Empire
acra (citadel), 252, 262, 263, 293
Adad-nirari III, king of Assyria, 149–50
Adam, as name, 77
Adoni, as name, 66, 67, 293. *See also* God
Afro-Asiatic region
  chronology of, 32
  map of, *35*
  as term, 31, 293
agriculture
  animals, 58–59, 103–4
  climate and, 47–48, 58, 129
  crops, 58, 60
  food storage and, 62
  growth in production, 163
  in Hellenistic period, 233, 234
  in highland settlements, 101, *102*
Ahab, king of Israel, 119, 133, 135, 136, 140, 144
Ahaziah, king of Israel, 136, 138, 140
Ahaziah, king of Judah, 138, 143–45, 147
Ahaz/Jehoahaz I, king of Judah, 153–54
Albright, William, 120
Alcimus, high priest, 253, 254, 256, 258
Alexander Balas, Seleucid leader, 258–60
Alexander IV, son of Alexander the Great, 228
Alexander Jannaeus, Hasmonean high priest, 267–69

Alexander the Great, 27, 222, 225–27
Alexandra, Hasmonean ruler, 269–70
Alexandria (city), 243, 254
altars in homes, 70
Ālu-ša-Našar (city), 220
Āl-Yāḫdu (city), 220
Amal (city), 70
Amarna letters, 85–86
Amaziah, king of Judah, 148
Amelmarduk, king of Babylon, 191
Ammon/Ammonites, 40–42, 293
Amon, king of Judah, 170, 178, 281
Ancient Age, overview, 33
Andronicus, Seleucid deputy, 242–43
animal husbandry, 58–59, 103–4
Athanasius, 291
Antigonus, Hasmonean prince, 266
Antiochus I, Seleucid king, 230
Antiochus II, Seleucid king, 230
Antiochus III, Seleucid king, 231–32, 237–38
Antiochus IV, Seleucid king, 239–40, 241, 242–46, 250, 251, 252
Antiochus V, Seleucid king, 253–54
Antiochus VI, Seleucid king, 261, 262
Antiochus VII, Seleucid king, 263–64, 265
Antiochus XII, Seleucid king, 269
Antipater the Idumean, 270
Anu (god), 154
apocryphal/deuterocanonical literature, defined, 293
apodictic laws, 53–54

308

Index of Subjects

Apollonius, governor of Syria, 260
Arabian Desert, 44
Arad (city), 61, 71, 72, 137
Aram
  conquest of, 154, 155
  growth of, 133–34
  location of, 40
  overview, 293
  relationship with Assyria, 149–50, 152–53
  relationship with Israel, 132, 134, 138, 143, 145–46, 149, 151
  relationship with Judah, 134, 143, 148
Aramaic language, 157–59, 188, 189, 198–200, 242, 246, 286–87
archaeological evidence
  for Babylonian destruction of Judah, 185–86
  and biblical narrative discrepancies, 99–100, 122–24, 131, 139, 175, 207
  chronology of, 82, 82n15, 119–23, 119n22, 121nn27–28
  for David-Solomon reigns, 113–14, 116–23
  for exodus event, 84
  for Hezekiah's reign, 162
  for Israel prosperity, 151
  for Israel territory, 98, 103, 107
  for Jerusalem, 118, 164, 216n93
  for Mount Gerizim temple, 210
  for Nehemiah's rebuilding program, 215–16
  for Omride dynasty, 134, 135–36, 144
  remains, physical, 50, 82, 118–19, 185, 207, 215, 297
  as source, 49–51
  for worship practices, 67–68, 71, 140–41
archaeologists, work of, 293
archivists, work of, 293
area names, 156n39
Aristobulus II, Hasmonean high priest, 269, 270–71
Armenians, 269–70, 271
Arnold, John, 12, 16
Arses, king of Persia, 222
Artaxerxes I, king of Persia, 211, 213
Artaxerxes II, king of Persia, 211, 222

Artaxerxes III, king of Persia, 222
artifacts, defined, 12, 294, 295, 297
Asa, king of Judah, 132, 137, 289
Ashdod (city), 96, 119n21
Asherah (goddess), 68, 140, 170, 294
Ashkelon (city), 96
ashlar stone, 134, 294
Ashurbanipal, king of Assyria, 173, 177
Ashurnasirpal II, king of Assyria, 134
Assyrian Empire
  attack on Judah, 166–69
  collapse of, 177
  common language in, 157–59
  conquest of Aram, 154, 155
  conquest of Israel, 155–57
  growth of, 134, 136–37, 148, 151, 157, 164
  map of, *158*
  military, 52
  multi-country alliance against, 164–66, 167
  plague of, 168nn32, 34
  relationship with Aram, 150, 152–53
  relationship with Israel, 145, 149, 151, 152–54
  relationship with Judah, 153–54, 161–62, 164, 170, 173
  relief, "Son of Omri," 144
  writings from, 279
Athaliah, queen of Judah, 138, 147, 178
Atkinson, Kenneth, 266n79
Atlas, George, 242
Azariah/Uzziah, king of Judah, 148, 151

Baal (god), 68, 133, 135, 140, 144, 154, 170
Baasha, king of Israel, 132–33, 137
Babota, Vasile, 254n26
Babylon
  Alexander the Great in, 226, 227
  business records of Jews, 219, 219–20n107, 220, 220n108
  calendar, 181n33
  collapse of, 191–92
  conflict with Assyria, 151, 164–65, 166, 177
  conflict with Egypt, 179–80
  conflict with Judah, 180–81, 183–86

Babylon (*continued*)
  cosmology, 285
  documents, 189n69
  Jewish community in, 219–20
  overview, 294
  Parthian conquest of, 263
  reports re exiles, 188n65
  Seleucid control of, 228
Babylonian exile, 181–82, 184–91
Bacchides, Seleucid general, 254, 255, 257, 258
Bailey, Randall, 19
Bailey, Wilma, 55
Barker, Margaret, 168
Barkay, Gabriel, 185–86
Bar-Kochva, Bezalel, 251, 252n18
barter system, 58, 61
Barth, Karl, 27
Becking, Bob, 157
Beersheba (city), 61
Bel-shar-usar, king of Babylon, 192
Ben-Hadad, 133–34, 137n26, 294
Berlin, Andrea, 234
Berquist, Jon, 189, 212
Bethel (city), 131
Beth-Shean (city), 38
Beth-Shemesh (city), 61, 163
Bible/texts, development of, 6, 273–74, 276, 278
Bīt-Abī-râm (city), 220
Black Obelisk, 137n26, 145, 149, *150*
Blenkinsopp, Joseph, 56, 196
Book of the Covenant, 53, 54n10, 55, 90
Bright, John, 175
Briant, Pierre, 196–97
Bronze Age, defined, 33
Broshi, Megen, 163
bullae (seal impressions), 118, 162, 186–87

Calvin, John, 79–80
Cambyses II, king of Persia, 197, 220
Canaan
  collapse of, 95, 96
  early inhabitants, 34–37
  empires surrounding, 37–38
  genetic pool of, 39
  highland settlements in, 86–87
  maps of, *36, 41*
  as name, 34
  nation-states of, 38–43
  roads in, 44–47, *46*
  topography and climate, 43–44, *44, 45,* 47–48, 58, 129
canon, 3–7, 294
carbon 14 dating, 121, 185n54
Carmel Mountain Range, 44
Carr, David, 275
Cassander, Macedonian Greek general, 228
casuistic/case laws, 54
Catholic Bible, 3–7
cave drawings/paintings, 26n23, 33
children, mortality rates, 55–56
Christianity, canonical traditions, 3–7
cities
  growth of, 60–61
  layout of, 61–64
  See also specific cities
clans
  defined, 294
  formation of, 102–3
Cleopatra III of Egypt, 267
Cleopatra Thea, 259–60
climate and topography, 43–44, *44, 45,* 47–48, 58, 129
Cline, Eric, 86, 95–96
coastal plain, 200
Code of Hammurabi, 33, 53
codex/book form, 283n29
Coele-Syria, 228. *See also* Syria/Aram-Palestine
comparative studies, 52–53, 275, 294
compounds. *See* houses
copper mining, 42
Covenant Code, 53, 54n10, 55, 90
crafts and trades, 62–63
creation accounts, 76–80
cult, defined, 70, 294
cultic activity, defined, 294. *See also* worship practices and beliefs
cultic sites, 70–72, *71, 72,* 294
culture
  complexities of interpreting, 20–25
  defined, 19–20, 294
  identity formation in Israel, 103–6

Index of Subjects

cuneiform, 26, 294
currency, 61
Cyprus, 197, 222, 258, 267
Cyrus the Great, king of Persia, 192, 196–97, 204

daily life
  archaeological evidence, 49–51
  in exile, 188–89
  literary evidence, 51–55
  rural settings, 55–60
  urban settings, 60–64
  See also worship practices and beliefs
Damascus (city), 61
Damascus, Kingdom of. *See* Aram
Dan (city), 38, 61, 70, 131
Darius I, king of Persia, 197–98, 204
Darius II, king of Persia, 211
Darius III, king of Persia, 222, 225, 226
David, king of Israel
  archaeological evidence for reign of, 113–14, 116–22
  biblical account, 108, 111–12, 124
  dating reign of, 114–16
Davies, Graham, 88–89
Dead Sea Scrolls, 256, 294
death rates and life expectancy, 55–56
deities. *See specific deities*
Demetrius I, Seleucid king, 239–40, 254–55, 258, 259
Demetrius II, Seleucid king, 254, 260–61, 262, 263
Demetrius III, Seleucid king, 268, 269
depositories for literature, 277
deuterocanonical/apocryphal literature, defined, 293
Deuteronomistic source, 131, 295
Dever, William, 60, 64, 65, 68, 69, 102
Diaspora
  defined, 187–88, 295
  Hellenistic period, 235–36
  Persian period, 198–200, 219–21
  See also exile
diet, 58, 103–4
Dobbs-Allsopp, F. W., 15

economy
  barter system, 58, 61

currency, 61
  See also agriculture
Edom/Edomites, 42, 154, 295
Egypt
  Alexander the Great in, 226
  in Bronze Age, 33
  commerce evidence in, 233–34
  conflict with Assyria, 167, 168
  conflict with Babylon, 179–80, 183–84
  conflict with Judah, 177–79
  conflict with Persia, 198, 211, 213, 222
  in Exodus narrative, 83–89
  influence in Canaan, 37
  Jewish community in, 189, 219, 220, 235, 236–37, 254
  political alliance with Judah, 165
  Ptolemaic control of, 228, 233, 258, 267
  pyramids, Sphinx, 33
  road stations in the south, 233
  Seleucid control of, 243–44
  Tahpanhes evidence, 220
  tomb relief, Egypt, 85
  War of the Scepters, 267–68
Ekron (city), 96
Elah, king of Israel, 133
Elephantine Jewish community, 189, 219, 220–21, 235
Eliakim/Jehoiakim, king of Judah, 178, 179–81
Elijah (biblical figure), 136
Elisha (biblical figure), 136, 143–44
elite class, houses, 63–64
Elohim, as name, 66, 280
enslavement, 20, 84, 85, 88
Enuma Elish, 78
Eph'al, Israel, 188n65
Ephraimites, 208
Epic of Gilgamesh, 33, 295
epigraphers, work of, 295
epigraphic artifacts, 12, 176, 276, 295
Essenes, 256–57
Ethiopia, 167
ethnogenesis, 104–5
Euphrates River, 43
Eve, as name, 77
exegesis, defined, 295

exile
  Assyrian, 157, 181, 208–9
  Babylonian, 181–82, 184–91
  Persian end of, 196, 202
  See also Diaspora
exodus event
  debates on history of, 88–89
  size of, 87–88
  time frame for, 83–87
  wilderness and lawgiving narratives, 89–91
Ezekiel (biblical figure), 181, 285
Ezra (biblical figure), 212, 216–18, 220, 288

family structure, 55–60, 63, 102, 296
family worship, 64–69, 236
farming. *See* agriculture
Fea, John, 11, 15
Fertile Crescent, 43–44, *44*, 295
fertility gods, 68
Finkelstein, Israel, 60, 87, 92, 117–18, 119–20, 123, 125n39, 139, 148, 163, 169, 170, 186, 216
flood accounts, 81
Foley, John, 274
food and diet, 58, 103–4
forty, as symbolic number, 91, 115

Garbini, Giovanni, 286n38
Garfinkel, Yosef, 120
gates and walls, city, 61–62, 119, 120
Gath (city), 96
Gaza (city), 96, 232, 233, 267
Gedaliah, governor of Judah, 185, 186–87, 206
gender roles, 59, 63, 65–66
genealogies, 105
Genesis creation account, 76–80
Geshem the Arab, 214
Gezer (city), 47, 61, *71*, 96, 119–21, 136, 263, 264, 265
Ghassulian tribe, 37
Gibeon (city), 124
God
  as creator, 76, 78, 80
  Cyrus as instrument of, 196
  kingship under authority of, 108–9, 130
  names for, 66–67, 280, 293
  polytheism and, 68, 140, 218
Gorgias, Seleucid general, 250–51
Grabbe, Lester L., 150n19, 165, 205, 208, 212–13, 214, 215, 228, 244n111, 251, 255n27, 263n60, 268n92
Greek Empire. *See* Hellenistic Empire
Greek language, 235, 237, 242, 246, 289, 290
Guillaume, Philippe, 163n15
Guardiola-Sáenz, Leticia, 21
Gunkel, Hermann, 28
gymnasiums, 241, 246, 295

Halpern, Baruch, 175n5
Hammurabi, Code of, 33, 53, 90, 295
Hanani (biblical figure), 213–14
Hanukkah, 252
Haran (city), 39, 40
Hartley, John, 91
Hasideans, 250, 253, 256
Hasmonean Dynasty
  Alexander Jannaeus, 267–69
  Aristobulus II, 269, 270–71
  collapse of, 270–71
  John Hyrcanus I, 264–66
  John Hyrcanus II, 269, 270–71
  Jonathan Maccabeus, 258–61
  Judah Aristobulus, 266–67
  Maccabean Revolt, 250–55
  Shelamzion (Salome) Alexandra, 269–70
  Simon Maccabeus, 261–64
Hatti Land, 179
Hayes, John H., 17, 108n38, 123, 130, 145–46, 155n32, 164, 165, 187
Hays, Christopher, 52, 77
Hazael, king of Aram, 113, 145–46, 148, 149
Hazor (city), 38, 47, 61, 96, 119–21, 136
Hebrew Bible
  academic study of, 7–10
  canonical traditions, 3–7, 291

Index of Subjects

literary genres in, 27–30
Hebrew Bible, composition process
  earliest narratives, 274–75
  Greek translation, 237, 283, 290
  Hebrew ≠ Greek, 284
  official narratives during state formation, 276–82
  overview, 2–3
  postexilic edits/additions, Babylonian period, 282–86
  postexilic edits/additions, Hellenistic period, 290–91
  postexilic edits/additions, Persian period, 286–89
Hebrew Bible, historical context
  chronology, 32
  complexities of cultural interpretation, 20–25
  historiography, as discipline, 13–17, 29–30, 296
  importance of, 19–20
  scholarly debates on, 17–19
  sources, 11–13
Hebrew language, 198–200, 209, 286–87, 289
Hebron (city), 124
Heliodorus, Seleucid tax collector, 239, 240
Hellenistic Empire
  Alexander the Great's conquests, 225–27
  Diadochi divisions, 227–29
  overview, 296
  Ptolemaic Empire, 228–33, 243–44, 258, 260, 267
  See also Seleucid Empire
hellenization, 234–35, 239, 241–42, 246, 256, 272
Hendel, Ronald, 85, 122
henotheism, 68, 296
Herod the Great, 207
Herodotus, 26–27, 29
Hertzberg, Hans, 108n36
Hesse, Brian, 103–4
Hezekiah, king of Judah, 161–62, 164–69, 281
high priests
  position of, 208, 235, 263
  Seleucid oversight of, 238, 240–43, 244, 253, 258, 259
  Zadokite, 254, 256
  See also Hasmonean Dynasty
highland settlements, 96–98, *97*, 101–2
historical books, as genre, 29
historiography, as discipline, 13–17, 29–30, 296
Hittites, 95
Hoffmeier, James, 84, 85
Hoshea, king of Israel, 155
houses
  structure of, 56–58, *57*, 62–63, 101, 295
  worship in, 64–68, *65*
human fossils, 32–34

identity formation, 103–6
infant mortality rates, 55–56
Iron Age, defined, 95
Israel
  Assyrian conquest of, 155–57
  attack on Judah, 153–55
  clan and tribal formation, 102–3, 106
  cultural survivals, after Assyrian conquest, 208–10
  early rivalry with Judah, 111–12
  growth of, 133–39, 151
  highland settlements, 96–98, *97*, 101–2
  identity formation, 103–6
  Jehu's coup, 143–47
  kings of, dating, 108, 114–16
  kings of, list, 132, 146, 152
  kingship theology in, 108–9
  as label, 159–60
  location of, 40, 128–29
  political instability in, 130–31, 132–33, 152
  population, 60–61, 87, 98, 101, 129
  separation from Judah, 127–28
  Seleucid stela in Israel, 239
  territorial conflict, with Assyria, 149–50
  territorial conflict, with Philistines, 102, 106, 112
  territorial state formation, 106–7

Israel (*continued*)
    unification with Judah, 124–25
    See also Judah; Samaria/Samaritans
Israelian Hebrew dialect, 209
"Israel/Israelite" label, 159–60, 236

Jannaeus, Hasmonean high priest, 267–69
Japhet, Sara, 203
Jason, high priest, 241–42, 244
Jebusites, 98, 116, 118
Jedaniah, Elephantine Jewish leader, 221
Jehoahaz, king of Israel, 149, 150
Jehoahaz I/Ahaz, king of Judah, 153–54
Jehoahaz II, king of Judah, 178–79
Jehoash, king of Israel, 150
Jehoiachin, king of Judah, 180–81, 202–3, 284–85
Jehoiakim/Eliakim, king of Judah, 178, 179–81
Jehoram, king of Israel, 138, 140, 143–45
Jehoram, king of Judah, 136n25, 138
Jehoshaphat, king of Judah, 136, 137
Jehosheba/Jehoshabeath (biblical figure), 147
Jehu, king of Israel, 143–47, 149, *150*
Jeremiah (biblical figure), 283
Jericho (city), 37, 38, 100
Jeroboam, king of Israel, 125, 128
Jeroboam II, king of Israel, 151
Jerusalem (city), *63*
    Assyrian attack on, 167–68
    Babylonian attack on (598–597), 180–81
    Babylonian destruction of (587), 175, 183–85, 190, 283, 285
    building projects in, 112, 116–19, 122, 124–25, 127–28, 137, 162, 164
    burial caves at Jerusalem, 185
    as capital, 124
    early conflict over, 98–99
    fortification of, 118, 122, 137, 162, 164, 204, 213–16, 259
    Hasmonean control of, 262, 263, 265, 268–69, 271
    hellenization of, 239, 241–42, 245, 256
    Maccabean Revolt, 251–55
    map of, *117, 165*
    palaces in, 63
    population, 61, 162, 175, 216, 238
    Ptolemaic control of, 233–35
    return of exiles, 196, 202–4, 205–6, 217–18
    Seleucid control of, 232, 238–43, 244–46, 259, 260, 265
    See also temple of Jerusalem
"Jew/Jewish," as term, 200, 235
Jezebel, queen of Israel, 135, 136, 144
Jezreel (city), 135
Joash/Jehoash, king of Judah, 147–48, 150
John Hyrcanus I, Hasmonean high priest, 264–66
John Hyrcanus II, Hasmonean high priest, 269, 270–71
Johoiada (biblical figure), 147–48
Jonathan Maccabeus, 258–61
Joppa (city), 263, 264, 265
Jordanian mountains, 44
Jordan River, 44
Josephus, Flavius, 225
Joshua (biblical figure), 98, 105
Josiah, king of Judah, 118, 174–78, 279, 281
Jotham, king of Judah, 148, 153
Judah
    anti-Assyrian alliance, 164–66
    Assyrian attack on, 166–69
    Assyrian control of, 153–54, 161–62, 164, 170, 173, 175
    Babylonian attacks on, 180–81, 183–86
    Babylonian control of, 179–80, 182
    coins minted by, 266
    dynastic succession in, 130, 132
    early rivalry with Israel, 111–12
    Egyptian control of, 177–79
    exile and Diaspora, 181–82, 184–91
    under Ezra, 216–19
    growth of, 137, 148–49, 151, 162–63, 170
    Hasmonean control of, 262–71

Israel and Aram attack on, 153–55
"Israel" label, 159
Jehu's coup, 143–47
Jewish sect development in, 255–57
kings of, list, 132, 146, 152, 161, 173
location of, 40, 129
Maccabean Revolt, 250–55
under Nehemiah, 212–16
Persian control of, 196–97, 198–205, *201*, 286
population, 87, 98, 129–30, 162, 169, 175, 186
Ptolemaic control of, 234
religious reforms in, 166, 170, 174–77
return of exiles, 196, 202–4, 205–6, 217–18
Roman control of, 271
Seleucid control of, 238–42, 257–61, 265
Seleucid-Ptolemaic dispute over, 228–29, 232, 240
separation from Israel, 127–28
stories/songs, 280
territorial conflict, with Philistines, 112
unification with Israel, 124–25
Judah Aristobulus, Hasmonean high priest, 266–67
Judas Maccabeus, 250–51, 252, 253, 254–55, 258
Justinian I, Byzantine Emperor, 89

Kenyon, Kathleen, 117
Khirbet Qeiyafa site, 120–21
Killebrew, Ann, 104
King, Philip, 55
King's Highway (Transjordanian Route), 44–45, *46*, 129, 170, 200, 233, 298
King's Land, Galilee, 234
kingship theology, 108–9, 130
Kletter, Raz, 125
Kluckhohn, Clyde, 19–20
Knoppers, Gary, 209, 210, 214
kosher dietary restrictions, 103
Kurkh Monolith, 135

Lachish (city), 38, *51*, 61, 63, 70, 96, 137, 167
Lachish Ostracon 3, 176n10, 277

land bridges, 43–44, 295
language
  Aramaic, 157–59, 188, 189, 198–200, 242, 286–87
  Greek, 235, 237, 242, 290
  Hebrew, 198–200, 209, 286–87
Laodicean War (Third Syrian War), 230
law codes
  comparative study of, 53, 90
  in Deuteronomy, 175–76, 279, 281
  in Exodus, 90–91
  as genre, 28
  Hammurabi, 33, 53, 295
  in Leviticus, 91
  postexilic emphasis on, 218
  types, 53–54
legends, as genre, 28, 296
Lemaire, André, 135n18, 136n25
Lemche, Niels, 88
Leontopolis (city), 254
Leuchter, Mark, 197n11
Levant, as name, 34
Levenson, Jon, 289n47
Levinskaya, Irina, 189
life expectancy and mortality, 55–56
Lipit-Istar, Code of, 90
Lipschits, Oded, 184–85
literacy, 2, 99, 162–63, 176, 276
longue durée, 296
Luce, T. James, 26–27
Luther, Martin, 7, 79, 81
Lysias, governor of Syria, 250, 251–52, 253–54
Lysimachus, high priest, 242, 243

Maccabean Revolt, 250–55. *See also* Hasmonean Dynasty
Manasseh, king of Judah, 169–70, 175, 281
Manassites, 208
Manot Cave skull, 34, 34n10, 44
Marduk (god), 78, 191
marriage, 55, 56, 217
masseboth (maṣṣēbôt), 64, 296
Matthews, Victor, 18, 59, 80–81
maximalist-minimalist debates, 17–18
Mazar, Amihai, 85, 183n44
Medes, 177, 192, 296

medinahs, 197, 198, 296
Megiddo (city), 38, 47, 61, 62, 63, 70, 96, 119–21, 129, 136, 177–79
men
  labor roles, 59, 63
  religious roles, 65, 66
Menahem, king of Israel, 152–53
Menelaus, high priest, 242–43, 244, 245, 251, 252, 253, 256
Merenptah Stela, 82, 86, 101
Merodach-baladan II, king of Babylon, 164
Mesad Hashavyahu ostracon, 176n10
Mesha, king of Moab, 135
Mesha Stela (Moabite Stone), 135–37
Mesolithic Age, 32, 37
Mesopotamia, 296. *See also* Assyrian Empire; Babylon
metaphors, defined, 29
Meyers, Carol, 55n14
military service, 60, 235
Miller, J. Maxwell, 17, 108n38, 123, 130, 145–46, 155n32, 164, 165, 187
Miller, Patrick, 54n10
minimalist-maximalist debates, 17–18
Mizpah (city), 186, 200
mnemohistory, 122
Moabite Stone (Mesha Stela), 135, 136, 137
Moab/Moabites, 42, 135, 136, 296
money, 61
monotheism *vs.* polytheism, 67–69, 139–41, 218, 297
mortality and life expectancy, 55–56
Moses (biblical figure), 79, 81
Mount Gerizim, 210, 219, 236, 245, 265
Mount Sinai, 89–90
Mycenaeans, 95
myths, as genre, 27, 297

Nabonidus, king of Babylon, 191–92
  stela to mother, 191n74
Nabopolassar, king of Babylon, 177, 179
Nadad, king of Israel, 132
Nathan-Melech (biblical figure), 118
Nebuchadrezzar, king of Babylon, 179–81, 182, 183–84, 191

Neco II, Pharaoh, 177–79
Nehemiah (biblical figure), 212–16
Neo-Assyrian Empire, 297
Neolithic Age, 33, 37
Neriglissar, king of Babylon, 191
Nicanor, governor of Syria, 254–55
Niditch, Susan, 176
Noll, K. L., 103, 176n9
nomadic culture, 42, 82, 103
Noth, Martin, 275
numerical symbolism, 91, 115
Nuzi texts, 83n16

O'Brien, Brandon, 93
offerings and sacrifices, 64, 65, 207–8, 221, 236, 245
olives and olive oil, 58, 60
Olmstead, A. T., 168
Omri, king of Israel, 119, 133, 134–36
Omride dynasty, 121, 122, 134–39, 144
Onias III, high priest, 240–41, 242
Onias IV, high priest, 254
oral tradition, 2, 18, 28, 82, 99, 105, 176, 274–75, 297
Orthodox Bible, 3–7
ostraca, 151, 162, 176n10, 277, 297

palaces, 63
Paleolithic Era, 32
Palestine
  Hellenistic region of, 228
  as name, 34, 297
  See also Syria/Aram-Palestine
Parthians, 263, 265
Passover celebration, 174, 220–21
patriarchal social system, 55, 64
Pearce, Laurie, 220
peer reviews, 297
Pekah, king of Israel, 153, 154, 155
Pekahiah, king of Israel, 153
Pentateuch, defined, 297
"people of the land"
  postexilic label, 205–6, 218
  preexilic label, 178
Perdue, Leo, 65–66
pericope, defined, 297
Persepolis (city), 226

Index of Subjects   317

Persian Empire
  collapse of, 222, 225, 226
  extrabiblical sources during, 195
  growth of, 197–98, 200
  Hebrew documents in, 189n69, 286n38
  map of, *199, 201*
  organization of, 197, 222–23
  political instability in, 211
  relationship with Judah, 196–97, 198, 204–5
  rise of, 192, 195
Pharisees, 257, 257n36, 268, 269
Philip I, Seleucid king, 268, 269
Philip of Macedon, 222
Philistia
  arrival in Afro-Asiatic region, 96
  conflict with Assyria, 155, 167
  conflict with Israel, 102, 106, 112
  conflict with Judah, 154
  grave testing in, 42, 96
  Hasmonean control of, 260
  location of, 42–43
  overview, 297
  political alliance with Judah, 165
  pottery of, 43n26, 96n5
  trade and commerce, 200
Phoenicia/Phoenicians, 40, 135, 140, 200, 222, 225, 233, 297
physical artifacts, defined, 12, 297
Pithom (city), 84
Placher, William, 27
poetry, as genre, 29
polis, defined, 297
polytheism *vs.* monotheism, 67–69, 139–41, 218, 297
Pompey, Roman general, 271
population, 60–61, 87, 101, 129–30, 162, 169, 175, 186, 208–9, 216, 238
pork consumption, 103–4
priests
  in household worship, 65–66
  temple, 208, 235
primary sources, defined, 11–12, 297
Protestants
  biblical canon, 4–7
  biblical interpretation, 79
proverbs, as genre, 28–29

Psammetichus II, Pharaoh, 182
Psamtik I, Pharaoh, 173
Ptolemaic Empire, 228–33, 243–44, 258, 260, 267
Ptolemais (city), 259, 260, 261, 267
Ptolemy, Macedonian Greek general, 228–29
Ptolemy (son of) Abubus, 264, 265
Ptolemy II, 229, 230
Ptolemy III, 230, 236
Ptolemy IV, 231
Ptolemy V, 231
Ptolemy VI, 243, 244, 258, 260
Ptolemy IX, 267
purity, cultural and religious, 103, 217

Queen of Sheba, 112–13
Qumran community, 297

Rad, Gerhard von, 275
radiocarbon dating, 50n3
Rainey, Anson, 100n11
Ramah (city), 132
Rameses (city), 84, 85
Rameses II, Pharaoh, 84, 85
Ramoth-Gilead (city), 143
reception history, 21, 298
Rehoboam, king of Judah, 125, 128
religion. *See* worship practices and beliefs; *specific deities*
Rendsburg, Gary, 84
Rezin, king of Aram, 152, 153, 154
Richards, Randolph, 93
roads
  overview, 44–47, *46*
  Transjordanian Route (King's Highway), 44–45, *46*, 129, 170, 200, 233, 298
  Way of the Sea, 45–47, *46*, 62, 129, 134, 148, 155, 200, 225, 299
Roberts, Jimmy J. M., 23–24, 53, 90, 164–65
Roman Empire
  control of Judah, 271
  relationship with Hasmoneans, 261, 262, 263, 271
  relationship with Seleucids, 237–38, 239–40, 243–44, 255, 258–59

Rosh Hashanah, 288
Rupp, Rebeca, 21
rural life, 55–60

sacrifices and offerings, 64, 65, 207–8, 221, 236, 245
Sadducees, 257, 257n36, 268, 269
sagas, as genre, 27, 298
Samaria (city), 61, 63, 134–35, 266
Samaria ostraca, 151, 277
Samaria/Samaritans
   Alexander the Great in, 226
   Elephantine community and, 221
   Hasmonean control of, 260, 265–66
   as name, 298
   origin of, 208–9
   Persian control of, 197
   Ptolemaic control of, 234
   relationship with Judah, 204, 206, 210, 214–15
   Seleucid control of, 239, 245, 254
   Seleucid-Ptolemaic dispute over, 228–29, 232, 240
   site surveys, 186, 209
   trade and commerce, 200
   worship practices, 209–10, 236
Samuel (biblical figure), 107, 108, 109, 112
Sanballat the Horonite, 204, 213, 214–15
Sanhedrin, 243
Sargon II, king of Assyria, 156, 157–59, 161–62, 164, 166
satrapies, 197, 222–23, 298
Saul, king of Israel, 107–8, 109, 111–12
Scaurus, Roman general, 271
Schneider, Tammi, 144
Schniedewind, William, 113, 146, 163, 176, 278–79, 281, 284–85
Scripture, defined, 298
scroll, 281, 283
seal impressions (bullae), 118, 162, 186–87
Seleucid Empire
   collapse of, 269–70
   control of Syria/Aram-Palestine, 237–46, 257–58
   Maccabean Revolt against, 250–55

   map of, *229*
   political instability in, 258–60, 261, 263–64, 265, 267–69
   territorial conflict with Ptolemies, 228–32, 240, 243–44, 258, 260
Seleucus, Macedonian Greek general, 228–29
Seleucus II, 230–31
Seleucus III, 231
Seleucus IV Philopater, 239, 240
Sennacherib, king of Assyria, 166–69
Septuagint, 237, 283–84, 289n47, 290
Shallum, king of Israel, 152
Shalmaneser III, king of Assyria, 52, 135, 136–37, 148, 149, *150*
Shalmaneser V, king of Assyria, 155–56
Shanks, Hershel, 120
Sharp, Carolyn, 13
Shechem (city), 128, 234, 265
Shelamzion (Salome) Alexandra, Hasmonean ruler, 269–70
Sheshbazzar (biblical figure), 202, 203
Sheshonq, Pharaoh, 115, 116
Shiloh (city), 107
Shiloh, Yigal, 60
Shishak, Pharaoh, 115, 116
shrines, 64–65, *65*
Sidon (city), 232
Silberman, Neil, 125n39, 163
Siloam (Hezekiah) tunnel, 162
silver currency, 61
Simon II, high priest, 238, 240
Simon Maccabeus, Hasmonean high priest, 261–64
Sin (god), 191
Sin-shar-ishkun, king of Assyria, 177
slavery, 20, 84, 85, 88
Smith-Christopher, Daniel, 190
Solomon, king of Israel
   archaeological evidence for reign of, 116–22, 123
   biblical account, 112–13, 124–25, 128
   dating reign of, 114–16
Stager, Lawrence, 55, 106
Saint Catherine's Monastery, 89
Stith, Matthew, 146
Sumerian Empire, 37
Susa (city), 219, 226, 227

symbolic numbers, 91, 115
synagogues, 236
Syria/Aram-Palestine
   Jewish life under Ptolemies, 235–37
   Maccabean Revolt in, 250–55
   Ptolemaic control of, 233–35, 237
   Seleucid control of, 237–46, 257–58
   Seleucid political instability in, 258–60, 261, 263–64, 265, 267–69
   Seleucid-Ptolemaic dispute over, 228–32, 240, 243–44, 258–60
   Syrian (Aramaean) Wars, 230–32, 243–44, 246, 260–61

Taanach (city), 70
Tahpanhes (city), 220
TaNaKh/Tanakh (Jewish canon), 3–7, 298
Tattenai (biblical figure), 204–5
taxation, 58, 60, 124, 127–28, 223, 234, 238, 260, 262
Tel al-Rimah Stela, 150
Tel Dan Stela, 113, *114*, 127, 135n21, 145
Tell Beit Mirsim (city), 163
Tell el-Dabʻa (city), 84
Tell el-Fūl (city), 107
Tell el-Maskhuta (city), 84
Tell el-Retaba, 84
tels/tells, 50, *51*, 61, 298
temple of Jerusalem
   construction of, 112, 116
   destruction of, Babylonian, 184, 283
   diminished importance of, 218–19
   leadership, 208
   location of, *117*
   monotheism in, 69
   rebuilding of, 197, 200–202, 203–7, 210, 213–14
   rededication of, Hasmonean, 252
   and religious devotion of kings, 131
   renovation of, Seleucid period, 238
   restoration of, under Josiah, 174, 208
   sacrifices at, 207–8, 236
   stripping and rededication of, by Antiochus IV, 244–46
   tax collection, 234
   See also high priests

temples, outside of Jerusalem
   Arad, 71–72, 71n69
   Elephantine (in Egypt)
      destroyed, 221
      letter on rebuilding, 221
      real estate receipt, 221
   Ghassulian, Ein Gedi, 37n15
   home worship, 236
   Jerusalem, expanded under Simon II, 238
   Leontopolis, 254
   multiple in Persian period, 219, 219n103
   places of worship, 64–65, 68
   Samaritan temple
      aconomy, 234
      evidence, 210, 210n59
   Second Temple remains, 207
   signs of temple worship, 236
   standing stones, 64, 68, 70–71, 296
   stories, Northern Kingdom, 280
   Temple of Amun, Karnak, 115–16, 115n10
   temple under Jerusalem, 71
   temples as banks, 167n24
Ten Commandments, 53–54, 90
terra-cotta figurines, 67–68, 140–41, 218
theocracy, 108–9, 130, 298
theophany, 298
Tibni, king of Israel, 133, 134
Tiglath-Pileser III, king of Assyria, 151, 152–54, 155
Tigranes of Armenia, 269–70
Tigris River, 43
Tirzah (city), 133, 134
Tobiah the Ammonite, 215
topography and climate, 43–44, *44*, *45*, 47–48, 58, 129
Torah, 3, 53, 90, 257, 279, 281, 288, 289, 298
trade routes, 45–47, 129, 136, 148, 170, 184, 200, 233
trades and crafts, 62–63
traditional site, defined, 298
Transjordanian Route (King's Highway), 44–45, *46*, 129, 170, 200, 233, 298

tribes
    defined, 298
    formation of, 103, 106
Tryphon, Seleucid general, 261, 262, 263–64

Ugarit (city-state), 95
urban centers. *See* cities
Ur-Kasdim (city), 39
Ur-Nammu, Code of, 90
Ussishkin, David, 43n26, 96n5, 119–20
Uzziah/Azariah, king of Judah, 148, 151

vassal, defined, 298–99
villages
    development of, 60
    highland, 101–2

walls and gates, city, 61–62, 119, 120
Wapnish, Paula, 103–4
water supply, 58, 62, *63*
Watts, John, 196
Way of the Sea, 45–47, *46*, 62, 129, 134, 148, 155, 200, 225, 299
Weinberg, Joel, 186
Wenham, Gordon, 20, 22
Westermann, Claus, 77
wilderness narrative, 89–92
Williamson, H. G. M., 204
wine, 58, 60
Winitzer, Abraham, 285
Wolfram, Herwig, 104
women
    labor roles, 59, 63
    religious roles, 65–66
worship practices and beliefs
    cultic sites, 70–72, *71*, *72*
    diasporic, 219, 220–21, 223, 236–37, 254
    of Essenes, 256–57
    in exile, 188, 189
    family/household, 64–68, 236
    in highland settlements, 102
    and identity formation, 105–6
    monotheism *vs.* polytheism, 67–69, 139–41, 218, 297
    Passover, 174, 220–21
    of Pharisees, 257
    religious reforms, 166, 170, 174–77
    Rosh Hashanah, 288
    sacrifices and offerings, 64, 65, 207–8, 221, 236, 245
    of Sadducees, 257
    of Samaritans, 209–10
    terminology, 70
    See also temple of Jerusalem
writing surfaces, 277
Wunsch, Cornelia, 220

Xerxes, king of Persia, 204, 211
Xerxes II, king of Persia, 211

Yadin, Yigael, 119
Yamada, Frank, 21
YHWH, as name, 66–67
Younger, K., 155n33

Zadokite priests, 254, 256
Zechariah, king of Israel, 152
Zedekiah, king of Judah, 182–83, 184
Zerubbabel (biblical figure), 202–3, 207, 210
Zeus (god), 239, 245
Zimri, king of Israel, 133

www.ingramcontent.com/pod-product-compliance
Lightning Source LLC
Chambersburg PA
CBHW051912220925
32992CB00001B/1